MEDITERRANEAN
Diet Cookbook
for Beginners

The Complete Guide to Cook Quick & Easy Mouth-Watering Recipes on a Budget 30-Day Meal Plan to Jumpstart Your Well-being

Greta Davies

© **Copyright 2021 by Greta Davies - All rights reserved.**

This document is geared towards providing exact and reliable information in regard to the topic and issue covered.

- From a Declaration of Principles which was accepted and approved equally by a Committee of the American Bar Association and a Committee of Publishers and Associations.

In no way is it legal to reproduce, duplicate, or transmit any part of this document in either electronic means or in printed format. All rights reserved.

The information provided herein is stated to be truthful and consistent, in that any liability, in terms of inattention or otherwise, by any usage or abuse of any policies, processes, or directions contained within is the solitary and utter responsibility of the recipient reader. Under no circumstances will any legal responsibility or blame be held against the publisher for any reparation, damages, or monetary loss due to the information herein, either directly or indirectly.

Respective authors own all copyrights not held by the publisher.

The information herein is offered for informational purposes solely and is universal as so. The presentation of the information is without contract or any type of guarantee assurance.

The trademarks that are used are without any consent, and the publication of the trademark is without permission or backing by the trademark owner. All trademarks and brands within this book are for clarifying purposes only and are owned by the owners themselves, not affiliated with this document.

Table of Contents

Introduction	Pag 5
Chapter 1. Bases of the Mediterranean Diet	Pag. 7
Chapter 2. 30-Day Meal Plan	Pag. 10
Chapter 3. Breakfast Recipes	Pag. 14
Chapter 4. Snack and Appetizers	Pag. 50
Chapter 5. Pasta and Rice Recipes	Pag. 77
Chapter 6. Soups	Pag. 127
Chapter 7. Saladsc and Sides	Pag. 140
Chapter 8. Vegetables	Pag. 180
Chapter 9. Poultry and Meat Recipes	Pag. 200
Chapter 10. Fish and Seafood	Pag. 274
Chapter 11. Bread and Pizza Recipes	Pag. 338
Chapter 12. Desserts	Pag. 376
Conclusion	Pag. 404
Measurement Conversion Table	Pag. 406
Index of Recipes	Pag. 407

Introduction

The Mediterranean diet is inspired by the eating habits of the populations that live around the Mediterranean Sea. The people of southern Italy and Greece are the central regions that influence this diet. But, it isn't the diet consumed today in many of these regions that gained so much attention. The Mediterranean diet refers to these areas' traditional eating habits and lifestyles in the 1950s and 1960s. During this time, researchers noticed a significant difference in the health of populations in these areas compared to those living in America. Many of the individuals in the Mediterranean regions were healthier, and the critical difference between those living in the Mediterranean and those living in America was their diet.

Suppose you decide to follow the Mediterranean diet. In that case, the basis of your diet will be natural products, vegetables, entire grain pieces of bread, pasta, rice, grains, and potatoes, alongside beans, nuts, vegetables, and seeds. These foods ought to be consumed day by day and will shape the premise of each meal you eat, with crisp vegetables becoming the overwhelming focus. While carbohydrates are a piece of this diet, they will generally be entire, unpredictable, high in fiber, and consumed with protein or fats simultaneously.

Fish and seafood are the staple proteins in this diet. Regular consumption of greasy fish, similar to salmon, mackerel, and fish, assists with satiety and lifts admission of heart solid omega-3 unsaturated fats. When looking for fish, be that as it may, avoid ranch-raised at whatever point conceivable. Extra wellsprings of fat incorporate olive and canola oil, which replace margarine and grease for cooking and dressing food.

With some restraint, you'll eat poultry, eggs, cheddar, and plain, unsweetened yogurt each other day or a couple of times each week, relying upon your inclination. Decide on characteristic dairy and cheddar, not vigorously handled or seasoned assortments, to avoid added additives, sugars, or synthetics. Goat cheddar and feta cheddar are generally observed on Mediterranean diet menus.

Desserts, for example, crude nectar, are appreciated in strict control, while different treats are eaten distinctly during extraordinary events. Red meat is barely consumed in the Mediterranean diet, alongside exceptionally handled meats like wieners and bacon. A solitary glass of wine is considered a staple in the diet and part of what makes the diet so heart solid, so don't feel awful about presenting yourself with a glass with your supper.

Who Is This Diet Well Suited For?

This diet will work well for someone who wants to boost their heart well-being, reduce their cholesterol, lose some weight, and do without feeling insulted as such. Note, though, if you consume too many processed grains in your diet (white bread, white pasta, and so on), this will potentially build up your cholesterol level, so it's essential to concentrate on healthier grains that have been handled as poorly as you would expect under the circumstances.

This diet is likewise extraordinary for individuals who don't react well to a conventional low-carb diet. A significant piece of the Mediterranean diet is the worth set on regular exercise, which is bolstered by the vitality you'll get from complex carbohydrates and common natural product sugars. Try not to be amazed if 50-60% of your all-out everyday calorie consumption originates from carbohydrates while on this plan.

At last, the plan is extraordinary for the individuals hoping to keep up their weight utilizing a dietary convention that can be supported for quite a long time to come. Since you are not dispensing with any food bunches altogether, it's genuinely conceivable to get balanced nutrition with this plan.

Chapter 1

Bases of the Mediterranean Diet

A helpful illustration of what you're allowed to eat, how much, and how often is the food pyramid. I particularly like the fact that social aspects like eating with your family and physical activity make up the pyramid's foundation. It just drives home the point that the Mediterranean Diet is not just a way of eating; it is a way of living.

The pyramid is divided proportionally into groups containing foods you can choose from. The base is the lifestyle aspect. However, I adjusted the other levels somewhat. That is because, in addition to trusting the Mediterranean Diet, I also feel that limiting carbohydrate intake will have a significant impact on your overall health.

Before we move on to the other tiers on the food pyramid, let me explain why carbohydrates may be harming your body.

First, let me make it clear that I am not against all carbs. Carbohydrates are essential sources of energy and nutrition. My issue lies with the simple carbs that make up so much of an American plate nowadays. Loaves of bread baked with white flour, heaps of sugar, soda, sweets, cookies, doughnuts, and cake are all things that we quickly become addicted to. They jolt our blood sugar too high heaven and then crash just as fast.

This increase and drop of blood sugar play havoc on your insulin levels, leading to insulin resistance and diabetes.

Complex carbohydrates like whole grains and oatmeal, on the other hand, are excellent to eat. This form of carbohydrates gets broken down slower and will not cause your blood sugar to spike. It will also make you feel fuller for longer.

Considering the adverse effects of simple carbs, I suggest limiting bread, pasta, rice, and products made with flour to only a few times a month. In contrast, the original pyramid states you can eat it daily.

Now that you know what slight modifications I suggest, I can break down the levels for you.

After the foundation tier, you get your fruits, vegetables, grains, beans, nuts, legumes, seeds, herbs and spices, olive oil, and other good fats. You can eat foods on this tier every day. Then you get your fish, seafood, poultry, eggs, and dairy. Limit this row to three to five times a week, and keep the poultry, eggs, and dairy portions small when you do eat them. Lastly and in this case, we have meat, potatoes, rice, pasta, flour products, and sweets.

Benefits

Boosts Your Brain Health: Preserve memory and prevent cognitive decline by following the Mediterranean diet that will limit processed foods, refined bread, and red meats. Have a glass of wine versus hard liquor.

Improves Poor Eyesight: Older individuals suffer from poor eyesight, but the Mediterranean diet has provided notable improvement in many cases. An Australian Center for Eye Research discovered that the individuals who consumed a minimum of 100 ml (0.42 cup) of olive oil weekly were almost 50% less likely to develop macular degeneration versus those who ate less than one ml each week.

Helps to Reduce the Risk of Heart Disease: The New England Journal of Medicine provided evidence in 2013 from a randomized clinical trial. The trial was implemented in Spain, whereas individuals did not have cardiovascular disease at enrollment but were in the 'high risk' category. The incidence of major cardiovascular events was reduced by the Mediterranean diet supplemented with extra-virgin olive oil or nuts. In one study, men who consumed fish in this manner reduced the risk by 23% of death from heart disease.

The Risk of Alzheimer's disease is reduced: In 2018, the journal Neurology studied 70 brain scans of individuals who had no signs of dementia at the onset. They followed the eating patterns in a two-year study resulting in individuals on the Med diet having a lesser increase of the depots and reduced energy use - potentially signaling risk for Alzheimer's.

Helps Lessen the Risk of Some Types of Cancer: According to the results of a group study, the diet is associated with a lessened risk of stomach cancer (gastric adenocarcinoma).

Decreases Risks for Type 2 Diabetes: It can help stabilize blood sugar while protecting against type 2 diabetes with its low-carb elements. The Med diet maintains a richness in fiber, which will digest slowly while preventing variances in your blood sugar. It also can help you maintain a healthier weight, which is another trigger for diabetes.

Suggests Improvement for Those with Parkinson's disease: By consuming foods on the Mediterranean diet, you add high antioxidants that can prevent your body from undergoing oxidative stress, which is a damaging process that will attack your cells. The menu plan can reduce your risk factors in half.

Chapter 2

30-Day Meal Plan

Day	Breakfast	Lunch	Dinner	Dessert
1	Cheesy Avocado Omelet	Cauliflower Tomato Beef	Chicken with Peas	Deliciously Cold Lychee Sorbet
2	Barley Porridge	Three Sauces Lasagna	Elegant Pork Loin	Blueberry Frozen Yogurt
3	Tomato, Herb, and Goat Cheese Frittata	Grilled Steak	Roasted Root Vegetable Soup	Mixed Berry and Orange Compote
4	Prosciutto Breakfast Bruschetta	Spicy Mustard Chicken	Moist Shredded Beef	Apple Couscous Pudding
5	Low Carb Taco Bowls	Chopped Israeli Mediterranean Pasta Salad	Pecan Salmon Fillets	Butterscotch Lava Cakes
6	Tuna and Avocado Salad Sandwich	Parmesan Chicken	Sweet Veggie-Stuffed Peppers	Crème Caramel
7	Artichoke Frittatas	Dill Beef Brisket	Mushroom Spinach Soup	Honey Stewed Apples
8	Hearty Honey-Apricot Granola	Chicken and Quinoa Salad	Pan-Fried Pork Chops with Orange Sauce	Decadent Croissant Bread Pudding
9	Ricotta Breakfast Casserole	Rosemary Pork Chops	Tuna with Vegetable Mix	Mexican Chocolate Mousse
10	Vanilla Raspberry Overnight Oats	Quick Shrimp Fettuccine	Italian Beef Roast	Cardamom Date Bites
11	Sausage Stuffed Mushrooms	Green Curry Beef	Leek, Potato, and Carrot Soup	Banana Ice Cream with Chocolate Sauce
12	Sweet Potato Toast	Tortoreto Mushrooms with Cheddar	Tarragon Cod Fillets	Chocolate Peanut Butter Cups
13	Spiced Almond Pancakes	Sweet Veggie-Stuffed Peppers	Buttery Herb Lamb Chops	Fruit Crepes
14	Spinach Curry Pancakes with Apple, Raisins, And Chickpeas	Roasted Vegetarian Lasagna	Salmon and Corn Salad	Vanilla Bread Pudding with Apricots

15	Polenta with Arugula, Figs, and Blue Cheese	Prime BBQ	Kale Chicken Soup	Fig and Honey Buckwheat Pudding
16	Ricotta Breakfast Casserole	Mediterranean Salad With Peppers And Tomatoes	Jalapeno Beef Chili	Honey Stewed Apples
17	Low Carb Taco Bowls	Chicken and Onion Casserole	Dill Beef Brisket	Cardamom Date Bites
18	Sausage Stuffed Mushrooms	Pecan Salmon Fillets	Mushroom and Vegetable Penne Pasta	Blueberry Frozen Yogurt
19	Barley Porridge	Halibut and Quinoa Mix	Elegant Pork Loin	Chocolate Peanut Butter Cups
20	Spiced Almond Pancakes	Chicken Quesadilla	Chickpea & Lentil Salad	Mixed Berry and Orange Compote
21	Tomato, Herb, and Goat Cheese Frittata	Mozzarella Eggplants	Buttery Herb Lamb Chops	Banana Ice Cream with Chocolate Sauce
22	Hearty Honey-Apricot Granola	Tuna with Vegetable Mix	Parmesan Chicken	Vanilla Bread Pudding with Apricots
23	Prosciutto Breakfast Bruschetta	White Bean Alfredo Pasta	Spicy Mustard Chicken	Deliciously Cold Lychee Sorbet
24	Polenta with Arugula, Figs, and Blue Cheese	Mediterranean Veggie Bowl	Rustic Lamb Shanks Elegant Pork Loin	Mexican Chocolate Mousse
25	Cheesy Avocado Omelet	Mozzarella Eggplants	Italian Beef Roast	Butterscotch Lava Cakes
26	Vanilla Raspberry Overnight Oats	Spicy Baked Feta with Tomatoes	Green Curry Beef	Fig and Honey Buckwheat Pudding
27	Tuna and Avocado Salad Sandwich	Greek Baked Cod	Baked Chicken Paella	Apple Couscous Pudding
28	Spinach Curry Pancakes with Apple, Raisins, And Chickpeas	Tarragon Cod Fillets	Roasted Cauliflower and Tomatoes	Crème Caramel
29	Artichoke Frittatas	Lemon Chicken Mix	Mediterranean Snapper With Olives And Feta	Decadent Croissant Bread Pudding
30	Sweet Potato Toast	Baked Rice With Swordfish And Mussels	Chicken and Mushrooms	Fruit Crepes

Recipes

Chapter 3. Breakfast Recipes

1. Smoky Shrimp Chipotle

Preparation Time: 5 minutes

Cooking Time: 15 minutes

Servings: 4

Ingredients:

- 1 capful (1 tablespoon) Cinnamon Chipotle or a small amount of chipotle pepper,
- cinnamon, salt, and pepper to taste
- 4 teaspoons Olive Oil or oil of your choice and fresh garlic
- 4 tbsp. fresh cilantro (optional)
- 2 lbs. wild-caught, raw shrimp shelled; deveined & tails removed
- 1 can (16 oz.) diced tomatoes (unflavored, no sugar added)
- 1 cup chopped chives or scallions (greens only)
- 4 lime wedges (optional)

Directions:

1. Heat oil over medium-high heat in a medium-sized frying pan.
2. Put the scallions and roast, until mildly wilted and glistening, for one minute.
3. Include the shrimp and cook on each side for 1 minute.
4. Add the sauce with the tomatoes and Cinnamon Chipotle. Cook an extra 3-5 minutes, stirring regularly, until the tomatoes are hot and the shrimp is thoroughly cooked and opaque. As it can make the shrimp tough and dry, be careful not to overcook it.
5. If needed, sprinkle with cilantro and spritz with a wedge of lime (or for a beautiful and practical garnish, serve the lime wedge on the plate.
6. Serve it warm.

7. Make 4 servings or so.

Nutrition: Energy (calories): 632 kcal
Protein: 44.58 g Fat: 8.71 g
Carbohydrates: 176.33 g

2. Low Carb Taco Bowls

Preparation Time: 5 minutes

Cooking Time: 15-20 minutes

Servings: 4

Ingredients:

- cauliflower rice:
- 1 large head cauliflower, steamed until soft or frozen ready-to-cook
- 1 1/2 pounds lean ground beef
- 2 C canned, diced tomatoes (no sugar added; no flavor added)
- 1-2 capfuls Sunrise or Southwestern Seasoning or low salt taco seasoning
- Your favorite approved condiments.

Directions:

1. Over medium-high heat, position a large frying pan. In a wide (preferably Nonstick) skillet, add ground beef and sauté for 8-12 minutes until lightly browned. Using a spatula or a cutting implement, cut the more significant bits into smaller parts.
2. Add the tomatoes, then season. Stir to blend.
3. Reduce the heat to low and allow the mixture to simmer until the liquid is reduced by 1/2 and pleasant & solid for 5 minutes.
4. Use a food processor or chopping instrument to chop steamed cauliflower into rice-sized bits while cooking. Prepare it according to box Directions for using ready-to-cook cauli rice.
5. In a cup, add 1/2 C of cauliflower rice and finish with 1/4 of the meat mixture. Top with your favorite condiments and serve sweet.

Nutrition: Energy (calories): 420 kcal
Protein: 46.54 g Fat: 19.06 g
Carbohydrates: 12.24 g

3. Artichoke Frittatas

Preparation Time: 10 minutes

Cooking Time: 30 minutes

Servings: 1

Ingredients:

- 2.5 oz. dry spinach
- 1/4 red bell pepper
- 1 Artichoke (drain the liquid)
- 2 green onions
- 2 dried tomatoes
- 2 eggs
- 1 tsp. Italian seasoning
- Salt - Pepper to taste

Directions:

1. Preheat oven to medium heat.
2. Brush a bit of oil on the cast-iron skillet.
3. Mix all the vegetables.
4. Add some seasoning.
5. Spread the vegetables evenly in the pan.
6. Whisk the eggs and add some milk.
7. Add some salt and pepper.
8. Mix in some cheese (helps to make it fluffier).
9. Pour the egg mixture into the saucepan.
10. Place the pan inside the oven for about 30 minutes.
11. Enjoy!

Nutrition: Calories: 160 Protein: 7g Carbohydrates: 4g Fat: 3.5g

4. Chocolate Sweet Potato Pudding

Preparation Time: 5 minutes

Cooking Time: 2 minutes

Servings: 1

Ingredients:

- 2 well-cooked sweet potatoes
- 2 tablespoons cocoa powder
- 2 tablespoons maple syrup
- 1/4 cups plant-based milk (for example, almond milk)
- 1/4 tablespoons salt
- 1/4 tablespoons vanilla extract

Directions:

1. Inside the food processor, put all the ingredients.
2. Blend thoroughly for about 30 seconds to 1 minute.

3. Voilà!

Nutrition: Calories: 200 Fat: 1.5g Carbohydrates: 23.4g Fiber: 1.3g

5. Peanut Butter and Protein Pancake

Preparation Time: 10 minutes

Cooking Time: 15 minutes

Servings: 1

Ingredients:

- 1/2 cup oat flour
- 1/2 cup gluten-free chocolate pancake mix
- 1/2 cup almond milk
- 1 egg
- 1 tablespoon coconut water
- 1 tablespoon peanut butter
- Fresh fruits slices

Directions:

1. Preheat a saucepan to medium heat.
2. Mix the flour and the pancake mix in a mixing bowl.
3. Mix the almond milk and eggs with coconut water in another bowl.
4. Mix the dry and wet ingredients thoroughly to form a delicate batter.
5. Spray the preheated saucepan with some coconut oil.
6. Put the batter into the saucepan with a measuring cup and allow it to cook for a few minutes.
7. Allow to cool and top with peanut butter and fresh fruit slices.

Nutrition: Calories: 380 Protein: 22g Carbohydrates: 16g

6. Tex-Mex Tofu Breakfast Tacos

Preparation Time: 10 minutes

Cooking Time: 15 minutes

Servings: 1

- **Ingredients:**
- 8 oz. firm tofu
- 1 cup well-cooked black bean
- 1/4 red onion
- 1 cup fresh coriander
- 1 ripe avocado
- 1/2 cup salsa
- 1 medium-sized lime

- 5 whole corn tortillas
- 1/2 teaspoon garlic powder
- 1/2 teaspoon chili powder
- 1/8 teaspoon of sea salt
- 1 tablespoon salsa
- 1 tablespoon water

Directions:

1. Dice the red onions, avocados, coriander, and keep in separate bowls.
2. Also, slice the limes and keep them in individual bowls.
3. In a clean towel. Wrap the tofu and place it under a cast-iron skillet.
4. In the meantime, heat a saucepan to medium heat.
5. Cook the black beans in the saucepan and add a little salt, cumin, and chili powder.
6. Then decrease the heat to a low simmer and set aside.
7. Add the tofu spices and salsa into a bowl, then add some water and set aside.
8. Heat another skillet to medium heat.
9. Pour some oil into the skillet, and then crumble the tofu into it.
10. Stir-fry for about 5 minutes until the tofu begins to brown.
11. Add some seasoning and continue to cook for about 5 to 10 minutes, and then set aside.
12. Heat the tortillas in the oven to 250°F.
13. Top the tortillas with tofu scramble, avocado, salsa, coriander, black beans, and lime juice.
14. Serve immediately.

Nutrition: Calories: 350 Fat: 6.5g Carbohydrates: 23.6g Protein: 21.5g

7. Mocha Oatmeal

Preparation Time: 5 minutes

Cooking Time: 10 minutes

Servings: 1

Ingredients:

- 1 banana
- 1/2 cup oats
- 1 cup coffee
- 1/4 teaspoon salt

- 1 teaspoon walnut
- 1/2 teaspoon cacao powder
- 1 cup milk
- Honey

Directions:

1. Preheat a saucepan to medium heat.
2. Put the oats in a saucepan.
3. Slice the banana, mash them, and add them to the oats.
4. Add coffee, walnuts, cacao powder, and salt.
5. Stir and you may want to wait for it to simmer, practically until the mixture becomes sticky inconsistency.
6. Serve in a bowl and add milk and honey as desired.
7. Enjoy!

Nutrition: Calories: 400 Carbohydrates: 51g Fats: 5g Fiber: 8g

8. Black and Blueberry Protein Smoothie

Preparation Time: 5 minutes

Cooking Time: 0 minutes

Servings: 1

Ingredients:

- 1 cup sugar-free coconut milk (or any other plant-based milk of your choice)
- 1 scoop vanilla or natural protein powder
- 6 oz. fat-free vanilla Greek yogurt
- 2 tablespoons of milled flaxseed
- 1 cup berries (black or blue)
- 1 cup ice

Directions:

In the food processor, place all the ingredients.

Blend until smooth.

Pour into a cup and enjoy.

Nutrition: Calories: 360 Fats: 1.5g Protein: 49g Carbohydrates: 40g

9. Barley Porridge

Preparation Time: 5 minutes

Cooking Time: 25 minutes

Servings: 4

Ingredients:

- 1 cup barley
- 1 cup wheat berries
- 2 cups unsweetened almond milk, plus more for serving
- 2 cups water
- 1/2 cup blueberries
- 1/2 cup pomegranate seeds
- 1/2 cup hazelnuts, toasted and chopped
- 1/4 cup honey

Directions:

1. Place the barley, wheat berries, almond milk, and water in a medium saucepan over medium-high heat. Bring to a boil, reduce the heat to low, and simmer for about 25 minutes, frequently stirring until the grains are very tender.
2. 2.Top each serving with almond milk, 2 tablespoons of blueberries, 2 tablespoons of pomegranate seeds, 2 tablespoons of hazelnuts, and 1 tablespoon of honey.
3. Substitution tip: Bulgur is a healthy protein and fiber-packed substitution for the barley in this hot breakfast. Bulgur is a cracked, partially cooked wheat kernel.

Nutrition: Calories: 354 Total Fat: 8g Saturated Fat: 1g Carbohydrates: 63g Fiber: 10g Protein: 11g

10. Ricotta Breakfast Casserole

Preparation Time: 15 minutes

Cooking Time: 25 minutes

Servings: 4

Ingredients:

- 1 teaspoon extra-virgin olive oil
- 1 zucchini, chopped
- 1 cup broccoli florets, blanched or steamed
- ½ cup diced cooked carrots
- ½ red bell pepper, seeded and diced
- 8 large eggs
- ½ cup low-fat ricotta cheese
- 1 teaspoon chopped fresh basil

- 1 teaspoon chopped fresh oregano
- 1 teaspoon chopped fresh chives
- Pinch sea salt
- Pinch freshly ground black pepper

Directions:

1. Preheat the oven to 350°F.
2. Lightly grease an 8-by-8-inch baking dish with olive oil. Evenly distribute the zucchini, broccoli, carrots, and red bell pepper over the bottom of the dish.
3. Whisk together the eggs, ricotta, basil, oregano, chives, sea salt, and pepper in a large bowl. Pour the eggs into the prepared dish over the vegetables.
4. Bake, the casserole for about 25 minutes, or until a knife inserted near the center comes out clean.
5. Substitution tip: Ricotta adds an interesting texture, but you can easily substitute goat cheese, feta cheese, or even plain cottage cheese with equally superb results.

Nutrition: Calories: 220 Total Fat: 14g Saturated Fat: 5g Carbohydrates: 7g Fiber: 2g Protein: 17g

11. Mango-Pear Smoothie

Preparation Time: 10 minutes

Cooking Time: 3 minutes

Servings: 1

Ingredients:

- 1 ripe pear, cored and chopped
- 1/2 mango, peeled, pitted, and chopped
- 1 cup chopped kale
- 1/2 cup plain Greek yogurt
- 2 ice cubes

Directions:

1.In a blender, purée the pear, mango, kale, and yogurt.

2.Add the ice and blend until thick and smooth. Pour the smoothie into a glass and serve cold.

Substitution tip: Apples can be used instead of pear. For some extra fiber, leave the skin on the fruit. Wash the skin thoroughly, though, to remove any pesticide residue if your apples are not organic.

Nutrition: Calories: 293 Total Fat: 8g Saturated Fat: 5g Carbohydrates: 53g Fiber: 7g Protein: 8g

12. Strawberry-Rhubarb Smoothie

Preparation Time: 5 minutes

Cook Time: 3 minutes

Servings: 1

Ingredients:

- 1 rhubarb stalk, chopped
- 1 cup sliced fresh strawberries
- 1/2 cup plain Greek yogurt
- 2 tablespoons honey
- Pinch ground cinnamon
- 3 ice cubes

Directions:

1. Place a small saucepan filled with water over high heat and bring to a boil. Add the rhubarb and boil for 3 minutes. Drain and transfer the rhubarb to a blender.
2. Add the strawberries, yogurt, honey, and cinnamon and pulse the mixture until it is smooth.
3. Add the ice and blend until thick, with no ice lumps remaining. Pour the smoothie into a glass and enjoy the cold.
4. Ingredient tip: Rhubarb leaves contain a compound called oxalic acid, which is toxic—use only the plant's stems in your recipes.

Nutrition: Calories: 295 Total Fat: 8g Saturated Fat: 5g Carbohydrates: 56g Fiber: 4g Protein: 6g

13. Pumpkin-Gingerbread Smoothie

Preparation Time: 5 minutes, Plus 1 Hour Or Overnight Soaking

Cooking Time: 10 minutes

Servings: 1

Ingredients:

- 1 cup unsweetened almond milk
- 2 teaspoons chia seeds
- 1 banana
- 1/2 cup canned pure pumpkin
- 1/4 teaspoon ground cinnamon
- 1/4 teaspoon ground ginger
- Pinch ground nutmeg

Directions:

1. In a small bowl, mix the almond milk and chia seeds. Soak the seeds for at least 1 hour. Transfer the seeds to a blender.

2. Add the banana, pumpkin, cinnamon, ginger, and nutmeg.

Blend until smooth. Pour the smoothie into a glass and serve.

Substitution tip: Cooked sweet potato or butternut squash works as an alternative if you do not have pumpkin handy.

Nutrition: Calories: 200 Total Fat: 5g Saturated Fat: 1g Carbohydrates: 41g Fiber: 10g Protein: 5g

14. Low Carb Sloppy Joes

Preparation Time: 5 minutes

Cooking Time: 25 minutes

Servings: 4

Ingredients:

- Salt and Pepper to taste
- 1 Cup low sodium beef broth
- 1 Tablespoon of wine vinegar
- 1/2 Tablespoon Cinnamon Chipotle Seasoning or ground cinnamon, chipotle paste and garlic
- 1 Tablespoon (one Capful) Garlic & Spring Onion Seasoning or salt, pepper, crushed garlic, garlic powder and onion to taste
- 1 Tablespoon yellow mustard
- 1 teaspoon (one packet) powdered stevia
- 2 Tablespoons tomato paste
- 1/2 C diced green bell pepper
- 1 1/2 pounds lean ground beef

Directions:

1. In a frying pan, place the ground beef and place it over

medium heat on the burner. When it is frying, split up the larger pieces of beef.
2. Cook the meat for about 7 minutes, then add the rest of the ingredients (EXCEPT the broth) and whisk to mix. Add the water and transform the
3. Heat up to medium-high until combined.
4. When the liquid is boiling, reduce the heat to low and let it steam until the liquid is somewhat reduced and you have a lovely sauce, uncovered for around 10-15 minutes.
5. Serve warm & have fun!

Nutrition: Energy (calories): 413 kcal Protein: 46.92 g Fat: 19.17 g Carbohydrates: 11.08 g

15. Tex-Mex Seared Salmon

Preparation Time: 5 minutes

Cooking Time: 15 minutes

Servings: 4

Ingredients:

- 1 Tablespoon (one Capful) Phoenix Sunrise Seasoning or salt, pepper, garlic, cumin, paprika, cayenne, and onion to taste
- 1 1/2 pounds wild-caught salmon filet (will cook best if you have it at room temp)

Directions:

1. Preheat a nonstick pan for 1 min over high heat.
2. Swirl seasoning over the salmon during the heating process (NOT on the skin side)
3. Decrease the heat to medium height.
4. Put the fish in the pan and let it cook for about 4-6 minutes depending on the size. Seasoned side down. When a "crust" has been created from the seasoning, and the fish is quickly released from the pan, you will know it's ready to flip.
5. Lower the heat to medium-low. Turn the fish down to the side of the skin and cook for about

4-6 more minutes. (Less for medium / rare and more for well done.) Using a meat thermometer is the safest way to search for crispiness.
6. We cook to 130 degrees and then let it rest for 5 minutes, not overcooked and softly yellow.
7. Withdraw from the flame and serve. Fish can slip onto the plate right off the skin.

Nutrition: Energy (calories): 244 kcal Protein: 42.94 g Fat: 7.91 g Carbohydrates: 0.23 g

16. Tomato, Herb, and Goat Cheese Frittata

Preparation Time: 15 minutes

Cooking Time: 25 minutes

Servings: 2

Ingredients:

- 1 tablespoon olive oil
- 1/2-pint cherry or grape tomatoes
- 2 garlic cloves, minced
- 5 large eggs, beaten
- 3 tablespoons unsweetened almond milk
- 1/2 teaspoon salt
- Pinch freshly ground black pepper
- 2 tablespoons minced fresh oregano
- 2 tablespoons minced fresh basil
- 2 ounces (57 g) crumbled goat cheese (about ½ cup)

Directions:

1. Heat the oil in a nonstick skillet over medium heat. Add the tomatoes. As they start to cook, pierce some of them, giving off some of their juice. Reduce the heat to medium-low, cover the pan, and let the tomatoes soften.
2. When the tomatoes are mostly softened and broken down, remove the lid, add the garlic and continue to sauté.
3. Combine the eggs, milk, salt, pepper, and herbs in a medium bowl and whisk well to combine.

4. Turn the heat up to medium-high. Add the egg mixture to the tomatoes and garlic, then sprinkle the goat cheese over the eggs.
5. Cover the pan and let cook for about 7 minutes.
6. Uncover the pan and continue cooking for another 7 to 10 minutes, or until the eggs are set. Run a spatula around the edge of the pan to make sure it won't stick.
7. Let the frittata cool for about 5 minutes before serving. Cut it into wedges and serve.

Nutrition: calories: 417 fat: 31g Protein: 26g carbs: 12g fiber: 3g Sodium: 867mg

17. Prosciutto Breakfast Bruschetta

Preparation Time: 10 minutes

Cooking Time: 20 minutes

Servings: 4

Ingredients:

- 1/4 teaspoon kosher or sea salt
- 6 cups broccoli rabe, stemmed and chopped (about 1 bunch)
- 1 tablespoon extra-virgin olive oil
- 2 garlic cloves, minced (about 1 teaspoon)
- 1-ounce (28 g) prosciutto, cut or torn into ½-inch pieces
- 1/4 teaspoon crushed red pepper
- Nonstick cooking spray
- 3 large eggs
- 1 tablespoon unsweetened almond milk
- 1/4 teaspoon freshly ground black pepper
- 4 teaspoons grated Parmesan or Pecorino Romano cheese
- 1 garlic clove, halved
- 8 slices baguette-style whole-grain bread or 4 slices larger Italian-style whole-grain bread

Directions:

1. Bring a large stockpot of water to a boil. Add the salt and broccoli rabe, and boil for 2 minutes. Drain in a colander.

2. In a large skillet over medium heat, heat the oil. Add the garlic, prosciutto, and crushed red pepper, and cook for 2 minutes, stirring often. Add the broccoli rabe and cook for an additional 3 minutes, stirring a few times. Transfer to a bowl and set aside.
3. Place the skillet back on the stove over low heat and coat with nonstick cooking spray.
4. In a small bowl, whisk together the eggs, milk, and pepper. Pour into the skillet. Stir and cook until the eggs are soft-scrambled, 3 to 5 minutes. Add the broccoli rabe mixture back to the skillet along with the cheese. Stir and cook for about 1 minute, until heated through. Remove from the heat.
5. Toast the bread, then rub the cut sides of the garlic clove halves onto one side of each slice of the toast. (Save the garlic for another recipe.) Spoon the egg mixture onto each piece of toast and serve.

Nutrition: calories: 313 fat: 10g Protein: 17g carbs: 38g fiber: 8g Sodium: 559mg

18. Prosciutto, Avocado, and Veggie Sandwiches

Preparation Time: 10 minutes

Cooking Time: 0 minutes

Servings: 4

Ingredients:

- 8 slices whole-grain or whole-wheat bread
- 1 ripe avocado, halved and pitted
- 1/4 teaspoon freshly ground black pepper
- 1/4 teaspoon kosher or sea salt
- 4 romaine lettuce leaves, torn into 8 pieces total
- 1 large, ripe tomato, sliced into 8 rounds
- 2 ounces (57 g) prosciutto, cut into 8 thin slices

Directions:

1. Toast the bread and place it on a large platter.

2. Scoop the avocado flesh out of the skin into a small bowl. Add the pepper and salt. Using a fork or a whisk, gently mash the avocado until it resembles a creamy spread. Spread the avocado mash over all 8 pieces of toast.
3. to make one sandwich, take one slice of avocado toast, and top it with a lettuce leaf, tomato slice, and prosciutto slice. Top with another slice of lettuce, tomato, and prosciutto, then cover with a second piece of avocado toast (avocado-side down on the prosciutto). Repeat with the remaining ingredients to make three more sandwiches and serve.

Nutrition: calories: 262 fat: 12g Protein: 8g carbs: 35g fiber: 10g Sodium: 162mg

19. Chickpea and Hummus Patties in Pitas

Preparation Time: 15 minutes

Cooking Time: 13 minutes

Servings: 4

Ingredients:

- 1 can chickpeas, drained and rinsed
- 1/2 cup lemony garlic hummus or ½ cup prepared hummus
- 1/2 cup whole-wheat panko bread crumbs
- 1 large egg
- 2 teaspoons dried oregano
- 1/4 teaspoon freshly ground black pepper
- 1 tablespoon extra-virgin olive oil
- 1 cucumber, unpeeled (or peeled if desired), cut in half lengthwise
- 1 (6-ounce / 170-g) container 2% plain Greek yogurt
- 1 garlic clove, minced
- 2 whole-wheat pita bread, cut in half
- 1 medium tomato, cut into 4 thick slices

Directions:

1. In a

2. large bowl, mash the chickpeas with a potato masher or fork until coarsely smashed (they should still be somewhat chunky). Add the hummus, bread crumbs, egg, oregano,
3. In a large skillet over medium-high heat, heat the oil until very hot, about 3 minutes. Cook the patties for 5 minutes, then flip with a spatula—Cook for an additional 5 minutes.
4. While the patties are cooking, shred half of the cucumber with a box grater or finely chop with a knife. Stir together the shredded cucumber, yogurt, and garlic to make the tzatziki sauce in a small bowl. Slice the remaining half of the cucumber into ¼-inch-thick slices and set aside.
5. Toast the pita bread. To assemble the sandwiches, lay the pita halves on a work surface. Place a few slices of cucumber, a chickpea patty, and a tomato slice into each pita, then drizzle the sandwich

and pepper. Stir well to combine. With your hands, form the mixture into 4 (½-cup-size) patties. Press each patty flat to about ¾ inch thick and put it on a plate.
with the tzatziki sauce and serve.

Nutrition: calories: 308 fat: 8g Protein: 15g carbs: 45g fiber: 78g Sodium: 321mg

20. Morning Creamy Iced Coffee

Preparation Time: 5 minutes

Cooking Time: 0 minutes

Servings: 1

Ingredients:

- 1 cup freshly brewed strong black coffee, cooled slightly
- 1 tablespoon extra-virgin olive oil
- 1 tablespoon half-and-half or heavy cream (optional)
- 1 teaspoon MCT oil (optional)
- 1/8 teaspoon almond extract
- 1/8teaspoon ground cinnamon

Directions:

1. Pour the slightly cooled coffee into a blender or large glass (if using an immersion blender).
2. Add the olive oil, half-and-half (if using), MCT oil (if using), almond extract, and cinnamon.
3. Blend well until smooth and creamy. Drink warm and enjoy.

Nutrition: calories: 128 fat: 14g Protein: 0g carbs: 0g fiber: 0g Sodium: 5mg

21. Versatile Sandwich Round

Preparation Time: 5 minutes

Cooking Time: 2 minutes

Servings: 1

Ingredients:

- 3 tablespoons almond flour
- 1 tablespoon extra-virgin olive oil
- 1 large egg
- 1/2 teaspoon dried rosemary, oregano, basil, thyme, or garlic powder (optional)
- 1/4 teaspoon baking powder
- 1/8 teaspoon salt

Directions:

In a microwave-safe ramekin, combine the almond flour, olive oil, egg, rosemary (if using), baking powder, and salt. Mix well with a fork.

Microwave for 90 seconds on high.

Slide a knife around the edges of the ramekin and flip to remove the bread.

Slice in half with a serrated knife if you want to use it to make a sandwich.

22. Tuna and Avocado Salad Sandwich

Preparation Time: 10 minutes

Cooking Time: 2 minutes

Servings: 4

Ingredients:

- 4 versatile sandwich rounds
- 2 (4-ounce/ 113-g) cans tuna, packed in olive oil
- 2 tablespoons roasted garlic aioli or avocado oil mayonnaise with 1 to 2 teaspoons freshly

squeezed lemon juice and/or zest
- 1 very ripe avocado, peeled, pitted, and mashed
- 1 tablespoon chopped fresh capers (optional)
- 1 teaspoon chopped fresh dill or ½ teaspoon dried dill

Directions:

1. Make sandwich rounds according to a recipe. Cut each round in half and set it aside.
2. In a medium bowl, place the tuna and the oil from cans. Add the aioli, avocado, capers (if using), and dill and blend well with a fork.
3. Toast sandwich rounds and fills each with one-quarter of the tuna salad, about 1/3 cup.

Nutrition: calories: 436 fat: 36g Protein: 23g carbs: 5g fiber: 3g Sodium: 790mg

23. Protein Oatcakes

Preparation Time: 10 minutes

Cooking Time: 5 minutes

Servings: 1

Ingredients:

- 70g oatmeal
- 15g protein
- 1 egg white
- 1/2 cup water
- 1/2 teaspoon cinnamon
- 60g curd
- 1 teaspoon cacao powder
- 15g sugar

Directions:

1. Mix the oatmeal, protein, egg white, and water in a bowl.
2. Preheat a saucepan to medium heat.
3. Place the mixture into the saucepan.
4. While waiting, prepare the topping by mixing the curd, cinnamon, and sugar in a second bowl.
5. Remove the oatcake from the saucepan when it becomes golden-brown.
6. Serve on a plate.
7. Add the topping and cocoa powder.

Nutrition: Calories: 440 Protein: 1.1g Fiber: 0.8g Carbohydrates: 6.1g

24. Polenta with Arugula, Figs, and Blue Cheese

Preparation Time: 10 minutes

Cooking Time: 40 minutes

Servings: 4

Ingredients:

- 1 cup coarse-ground cornmeal
- 1/2 cup oil-packed sun-dried tomatoes, chopped
- 1 teaspoon minced fresh thyme or ¼ teaspoon dried
- 1/2 teaspoon table salt
- 1/4 teaspoon pepper
- 3 tablespoons extra-virgin olive oil, divided
- 2 ounces (57 g) baby arugula
- 4 figs, cut into ½-inch-thick wedges
- 1 tablespoon balsamic vinegar
- 2 ounces (57 g) blue cheese, crumbled
- 2 tablespoons pine nuts, toasted

Directions:

1. Add 1 cup of water to a pot. Fold a sheet of aluminum foil into a 16 by 6-inch sling, then rest 1½-quart round soufflé dish in the center of the sling. Whisk 4 cups of water, cornmeal, tomatoes, thyme, salt, and pepper together in a bowl, then transfer mixture to soufflé dish. Using sling, lower soufflé dish into a pot and onto trivet; allow narrow edges of a sling to rest along sides of the insert.
2. Cover the pot—Cook for 40 minutes at high heat. Turn off the heat. Carefully remove the lid, allowing steam to escape away from you.
3. I am using a sling, transfer the soufflé dish to the wire rack. Whisk 1 tablespoon oil into polenta, smoothing out any lumps. Let sit until thickened slightly, about 10 minutes—season with salt and pepper to taste.

4. Toss arugula and figs with vinegar and the remaining 2 tablespoons of oil in a bowl, and season with salt and pepper to taste. Divide polenta among individual serving plates and top with arugula mixture, blue cheese, and pine nuts. Serve.

Nutrition: calories: 360 fat: 21g Protein: 7g carbs: 38g fiber: 8g Sodium: 510mg

25. Pumpkin Layers with Honey Granola

Preparation Time: 5 minutes

Cooking Time: 0 minutes

Servings: 4

Ingredients:

- 1 (15-ounce / 425-g) can pure pumpkin purée
- 4 teaspoons honey, additional to taste
- 1 teaspoon pumpkin pie spice
- 1/4 teaspoon ground cinnamon
- 2 cups plain, unsweetened, full-fat Greek yogurt
- 1 cup honey granola

Directions:

1. In a large bowl, mix the pumpkin purée, honey, pumpkin pie spice, and cinnamon. Cover and refrigerate for at least 2 hours.
2. To make the parfaits, pour ¼ cup pumpkin mix, ¼ cup yogurt, and ¼ cup granola in each cup. Repeat Greek yogurt and pumpkin layers and top with honey granola.

Nutrition: calories: 264 fat: 9g Protein: 15g carbs: 35g fiber: 6g Sodium: 90mg

26. Shakshuka with Cilantro

Preparation Time: 15 minutes

Cooking Time: 18 minutes

Servings: 4

Ingredients:

- 2 tablespoons extra-virgin olive oil

- 1 cup chopped shallots
- 1 cup chopped red bell peppers
- 1 cup finely diced potato
- 1 teaspoon garlic powder
- 1 can diced tomatoes, drained
- 1/4 teaspoon turmeric
- 1/4 teaspoon paprika
- 1/4 teaspoon ground cardamom
- 4 large eggs
- 1/4 cup chopped fresh cilantro

Directions:

1. Preheat the oven to 350ºF (180ºC).
2. In an oven-safe sauté pan or skillet, heat the olive oil over medium-high heat and sauté the shallots, occasionally stirring, for about 3 minutes, until fragrant. Add the bell peppers, potato, and garlic powder. Cook, uncovered, for 10 minutes, stirring every 2 minutes.
3. Add the tomatoes, turmeric, paprika, and cardamom to the skillet and mix well. Once bubbly, remove from heat and crack the eggs into the skillet so the yolks face up.
4. Put the skillet in the oven and cook for an additional 5 to 10 minutes, until eggs are cooked to your preference. Garnish with the cilantro and serve.

Nutrition: calories: 224 fat: 12g Protein: 9g carbs: 20g fiber: 3g Sodium: 278mg

27. Pumpkin Muffins

Preparation Time: 15 minutes

Cooking Time: 15 minutes

Servings: 12 muffins

Ingredients:

- Nonstick cooking spray
- 1½ cups granulated sugar
- 1/2 cup sugar
- 3/4 cup all-purpose flour
- 2 teaspoons pumpkin pie spice
- 1 teaspoon baking soda
- 1/4 teaspoon salt
- Pinch nutmeg
- 3 mashed bananas
- 1 (15-ounce / 425-g) can pure pumpkin purée

- 1/2 cup plain, unsweetened, full-fat yogurt
- 1/2 cup butter, melted (optional)
- 2 large egg whites

Directions:

1. Preheat the oven to 350ºF (180ºC). Spray a muffin tin with cooking spray.
2. Mix the sugars, flour, pumpkin pie spice, baking soda, salt, and nutmeg in a large bowl. Mix the bananas, pumpkin purée, yogurt, and butter (if desired). Slowly mix the wet ingredients into the dry ingredients.
3. Using a mixer on high, whip the egg whites until stiff and fold them into the batter in a large glass bowl.
4. Pour the batter into a muffin tin, filling each cup halfway. Bake for 15 minutes, or until a fork inserted in the center comes out clean.

Nutrition: calories: 259 fat: 8g Protein: 3g carbs: 49g fiber: 3g Sodium: 226mg

28. Cardamom-Cinnamon Overnight Oats

Preparation Time: 10 minutes

Cooking Time: 0 minutes

Servings: 2

Ingredients:

- 1/2 cup vanilla, unsweetened almond milk (not Silk brand)
- 1/2 cup rolled oats
- 2 tablespoons sliced almonds
- 2 tablespoons simple sugar liquid sweetener
- 1 teaspoon chia seeds
- 1/4 teaspoon ground cardamom
- 1/4 teaspoon ground cinnamon

Directions:

1. Combine the almond milk, oats, almonds, liquid sweetener, chia seeds, cardamom, and cinnamon in a mason jar and shake well. Store in the refrigerator for 8 to 24 hours, then serve cold or heated.

Nutrition: calories: 131 fat: 6g Protein: 5g carbs: 17g fiber: 4g Sodium: 45mg

29. Vanilla Raspberry Overnight Oats

Preparation Time: 10 minutes

Cooking Time: 0 minutes

Servings: 2

Ingredients:

- 2/3 cup vanilla, unsweetened almond milk
- 1/3 cup rolled oats
- 1/4 cup raspberries
- 1 teaspoon honey
- 1/4 teaspoon turmeric
- 1/8 teaspoon ground cinnamon
- Pinch ground cloves

Directions:

1. In a mason jar, combine the almond milk, oats, raspberries, honey, turmeric, cinnamon, and cloves and shake well. Store in the refrigerator for 8 to 24 hours, then serve cold or heated.

Nutrition: calories: 82 fat: 2g Protein: 2g carbs: 14g fiber: 3g Sodium: 98mg

30. Toasted Sesame Ginger Chicken

Preparation Time: 10 minutes

Cooking Time: 15 minutes

Servings: 4

Ingredients:

- 1 Tablespoon Toasted Sesame Ginger Seasoning (or toasted sesame seeds, garlic, onion powder, red pepper, ground ginger, salt, pepper, and lemon)
- 1 1/2 lbs. boneless, skinless chicken breast
- 4 teaspoons Olive Oil

Directions:

1. On a clean, dry cutting board put the chicken breasts.
2. Softly flatten the chicken breasts to the approx. The thickness of 3/8 using a beef hammer or a frying pan's backside.
3. Dust with some seasoning.

4. Heat the Olive Oil over medium-high flame in a big, nonstick frying pan.
5. Add the chicken and cook on one side for about 7-8 minutes, until a beautiful crust has created — it will be mildly orange.
6. Turn the chicken softly and cook on the other side for a further 5-6 minutes before the chicken is thoroughly cooked.
7. Serve hot or cooled over salad with your favorite side dish. Makes about 4 servings.

Nutrition: Energy (calories): 310 kcal Protein: 16.14 g Fat: 10.64 g Carbohydrates: 36.65 g

31. Tender and Tasty Fish Tacos

Preparation Time: 15 minutes

Cooking Time: 15 minutes

Servings: 4

Ingredients:
- 2 teaspoons Olive Oil or oil and fresh garlic your favorite taco condiments
- 1 capful (1 Tablespoon) Southwestern Seasoning or Phoenix Sunrise Seasoning or cumin, garlic, cilantro, red pepper, onion, parsley, paprika, salt & pepper (or low sodium taco seasoning)
- 1 3/4 lbs. cod or haddock (wild-caught)

Directions:
1. Clean your fish and slice it into 1" pieces.
2. Sprinkle with the seasoning and toss over to coat the fish thoroughly.
3. Heat the Olive Oil over medium-high flame in a big, nonstick frying pan.
4. Add the fish and cook for about 10 to 12 minutes until the fish is transparent and splits into pieces. Be cautious not to overcook; otherwise, the fish may be dry and chewy.

5. With your favorite condiments, serve warm.
6. Makes about 4 servings.

Nutrition: Energy (calories): 748 kcal Protein: 29.23 g Fat: 6.64 g Carbohydrates: 148.64 g

32. Sausage Stuffed Mushrooms

Preparation Time: 5 minutes

Cooking Time: 25 minutes

Servings: 4

Ingredients:

- 4 large Portobello mushrooms (caps and stems)
- 1 capful (1 Tablespoon) Garlic & Spring Onion Seasoning or Garlic Gusto Seasoning or chopped garlic, chopped chives, garlic powder, onion powder, salt, and pepper to taste
- 1 1/2 pounds lean Italian sausage (85-94% lean)

Directions:

1. Preheat the oven to 350 ° C. Cut the mushroom stems carefully and clean both the tops and stems,
2. The stems are chopped into tiny pieces and placed in a bowl. Put the meat and spices into the bowl and mix all the spices well, using your fingertips. Set the smooth side of the mushroom caps on a wide cookie sheet or baking tray.
3. Divide 4 equal sections of the meat mixture and lightly press one section into each mushroom head.
4. Bake with your favorite side dishes for about 25 minutes & serve crispy. Make 4 servings or so.

Nutrition: Energy (calories): 437 kcal Protein: 31.52 g Fat: 30.89 g Carbohydrates: 16.74 g

33. Orange French Toast

Preparation Time: 5 minutes

Cooking Time: 15 minutes

Servings: 6

Ingredients:

- 1 cup unsweetened almond milk
- 3 large eggs
- 2 teaspoons grated orange zest
- 1 teaspoon vanilla extract
- 1/4 teaspoon ground cardamom
- 1/4 teaspoon ground cinnamon
- 1 loaf of boule bread, sliced 1 inch thick (gluten-free preferred)
- 1 banana, sliced
- ¼ cup Berry and Honey Compote

Directions:

1. Heat a large nonstick sauté pan or skillet over medium-high heat.
2. Mix the milk, eggs, orange zest, vanilla, cardamom, and cinnamon in a large, shallow dish. Working in batches, dredge the bread slices in the egg mixture and put them in the hot pan.
3. Cook for 5 minutes on each side, until golden brown. Serve, topped with banana and drizzled with honey compote.

Nutrition: calories: 394 fat: 6g Protein: 17g carbs: 68g fiber: 3g Sodium: 716mg

34. Sweet Potato Toast

Preparation Time: 5 minutes

Cooking Time: 15 minutes

Servings: 4

Ingredients:

- 2 plum tomatoes, halved
- 6 tablespoons extra-virgin olive oil, divided
- Salt and freshly ground black pepper, to taste
- 2 large sweet potatoes, sliced lengthwise
- 1 cup fresh spinach
- 8 medium asparagus, trimmed

- 4 large cooked eggs or egg substitute (poached, scrambled, or fried)
- 1 cup arugula
- 4 tablespoons pesto
- 4 tablespoons shredded Asiago cheese

Directions:

1. Preheat the oven to 450ºF (235ºC).
2. Brush the plum tomato halves with 2 tablespoons of olive oil on a baking sheet and season with salt and pepper. Roast the tomatoes in the oven for approximately 15 minutes, then remove from the oven and allow to rest.
3. Put the sweet potato slices on a separate baking sheet, brush about 2 tablespoons of oil on each side, and season with salt and pepper. Bake the sweet potato slices for about 15 minutes, flipping once after 5 to 7 minutes, until just tender. Remove from the oven and set aside.
4. In a sauté pan or skillet, heat the remaining 2 tablespoons of olive oil over medium heat and sauté the fresh spinach until just wilted. Remove from the pan and rest on a paper towel-lined dish. In the same pan, add the asparagus and sauté, turning throughout. Transfer to a paper towel-lined dish.
5. Place the grilled sweet potato slices on serving plates and divide the spinach and asparagus evenly among the slices. Place a prepared egg on top of the spinach and asparagus. Top this with ¼ cup of arugula.
6. Finish by drizzling with 1 tablespoon of pesto and sprinkle with 1 tablespoon of cheese. Serve with 1 roasted plum tomato.

Nutrition: calories: 441 fat: 35g Protein: 13g carbs: 23g fiber: 4g Sodium: 481mg

35. Cheesy Mini Frittatas

Preparation Time: 10 minutes

Cooking Time: 25 minutes

Servings: 6

Ingredients:

- Nonstick cooking spray
- 1 1/2 tablespoons extra-virgin olive oil
- 1/4 cup chopped red potatoes (about 3 small)
- 1/4 cup minced onions
- 1/4 cup chopped red bell pepper
- 1/4 cup asparagus, sliced lengthwise in half and chopped
- 4 large eggs
- 4 large egg whites
- 1/2 cup unsweetened almond milk
- Salt and freshly ground black pepper, to taste
- 1/2 cup shredded low-moisture, part-skim Mozzarella cheese, divided

Directions:

1. Preheat the oven to 350ºF (180ºC). Using nonstick cooking spray, prepare a 12-count muffin pan.
2. In a medium sauté pan or skillet, heat the oil over medium heat and sauté the potatoes and onions for about 4 minutes, until the potatoes are fork-tender.
3. Add the bell pepper and asparagus and sauté for about 4 minutes, until just tender. Transfer the contents of a pan onto a paper-towel-lined plate to cool.
4. Whisk together the eggs, egg whites, and milk in a bowl—season with salt and pepper.
5. Once the vegetables are cooled to room temperature, add the vegetables and ¼ cup of Mozzarella cheese.
6. Using a spoon or ladle, evenly distribute the contents of the bowl into the prepared muffin pan, filling the cups about halfway.

7. Sprinkle the remaining ¼ cup of cheese over the top of the cups.
8. Bake for 20 to 25 minutes, or until eggs reach an internal temperature of 145ºF (63ºC) or the center is solid.
9. Allow the mini frittatas to rest for 5 to 10 minutes before removing the muffin pan and serving.

Nutrition: calories: 133 fat: 9g Protein: 10g carbs: 4g fiber: 1g Sodium: 151mg

36. Savory Lentil Waffles

Preparation Time: 10 minutes

Cooking Time: 20 minutes

Servings: 4

Ingredients

- 1 14.5-oz. can lentils, rinsed
- 1/4 small red onion, thinly sliced
- 1/4 c. golden raisins, chopped
- 3 tbsp. olive oil
- 3 tbsp. sherry vinegar
- 1 c. store-bought waffle mix
- 1/8 tsp. salt
- 1/8 tsp. pepper
- 4 c. baby arugula
- 1/4 c. roasted almonds, chopped
- plain Greek yogurt, for serving

Directions

1. In a medium bowl, red onion, combine lentils, raisins, olive oil, and sherry vinegar.
2. Beat waffle mix, curry powder, ground coriander, salt, and pepper in a large bowl. Prepare and cook 2-waffles in the waffle iron according to the manufacturer's directions.
3. Cut the waffles into pieces and divide them with Greek yogurt if desired. Top with lentil salad.

Nutrition

389 calories, 13 g pro, 50 g carbohydrates, 10 g fiber, 14 g sugars (0 g added sugars), 16 g fat (2 g saturated fat), 0 mg Chol, 503 mg sodium

37. Baked Dandelion Toast

Preparation Time: 10 minutes

Cooking Time: 15 minutes

Servings: 4

Ingredients

- 2 tbsp. olive oil
- 1 small red onion, thinly sliced
- 1/8 tsp. red pepper flakes
- 2 tbsp. lemon juice
- 1 bunch dandelion greens
- 1/4 tsp. salt
- 1/4 tsp. pepper
- 4 oz. feta cheese
- 1/4 c. plain yogurt (not Greek)
- 1 tsp. grated lemon zest
- 1 loaf ciabatta, split and toasted
- 2 tbsp. small mint leaves

Directions

1. You need to heat olive oil in a large skillet over medium heat. Add red onion and red pepper flakes and cook, occasionally stirring, until softened, 4 to 5 minutes.
2. Add lemon juice and cook until evaporated, about 30 seconds. Remove from heat, add dandelion greens (about 8 oz, with 5 inches of stem discarded), season with salt and pepper, and toss until it starts to wilt.
3. Meanwhile, crumble feta cheese in a mini food processor and pulse four times. While the food processor is running, add yogurt and the lemon zest; puree until smooth and creamy. (You can also crumble feta very finely in a bowl and beat with yogurt and lemon zest.)
4. Spread over ciabatta, cover with green, and sprinkle with mint.

Nutrition

148 calories, 4.69 g pro, 2.91 g carbohydrates, 0.1 g fiber, 2.32 g sugars 13.31 g fat 27 mg Chol, 413mg sodium

38. Spiced Almond Pancakes

Preparation Time: 10 minutes

Cooking Time: 20 minutes

Servings: 6

Ingredients:

- 2 cups unsweetened almond milk, at room temperature
- ½ cup melted coconut oil, plus more for greasing the skillet
- 2 large eggs, at room temperature
- 2 teaspoons honey
- 1 ½ cups whole-wheat flour
- ½ cup almond flour
- 1 ½ teaspoons baking powder
- ½ teaspoon baking soda
- ¼ teaspoon sea salt
- ¼ teaspoon ground cinnamon

Directions:

1. Whisk the almond milk, coconut oil, eggs, and honey in a large bowl until blended.
2. Sift together the whole-wheat flour, almond flour, baking powder, baking soda, sea salt, and cinnamon in a medium bowl until well mixed.
3. Add the flour mixture to the milk mixture and whisk until just combined.
4. Grease a large skillet with coconut oil and place it over medium-high heat.
5. Add the pancake batter in ½-cup measures, about 3 for a large skillet. Cook for about 3 minutes until the edges are firm, the bottom is golden, and the bubbles on the surface break. Flip and cook for about 2 minutes more until the other side is golden brown and the pancakes are cooked through. Transfer to a plate and wipe the skillet with a clean paper towel.
6. Regrease the skillet and repeat until the remaining batter is used.
7. Serve the pancakes warm with fresh fruit, if desired.
8. Cooking tip: The pancakes can be made ahead. After they cool, keep refrigerated for a cold treat topped with a spoonful of

honey. You can also quickly reheat the cooked pancakes in a toaster if you prefer them warm.

Nutrition: Calories: 286 Total Fat: 17g Saturated Fat: 12g Carbohydrates: 27g Fiber: 1g Protein: 6g

39. Crustless Sun-Dried Tomato Quiche

Preparation Time: 15 minutes

Cooking Time: 25 minutes

Servings: 4

Ingredients:

- 6 large eggs
- ¼ cup goat cheese
- 2 tablespoons milk
- Pinch cayenne pepper
- 1 teaspoon extra-virgin olive oil
- 2 shallots, finely chopped
- ½ teaspoon minced garlic
- 10 sun-dried tomatoes, quartered
- 1 teaspoon chopped fresh parsley
- Pinch sea salt
- Pinch freshly ground black pepper

Directions:

1. Preheat the oven to 375°F.
2. Whisk the eggs, goat cheese, milk, and cayenne pepper to blend in a medium bowl.
3. Place a 9-inch ovenproof skillet over medium-high heat and add the olive oil.
4. Add the shallots and garlic to the skillet, and sauté for about 2 minutes until tender.
5. Pour in the egg mixture. Scatter the sun-dried tomatoes and parsley evenly over the top.
6. Season the quiche with sea salt and pepper.
7. Cook the quiche, lifting the edges to allow the uncooked egg to flow underneath, for about 3 minutes until the bottom is firm.
8. Place the skillet in the oven and bake for about 20 minutes until the egg is cooked through, golden, and puffy.

9. Cooking tip: If you have leftover quiche, wrap it in a tortilla the next day for a leisurely, hearty lunch or breakfast.

Nutrition: Calories: 171 Total Fat: 11g Saturated Fat: 4 Carbohydrates: 5g Fiber: 1g Protein: 13g

40. Spinach Curry Pancakes with Apple, Raisins, And Chickpeas

Preparation Time: 20 minutes

Cooking Time: 40 minutes

Servings: 6

Ingredients

- 2 LG eggs
- 1/3 C finely chopped fresh cilantro
- 1/4 tsp. black pepper
- 2 1/2 C 1% milk
- 1 C plus 2 tbsp all-purpose flour
- 1 yellow onion, chopped
- 1 can (15.5 oz) chickpeas, rinsed and drained
- 1 granny smith apple, diced
- 1/4 C golden raisins
- 2 tbsp. madras curry powder
- 10 oz. fresh spinach
- lemon wedges, for serving

Directions

1. In a blender, puree eggs, cilantro, pepper, 1 cup of milk and flour, 2- tablespoons of oil, and 1/4 teaspoon of salt. Lightly brush the 10 "non-stick skillet with cooking spray and heat over medium heat. Pour 1/3 cup of batter evenly into pan and cook until edges set, 1 minute. Flip and cook for 30 seconds. Repeat for remaining pancakes. Cover to keep warm.
2. Heat the remaining 1-tablespoon of oil in a skillet over medium heat. Add onion and keep cooking until soften, 5-minutes. Add chickpeas, apple, raisins, and curry powder—Cook for 3 minutes. Stir in the remaining 2-tablespoons of flour through and cook for 30 seconds. Stir in the remaining 1-1/2 cup milk. Cook until thick, 2 minutes.

Add spinach and the remaining 1/2 teaspoon of salt.

Nutrition: 106 calories, 5.04 g pro, 14.66 g carbohydrates, 2.4 g fiber, 4.08 g sugars 3.27 g fat 80 mg Chol, 85mg sodium

41. Swiss Chard Gingerbread Pan with Egg, Onion, And Tomato

Preparation Time: 0 minutes

Cooking Time: 28 minutes

Servings: 4

Ingredients

- 1 1/4 c. quartered cherry tomatoes
- 1 tbsp. red wine vinegar
- 2 bunches Swiss chard or rainbow chard
- 2 c. large chopped yellow onion
- 3 tbsp. extra-virgin olive oil
- 4 cloves garlic, minced
- 1/2 tsp. sea salt
- 1/2 tsp. freshly ground black pepper
- 4 large eggs

Directions

1. Toss cherry tomatoes with vinegar in a small bowl. Put aside.
2. Remove chard leaves from stems. Chop the leaves, put them in a large bowl of cold water, and flip to rinse. Transfer to a colander and leave a little water on the leaves. Rinse, dry, and thinly slice the stems.
3. Take a large cast-iron pan over medium heat, sauté chard stalks, and olive oil onion until soft, about 10 minutes. Lower the heat. Add garlic and cook for 1 minute. Add chard leaves, salt, and pepper. Turn up the heat and toss with tongs until the leaves wilt.
4. Make four notches or "nests" in Swiss chard with the back of a spoon. Break one egg in each nest. Cover pan, reduce heat slightly and cook until yolks are medium-hard about 4 minutes.

5. Add cherry tomatoes and vinegar to the pan and serve.

Nutrition: calories, 11 grams, 17 g carbohydrates (5 g fiber), 16 g fat (3 g saturated fat), 635 mg sodium

42. Cheesy Avocado Omelet

Preparation Time: 5 minutes

Cooking Time: 15 minutes

Servings: 2

Ingredients

- 1 tsp. olive oil
- 1 small red onion, finely chopped
- Kosher salt and pepper
- 6 cremini mushrooms, sliced
- 1 c. baby spinach
- 4 large eggs plus 2 egg whites
- 2 oz. sharp Cheddar, coarsely grated
- 1 c. grape tomatoes halved
- 1/4 c. fresh flat-leaf parsley, chopped
- 1/2 small avocado

Directions

1. You need to heat oil in a large non-stick frying pan over medium heat. Add the onion, season with 1/4 teaspoon salt and pepper, and cook, occasionally stirring for 4 minutes. Add the mushrooms and cook, occasionally stirring, until soft, 4 minutes. Stir in the spinach and cook until it starts to wilt.
2. Add eggs & start cooking; keep stirring for 1-minute, then cook without stirring until edges are browned, 2-3 minutes. Sprinkle with cheese and fold half over the other to make a semicircle.
3. Toss tomatoes with parsley and avocado and serve with a spoon over the omelet.

Nutrition: calories, 351 grams, 30.43 g carbohydrates (6.3 g fiber), 19.74 g fat (6.93 g saturated fat), 402 mg sodium

43. Bircher Muesli

Preparation Time: 10 minutes, Plus 6 Hours Or Overnight Soaking

Cooking Time: 5 mins

Servings: 4

Ingredients:

- 1½ cups rolled oats
- ½ cup unsweetened shredded coconut
- 2 cups unsweetened almond milk
- 2 bananas, mashed
- ½ cup chopped almonds
- ½ cup raisins
- ½ teaspoon ground cinnamon

Directions:

1. In a large sealable container, stir together the oats, coconut, and almond milk until well combined. Refrigerate the mixture to soak overnight.
2. In the morning, stir in the banana, almonds, raisins, and cinnamon to serve.
3. Substitution tip: If you do not want a vegetarian breakfast, use 2 percent milk instead of nut milk.

Nutrition: Calories 397 Total Fat: 18g Saturated Fat: 8g Carbohydrates: 55g Fiber: 10g Protein: 9g

Chapter 4. Snacks And Appetizers

44. Mediterranean Mezze Dish

Preparation Time: 20 minutes

Cooking Time: 30 minutes

Servings: 4

Ingredients

- 1/2 cup of kalamata or other flavorful olives
- ½-cup plain Greek yogurt stirred with a pinch of salt and a drizzle of olive oil
- 1 cup of hummus (homemade or store-bought)
- 1 cup of Easy Muhammara
- 2/3 of an English cucumber, sliced
- 1 cup of cherry tomatoes
- 1-large carrot, sliced diagonally
- A small bunch of grapes
- 4 ounces of feta cheese, broken into pieces, lightly drizzled with olive oil and a pinch of herbs
- 3-pita bread, quartered, lightly brushed with olive oil, and heated in the oven

Directions

1. Set out a large bowl or a generous cutting board. Place the olives, yogurt, hummus, and muhammara in small bowls and add to the bowl. Arrange the cucumber, tomatoes, carrots, grapes, and feta on the dish. Fill in the warm pita bread just before serving.

Nutrition: 307 Calories 16.06g Fat 30.52g Carbohydrates 10.07g Protein

45. Marinated Feta and Artichokes

Preparation Time: 10 minutes + 4 hours

Cooking Time: 0 minute

Servings: 3

Ingredients:

- 4 ounces traditional Greek feta, cut into ½-inch cubes
- 4 ounces drained artichoke hearts, quartered lengthwise
- 1/3 cup extra-virgin olive oil
- Zest and juice of 1 lemon
- 2 tablespoons roughly chopped fresh rosemary
- 2 tablespoons roughly chopped fresh parsley
- ½ teaspoon black peppercorns

Directions:

1. In a glass bowl, combine the feta and artichoke hearts. Add the olive oil, lemon zest and juice, rosemary, parsley, and peppercorns and toss gently to coat, being sure not to crumble the feta.
2. Cover and chill for 4 hours before serving.

Nutrition: 235 Calories 23g Fat 4g Protein 11g Carbohydrates

46. Citrus-Marinated Olives

Preparation Time: 10 minutes + 4 hours

Cooking Time: 0 minute

Servings: 4

Ingredients:

- 2 cups mixed green olives with pits
- ¼ cup red wine vinegar
- ¼ cup extra-virgin olive oil
- 4 garlic cloves, finely minced
- Zest and juice orange
- 1 teaspoon red pepper flakes
- 2 bay leaves
- ½ teaspoon ground cumin
- ½ teaspoon ground allspice

Directions:

1. Mix olives, vinegar, oil, garlic, orange zest and juice, red pepper flakes, bay leaves, cumin, and allspice in a jar. Cover and chill for 4 hours, tossing again before serving.

Nutrition: 133 Calories 14g Fat 1g Protein 4g Carbohydrates

47. Labneh and Veggie Parfaits

Preparation Time: 10 minutes

Cooking Time: 0 minutes

Servings: 2

Ingredients:

For the Labneh:

- 8 ounces (227 g) plain Greek yogurt (full-fat works best)
- Generous pinch salt
- 1 teaspoon za'atar seasoning
- 1 teaspoon freshly squeezed lemon juice
- Pinch lemon zest

For the Parfaits:

- ½ cup peeled, chopped cucumber
- ½ cup grated carrots
- ½ cup cherry tomatoes halved

Directions:

1. Make the Labneh
2. Line a strainer with cheesecloth and place it over a bowl.
3. Stir together the Greek yogurt and salt and place them in the cheesecloth. Wrap it up and let it sit for 24 hours in the refrigerator.
4. When ready, unwrap the labneh and place it into a clean bowl. Stir in the za'atar, lemon juice, and lemon zest.
5. Make the Parfaits
6. Divide the cucumber between two transparent glasses.
7. Top each portion of cucumber with about 3 tablespoons of labneh.
8. Divide the carrots between the glasses.
9. Top with another 3 tablespoons of the labneh.
10. Top parfaits with cherry tomatoes.

Nutrition:

Calories: 143; Total fat: 7g; Total carbs: 16g; Fiber: 2g; Sugar: 13g; Protein: 5g; Sodium: 187mg; Cholesterol: 25mg

48. Mediterranean Nachos

Preparation Time: 20 minutes

Cooking Time: 30 minutes

Servings: 4

Ingredient

- 4-5 pita bread, each cut into 8-triangles
- 1/2 cup chickpeas, drained and rinsed
- 1-teaspoon of olive oil + more for drizzle
- Salt and pepper to taste
- 1-teaspoon of onion powder
- 1-teaspoon of garlic powder
- 1-teaspoon paprika
- 1/2 medium cucumber, cut into small cubes
- 1/4 cup kalamata olives, pitted and sliced
- ¼ cup of green olives
- 1-large tomato, finely chopped
- 1/2 cup banana peppers, sliced
- ¼ red onion, thinly sliced
- 1/2 cup of feta crumbles
- 2-green onions, sliced for garnish
- Paperchains for garnish
- 2–3 TBSP fresh parsley, chopped for garnish
- Pinch of Za'atar spice for garnish
- Hummus, Tzatziki for serving

Directions

1. Start with preheating the oven to 375° F. Then line 2-baking trays with parchment paper and divide pita triangles over them; Lightly drizzle olive oil along with salt and pepper and toss evenly. Place the chickpeas on a second baking tray and mix with 1-teaspoon olive oil, salt, pepper, garlic powder, paprika, and onion powder. Now place both sheets in the oven & bake. Bake pita bread for 10 minutes and chickpeas for 15-20 minutes, stirring in between. Check for desired crunchiness and remove from the oven.
2. When the pita bread comes out of the oven, place them on a tray/plate.
3. Top pita nachos with all toppings (optional: you can return the nachos to the oven for 4 minutes if you want the toppings to be warm too!). Garnish with a pinch of za'atar evenly spread over French

fries, freshly ground pepper, green onion, and chopped parsley. Serve immediately with hummus and tzatziki sauce. See images for plating inspiration

Nutrition: 211 Calories 6.63g Fat 30.14g Carbohydrates 8.78g Protein

49. Smoked Salmon and Avocado Summer Rolls

Preparation Time: 15 minutes

Cooking Time: 30 minutes

Servings: 4

Ingredients

- 12 round rice paper wrappers
- 6-slices of smoked salmon
- 1-avocado, thinly sliced
- 2-3 cups of raw sprouts or cooked vermicelli
- 1-cucumber, seeded, and cut into strips
- miso sesame dressing or vissaus vinaigrette, dipping into

Directions

1. Take a rice paper wrapper and immerse it completely in a bowl of hot tap water for 10-15 seconds. Place the wrapper on a plate or cutting board - it will get softer as you assemble your roll. Add fillings as desired: avocado smoked salmon, cucumbers, Brussels sprouts, or noodles. Start folding the bottom half of the wrap over the filling, holding the fold in place, fold in the sides, and roll. Repeat if necessary. Dip in the miso sesame dressing or fish sauce vinaigrette and enjoy!
2. Roll the mixture into small balls, about 1-2 tablespoons per ball. Place in an airtight container and store in the refrigerator for up to 2 weeks. You can also store the balls in the freezer for up to 1 month.

Nutrition: Calories: 165kcal, Carbohydrates: 19g, Protein: 4g, Fat: 9g, Saturated Fat: 1g, Sodium: 9mg,

Potassium: 185mg, Fiber: 4g, Sugar: 10g, Calcium: 63mg Iron: 1 mg

50. Healthy Lemon Bars

Preparation Time: 15 minutes

Cooking Time: 40 minutes

Servings: 12

Ingredients

For the crust:

- ¼ cup coconut sugar (or 2-3 tablespoons honey or maple syrup)
- ¼-cup melted and cooled coconut oil
- 1-egg, at room temperature
- ¼ teaspoon of almond extract
- 1-cup packed fine almond flour
- 3-tablespoons of coconut flour
- 1/4 teaspoon of salt

For the filling:

- Peel of 1 lemon
- ½-cup freshly squeezed lemon juice
- ½ cup of honey
- 4-large eggs
- 1-egg yolk
- 1-tablespoon coconut flour, sifted (or sub tapioca flour or arrowroot flour)
- to garnish:
- Icing sugar (sifted)
- Lemon peel

Directions

1. Start with preheating the oven to 325 degrees F. Line an 8x8 inch pan with parchment paper. (Do not use a glass pan as this will likely burn the bottom of the crust.)
2. You need to make the crust: In a medium bowl, add the coconut oil, coconut sugar, egg, and almond extract. Mix until smooth. Add almond flour, coconut flour, and salt. Mix again until a dough forms. Then start pressing the dough evenly into the prepared pan with your hands. Bake for 10 minutes, remove from oven and let cool for two minutes before adding your filling.
3. While your crust is baking, you can make the filling: In a

medium bowl, whisk the lemon zest, lemon juice, honey, eggs, egg yolks, and coconut flour. Pour over the crust. Bake for 18-25 minutes or until filling is set and no longer shaking. Allow to cool completely on a wire rack, then refrigerate for at least 4 hours to set the bars. Once ready to serve, use a sharp knife to cut into 12 bars. I recommend garnishing them with icing sugar and a little lemon zest before serving. To enjoy!

Nutrition: Calories: 189kcal Fat: 11.5 g Saturated fat: 4.9 g Carbohydrates: 18.9 g Fiber: 1.5 g

51. Mediterranean Baking Tray With Halloumi Pieces

Preparation Time: 0 minutes

Cooking Time: 45 minutes

Servings: 2

Ingredients

- 400 g (14 oz) baby potatoes, waxed
- 4-carrots tops removed and scrubbed
- 2-red (paprika) peppers (paprika), core and seeds removed
- 1-zucchini (zucchini), garnished with a tail
- 1-garlic bulb
- 1-lemon washed
- 2-sprigs of fresh rosemary
- 60 ml extra virgin olive oil
- sea salt and freshly ground black pepper
- 250 g (8¾ oz) Haloumi
- 12 black Kalamata olives, drained and pitted
- to serve
- rocket (arugula) or mesclun
- roasted pine nuts
- sea salt and freshly ground black pepper
- balsamic vinegar from extra virgin olive oil

Directions

1. Start heating the oven to 200° C (400° F / Gas mark 6) & line a baking tray with parchment paper.

2. Cut the potatoes, carrots, bell pepper (bell pepper), & zucchini into bite-sized pieces, cut the garlic crosswise in half, and cut the lemon into thin wedges. Place on the baking tray and add the rosemary. Drizzle over the oil, season with salt and pepper, and mix until well coated. Bake for 25-30 minutes or until vegetables are almost cooked.
3. Divide the halloumi into bite-sized pieces and divide it over the vegetables along with the olives. Change the oven setting to grill, increase the temperature and grill the halloumi, olives, and vegetables for 5–10 minutes or until the halloumi is soft and golden and the vegetables are soft and golden brown.
4. Serve with a handful of arugulas, a drizzle of pine nuts and herbs, and a drizzle of oil and vinegar.

Nutrition: Calories: 217kcal Fat: 2.98 g Saturated fat: 0.43 g Carbohydrates: 44.96 g Fiber: 7.8 g

52. Burrata Caprese Stack

Preparation Time: 5 minutes

Cooking Time: 0 minutes

Servings: 4

Ingredients:

- 1 large organic tomato
- ½ teaspoon salt
- ¼ teaspoon black pepper
- 1 (4-ounce) ball burrata cheese
- 8 fresh basil leaves
- 2 tablespoons extra-virgin olive oil
- 1 tablespoon red wine

Direction

1. Slice the tomato into 4 thick slices, removing any rigid center core and sprinkle with salt and pepper. Place the tomatoes, seasoned-side up, on a plate.
2. Slice the burrata into 4 thick slices on a separate rimmed plate and place one slice on top

of each tomato slice. Top each with one-quarter of the basil and pour any reserved burrata cream from the rimmed plate over the top.
3. Drizzle with olive oil and vinegar and serve with a fork and knife.

Nutrition: 153 Calories 13g Fat 7g Protein 6g Carbohydrates

53. Zucchini-Ricotta Fritters with Lemon-Garlic Aioli

Preparation Time: 30 minutes

Cooking Time: 25 minutes

Servings: 4

Ingredient:

- 1 large zucchini
- 1 teaspoon salt, divided
- ½ cup whole-milk ricotta cheese
- 2 scallions
- 1 large egg
- 2 garlic cloves
- 2 tablespoons fresh mint (optional)
- 2 teaspoons grated lemon zest
- ¼ teaspoon freshly ground black pepper
- ½ cup almond flour
- 1 teaspoon baking powder
- 8 tablespoons extra-virgin olive oil
- 8 tablespoons Roasted Garlic Aioli

Direction

1. Place the shredded zucchini in a colander or on several layers of paper towels. Sprinkle with ½ teaspoon salt and let sit for 10 minutes. Using another layer of paper towel, press down on the zucchini to release any excess moisture and pat dry.
2. In a large bowl, combine the drained zucchini, ricotta, scallions, egg, garlic, mint (if using), lemon zest, remaining ½ teaspoon salt, and pepper and stir well.
3. Blend almond flour and baking powder. Mix in flour mixture

into the zucchini mixture and let rest for 10 minutes.
4. In a large skillet, working in four batches, fry the patties. For each batch of four, heat 2 tablespoons of olive oil over medium-high heat. Add 1 heaping tablespoon of zucchini batter per fritter, pressing down with the back of a spoon to form 2- to 3-inch fritters. Cover and let fry 2 minutes before flipping. Fry another 2 to 3 minutes, covered.
5. Repeat for the remaining three batches, using 2 tablespoons of olive oil for each batch.
6. Serve with aioli.

Nutrition: 448 Calories 42g Fat 8g Protein 8g Carbohydrates

54. Salmon-Stuffed Cucumbers

Preparation Time: 10 minutes

Cooking Time: 0 minute

Servings: 4

Ingredients:
- 2 large cucumbers, peeled
- 1 (4-ounce) can red salmon
- 1 medium very ripe avocado
- 1 tablespoon extra-virgin olive oil
- Zest and juice of 1 lime
- 3 tablespoons chopped fresh cilantro
- ½ teaspoon salt
- ¼ teaspoon black pepper

Directions:
1. Slice the cucumber into 1-inch-thick segments and using a spoon, scrape seeds out of the center of each segment and stand up on a plate.
2. Mix salmon, avocado, olive oil, lime zest and juice, cilantro, salt, and pepper in a medium bowl.
3. Spoon the salmon mixture into the center of each cucumber segment and serve chilled.

Nutrition: 159 Calories 11g Fat 9g Protein 20g Carbohydrates

55. Goat Cheese–Mackerel Pâté

Preparation Time: 10 minutes

Cooking Time: 0 minute

Servings: 4

Ingredients:

- 4 ounces olive oil-packed wild-caught mackerel
- 2 ounces goat cheese
- Zest and juice of 1 lemon
- 2 tablespoons chopped fresh parsley
- 2 tablespoons chopped fresh arugula
- 1 tablespoon extra-virgin olive oil
- 2 teaspoons chopped capers
- 2 teaspoons fresh horseradish (optional)

Directions:

1. In a food processor, blender, or large bowl with an immersion blender, combine the mackerel, goat cheese, lemon zest and juice, parsley, arugula, olive oil, capers, and horseradish (if using). Process or blend until smooth and creamy.
2. Serve with crackers, cucumber rounds, endive spears, or celery.

Nutrition: 118 Calories 8g Fat 9g Protein 15g Carbohydrates

56. Baba Ghanoush

Preparation Time: 9 minutes

Cooking Time: 11 minutes

Servings: 8

Ingredients:

- 2 tablespoons extra-virgin olive oil
- 1 large eggplant
- 3 cloves garlic
- ½ cup water
- 3 tablespoons fresh flat-leaf parsley
- ½ teaspoon salt
- ¼ teaspoon smoked paprika
- 2 tablespoons lemon juice
- 2 tablespoons tahini

Direction

1. Add 1 tablespoon oil to a pot. Add eggplant and cook until it begins to soften about 5 minutes. Add garlic and cook for 30 seconds.
2. Add water and close lid; cook for 6 minutes.
3. Strain cooked eggplant and garlic and add parsley, salt, smoked paprika, lemon juice, and tahini to a food processor or blender. Add remaining 1 tablespoon oil and process. Serve warm or at room temperature.

Nutrition: 79 Calories 6g Fat 2g Protein 3g Carbohydrates

57. Taste of the Mediterranean Fat Bombs

Preparation Time: 15 minutes + 4 hours

Cooking Time: 0 minute

Servings: 6

Ingredients:

- 1 cup crumbled goat cheese
- 4 tablespoons jarred pesto
- 12 pitted Kalamata olives
- ½ cup finely chopped walnuts
- 1 tablespoon chopped fresh rosemary

Directions:

1. Mix goat cheese, pesto, and olives. Cool for 4 hours to harden.
2. Create the mixture into 6 balls, about ¾-inch diameter. The mixture will be sticky.
3. Place the walnuts and rosemary in a small bowl and roll the goat cheese balls in the nut mixture to coat.

Nutrition: 166 Calories 15g Fat 5g Protein 8g Carbohydrates

58. Cream of Cauliflower Gazpacho

Preparation Time: 15 minutes

Cooking Time: 25 minutes

Servings: 6

Ingredients:

- 1 cup raw almonds

- ½ teaspoon salt
- ½ cup extra-virgin olive oil
- 1 small white onion
- 1 small head cauliflower
- 2 garlic cloves
- 2 cups chicken stock
- 1 tablespoon red wine vinegar
- ¼ teaspoon freshly ground black pepper

Directions:

1. Boil almonds in the water for 1 minute. Drain in a colander and run under cold water. Pat dry. Discard the skins.
2. In a food processor or blender, blend the almonds and salt. With the processor running, drizzle in ½ cup extra-virgin olive oil, scraping down the sides as needed. Set the almond paste aside.
3. In a stockpot, cook the remaining 1 tablespoon olive oil over medium-high heat. Sauté onion for 4 minutes. Add the cauliflower florets and sauté for another 3 to 4 minutes—Cook garlic for 1 minute more.
4. Add 2 cups stock and bring to a boil. Cover, reduce the heat to medium-low and simmer the vegetables until tender, 8 to 10 minutes. Pull out from the heat and allow to cool slightly.
5. Blend vinegar and pepper with an immersion blender. With the blender running, add the almond paste and blend until smooth, adding extra stock if the soup is too thick.
6. Serve warm, or chill in refrigerator for at least 4 to 6 hours to serve a cold gazpacho.

Nutrition: 505 Calories 45g Fat 10g Protein 11g Carbohydrates

59. Passion Fruit and Spicy Couscous

Preparation Time: 15 minutes

Cooking Time: 15 minutes

Servings: 4

Ingredients:

- 1 pinch of salt

- 1 pinch of allspice
- 1 teaspoon of mixed spice
- 1 cup of boiling water
- 2 teaspoons of extra-virgin olive oil
- ½ cup of full-fat Greek yogurt
- ½ cup of honey
- 1 cup of couscous
- 1 teaspoon of orange zest
- 2 oranges, peeled and sliced
- 2 tablespoons of passion fruit pulp
- ½ cup of blueberries
- ½ cup of walnuts, roasted and unsalted
- 2 tablespoons of fresh mint

Directions:

1. Combine the salt, allspice, mixed spice, honey, couscous, and boiling water in a mixing bowl. Cover the bowl and rest for five to ten minutes, or until the water has been absorbed. Using a fork, give the mixture a good stir, then add the diced walnuts.
2. In a separate bowl, combine the passion fruit, yogurt, and orange zest.
3. To serve, dish the couscous up into four bowls, add the yogurt mixture, and top with the sliced orange, blueberries, and mint leaves.

Nutrition: 100 calories 10.5g fat 2.1g protein 8.7g Carbohydrates

60. Honey and Vanilla Custard Cups with Crunchy Filo Pastry

Preparation Time: 25 minutes

Cooking Time: 2 hours

Servings: 4

Ingredients:

- 1 vanilla bean, cut lengthways
- 2 cups of full-fat milk
- 1/3 cup of honey
- 1 tablespoon of brown sugar
- 2 tablespoons of custard powder
- 4 to 6 ripe figs, quartered
- 1 sheet of filo pastry
- 2 tablespoons of raw pistachios

Directions:

1. Situate saucepan over medium heat, simmer vanilla bean, milk, and honey
2. In a heatproof dish, combine the sugar and custard powder. Transfer the milk mixture into the bowl containing the custard powder. Using a whisk, combine well and then transfer back into the saucepan.
3. Bring to a boil, constantly whisking until the custard thickens. Remove the vanilla bean.
4. Pour the custard into cups and allow to chill in the refrigerator for 2 hours.
5. Heat your oven to 350 F and line a baking tray with parchment.
6. Put the pastry sheet onto an even surface and spray lightly with olive oil cooking spray.
7. Sprinkle half the pistachios over the pastry and then fold the pastry in half. Heat 2 tablespoons of honey in the microwave, then coat the pastry.
8. Place the pastry into the oven and allow to bake for 10 minutes. Remove from heat and allow it to cool.
9. Gently break the filo pastry into pieces, then top the custard with the shards and fresh-cut figs.

Nutrition: 307 calories   17g fat   4g protein 6.5g Carbohydrates

61. Citrus Cups

Preparation Time: 15 minutes

Cooking Time: 15 minutes

Servings: 4

Ingredients:

- ½ cup of water
- 1 tablespoon of orange juice
- 3 cups of full-fat Greek yogurt
- 1 vanilla bean
- 1 ruby grapefruit
- 2 mandarins
- 1 orange
- 6 strips of mandarin rind
- 1/3 cup of powdered sugar

- 1 small handful of fresh mint leaves

Directions:

1. Slice open the vanilla bean lengthways and transfer the seeds into a medium saucepan. Add the pod to the saucepan, followed by the water, sugar, and mandarin rind.
2. Bring the mixture to a boil, turn it down to a simmer, and cook for five minutes or until the syrup thickens.
3. Allow to cool, remove the pod, and stir in the orange juice.
4. Pour the syrup over the sliced citrus fruits and allow to rest.
5. Dish the yogurt up into four bowls, top with the citrus and syrup, sprinkle with a bit of mint, then serve.

Nutrition: 217 calories 16g fat 4g protein 3.2g Carbohydrates

62. Bananas Foster

Preparation Time: 5 minutes

Cooking Time: 6 minutes

Servings: 4

Ingredients

- 2/3 cup dark brown sugar
- 1/4 cup butter
- 3 1/2 tablespoons rum
- 1 1/2 teaspoons vanilla extract
- 1/2 teaspoon of ground cinnamon
- 3 bananas, peeled and cut lengthwise and broad
- 1/4 cup coarsely chopped nuts
- vanilla ice cream

Direction

1. Melt the butter in a deep-frying pan over medium heat. Stir in sugar, rum, vanilla, and cinnamon.
2. When the mixture starts to bubble, place the bananas and nuts in the pan. Bake until the bananas are hot, 1 to 2 minutes. Serve immediately with vanilla ice cream.

Nutrition: 534 calories 23.8g fat 4.6g protein 5.7g Carbohydrates

63. Cranberry Orange Cookies

Preparation Time: 20 minutes

Cooking Time: 16 minutes

Servings: 24

Ingredients

- 1 cup of soft butter
- 1 cup of white sugar
- 1/2 cup brown sugar
- 1 egg
- 1 teaspoon grated orange peel
- 2 tablespoons orange juice
- 2 1/2 cups flour
- 1/2 teaspoon baking powder
- 1/2 teaspoon salt
- 2 cups chopped cranberries
- 1/2 cup chopped walnuts (optional)

Icing:

- 1/2 teaspoon grated orange peel
- 3 tablespoons orange juice
- 1 ½ cup confectioner's sugar

Direction

1. Preheat the oven to 190 ° C.
2. Blend butter, white sugar, and brown sugar. Beat the egg until everything is well mixed. Mix 1 teaspoon of orange zest and 2 tablespoons of orange juice. Mix the flour, baking powder, and salt; stir in the orange mixture.
3. Mix the cranberries and, if used, the nuts until well distributed. Place the dough with a spoon on ungreased baking trays.
4. Bake in the preheated oven for 12 to 14 minutes. Cool on racks.
5. In a small bowl, mix icing ingredients. Spread over cooled cookies.

Nutrition: 110 calories 4.8g fat 1.1 g protein 2.3g Carbohydrates

64. Vinegar Beet Bites

Preparation Time: 10 minutes

Cooking Time: 30 minutes

Servings: 4

Ingredients:

- 2 beets, sliced
- Pinch of sea salt and black pepper
- 1/3 cup balsamic vinegar
- 1 cup olive oil

Directions:

1. Spread the beet slices on a baking sheet lined with parchment paper, add the rest of the ingredients, toss and bake at 350 degrees F for 30 minutes.
2. Serve the beet bites cold as a snack.

Nutrition: calories 199, fat 5.4, fiber 3.5, carbs 8.5, protein 3.5

65. Mediterranean White Bean Harissa Dip

Preparation Time: 5 minutes

Cooking Time: 1 hour

Servings: 1½ cups

Ingredients:

- 1 whole head of garlic
- ½ cup olive oil, divided
- 1 (15-ounce / 425-g) can cannellini beans, drained and rinsed
- 1 teaspoon salt
- 1 teaspoon harissa paste (or more to taste)

Directions:

1. Preheat the oven to 350ºF (180ºC).
2. Cut about ½ inch off the top of a whole head of garlic and lightly wrap it in foil. Drizzle 1 to 2 teaspoons of olive oil over the top of the cut side. Place it in an oven-safe dish and roast it in the oven for about 1 hour or until the cloves are soft and tender.
3. Remove the garlic from the oven and let it cool. The garlic can be roasted up to 2 days ahead of time.
4. Remove the garlic cloves from their skin and place them in the bowl of a food processor along with the beans, salt, and harissa. Purée, drizzling in as much olive oil as needed until

the beans are smooth. If the dip seems too stiff, add additional olive oil to loosen the dip.

5. Taste the dip and add additional salt, harissa, or oil as needed.
6. Store in the refrigerator for up to a week.
7. Portion out ¼ cup of dip and serve with a mixture of raw vegetables and mini pita bread.

Nutrition: (¼ cup): Calories: 209 Total fat: 17g Total carbs: 12g Fiber: 3g; Sugar: 0g Protein: 4g Sodium: 389mg Cholesterol: 0mg

66. Apple Chips with Maple Chocolate Tahini

Preparation Time: 10 minutes

Cooking Time: 0 minutes

Servings: 2

Ingredients:

- 2 tablespoons tahini
- 1 tablespoon maple syrup
- 1 tablespoon unsweetened cocoa powder
- 1 to 2 tablespoons warm water (or more if needed)
- 2 medium apples
- 1 tablespoon roasted, salted sunflower seeds

Directions:

1. In a small bowl, mix the tahini, maple syrup, and cocoa powder. Add warm water, a little at a time, until thin enough to drizzle. Do not microwave it to thin it; it won't work.
2. Slice the apples crosswise into round slices, and then cut each piece in half to make a chip.
3. Lay the apple chips out on a plate and drizzle them with the chocolate tahini sauce.
4. Sprinkle sunflower seeds over the apple chips.

Nutrition: Calories: 261 Total fat: 11g Total carbs: 43g Fiber: 8g Sugar: 29g Protein: 5g Sodium: 21mg Cholesterol: 0mg

67. Strawberry Caprese Skewers with Balsamic Glaze

Preparation Time: 5 minutes

Cooking Time: 10 minutes

Servings: 2

Ingredients:

- ½ cup balsamic vinegar
- 16 whole, hulled strawberries
- 12 small basil leaves or 6 large leaves, halved
- 12 pieces of small Mozzarella balls (ciliegine)

Directions:

1. to make the balsamic glaze, pour the balsamic vinegar into a small saucepan and bring it to a boil. Reduce the heat to medium-low and simmer for 10 minutes, or until it's reduced by half and is thick enough to coat the back of a spoon.
2. On each of the 4 wooden skewers, place a strawberry, a folded basil leaf, and a Mozzarella ball, repeating twice and adding a strawberry on end. (Each skewer should have 4 strawberries, 3 basil leaves, and 3 Mozzarella balls.)
3. Drizzle 1 to 2 teaspoons of balsamic glaze over the skewers.

Nutrition: Calories: 206 Total fat: 10g Total carbs: 17g Fiber: 1g Sugar: 14g Protein: 10g Sodium: 282mg Cholesterol: 34mg

68. Eggplant Dip

Preparation Time: 10 minutes

Cooking Time: 40 minutes

Servings: 4

Ingredients:

- 1 eggplant, poked with a fork
- 2 tablespoons tahini paste
- 2 tablespoons lemon juice
- 2 garlic cloves, minced
- 1 tablespoon olive oil
- Salt and black pepper to the taste
- 1 tablespoon parsley, chopped

Directions:

1. Put the eggplant in a roasting pan, bake at 400 degrees F for 40 minutes, cool down, peel and transfer to your food processor. Blend the rest of the ingredients except the parsley, pulse well, divide into small bowls and serve as an appetizer with the parsley sprinkled on top.

Nutrition: 121 Calories 4.3g Fat 1.4g Carbohydrates 4.3g Protein

69. Veggie Fritters

Preparation Time: 10 minutes

Cooking Time: 10 minutes

Servings: 8

Ingredients:

- 2 garlic cloves, minced
- 2 yellow onions, chopped
- 4 scallions, chopped
- 2 carrots, grated
- 2 teaspoons cumin, ground
- ½ teaspoon turmeric powder
- Salt and black pepper to the taste
- ¼ teaspoon coriander, ground
- 2 tablespoons parsley, chopped
- ¼ teaspoon lemon juice
- ½ cup almond flour
- 2 beets, peeled and grated
- 2 eggs, whisked
- ¼ cup tapioca flour
- 3 tablespoons olive oil

Directions:

1. In a bowl, combine the garlic with the onions, scallions and the rest of the ingredients except the oil; stir well and shape medium fritters out of this mix.
2. Preheat pan over medium-high heat, place the fritters, cook for 5 minutes on each side, arrange on a platter and serve.

Nutrition: 209 Calories 11.2g Fat 4.4g Carbohydrates 4.8g Protein

70. Peppery Potatoes

Preparation Time: 10 minutes

Cooking Time: 18 minutes

Servings: 4

Ingredients:

- 4-pcs large potatoes, cubed
- 4-tbsp extra-virgin olive oil (divided)
- 3-tbsp garlic, minced
- ½-cup coriander or cilantro, finely chopped
- 2-tbsp fresh lemon juice
- 1¾-tbsp paprika
- 2-tbsp parsley, minced

Directions:

1. Place the potatoes in a microwave-safe dish. Pour over a tablespoon of olive oil. Cover the dish tightly with plastic wrap. Heat the potatoes for seven minutes in your microwave to par-cook them.
2. Cook 2 tablespoons of olive oil in a pan placed over medium-low heat. Add the garlic and cover—Cook for 3 minutes. Add the coriander, and cook for 2 minutes. Transfer the garlic-coriander sauce to a bowl, and set aside.
3. In the same pan placed over medium heat, heat 1 tablespoon of olive oil. Add the par-cooked potatoes. Do not stir! Cook for 3 minutes until browned, flipping once with a spatula. Continue cooking until browning all the sides.
4. Take out the potatoes and place them on a dish. Pour over the garlic-coriander sauce and lemon juice. Add the paprika, parsley, and salt. Toss gently to coat evenly.

Nutrition: 316.2 Calories 14.2g Fats 4.5g Protein

71. Turkey Spheroids with Tzatziki Sauce

Preparation Time: 10 minutes

Cooking Time: 20 minutes

Servings: 8

Ingredients:

For Meatballs:

- 2-lbs ground turkey
- 2-tsp salt
- 2-cups zucchini, grated
- 1-tbsp lemon juice
- 1-cup crumbled feta cheese

- 1½-tsp pepper
- 1½-tsp garlic powder
- 1½-tbsp oregano
- ¼-cup red onion, finely minced

For Tzatziki Sauce:

- 1-tsp garlic powder
- 1-tsp dill
- 1-tbsp white vinegar
- 1-tbsp lemon juice
- 1-cup sour cream
- ½-cup grated cucumber
- Salt and pepper

Directions:

Preheat your oven to 350 ºF.

For the Meatballs:

1. Incorporate all the meatball ingredients in a large mixing bowl. Mix well until thoroughly combined. Form the turkey mixture into spheroids, using ¼-cup of the mixture per spheroid.
2. Heat a non-stick skillet placed over high heat. Add the meatballs, and sear for 2 minutes.
3. Transfer the meatballs to a baking sheet. Situate the sheet in the oven, and bake for 15 minutes.

For the Tzatziki Sauce:

Combine and whisk together all the sauce ingredients in a medium-sized mixing bowl. Mix well until thoroughly combined. Refrigerate the sauce until ready to serve and eat.

Nutrition: 280 Calories 16g Fats 26.6g Protein

72. Cheesy Caprese Salad Skewers

Preparation Time: 15 minutes

Cooking Time: 0 minute

Servings: 10

Ingredients:

- 8-oz cherry tomatoes, sliced in half
- A handful of fresh basil leaves, rinsed and drained
- 1-lb fresh mozzarella, cut into bite-sized slices
- Balsamic vinegar

- Extra virgin olive oil
- Freshly ground black pepper

Directions:

1. Sandwich a folded basil leaf and mozzarella cheese between the halves of tomato onto a toothpick.
2. Drizzle with olive oil and balsamic vinegar on each skewer. to serve, sprinkle with freshly ground black pepper.

Nutrition: 94 Calories 3.7g Fats 2.1g Protein

73. Leafy Lacinato Tuscan Treat

Preparation Time: 10 minutes

Cooking Time: 0 minute

Servings: 1

Ingredients:

- 1-tsp Dijon mustard
- 1-tbsp light mayonnaise
- 3-pcs medium-sized Lacinato kale leaves
- 3-oz. cooked chicken breast, thinly sliced
- 6-bulbs red onion, thinly sliced
- 1-pc apple, cut into 9-slices

Directions:

1. Mix the mustard and mayonnaise until thoroughly combined.
2. Spread the mixture generously on each of the kale leaves. Top each leaf with 1-oz. chicken slices, 3-apple slices, and 2-red onion slices. Roll each kale leaf into a wrap.

Nutrition: 370 Calories 14g Fats 29g Protein

74. Greek Guacamole Hybrid Hummus

Preparation Time: 10 minutes

Cooking Time: 0 minute

Servings: 1

Ingredients:

- 1-15 oz. canned chickpeas
- 1-pc ripe avocado
- ¼-cup tahini paste
- 1-cup fresh cilantro leaves
- ¼-cup lemon juice

- 1-tsp ground cumin
- ¼-cup extra-virgin olive oil
- 1-clove garlic
- ½ tsp salt

Directions:

1. Drain the chickpeas and reserve 2-tablespoons of the liquid. Pour the reserved liquid into your food processor and add in the drained chickpeas.
2. Add the avocado, tahini, cilantro, lemon juice, cumin, oil, garlic, and salt. Puree the mixture into a smooth consistency.
3. Serve with pita chips, veggie chips, or crudités.

Nutrition: 156 Calories 12g Fats 3g Protein

75. Mediterranean-Style Trail Mix

Preparation Time: 10 minutes

Cooking Time: 0 minutes

Servings: 6

Ingredients:

- 1 cup roughly chopped unsalted walnuts
- ½ cup roughly chopped salted almonds
- ½ cup shelled salted pistachios
- ½ cup roughly chopped apricots
- 1/2 cup roughly chopped dates
- 1/3 cup dried figs, sliced in half

Directions:

In a large zip-top bag, combine the walnuts, almonds, pistachios, apricots, dates, and figs and mix well.

Nutrition: 348; Protein: 9g; Total Carbohydrates: 33g; Sugars: 22g; Fiber: 7g; Total Fat: 24g; Saturated Fat: 2g; Cholesterol: 0mg; Sodium: 95mg

76. Savory Mediterranean Spiced Popcorn

Preparation Time: 10 minutes

Cooking Time: 2 minutes

Servings: 4 to 6

Ingredients:

- 3 tablespoons extra-virgin olive oil
- 1/4 teaspoon garlic powder
- 1/4 teaspoon freshly ground black pepper
- 1/4 teaspoon sea salt
- 1/8 teaspoon dried thyme
- 1/8 teaspoon dried oregano
- 12 cups plain popped popcorn

Directions:

1. In a large sauté pan or skillet, heat the oil over medium heat, until shimmering, and then add the garlic powder, pepper, salt, thyme, and oregano until fragrant.
2. In a large bowl, drizzle the oil over the popcorn, toss, and serve.

Nutrition: 183; Protein: 3g; Total Carbohydrates: 19g; Sugars: 0g; Fiber: 4g; Total Fat: 12g; Saturated Fat: 2g; Cholesterol: 0mg; Sodium: 146mg

77. Hummus with Ground Lamb

Preparation Time: 10 minutes

Cooking Time: 15 minutes

Servings: 8

Ingredients:

- 10 ounces hummus
- 12 ounces lamb meat, ground
- ½ cup pomegranate seeds
- ¼ cup parsley, chopped
- 1 tablespoon olive oil
- Pita chips for serving

Directions:

1. Preheat pan over medium-high heat, cook the meat, and brown for 15 minutes, stirring often. Spread the hummus on a platter, spread the ground lamb all over, spread the pomegranate seeds and the parsley and serve with pita chips as a snack.

Nutrition: 133 Calories 9.7g Fat 6.4g Carbohydrates 5.4g Protein

78. The Ultimate Mediterranean Appetizer Dish

Preparation Time: 5 minutes

Cooking Time: 10 minutes

Servings: 17

Ingredients

Fruit and vegetables:

- Diced melon and slices wrapped in prosciutto
- green and purple grapes, fresh pears, sliced and an assortment of kalamata olives
- sliced carrots, cucumbers, celery, and cherry tomatoes

Bread and crackers:

Cheeses:

- Old gouda and raw gouda cut into cubes
- Greek feta drizzled with Mediterranean oregano
- Soft goat cheese topped with fig paste above link I Deli always about 120 grams of a piece of fresh soft goat cheese sliced

Directions

1. Freshly crumbled feta with jalapeno (preferably sheep's milk)
2. 8 oz feta, mix with chopped jalapeno (start with a teaspoon and add more to taste) or mix with chopped sun-dried tomatoes to taste. I also like to combine the two! Tomatoes and jalapeno together.
3. Drizzle the cheese mixture with extra virgin olive oil and spread it on crackers or as a dip for chips or pita bread.

Nutrition: 33 Calories 1.61g Fat 3.45g Carbohydrates 1.45g Protein

Chapter 5. Pasta and Rice Recipes

79. Bean and Veggie Pasta

Preparation Time: 10 minutes

Cooking Time: 15 minutes

Serves 2

Ingredients:

- 16 ounces (454 g) small whole-wheat pasta, such as penne, farfalle, or macaroni
- 5 cups water
- 1 (15-ounce / 425-g) can cannellini beans, drained and rinsed
- 1 (14.5-ounce / 411-g) can dice (with juice) or crushed tomatoes
- 1 yellow onion, chopped
- 1 red or yellow bell pepper, chopped
- 2 tablespoons tomato paste
- 1 tablespoon olive oil
- 3 garlic cloves, minced
- ¼ teaspoon crushed red pepper (optional)
- 1 bunch kale, stemmed and chopped
- 1 cup sliced basil
- ½ cup pitted Kalamata olives, chopped

Directions:

1. Add the pasta, water, beans, tomatoes (with juice if using diced), onion, bell pepper, tomato paste, oil, garlic, and crushed red pepper (if desired), to a large stockpot or deep skillet with a lid. Bring to a boil over high heat, stirring often.
2. Reduce the heat to medium-high, add the kale, and cook, continuing to stir often, until the pasta is al dente, about 10 minutes.
3. Remove from the heat and let sit for 5 minutes. Garnish with the basil and olives and serve.

Nutrition:

Calories: 565 fat: 17.7g Protein: 18.0g carbs: 85.5g fiber: 16.5g Sodium: 540mg

80. Roasted Ratatouille Pasta

Preparation Time: 10 minutes

Cooking Time: 30 minutes

Servings: 2

Ingredients:

- 1 small eggplant (about 8 ounces / 227 g)
- 1 small zucchini
- 1 portobello mushroom
- 1 Roma tomato, halved
- ½ medium sweet red pepper, seeded
- ½ teaspoon salt, plus additional for the pasta water
- 1 teaspoon Italian herb seasoning
- 1 tablespoon olive oil
- 2 cups farfalle pasta (about 8 ounces / 227 g)
- 2 tablespoons minced sun-dried tomatoes in olive oil with herbs
- 2 tablespoons prepared pesto

Directions:

1. Slice the ends off the eggplant and zucchini. Cut them lengthwise into ½-inch slices.
2. Place the eggplant, zucchini, mushroom, tomato, and red pepper in a large bowl and sprinkle with ½ teaspoon of salt. Using your hands, toss the vegetables well so that they're covered evenly with the salt. Let them rest for about 10 minutes.
3. While the vegetables are resting, preheat the oven to 400ºF (205ºC). Line a baking sheet with parchment paper.
4. When the oven is hot, drain off any liquid from the vegetables and pat them dry with a paper towel. Add the Italian herb seasoning and olive oil to the vegetables and toss well to coat both sides.

5. Lay the vegetables out in a single layer on the baking sheet. Roast them for 15 to 20 minutes, flipping them over after about 10 minutes or once they start to brown on the underside. When the vegetables are charred in spots, remove them from the oven.
6. While the vegetables are roasting, fill a large saucepan with water. Add salt and cook the pasta until al dente, about 8 to 10 minutes. Drain the pasta, reserving ½ cup of the pasta water.
7. When cool enough to handle, cut the vegetables into large chunks (about 2 inches) and add them to the hot pasta.
8. Stir in the sun-dried tomatoes and pesto and toss everything well. Serve immediately.

Nutrition:

Calories: 613 fat: 16.0g Protein: 23.1g carbs: 108.5g fiber: 23.0g Sodium: 775mg

81. Lentil and Mushroom Pasta

Preparation Time: 10 minutes

Cooking Time: 50 minutes

Servings: 2

Ingredients:

- 2 tablespoons olive oil
- 1 large yellow onion, finely diced
- 2 portobello mushrooms, trimmed and chopped finely
- 2 tablespoons tomato paste
- 3 garlic cloves, chopped
- 1 teaspoon oregano
- 2½ cups water
- 1 cup brown lentils
- 1 (28-ounce / 794-g) can diced tomatoes with basil (with juice if diced)
- 1 tablespoon balsamic vinegar
- 8 ounces (227 g) pasta of choice, cooked
- Salt and black pepper, to taste
- Chopped basil, for garnish

Directions:

1. Place a large stockpot over medium heat. Add the oil. Once the oil is hot, add the onion and mushrooms. Cover and cook until both are soft, about 5 minutes. Add the tomato paste, garlic, and oregano and cook for 2 minutes, stirring constantly.
2. Stir in the water and lentils. Bring to a boil, then reduce the heat to medium-low and cook for 5 minutes, covered.
3. Add the tomatoes (and juice if using diced) and vinegar. Replace the lid, reduce the heat to low and cook until the lentils are tender, about 30 minutes.
4. Remove the sauce from the heat and season with salt and pepper to taste. Garnish with the basil and serve over the cooked pasta.

Nutrition:

Calories: 463 fat: 15.9g Protein: 12.5g carbs: 70.8g fiber: 16.9g Sodium: 155mg

82. Spinach Pesto Pasta

Preparation Time: 10 minutes

Cooking Time: 10 minutes

Servings: 4

Ingredients:

- 8 oz whole-grain pasta
- 1/3 cup mozzarella cheese, grated
- 1/2 cup pesto
- 5 oz fresh spinach
- 1 3/4 cup water
- 8 oz mushrooms, chopped
- 1 tbsp olive oil
- Pepper
- Salt

Directions:

1. Add oil to a the pot.
2. Add mushrooms and sauté for 5 minutes.
3. Add water and pasta and stir well.
4. Seal pot with lid and cook on high for 5 minutes.
5. Once done, remove the lid.
6. Stir in remaining ingredients and serve.

Nutrition: Calories 213 Fat 17.3 g Carbohydrates 9.5 g Sugar 4.5 g Protein 7.4 g Cholesterol 9 mg

83. Authentic Pasta e Fagioli

Preparation Time: 6 minutes

Cooking Time: 15 minutes

Servings 4

Ingredients

- 2 tablespoons olive oil
- 1 teaspoon garlic, pressed
- 4 small-sized potatoes, peeled and diced
- 1 parsnip, chopped
- 1 carrot, chopped
- 1 celery rib, chopped
- 1 leek, chopped
- 1 (6-ounce) can tomato paste
- 4 cups water
- 2 vegetable bouillon cubes
- 8 ounces cannellini beans, soaked overnight
- 6 ounces elbow pasta
- 1/2 teaspoon oregano
- 1/2 teaspoon basil
- 1/2 teaspoon fennel seeds
- Sea salt, to taste
- 1/4 teaspoon freshly cracked black pepper
- 2 tablespoons Italian parsley, roughly chopped

Directions

1. Heat the oil in your pot and sauté the garlic, potatoes, parsnip, carrot, celery, and leek until they have softened.
2. Now, add the tomato paste, water, bouillon cubes, cannellini beans, elbow pasta, oregano, basil, fennel seeds, freshly cracked black pepper, and sea salt.
3. Secure the lid and cook for 9 minutes at high heat. Once cooking is complete, carefully remove the lid.
4. Serve with fresh Italian parsley. Bon appétit!

Nutrition: 486 Calories; 8.3g Fat; 95g Carbs; 12.4g Protein; 11.4g Sugars; 14.8g Fiber

84. Escarole And Cannellini Beans On Pasta

Preparation Time: 20 minutes

Cooking Time: 25 minutes

Servings: 8

Ingredients:

- Pepper and salt to taste
- 1 can 14.5-oz diced tomatoes with garlic and onion, drained
- 1 can 15.5-oz cannellini beans, with liquid
- 1 head escarole chopped
- 1 package 16-oz dry penne pasta

Directions:

1. Cook pasta according to package instructions, then drain and rinse under cold running water.
2. On medium-high fire, place skillet and cook diced tomatoes, cannellini beans with liquid and escarole.
3. Season with pepper and salt and cook until boiling.
4. Remove from fire and mix pasta.
5. Serve and enjoy.

Nutrition: Calories: 310; Carbs: 60.1g; Protein: 13.7g; Fat: 2.0g

85. Simple Pesto Pasta

Preparation Time: 10 minutes

Cooking Time: 10 minutes

Servings: 4

Ingredients:

- 1 lb. spaghetti
- 4 cups fresh basil leaves, stems removed
- 3 cloves garlic
- 1 tsp. salt
- 1/2 tsp. freshly ground black pepper
- 1/4 cup lemon juice
- 1/2 cup pine nuts, toasted
- 1/2 cup grated Parmesan cheese
- 1 cup extra-virgin olive oil

Directions:

1. Bring a large pot of salted water to a boil. Add the spaghetti to the pot and cook for 8 minutes.
2. Put basil, garlic, salt, pepper, lemon juice, pine nuts, and Parmesan cheese in a food processor bowl with a chopping blade and purée.
3. While the processor is running, slowly drizzle the olive oil through the top opening. Process until all the olive oil has been added.
4. Reserve ½ cup of the pasta water. Drain the pasta and put it into a bowl. Immediately add the pesto and pasta water to the pasta and toss everything together. Serve warm.

Nutrition: Calories: 113; Protein: 12.3g; Carbs: 3.4g; Fat: 6.3g

86. Meaty Baked Penne

Preparation Time: 10 minutes

Cooking Time: 40 minutes

Servings: 6

Ingredients:

- 1 lb. penne pasta
- 1 lb. ground beef
- 1 tsp. salt
- 1 (25-oz.) jar marinara sauce
- 1 (1-lb.) bag baby spinach, washed
- 3 cups shredded mozzarella cheese, divided

Directions:

1. Bring a large pot of salted water to a boil, add the penne, and cook for 7 minutes. Reserve 2 cups of e pasta water and drain the pasta.
2. Preheat the oven to 350°F.
3. In a large saucepan over medium heat, cook the ground beef and salt—Brown the ground beef for about 5 minutes.
4. Stir in marinara sauce and 2 cups of pasta water. Let simmer for 5 minutes.
5. Add a handful of spinach at a time into the sauce, and cook for another 3 minutes.

6. To assemble, in a 9-by-13-inch baking dish, add the pasta and pour the pasta sauce over it. Stir in 1½ cups of mozzarella cheese. Cover the dish with foil and bake for 20 minutes.
7. After 20 minutes, remove the foil, top with the rest of the mozzarella, and bake for another 10 minutes. Serve warm.

Nutrition: Calories: 173; Protein: 12.3g; Carbs: 3.4g; Fat: 6.3g

87. Mediterranean Pasta with Tomato Sauce and Vegetables

Preparation Time: 15 minutes

Cooking Time: 25 minutes

Servings: 8

Ingredients:

- 8 oz. linguine or spaghetti, cooked
- 1 tsp. garlic powder
- 1 (28 oz.) can whole peeled tomatoes, drained and sliced
- 1 tbsp. olive oil
- 1 (8 oz.) can tomato sauce
- ½ tsp. Italian seasoning
- 8 oz. mushrooms, sliced
- 8 oz. yellow squash, sliced
- 8 oz. zucchini, sliced
- ½ tsp. sugar
- ½ cup grated Parmesan cheese

Directions:

1. Mix tomato sauce, tomatoes, sugar, Italian seasoning, and garlic powder in a medium saucepan. Bring to boil on medium heat. Reduce heat to low. Cover and simmer for 20 minutes.
2. In a large skillet, heat olive oil on medium-high heat.
3. Add squash, mushrooms, and zucchini. Cook, stirring, for 4 minutes or until tender-crisp.
4. Stir vegetables into the tomato sauce.
5. Place pasta in a serving bowl.
6. Spoon vegetable mixture over pasta and toss to coat.
7. Top with grated Parmesan cheese.

Nutrition: Calories: 154 Protein: 6 g Fat: 2 g Carbs: 28 g

88. Cheesy Spaghetti with Pine Nuts

Preparation Time: 10 minutes

Cooking Time: 10 minutes

Servings: 4

Ingredients:

- 8 oz. spaghetti
- 4 tbsp. (½ stick) unsalted butter
- 1 tsp. freshly ground black pepper
- ½ cup pine nuts
- 1 cup fresh grated Parmesan cheese, divided

Directions:

1. Bring a large pot of salted water to a boil. Add the pasta and cook for 8 minutes.
2. In a large saucepan over medium heat, combine the butter, black pepper, and pine nuts. Cook for 2 to 3 minutes or until the pine nuts are lightly toasted.
3. Reserve ½ cup of the pasta water. Drain the pasta and put it into the pan with the pine nuts.
4. Add ¾ cup of Parmesan cheese and the reserved pasta water to the pasta and toss everything together to coat the pasta evenly.
5. Put the pasta in a serving dish and top with the remaining ¼ cup of Parmesan cheese.

Nutrition: Calories: 238; Protein: 12.3g; Carbs: 3.4g; Fat: 6.3g

89. Creamy Garlic-Parmesan Chicken Pasta

Preparation Time: 5 minutes

Cooking Time: 25 minutes

Servings: 6

Ingredients:

- 2 boneless, skinless chicken breasts
- 3 tbsp. extra-virgin olive oil
- 1½ tsp. salt
- 1 large onion, thinly sliced
- 3 tbsp. garlic, minced

- 1 lb. fettuccine pasta
- 1 cup heavy (whipping) cream
- ¾ cup freshly grated Parmesan cheese, divided
- ½ tsp. freshly ground black pepper

Directions:

1. Bring a large pot of salted water to a simmer.
2. Cut the chicken into thin strips.
3. In a large skillet over medium heat, cook the olive oil and chicken for 3 minutes.
4. Next, add the salt, onion, and garlic to the pan with the chicken—Cook for 7 minutes.
5. Bring the pot of salted water to a boil, add the pasta, and then cook for 7 minutes.
6. While the pasta is cooking, add the cream, ½ cup of Parmesan cheese, and black pepper to the chicken; simmer for 3 minutes.
7. Reserve ½ cup of the pasta water. Drain the pasta and add it to the chicken cream sauce.
8. Add the reserved pasta water to the pasta and toss it together. Let simmer for 2 minutes. Top with the remaining ¼ cup Parmesan cheese and serve warm.

Nutrition: Calories: 153; Protein: 12.3g; Carbs: 3.4g; Fat: 6.3g

90. Roasted Pepper Pasta

Preparation Time: 10 minutes

Cooking Time: 13 minutes

Servings: 6

Ingredients:

- 1 lb. whole wheat penne pasta
- 1 tbsp Italian seasoning
- 4 cups vegetable broth
- 1 tbsp garlic, minced
- 1/2 onion, chopped
- 14 oz jar roasted red peppers
- 1 cup feta cheese, crumbled
- 1 tbsp olive oil
- Pepper
- Salt

Directions:

1. Add roasted pepper into the blender and blend until smooth.

2. Add oil to your pot and heat it.
3. Add garlic and onion and sauté for 2-3 minutes.
4. Add blended roasted pepper and sauté for 2 minutes.
5. Add remaining ingredients except for feta cheese and stir well.
6. Seal pot with lid and cook on high heat. For 8 minutes.
7. Once done, remove the lid.
8. Top with feta cheese and serve.

Nutrition: Calories 459 Fat 10.6 g Carbohydrates 68.1 g Sugar 2.1 g Protein 21.3 g Cholesterol 24 mg

91. Italian Chicken Pasta

Preparation Time: 10 minutes

Cooking Time: 9 minutes

Servings: 8

Ingredients:

- 1 lb chicken breast, skinless, boneless, and cut into chunks
- 1/2 cup cream cheese
- 1 cup mozzarella cheese, shredded
- 1 1/2 tsp Italian seasoning
- 1 tsp garlic, minced
- 1 cup mushrooms, diced
- 1/2 onion, diced
- 2 tomatoes, diced
- 2 cups of water
- 16 oz whole wheat penne pasta
- Pepper
- Salt

Directions:

1. Add all ingredients except cheeses into the pot and stir well.
2. Seal pot with lid and cook on high heat for 9 minutes.
3. Once done, remove the lid.
4. Add cheeses and stir well and serve.

Nutritional Value (Amount per Serving): Calories 328 Fat 8.5 g Carbohydrates 42.7 g Sugar 1.4 g Protein 23.7 g Cholesterol 55 mg

92. Pesto Chicken Pasta

Preparation Time: 10 minutes

Cooking Time: 10 minutes

Servings: 6

Ingredients:

- 1 lb chicken breast, skinless, boneless, and diced
- 3 tbsp olive oil
- 1/2 cup parmesan cheese, shredded
- 1 tsp Italian seasoning
- 1/4 cup heavy cream
- 16 oz whole wheat pasta
- 6 oz basil pesto
- 3 1/2 cups water
- Pepper
- Salt

Directions:

1. Season chicken with Italian seasoning, pepper, and salt.
2. Add oil into the pot and heat.
3. Add chicken to the pot and sauté until brown.
4. Add remaining ingredients except for parmesan cheese, heavy cream, and pesto, and stir well.
5. Seal pot with lid and cook on high heat. For 5 minutes.
6. Once done, remove the lid.
7. Stir in parmesan cheese, heavy cream, and pesto, and serve.

Nutrition: Calories 475 Fat 14.7 g Carbohydrates 57 g Sugar 2.8 g Protein 28.7 g Cholesterol 61 mg

93. Fresh Sauce Pasta

Preparation Time: 15 minutes

Cooking Time: 15 minutes

Servings: 4

Ingredients:

- 1/8 teaspoon salt, plus more for cooking the pasta
- 1-pound penne pasta
- 1/4 cup olive oil
- 1 garlic clove, crushed
- 3 cups chopped scallions, white and green parts
- 3 tomatoes, diced
- 2 tablespoons chopped fresh basil
- 1/8 teaspoon freshly ground black pepper
- Freshly grated Parmesan cheese for serving

Directions:

1. Bring a large pot of salted water to a boil over high heat. Drop in the pasta, stir, and return the

water to a boil. Boil the pasta for about 6 minutes or until al dente.
2. A couple of minutes before the pasta is completely cooked, heat the olive oil in a medium saucepan over medium heat.
3. Add the garlic and cook for 30 seconds.
4. Stir in the scallions and tomatoes. Cover the pan and cook for 2 to 3 minutes.
5. Drain the pasta and add it to the vegetables. Stir in the basil and season with salt and pepper. Top with Parmesan cheese.

Nutrition: Calories: 477; Total Fat: 16g; Saturated Fat: 2g; Carbohydrates: 72g; Fiber: 3g; Protein: 15g; Sodium: 120mg

94. Three Sauces Lasagna

Preparation Time: 30 minutes

Cooking Time: 45 minutes

Servings: 8

Ingredients:

- 1 cup ricotta
- 1 cup Basil Pesto, or store-bought
- 4 cups Basic Tomato Basil Sauce, or store-bought, divided
- 2 (9-ounce) packages no-boil lasagna sheets
- 4 cups Béchamel Sauce, divided
- ½ cup freshly grated Parmesan cheese

Directions:

1. Preheat the oven to 375°F.
2. In a small mixing bowl, stir together the ricotta and pesto. Set aside.
3. Spread 1 cup of tomato sauce on the bottom of a 9-by-13-inch baking dish. Cover the sauce with a few lasagna sheets.
4. Spread 2 cups of béchamel sauce evenly on top of the lasagna sheets. Cover with a few more lasagna sheets.
5. Spread the ricotta and pesto mixture evenly over the lasagna sheets.
6. Pour 1 cup of tomato sauce over the ricotta layer and cover

the sauce with a few lasagna sheets.

7. Spread the remaining 2 cups of béchamel sauce over the lasagna sheets. Cover with a few more lasagna sheets.
8. Pour the remaining 2 cups of tomato sauce over the sheets. Top with Parmesan cheese.
9. Bake for 30 minutes or until the cheese on top is melted and golden brown. Let rest for 15 minutes before serving.

Nutrition: Calories: 616; Total Fat: 27g; Saturated Fat: 10g; Carbohydrates: 71g; Fiber: 4g; Protein: 16g; Sodium: 537mg

Variation tip: Add cooked spinach or other cooked vegetables as an extra layer.

Make ahead: Prepare in advance and freeze for up to 1 month. When ready to bake, thaw in the refrigerator overnight and bake for 40 minutes in a 375°F oven or cooked through.

95. Penne In Tomato And Caper Sauce

Preparation Time: 10 minutes

Cooking Time: 15 minutes

Serving 4

Ingredients:

- 2 tablespoons olive oil
- 2 garlic cloves, minced
- 1 cup sliced cherry tomatoes
- 2 cups Basic Tomato Basil Sauce, or store-bought
- 1 cup capers, drained and rinsed
- Salt
- 4 cups penne pasta

Directions:

1. Set a large pot of salted water over high heat to boil.
2. In a medium saucepan over medium heat, heat the olive oil. Add the garlic and cook for 30 seconds. Add the cherry tomatoes and cook for 2 to 3 minutes.
3. Pour in the tomato sauce and bring the mixture to a boil. Stir

in the capers and turn off the heat.

4. Once boiling add the pasta to the pot of water and cook for about 7 minutes until al dente.
5. Drain the pasta and stir it into the sauce. Toss gently and cook over medium heat for 1 minute or until warmed through.

Nutrition: Calories: 329; Total Fat: 8g; Saturated Fat: 1g; Carbohydrates: 55g; Fiber: 6g; Protein: 10g; Sodium: 612mg

Serving Tip: Serve this dish topped with shaved or grated Parmesan cheese; just note it will no longer be vegan.

Variation Tip: Add ½ cup chopped pitted green olives for a simple pasta puttanesca.

96. Chicken Spinach and Artichoke Stuffed Spaghetti Squash

Preparation Time: 10 mins.

Cook Time: 23 mins.

Total Time: 33 mins.

Servings: 4

Ingredients:

- 4 oz reduced-fat cream cheese, cubed and softened
- 1/4 tsp ground pepper
- 3 tbsp water
- 1/4 tsp salt
- Crushed red peppers
- 3 lb spaghetti squash, halved lengthwise and seeded
- 1/2 cup shredded parmesan cheese
- 5 oz pack baby spinach
- 10 oz pack artichoke hearts, chopped
- Diced fresh basil

Directions:

1. On a microwaveable dish, place your squash halves with the cut side facing up. Add 2 tbsp of water to the squash. Set the microwave to high and cook without covering the dish for about 15 minutes. You can also place the squash on a prepared baking sheet (rimmed) and bake at 400 degrees F for 40 minutes.

2. Set your stove to medium heat and place a large skillet containing 1 tbsp of water on it. Add spinach into the pan and stir while it cooks for about 5 minutes, or until the vegetable wilts. Drain the spinach and place it in a bowl.
3. Place the rack in the upper third region of your oven, then preheat your broiler.
4. Using a fork, scrape the squash from each shell half, and place them in a bowl. Add artichoke hearts, pepper, salt, cream cheese, and ¼ cup parmesan into the bowl of squash. Mix well. Place squash shells on a baking sheet, and add the squash mixture into the shells. Add the remaining parmesan on top and broil for 3 minutes.
5. Garnish with red pepper and basil, and serve.

Nutritional Information (per serving):

Cal: 223, Protein: 10.2g, Carbohydrates: 23.3g, Fiber: 8.6g, Fat: 10.9g, Sat. Fat: 5.7g

97. Angel Hair with Asparagus-Kale Pesto

Preparation Time: 10 minutes

Cooking Time: 10 minutes

Servings: 6

Ingredients:

- ¾ pound asparagus, woody ends removed, and coarsely chopped
- ¼ pound kale thoroughly washed
- ½ cup grated Asiago cheese
- ¼ cup fresh basil
- ¼ cup extra-virgin olive oil
- Juice of 1 lemon
- Sea salt
- Freshly ground black pepper
- 1-pound angel hair pasta
- Zest of 1 lemon

Directions:

1. In a food processor, pulse the asparagus and kale until very finely chopped.
2. Add the Asiago cheese, basil, olive oil, and lemon juice and pulse to form a smooth pesto.

3. Season with sea salt and pepper and set aside.
4. Cook the pasta al dente according to the package directions. Drain and transfer to a large bowl.
5. Add the pesto, tossing well to coat
6. Sprinkle with lemon zest and serve.
7. Cooking tip: You can make the asparagus pesto up to 3 days ahead. Keep it refrigerated until you need it.

Nutrition: Calories: 283; Total Fat: 12g; Saturated Fat: 2g; Carbohydrates: 33g; Fiber: 2g; Protein: 10g

98. Spicy Pasta Puttanesca

Preparation Time: 10 minutes

Cooking Time: 20 minutes

Servings: 4

Ingredients:

- 2 teaspoons extra-virgin olive oil
- ½ sweet onion, finely chopped
- 2 teaspoons minced garlic
- 1 (28-ounce) can sodium-free diced tomatoes
- ½ cup chopped anchovies
- 2 teaspoons chopped fresh oregano
- 2 teaspoons chopped fresh basil
- ½ teaspoon red pepper flakes
- ½ cup quartered Kalamata olives
- ¼ cup sodium-free chicken broth
- 1 tablespoon capers, drained and rinsed
- Juice of 1 lemon
- 4 cups cooked whole-grain penne

Directions:

1. In a large saucepan over medium heat, heat the olive oil.
2. Add the onion and garlic, and sauté for about 3 minutes until softened.
3. Stir in the tomatoes, anchovies, oregano, basil, and red pepper flakes. Bring the sauce to a boil and reduce the heat to low.

Simmer for 15 minutes, stirring occasionally.
4. Stir in the olives, chicken broth, capers, and lemon juice.
5. Cook the pasta according to the package directions and serve topped with the sauce.
6. Ingredient tip: Do not mistake sardines for anchovies, although they are both small, silvery fish sold in cans. Anchovies are usually salted in brine and matured to create a distinctive, rich taste.

Nutrition: Calories: 303; Total Fat: 6g; Saturated Fat: 0g; Carbohydrates: 54g; Fiber: 9g; Protein: 9g

99. Roasted Vegetarian Lasagna

Preparation Time: 25 minutes

Cooking Time: 50 minutes

Servings: 6

Ingredients:

- 1 eggplant, thickly sliced
- 2 zucchini, sliced lengthwise
- 1 yellow squash, sliced lengthwise
- 1 sweet onion, thickly sliced
- 2 tablespoons extra-virgin olive oil
- 1 (28-ounce) can sodium-free diced tomatoes
- 1 cup quartered, canned, water-packed artichoke hearts, drained
- 2 teaspoons minced garlic
- 2 teaspoons chopped fresh basil
- 2 teaspoons chopped fresh oregano
- Pinch red pepper flakes
- 12 no-boil whole-grain lasagna noodles
- ¾ cup grated Asiago cheese

Directions:

1. Preheat the oven to 400°F.
2. Line a baking sheet with aluminum foil and set it aside.
3. Toss together the eggplant, zucchini, yellow squash, onion, and olive oil to coat in a large bowl.

4. Arrange the vegetables on the prepared sheet and roast for about 20 minutes, or until tender and lightly caramelized.
5. Chop the roasted vegetables well and transfer them to a large bowl.
6. Stir in the tomatoes, artichoke hearts, garlic, basil, oregano, and red pepper flakes
7. Spoon one-quarter of the vegetable mixture into the bottom of a deep 9-by-13-inch baking dish.
8. Arrange 4 lasagna noodles over the sauce.
9. Repeat, alternating sauce and noodles, ending with sauce.
10. Sprinkle the Asiago cheese evenly over the top. Bake for about 30 minutes until bubbly and hot.
11. Remove from the oven and cool for 15 minutes before serving.
12. Substitution tip: If having a vegetarian meal is not a requirement, lean ground beef (92%) or ground chicken can be added to the roasted vegetable sauce for a more robust meal. Brown the ground meat in a skillet and add it to the finished sauce before assembling the lasagna.

Nutrition: Calories: 386; Total Fat: 11g; Saturated Fat: 3g; Carbohydrates: 59g; Fiber: 12g; Protein: 15g

100. Artichoke Chicken Pasta

Preparation Time: 20 minutes

Cooking Time: 5 minutes

Servings: 4

Ingredients:

- 2 cloves garlic, crushed
- 2 lemons, wedged
- 2 tbsp. lemon juice
- 14 oz. artichoke hearts, chopped
- 1-lb. chicken breast fillet, diced
- ½ cup feta cheese, crumbled
- 1 tbsp. olive oil
- 16 oz. whole-wheat (gluten-free) pasta of your choice
- 3 tbsp. parsley, chopped
- ½ cup red onion, chopped

- 2 tsp. oregano
- 1 tomato, chopped
- Ground black pepper and salt, to taste

Directions:

1. Pour the water into a deep saucepan and boil it. Add the pasta and some salt; cook it as per package directions. Drain the water and set aside the pasta.
2. Over medium stove flame, heat the oil in a skillet or saucepan (preferably of medium size).
3. Sauté the onions and garlic until softened and translucent; stir in between.
4. Add the chicken and cook until it is no longer pink.
5. Mix the tomatoes, artichoke hearts, parsley, feta cheese, oregano, lemon juice, and the cooked pasta.
6. Combine well and cook for 3-4 minutes, stirring frequently.
7. Season with black pepper and salt. Garnish with lemon wedges and serve warm.

Nutrition: Calories – 486|Fat – 10g|Carbs – 42g|Fiber – 9g|Protein – 37g

101. Spinach Beef Pasta

Preparation Time: 30 minutes

Cooking Time: 10 minutes

Servings: 4

Ingredients:

- 1 ¼ cups uncooked orzo pasta
- ¾ cup baby spinach
- 2 tbsp. olive oil
- 1 ½ lb. beef tenderloin
- ¾ cup feta cheese
- 2 quarts water
- 1 cup cherry tomatoes, halved
- ¼ tsp. salt

Directions:

1. Rub the meat with pepper and cut into small cubes.
2. Over medium stove flame, heat the oil in a deep saucepan (preferably of medium size).
3. Add and stir-fry the meat until it is evenly brown.

4. Add the water and boil the mixture; stir in the orzo and salt.
5. Cook the mixture for 7-8 minutes. Add the spinach and cook until it wilts.
6. Add the tomatoes and cheese; combine and serve warm.

Nutrition: Calories – 334 |Fat – 13g|Carbs – 36g|Fiber – 6g|Protein – 16g

102. Asparagus Parmesan Pasta

Preparation Time: 25 minutes

Cooking Time: 4 minutes

Servings: 2

Ingredients:

- 1 tsp. extra-virgin olive oil
- 1 tsp. lemon juice
- ¾ cup whole milk
- ½ bunch asparagus, trimmed and cut into small pieces
- ½ cup parmesan cheese, grated
- 2 tbsp. garlic, minced
- 2 tbsp. almond flour
- 2 tsp. whole grain mustard
- 4 oz. whole-wheat penne pasta
- 1 tsp. tarragon, minced
- Ground black pepper and salt, to taste

Directions:

1. Pour the water into a deep saucepan and boil it. Add the pasta and some salt; cook it as per package directions. Drain the water and set aside the pasta.
2. Take another pan, pour 8 cups of water and let it come to boiling. Add the asparagus and boil until it is soft. Drain and set aside.
3. In a mixing bowl, combine the milk, flour, mustard, black pepper and salt. Set aside.
4. Over medium stove flame, heat the oil in a skillet or saucepan (preferably of medium size).
5. Sauté the garlic until softened and fragrant, stirring in between.
6. Add the milk mixture and let it simmer. Add the tarragon,

lemon juice and lemon zest; mix to combine.
7. Add the cooked pasta, asparagus, and simmer until the sauce thickens, stirring frequently.
8. Top with parmesan cheese and serve warm.

Nutrition: Calories – 402|Fat – 31g|Carbs – 33g|Fiber – 6g|Protein – 44g

103. Caramelized Onion Flatbread with Arugula

Preparation Time: 10 minutes

Cooking Time: 25 minutes

Servings: 4

Ingredients:

- 4 tbsp. extra-virgin olive oil, divided
- 2 large onions, sliced into ¼-inch-thick slices
- 1 tsp. salt, divided
- 1 sheet puff pastry
- 1 (5-oz.) package goat cheese
- 8 oz. arugula
- ½ tsp. freshly ground black pepper

Directions:

1. Preheat the oven to 400°F.
2. In a large skillet over medium heat, cook 3 tbsp. Olive oil, the onions, and ½ tsp. of salt, stirring, for 10 to 12 minutes, until the onions are translucent and golden brown.
3. To assemble, line a baking sheet with parchment paper. Lay the puff pastry flat on the parchment paper. Prick the middle of the puff pastry all over with a fork, leaving a ½-inch border.
4. Evenly distribute the onions on the pastry, leaving the border.
5. Crumble the goat cheese over the onions. Put the pastry in the oven to bake for 10 to 12 minutes, or until you see the border become golden brown.
6. Remove the pastry from the oven, set it aside. In a medium bowl, add the arugula, remaining 1 tbsp and olive oil,

remaining ½ tsp. of salt, and ½ tsp. Black pepper; toss to dress the arugula evenly.

7. Cut the pastry into even squares. Top the pastry with dressed arugula and serve.

Nutrition: Calories: 63; Protein: 12.3g; Carbs: 3.4g; Fat: 6.3g

104. Quick Shrimp Fettuccine

Preparation Time: 10 minutes

Cooking Time: 10 minutes

Servings: 4

Ingredients:

- 8 oz. fettuccine pasta
- 1/4 cup extra-virgin olive oil
- 3 tbsp. garlic, minced
- 1 lb. large shrimp (21-25), peeled and deveined
- 1/3 cup lemon juice
- 1 tbsp. lemon zest
- 1/2 tsp. salt
- 1/2 tsp. freshly ground black pepper

Directions:

1. Bring a large pot of salted water to a boil. Add the fettuccine and cook for 8 minutes.
2. In a large saucepan over medium heat, cook the olive oil and garlic for 1 minute.
3. Add the shrimp to the saucepan and cook for 3 minutes on each side. Remove the shrimp from the pan and set it aside.
4. Add the lemon juice and lemon zest to the saucepan, along with the salt and pepper.
5. Reserve ½ cup of the pasta water and drain the pasta.
6. Add the pasta water to the saucepan with the lemon juice and zest and stir everything together. Add the pasta and toss it together to coat the pasta evenly. Transfer the pasta to a serving dish and top with the cooked shrimp. Serve warm.

Nutrition: Calories: 83; Protein: 12.3g; Carbs: 3.4g; Fat: 6.3g

105. Hearty Butternut Spinach, and Cheeses Lasagna

Preparation Time: 30 minutes

Cooking Time: 3 hours 45 minutes

Servings: 4 to 6

Ingredients:

- 2 tablespoons extra-virgin olive oil, divided
- 1 butternut squash, halved lengthwise and deseeded
- ½ teaspoon sage
- ½ teaspoon sea salt
- ¼ teaspoon ground black pepper
- ¼ cup grated Parmesan cheese
- 2 cups ricotta cheese
- ½ cup unsweetened almond milk
- 5 layers whole-wheat lasagna noodles (about 12 ounces / 340 g in total)
- 4 ounces (113 g) fresh spinach leaves, divided
- ½ cup shredded part-skim Mozzarella, for garnish

Directions:

1. Preheat the oven to 400ºF (205ºC). Line a baking sheet with parchment paper.
2. Brush 1 tablespoon of olive oil on the cut side of the butternut squash, then place the squash on the baking sheet.
3. Bake in the preheated oven for 45 minutes or until the squash is tender.
4. Allow to cool until you can handle it, then scoop the flesh out and put it in a food processor to purée.
5. Combine the puréed butternut squash flesh with sage, salt, and ground black pepper in a large bowl. Stir to mix well.
6. Combine the cheeses and milk in a separate bowl, then sprinkle with salt and pepper to taste.
7. Grease the slow cooker with 1 tablespoon of olive oil, then add a layer of lasagna noodles to coat the bottom of the slow cooker.

8. Spread half of the squash mixture on top of the noodles, then top the mixture with another layer of lasagna noodles.
9. Spread half of the spinach over the noodles, then top the spinach with half the cheese mixture. Repeat with the remaining 3 layers of lasagna noodles, squash mixture, spinach, and cheese mixture.
10. Top the cheese mixture with Mozzarella, then put the lid on and cook on low for 3 hours or until the lasagna noodles are al dente.
11. Serve immediately.
12. Tip: to make this a complete meal, you can serve it with fresh cucumber soup and a green leafy salad.

Nutrition:

calories: 657 fat: 37.1g Protein: 30.9g carbs: 57.2g fiber: 8.3g Sodium: 918mg

106. Minestrone Chickpeas and Macaroni Casserole

Preparation Time: 20 minutes

Cooking Time: 7 hours 20 minutes

Servings: 5

Ingredients:

- 1 (15-ounce / 425-g) can chickpeas, drained and rinsed
- 1 (28-ounce / 794-g) can diced tomatoes, with the juice
- 1 (6-ounce / 170-g) can no-salt-added tomato paste
- 3 medium carrots, sliced
- 3 cloves garlic, minced
- 1 medium yellow onion, chopped
- 1 cup low-sodium vegetable soup
- ½ teaspoon dried rosemary
- 1 teaspoon dried oregano
- 2 teaspoons maple syrup
- ½ teaspoon sea salt
- ¼ teaspoon ground black pepper
- ½ pound (227-g) fresh green beans, trimmed and cut into bite-size pieces

- 1 cup macaroni pasta
- 2 ounces (57 g) Parmesan cheese, grated

Directions:

1. Except for the green beans, pasta, and Parmesan cheese, combine all the ingredients in the slow cooker and stir to mix well.
2. Put the slow cooker lid on and cook on low for 7 hours.
3. Fold in the pasta and green beans. Put the lid on and cook on high for 20 minutes or until the vegetable are soft and the pasta is al dente.
4. Pour them in a large serving bowl and spread with Parmesan cheese before serving.
5. Tip: Instead of chickpeas, you can also use kidney beans, great northern beans, or cannellini beans.

Nutrition:

calories: 349 fat: 6.7g Protein: 16.5g carbs: 59.9g fiber: 12.9g Sodium: 937mg

107. Roasted Butternut Squash and Zucchini with Penne

Preparation Time: 15 minutes

Cooking Time: 30 minutes

Servings: 6

Ingredients:

- 1 large zucchini, diced
- 1 large butternut squash, peeled and diced
- 1 large yellow onion, chopped
- 2 tablespoons extra-virgin olive oil
- 1 teaspoon paprika
- 1/2 teaspoon garlic powder
- 1/2 teaspoon sea salt
- 1/2 teaspoon freshly ground black pepper
- 1-pound (454 g) whole-grain penne
- 1/2 cup dry white wine

- 2 tablespoons grated Parmesan cheese

Direction

1. Preheat the oven to 400ºF (205ºC). Line a baking sheet with aluminum foil.
2. Combine the zucchini, butternut squash, and onion in a large bowl. Drizzle with olive oil and sprinkle with paprika, garlic powder, salt, and ground black pepper. Toss to coat well.
3. Spread the vegetables in a single layer on the baking sheet, then roast in the preheated oven for 25 minutes or until the vegetables are tender.
4. Meanwhile, bring a pot of water to a boil, add the penne and cook for 14 minutes or until al dente. Drain the penne through a colander.
5. Transfer ½ cup of roasted vegetables in a food processor, then pour in the dry white wine. Pulse until smooth.
6. Pour the puréed vegetables in a nonstick skillet and cook with penne over medium-high heat for a few minutes to heat through.
7. Transfer the penne with the purée on a large serving plate, then spread the remaining roasted vegetables and Parmesan on top before serving.
8. Tip: Instead of dry white wine, you can use the same amount of low-sodium chicken broth to replace it.

Nutrition:

calories: 340 fat: 6.2g Protein: 8.0g carbs: 66.8g fiber: 9.1g Sodium: 297mg

108. Small Pasta and Beans Pot

Preparation Time: 20 minutes

Cooking Time: 15 minutes

Servings: 2 to 4

Ingredients:

- 1 pound (454 g) small whole wheat pasta
- 1 (14.5-ounce / 411-g) can diced tomatoes, juice reserved
- 1 (15-ounce / 425-g) can cannellini beans, drained and rinsed
- 2 tablespoons no-salt-added tomato paste
- 1 red or yellow bell pepper, chopped
- 1 yellow onion, chopped
- 1 tablespoon Italian seasoning mix
- 3 garlic cloves, minced
- ¼ teaspoon crushed red pepper flakes, optional
- 1 tablespoon extra-virgin olive oil
- 5 cups water
- 1 bunch kale, stemmed and chopped
- ½ cup pitted Kalamata olives, chopped
- 1 cup sliced basil

Directions:

1. Except for the kale, olives, and basil, combine all the ingredients in a pot. Stir to mix well. Bring to a boil over high heat. Stir constantly.
2. Reduce the heat to medium-high and add the kale. Cook for 10 minutes or until the pasta is al dente. Stir constantly.
3. Transfer all of them on a large plate and serve with olives and basil on top.
4. Tip: You can use small whole-wheat pasta like penne, farfalle, shell, corkscrew, macaroni, or alphabet pasta.

Nutrition:

calories: 357 fat: 7.6g Protein: 18.2g carbs: 64.5g fiber: 10.1g Sodium: 454mg

109. Garlic Shrimp Fettuccine

Preparation Time: 10 minutes

Cooking Time: 15 minutes

Servings: 4 to 6

Ingredients:

- 8 ounces (227 g) fettuccine pasta
- 1/4 cup extra-virgin olive oil
- 3 tablespoons garlic, minced
- 1 pound (454 g) large shrimp, peeled and deveined
- 1/3 cup lemon juice
- 1 tablespoon lemon zest
- 1/2 teaspoon salt
- 1/2 teaspoon freshly ground black pepper

Directions:

1. Bring a large pot of salted water to a boil. Add the fettuccine and cook for 8 minutes. Reserve ½ cup of the cooking liquid and drain the pasta.
2. In a large saucepan over medium heat, heat the olive oil. Add the garlic and sauté for 1 minute.
3. Add the shrimp to the saucepan and cook each side for 3 minutes. Remove the shrimp from the pan and set it aside.
4. Add the remaining ingredients to the saucepan. Stir in the cooking liquid. Add the pasta and toss it together to coat the pasta evenly.
5. Transfer the pasta to a serving dish and serve topped with the cooked shrimp.

Nutrition:

calories: 615 fat: 17.0g Protein: 33.0g carbs: 89.0g fiber: 4.0g Sodium: 407mg

110. Broccoli and Carrot Pasta Salad

Preparation Time: 5 minutes

Cooking Time: 10 minutes

Servings: 2

Ingredients:

- 8 ounces (227 g) whole-wheat pasta
- 2 cups broccoli florets
- 1 cup peeled and shredded carrots
- ¼ cup plain Greek yogurt
- Juice of 1 lemon
- 1 teaspoon red pepper flakes

- Sea salt and freshly ground pepper, to taste

Directions:

1. Bring a large pot of lightly salted water to a boil. Add the pasta to the boiling water and cook until al dente. Drain and let rest for a few minutes.
2. When cooled, combine the pasta with the veggies, yogurt, lemon juice, and red pepper flakes in a large bowl, and stir thoroughly to combine.
3. Taste and season to taste with salt and pepper. Serve immediately.

Nutrition:

calories: 428 fat: 2.9g Protein: 15.9g carbs: 84.6g fiber: 11.7g Sodium: 642mg

111. Mushroom and Vegetable Penne Pasta

Preparation Time: 5 minutes

Cooking Time: 8 minutes

Servings: 4

Ingredients:

- 6 ounces penne pasta
- 6 ounces shitake mushrooms, chopped
- 1 small carrot, cut into strips
- 4 ounces baby spinach, finely chopped
- 1 teaspoon ginger, grounded
- 3 tablespoons oil
- 2 tablespoons soy sauce
- 6 ounces zucchini, cut into strips
- 6 ounces leek, finely chopped
- ½ teaspoon salt
- 2 garlic cloves, crushed
- 2 cups of water

Directions:

1. Heat the oil
2. Sauté and stir-fry carrot and garlic for 3-4 minutes
3. Add remaining ingredients and pour in 2 cups of water
4. Cook on High pressure for 4 minutes
5. Quick-release the pressure
6. Serve and enjoy!

Nutrition: Calories: 429 Fat: 8 g Carbs: 64 g Protein: 25 g

112. Spaghetti With Garlic, Olive Oil, And Red Pepper

Preparation Time: 5 minutes

Cooking Time: 10 minutes

Servings: 2

Ingredients

- Salt
- 8 ounces spaghetti
- 1/4 cup extra-virgin olive oil
- garlic cloves, 3 lightly smashed, and 1 minced
- 1/2 teaspoon red pepper flakes
- 1/4 cup grated Parmesan cheese
- 1 tablespoon chopped fresh flat-leaf parsley

1. Directions
2. Bring a large pot of water to a boil over high heat. Once boiling, salt the water to your liking, stir, and return to a boil. Add the spaghetti and cook according to package directions until al dente. Drain, reserving about ½ cup of the cooking water.
3. In a large skillet, heat the olive oil over low heat. Add the smashed garlic cloves and cook until golden brown. Remove the garlic from the pan and discard.
4. Add the red pepper flakes to the garlic-infused oil and warm for 1 minute before turning off the heat.
5. Once the spaghetti is cooked, add it to the pan.
6. Add the minced garlic and toss the spaghetti in the oil to coat. Add the reserved pasta water, a little at a time, as needed to help everything combine.
7. Sprinkle with Parmesan and parsley.
8. COOKING TIP: When making pasta, it is essential to salt the water for a flavorful dish generally. I generally use about 2 tablespoons of salt per pound of pasta. Add the salt after the water boils, stir to dissolve,

wait for the water to return to a boil, and add the pasta.

Nutrition:

Calories: 722; Total Fat: 32g; Saturated Fat: 6g; Protein: 19g; Total Carbohydrates: 89g; Fiber: 4g; Sugar: 3g; Cholesterol: 11mg

113. Spaghetti With Anchovy Sauce

Preparation Time: 5 minutes

Cooking Time: 10 minutes

Servings: 4

Ingredients:

- Salt
- 1-pound spaghetti
- 1/4 cup extra-virgin olive oil
- 1 can oil-packed anchovy fillets, undrained
- 3 garlic cloves, minced
- 1/4 cup chopped fresh flat-leaf parsley
- 1 teaspoon red pepper flakes
- 1/4 teaspoon freshly ground black pepper
- 1 tablespoon bread crumbs

Directions:

1. Bring a large pot of water to a boil over high heat. Once boiling, salt the water to your liking, stir, and return to a boil. Add the spaghetti and cook according to package directions until al dente. Drain, reserving about ½ cup of the cooking water.
2. Meanwhile, in a large skillet, heat the olive oil over low heat. Add the anchovy fillets with their oil and the garlic. Cook for 7 to 10 minutes, until the pasta is ready, stirring until the anchovies melt away and form a sauce.
3. Add the spaghetti, parsley, red pepper flakes, black pepper, and a little of the reserved cooking water, as needed, and toss to combine all the ingredients.
4. Sprinkle with the bread crumbs.

Nutrition:

Calories: 581; Total Fat: 17g; Saturated Fat: 3g; Protein: 19g; Total Carbohydrates: 87g; Fiber: 4g; Sugar: 3g; Cholesterol: 12mg

114. White Bean Alfredo Pasta

Preparation Time: 10 minutes

Cooking Time: 15 minutes

Servings: 4

Ingredients:

- 1 teaspoon salt, plus more for the pasta water
- 1-pound fettuccine
- 2 tablespoons extra-virgin olive oil
- 2 garlic cloves, minced
- ¼ teaspoon red pepper flakes
- (15-ounce) cans cannellini beans, rinsed and drained
- 2 cups vegetable broth
- ½ cup almond milk
- ¼ cup low-fat Pecorino cheese
- ¼ teaspoon ground nutmeg
- Chopped fresh flat-leaf parsley for garnish

Directions:

1. Bring a large pot of water to boil over high heat. Once boiling, salt the water to your liking, stir, and return to a boil. Add the fettuccine and cook according to package directions until al dente. Drain, reserving about ½ cup of the cooking water.
2. Meanwhile, in a large skillet, heat the olive oil over medium heat. Add the garlic and red pepper flakes and cook for about 1 minute, until fragrant.
3. Add the beans, broth, and almond milk to the pan and bring to a boil. Remove the pan from the heat.
4. Using a slotted spoon, transfer the beans to a food processor or blender and process until smooth.
5. Return the pureed beans to the skillet. Add the Romano, salt, and nutmeg and bring to a simmer.

6. Add the cooked pasta to the bean mixture and stir to coat, adding the reserved cooking water, a little at a time, as needed—Cook for about 2 minutes.
7. Garnish with parsley.
8. VARIATION TIP: Try adding steamed broccoli florets or chopped sun-dried tomatoes for an extra burst of flavor, color, and nutrients.

Nutrition:

Calories: 697; Total Fat: 12g; Saturated Fat: 3g; Protein: 30g; Total Carbohydrates: 118g; Fiber:

12g; Sugar: 5g; Cholesterol: 5mg

115. Penne Pasta with Tomato Sauce and Mizithra cheese

Preparation Time: 15 minutes

Cooking Time: 20 minutes

Servings: 5

Ingredients:

- 2 tablespoons olive oil
- 2 scallion stalks, chopped
- 2 green garlic stalks, minced
- 10 ounces penne
- 1/3 teaspoon ground black pepper, to taste
- Sea salt, to taste
- 1/4 teaspoon cayenne pepper
- 1/4 teaspoon dried marjoram
- 1/2 teaspoon dried oregano
- 1/2 teaspoon dried basil
- 1/2 cup marinara sauce
- 2 cups vegetable broth
- 2 overripe tomatoes, pureed
- 1 cup Mitzithra cheese, grated

Directions:

1. Heat the oil in your pot until sizzling. Now, sauté the scallions and garlic until just tender and fragrant.
2. Stir in the penne pasta, spices, marinara sauce, broth, and pureed tomatoes; do not stir, but your pasta should be covered with the liquid.
3. Secure the lid and cook for 7 minutes at high heat. Once cooking is complete, carefully remove the lid.

4. Fold in the cheese and seal the lid. Let it sit in the residual heat until the cheese melts. Bon appetite

Nutrition: 395 Calories; 15.6g Fat; 51.8g Carbs; 14.9g Protein; 2.5g Sugars; 7.5g Fiber

116. Delicious Chicken Pasta

Preparation Time: 10 minutes

Cooking Time: 17 minutes

Servings: 4

Ingredients:

- 3 chicken breasts, skinless, boneless, cut into pieces
- 9 oz whole-grain pasta
- 1/2 cup olives, sliced
- 1/2 cup sun-dried tomatoes
- 1 tbsp roasted red peppers, chopped
- 14 oz can tomatoes, diced
- 2 cups marinara sauce
- 1 cup chicken broth
- Pepper
- Salt

Directions:

1. Add all ingredients except whole-grain pasta into the pot and stir well.
2. Seal pot with lid and cook on high heat for 12 minutes.
3. Once done, remove the lid.
4. Add pasta and stir well. Seal pot again and cook for 5 minutes.
5. Once cooked, remove the lid.
6. Stir well and serve.

Nutrition: Calories 615 Fat 15.4 g Carbohydrates 71 g Sugar 17.6 g Protein 48 g Cholesterol 100 mg

117. Spaghetti Pesto Cake

Preparation Time: 10 minutes

Cooking Time: 40 minutes

Serving 6

Ingredients:

- 12 ounces ricotta
- 1 cup Basil Pesto, or store-bought
- 2 tablespoons olive oil
- ¼ cup freshly grated Parmesan cheese
- Salt

- 1-pound spaghetti

Directions:

1. Preheat the oven to 400°F. Set a large pot of salted water to boil over high heat.
2. In a food processor, combine the ricotta and basil pesto. Purée into a smooth cream and transfer to a large bowl. Set aside.
3. Coat a 10-cup Bundt pan with olive oil and sprinkle with the Parmesan cheese. Set aside.
4. Once the water is boiling, add the pasta to the pot and cook for about 6 minutes until al dente.
5. Drain the pasta well and add it to the pesto cream. Mix well until all the pasta is saturated with the sauce.
6. Spoon the pasta into the prepared pan, pressing to ensure it is tightly packed—Bake for 30 minutes.
7. Place a flat serving platter on top of the cake pan. Quickly and carefully invert the pasta cake. Gently remove the pan. Cut into slices and serve topped with your favorite sauce, if desired.

Nutrition: Calories: 622; Total Fat: 30g; Saturated Fat: 7g; Carbohydrates: 67g; Fiber: 3g; Protein: 20g; Sodium: 425mg

Substitution Tip: For a dairy-free version of this cake: Purée 12 ounces firm tofu, 2 cups chopped fresh basil, 6 peeled garlic cloves, ½ teaspoon salt, and ½ cup olive oil into a smooth paste. Then follow steps 3 through 7 (just coat the pan with flour rather than Parmesan).

118. Artichokes, Olives & Tuna Pasta

Preparation Time: 10 minutes

Cooking Time: 15 minutes

Servings: 4

Ingredients:

- ¼ cup chopped fresh basil
- ¼ cup chopped green olives
- ¼ tsp freshly ground pepper
- ½ cup white wine
- ½ tsp salt, divided

- 1 10 oz package frozen artichoke hearts, thawed and squeezed dry
- 2 cups grape tomatoes, halved
- 2 tbsp lemon juice
- 2 tsp chopped fresh rosemary
- 2 tsp freshly grated lemon zest
- 3 cloves garlic, minced
- 4 tbsp extra virgin olive oil, divided
- 6 oz whole wheat penne pasta
- 8 oz tuna steak, cut into 3 pieces

Directions:

1. Cook penne pasta according to package instructions. Drain and set aside.
2. Preheat grill to medium-high.
3. In a bowl, toss and mix ¼ tsp pepper, ¼ tsp salt, 1 tsp rosemary, lemon zest, 1 tbsp oil, and tuna pieces.
4. Grill tuna for 3 minutes per side. Allow to cool and flake into bite-sized pieces.
5. On medium fire, place a large nonstick saucepan and heat 3 tbsp oil.
6. Sauté remaining rosemary, garlic olives, and artichoke hearts for 4 minutes. Add wine and tomatoes, bring to a boil and cook for 3 minutes while stirring once in a while.
7. Add remaining salt, lemon juice, tuna pieces and pasta. Cook until heated through.
8. To serve, garnish with basil and enjoy.

Nutrition: Calories 127.6; Carbohydrates 13 g; Protein 7.2 g; Fat 5.2 g

119. Broccoli Pesto Spaghetti

Preparation Time: 5 minutes

Cooking Time: 35 minutes

Servings: 4

Ingredients:

- 8 oz. spaghetti
- 1-pound broccoli, cut into florets
- 2 tablespoons olive oil
- 4 garlic cloves, chopped
- 4 basil leaves

- 2 tablespoons blanched almonds
- 1 lemon, juiced
- Salt and pepper to taste

Directions:

1. For the pesto, combine the broccoli, oil, garlic, basil, lemon juice and almonds in a blender and pulse until well mixed and smooth.
2. Cook the spaghetti in a large pot of salty water for 8 minutes or until al dente. Drain well.
3. Mix the warm spaghetti with the broccoli pesto and serve right away.

Nutrition: Calories:284, Fat:10.2g, Protein:10.4g, Carbohydrates:40.2g

120. Spaghetti all'Olio

Preparation Time:5 minutes

Cooking Time:30 minutes

Servings: 4

Ingredients:

- 8 oz. spaghetti
- 3 tablespoons olive oil
- 4 garlic cloves, minced
- 2 red peppers, sliced
- 1 tablespoon lemon juice
- Salt and pepper to taste
- ½ cup grated parmesan cheese

Directions:

1. Heat the oil in a skillet and add the garlic. Cook for 30 seconds then stir in the red peppers and cook for 1 more minute on low heat, making sure only to infuse them, not to burn or fry them.
2. Add the lemon juice and remove off heat.
3. Cook the spaghetti in a large pot of salty water for 8 minutes or as stated on the package, just until they become al dente.
4. Drain the spaghetti well and mix them with garlic and pepper oil.
5. Serve right away.

Nutrition: Calories:268, Fat:11.9g, Protein:7.1g, Carbohydrates:34.1g

121. Quick Tomato Spaghetti

Preparation Time: 5 minutes

Cooking Time: 15 minutes

Servings: 4

Ingredients:

- 8 oz. spaghetti
- 3 tablespoons olive oil
- 4 garlic cloves, sliced
- 1 jalapeno, sliced
- 2 cups cherry tomatoes
- Salt and pepper to taste
- 1 teaspoon balsamic vinegar
- ½ cup grated Parmesan

Directions:

1. Heat a large pot of water on medium flame. Add a pinch of salt and bring to a boil then add the pasta.
2. Cook for 8 minutes or until al dente.
3. While the pasta cooks, heat the oil in a skillet and add garlic and jalapeno. Cook for 1 minute then stir in the tomatoes, as well as salt and pepper.
4. Cook for 5-7 minutes until the tomatoes' skins burst.
5. Add the vinegar and remove off heat.
6. Drain the pasta well and mix it with the tomato sauce. Sprinkle with cheese and serve right away.

Nutrition: Calories:298, Fat:13.5g, Protein:9.7g, Carbohydrates:36.0g

122. Easy Rice Pilaf

Preparation Time: 5 minutes

Cooking Time: 20 minutes

Servings: 4

Ingredients:

- 2 tablespoons extra-virgin olive oil
- 1 small onion, diced
- 1½ cups long-grain white rice, such as jasmine
- 2 cups chicken broth
- 1 teaspoon dried oregano
- 1/2 teaspoon salt

- 1/4 teaspoon freshly ground black pepper

Directions:

1. In a large saucepan, heat the olive oil over medium heat. Add the onion and cook for about 3 minutes, until it starts to soften.
2. Add the rice and toss to coat it in the oil.
3. Add the chicken broth, oregano, salt, and pepper and bring to a boil. Reduce the heat to low, cover, and simmer for about 15 minutes until the liquid is fully absorbed into the rice.
4. Fluff with a fork before serving.
5. Variation tip: to spruce up this dish, you can add diced bell pepper and carrot when you cook the onion. Stir in some frozen peas at the end and cook for an additional 2 minutes.

Nutrition: Calories: 324; Total Fat: 9g; Saturated Fat: 1g; Protein: 6g; Total Carbohydrates: 55g; Fiber: 3g; Sugar: 1g; Cholesterol: 0mg

123. Baked Chicken Paella

Preparation Time: 15 minutes

Cooking Time: 1 hour 15 minutes

Servings: 4

Ingredients:

- 2 tablespoons extra-virgin olive oil
- 2 boneless, skinless chicken breasts, cut into bite-size pieces
- 1 teaspoon salt
- 1 teaspoon freshly ground black pepper
- 1 hot Italian pork sausage, sliced
- 1 medium onion, sliced
- 1 red or green bell pepper, seeded and sliced
- 3 garlic cloves, chopped
- 1/4 cup dry white wine
- 1 cup Arborio rice
- 3 cups chicken broth, divided
- 1 cup canned or cooked chickpeas
- 2 cup baby spinach
- 2 large eggs, beaten

Directions:

1. Preheat the oven to 350°F.
2. In a large ovenproof skillet or braising pan, heat the olive oil over medium heat. Add the chicken and season with salt and pepper. Brown the chicken on both sides, about 5 minutes total, then transfer to a plate.
3. Add the sausage, onion, bell pepper, and garlic to the skillet and cook for about 10 minutes, until the sausage is browned and the vegetables are softened. Transfer to the plate with the chicken.
4. Pour in the wine and deglaze the skillet, stirring to scrape up any browned bits on the bottom. Add the rice and mix with the wine until coated.
5. Add 1 cup of chicken broth, stir and cook for 5 minutes.
6. Add the chickpeas and another 1 cup of broth and stir again. Return the browned chicken to the skillet on top of the rice and chickpeas.
7. Add the sausage, onion, and bell pepper mixture on top of the chicken. Push the chicken, sausage, and vegetables down into the rice and chickpea mixture, but not stir. Add the remaining 1 cup of chicken broth and bring to a boil.
8. Cover the skillet, transfer to the oven and bake for 40 minutes.
9. Uncover the skillet and take a peek at the dish. If it looks dry, add 1/3 cup water to the skillet. Add the spinach and push it down into the mixture slightly. Pour the beaten eggs on top.
10. Return to the oven and bake for another 10 minutes, uncovered, until the egg is thoroughly cooked.
11. Let rest for 5 minutes before serving.

Nutrition: Calories: 539; Total Fat: 21g; Saturated Fat: 5g; Protein: 30g; Total Carbohydrates: 52g; Fiber: 5g; Sugar: 3g; Cholesterol: 166mg

124. Vegetable Rice Bake

Preparation Time: 15 minutes

Cooking Time: 50 minutes

Servings: 4

Ingredients:

- 1½ teaspoons paprika
- 1½ teaspoons dried thyme
- 1 teaspoon Italian Herb Blend
- 1 teaspoon salt
- 2 teaspoons freshly ground black pepper
- 2 carrots, chopped
- 1 turnip, peeled and chopped
- 2 garlic cloves, minced
- 1½ cups long-grain white rice
- 1½ cups chicken broth
- 1½ cups water
- 1 head broccoli, cut into florets
- 2 ears of corn, husks, and silks removed, cut into thirds
- 1 red onion, cut into large chunks
- Red bell pepper, seeded and cut into chunks
- 1/4 cup extra-virgin olive oil

Directions

1. Preheat the oven to 400°F.
2. Combine the paprika, thyme, Italian herb blend, salt, and pepper in a small bowl.
3. In a 9-by-13-inch baking pan, combine the carrots, turnip, garlic, rice, broth, and water. Stir in 1 teaspoon of the spice mix. Cover with aluminum foil and bake for 20 minutes.
4. In a large bowl, combine the broccoli, corn pieces, red onion, and bell pepper. Add the olive oil and the remaining 5 teaspoons of spice mix and toss to coat.
5. Remove the baking pan from the oven and remove the foil. Increase the oven temperature to 425°F.
6. Scatter the broccoli and corn mixture over the surface of the rice mixture. Be sure to cover the top fully so that the rice stays hidden underneath.
7. Return the dish to the oven, uncovered, and bake for 30 minutes.

Nutrition: Calories: 653; Total Fat: 23g; Saturated Fat: 4g; Protein: 30g; Total Carbohydrates: 86g; Fiber: 8g; Sugar: 6g; Cholesterol: 38mg

125. Farro With Porcini Mushrooms

Preparation Time: 15 minutes

Cooking Time: 40 minutes

Servings: 4

Ingredients:

- 1 and ½ cups vegetable broth
- 2 tablespoons extra-virgin olive oil
- 1 shallot, finely chopped
- 1 cup pearled farro
- 1/2 cup dry white wine
- 1/4 teaspoon red pepper flakes
- 1-pound porcini mushrooms, sliced
- 1/4 cup water
- 1/2 teaspoon salt
- 2 garlic cloves, minced
- 1 tablespoon cream sherry (optional)
- 1/4 cup grated Parmesan or Romano cheese
- Chopped fresh flat-leaf parsley for garnish

Directions:

1. In a small saucepan, bring the vegetable broth to a gentle simmer.
2. Heat the olive oil over medium heat in a large skillet and cook the shallot for about 2 minutes until softened.
3. Add the farro and stir until coated with oil—Cook for 1 minute.
4. Add the wine and cook until it is absorbed, stirring constantly. Add the red pepper flakes.
5. Mix in the hot broth, a ladleful at a time, and cook until absorbed,
6. stirring frequently. Each ladleful will probably take about 5 minutes to absorb.
7. Meanwhile, in another skillet, combine the mushrooms, water, and salt. Cover and cook for about 5 minutes until the mushrooms have softened.

Add the garlic and sherry (if using) and continue to cook, uncovered.

8. When you have about 1 ladleful of broth left, add the mushroom mixture to the farro and fold it in. Add the rest of the broth and continue to cook and stir until the liquid is absorbed.
9. Add the Parmesan and stir to combine. Garnish with parsley.
10. Ingredient tip: You can substitute cremini or white button mushrooms if porcini is not available.

Nutrition: Calories: 340; Total Fat: 9g; Saturated Fat: 2g; Protein: 10g; Total Carbohydrates: 52g; Fiber: 11g; Sugar: 5g; Cholesterol: 5mg

126. Sicilian Eggplant With Israeli Couscous

Preparation Time: 10 minutes

Cooking Time: 45 minutes

Servings: 2

Ingredients

- 1/4 cup extra-virgin olive oil
- 1/4 red onion, chopped
- 1 small Sicilian eggplant, cut into cubes
- 1 garlic clove, minced
- 1/2 teaspoon salt
- 1 cup canned crushed tomatoes
- 1/2 teaspoon dried oregano
- 1½ cups water
- 1 cup tricolor Israeli couscous
- fresh basil leaves, chopped
- 1/4 teaspoon smoked paprika
- Pinch cayenne pepper

Directions:

1. In a large skillet, heat the olive oil over medium heat. Add the red onion and cook for 3 to 5 minutes until it starts to soften.
2. Add the eggplant, garlic, and salt and cook for about 10 minutes until the eggplant softens and breaks down.
3. Add the tomatoes and oregano—cover and cook until thoroughly soft, about 20 minutes.

4. Meanwhile, in a saucepan, bring the water to a boil over high heat. Reduce the heat to a simmer and add the couscous. Cover and simmer for 10 minutes. Fluff it up using a fork, then remove from the heat and let stand, covered, for 3 minutes.
5. Add the couscous to the eggplant mixture. Stir in the basil, smoked paprika, and cayenne. Stir to combine and simmer for 10 minutes to meld all the flavors.
6. Ingredient tip: Sicilian eggplants are round and practically seedless, unlike the more common globe eggplant. If you can't find one, you can use a globe eggplant for this dish, but you may want to scoop out the seeds. You could also use 2 or 3 small Japanese eggplants.

Nutrition: Calories: 680; Total Fat: 28g; Saturated Fat: 4g; Protein: 16g; Total Carbohydrates: 94g; Fiber: 15g; Sugar: 16g; Cholesterol: 0mg

127. Polenta With Wild Greens

Preparation Time: 10 minutes

Cooking Time: 25 minutes

Servings: 2

Ingredients:

- 1 pound red or Swiss green chard, trimmed
- 1-pound dandelion greens, trimmed
- 1/4 cup extra-virgin olive oil
- 2 celery stalks, chopped
- 1 small onion, finely chopped
- 3 garlic cloves, minced
- 1 teaspoon red pepper flakes
- 1 teaspoon Italian Herb Blend
- 1/2 tube firm polenta, cut into 1-inch-thick slices
- Sea salt

Directions:

1. Bring a large pot of water to a boil over high heat. Add the chard and dandelion greens and cook for 3 to 5 minutes until the stems are soft. Drain and set aside to cool.

2. In a large skillet, heat the olive oil over low heat. Add the celery, onion, garlic, red pepper flakes, and Italian herb blend. Cook for 3 minutes, stirring until the vegetables soften.
3. Add the polenta to the pan and stir to combine—Cook for 5 minutes. Turn the polenta over and cook for another 5 minutes.
4. Roughly chop the cooled greens and add them to the skillet—season with salt.
5. Stir everything together—some of the polenta will break up into smaller pieces at this point. Cover and cook for about 10 minutes until the greens are tender.
6. Variation tip: This recipe can easily vary with the seasons. Use whatever greens are available at the time you make it.

Nutrition: Calories: 507; Total Fat: 29g; Saturated Fat: 4g; Protein: 14g; Total Carbohydrates: 52g; Fiber: 15g; Sugar: 8g; Cholesterol: 0mg

128. Baked Rice With Swordfish And Mussels

Preparation Time: 10 minutes

Cooking Time: 1 hour

Servings: 4

Ingredients:

- 2 tablespoons extra-virgin olive oil
- 2 swordfish steaks, cut into bite-size pieces
- 1 teaspoon salt
- 1 teaspoon freshly ground black pepper
- 1 hot Italian pork sausage, sliced
- 1 medium onion, sliced
- 1 yellow or orange bell pepper, seeded and sliced
- 3 garlic cloves, chopped
- ¼ cup dry white wine
- 1 cup Arborio rice
- 3 cups seafood or vegetable broth, divided
- 1-pound mussels, scrubbed and debearded
- 2 large eggs, beaten

Directions:

1. Preheat the oven to 325°F.
2. In a large, deep ovenproof skillet, heat the olive oil over medium heat. Add the swordfish and season with salt and pepper. Brown, the fish for about 1 minute on each side, then transfer to a plate.
3. Add the sausage, onion, bell pepper, and garlic to the skillet and cook for about 10 minutes, until the sausage is browned and the vegetables are softened. Transfer to the plate with the swordfish.
4. Pour in the wine and deglaze the skillet, stirring to scrape up any browned bits on the bottom. Add the rice and mix with the wine until coated.
5. Add 2 cups of broth and cook for 5 minutes without stirring.
6. Add the swordfish, sausage, onion, and bell pepper mixture on top of the rice. Pour in the remaining 1 cup of seafood broth and bring to a boil. Do not stir.
7. Cover, transfer to the oven, and bake for 30 minutes.
8. Uncover the skillet and take a peek at the dish. If it looks dry, add 1/3 cup water. Add the mussels, pushing the hinged-ends down into the rice. Pour the beaten eggs over the top of the dish.
9. Cook for another 10 minutes, uncovered, or until the mussels open and the egg is thoroughly cooked. Discard any mussels that do not open.

Nutrition: Calories: 508; Total Fat: 23g; Saturated Fat: 6g; Protein: 25g; Total Carbohydrates: 46g; Fiber: 2g; Sugar: 2g; Cholesterol: 160mg

129. Cucumber Olive Rice

Preparation Time: 20 minutes

Cooking Time: 10 minutes

Servings: 8

Ingredients:

- 2 cups rice, rinsed
- 1/2 cup olives, pitted
- 1 cup cucumber, chopped

- 1 tbsp red wine vinegar
- 1 tsp lemon zest, grated
- 1 tbsp fresh lemon juice
- 2 tbsp olive oil
- 2 cups vegetable broth
- 1/2 tsp dried oregano
- 1 red bell pepper, chopped
- 1/2 cup onion, chopped
- 1 tbsp olive oil
- Pepper
- Salt

Directions:

1. Add oil into the pot and heat.
2. Add onion and sauté for 3 minutes.
3. Add bell pepper and oregano and sauté for 1 minute.
4. Add rice and broth and stir well.
5. Seal pot with lid and cook on high heat. For 6 minutes.
6. Once done, remove the lid.
7. Add remaining ingredients and stir everything well to mix.
8. Serve immediately and enjoy it.

Nutrition: Calories 229 Fat 5.1 g Carbohydrates 40.2 g Sugar 1.6 g Protein 4.9 g Cholesterol 0 mg

130. Chorizo-kidney Beans Quinoa Pilaf

Preparation Time: 10 minutes

Cooking Time: 35 minutes

Servings: 4

Ingredients:

- ¼ pound dried Spanish chorizo diced (about 2/3 cup)
- ¼ teaspoon red pepper flakes
- ¼ teaspoon smoked paprika
- ½ teaspoon cumin
- ½ teaspoon sea salt
- 1 3/4 cups water
- 1 cup quinoa
- 1 large clove garlic minced
- 1 small red bell pepper finely diced
- 1 small red onion finely diced
- 1 tablespoon tomato paste
- 1 15-ounce can of kidney beans rinsed and drained

Directions:

1. Place a nonstick pot on medium high fire and heat for 2 minutes. Add chorizo and

sauté for 5 minutes until lightly browned.
2. Stir in peppers and onion. Sauté for 5 minutes.
3. Add tomato paste, red pepper flakes, salt, paprika, cumin, and garlic. Sauté for 2 minutes.
4. Stir in quinoa and mix well. Sauté for 2 minutes.
5. Add water and beans. Mix well. Cover and simmer for 20 minutes or until liquid is fully absorbed.
6. Turn off fire and fluff quinoa. Let it sit for 5 minutes more while uncovered.
7. Serve and enjoy.

Nutrition: Calories per serving: 260; Protein: 9.6g; Carbs: 40.9g; Fat: 6.8g

131. Belly-filling Cajun Rice & Chicken

Preparation Time: 45 minutes

Cooking Time: 20 minutes

Servings: 6

Ingredients:

- 1 tablespoon oil
- 1 onion, diced
- 3 cloves of garlic, minced
- 1-pound chicken breasts, sliced
- 1 tablespoon Cajun seasoning
- 1 tablespoon tomato paste
- 2 cups chicken broth
- 1 ½ cups white rice, rinsed
- 1 bell pepper, chopped

Directions:

1. Pour the oil into a pot and heat it.
2. Sauté the onion and garlic until fragrant.
3. Stir in the chicken breasts and season with Cajun seasoning.
4. Continue cooking for 3 minutes.
5. Add the tomato paste and chicken broth. Dissolve the tomato paste before adding the rice and bell pepper.
6. Close the lid.
7. Cook for 10 minutes.
8. Once cooled, evenly divide into serving size, keep in your preferred container, and refrigerate until ready to eat.

Nutrition: Calories per serving: 337; Carbohydrates: 44.3g; Protein: 26.1g; Fat: 5.0g

Chapter 6. Soups

132. Spinach and Feta Cheese Soup

Preparation Time: 8 minutes

Cooking Time: 24 minutes

Servings: 4

Ingredients:

- 14 oz frozen spinach
- oz feta cheese
- 1 large onion or 4-5 scallions
- 2 -3 tbsp light cream
- 3-4 tbsp olive oil
- 1-2 cloves garlic
- 4 cups water

Directions:

1. Heat the oil in a cooking pot.
2. Add the onion and spinach and sauté together for a few minutes until just softened.
3. Add garlic and stir for a minute. Remove from heat.
4. Add about 2 cups of hot water and season with salt and pepper.
5. Bring back to the boil, then reduce the heat and simmer for around 30 minutes.
6. Blend soup in a blender.
7. Crumble the cheese with a fork.
8. Stir in the crumbled feta cheese and the cream.
9. Serve hot.

Nutrition: 251 Calories 13g Fat 5g Protein

133. Moroccan Pumpkin Soup

Preparation Time: 7 minutes

Cooking Time: 54 minutes

Servings: 6

Ingredients:

- 1 leek, white part only
- 3 cloves garlic
- ½ tsp ground ginger
- ½ tsp ground cinnamon
- ½ tsp ground cumin
- 2 carrots
- 2 lb. pumpkin
- 1/3 cup chickpeas

- 5 tbsp olive oil
- juice of ½ lemon

Directions:

1. Heat oil in a large saucepan and sauté leek, garlic and 2 teaspoons of salt, occasionally stirring, until soft.
2. Add cinnamon, ginger and cumin and stir.
3. Add in carrots, pumpkin and chickpeas.
4. Stir to combine.
5. Add 5 cups of water, bring the soup to a boil, and then reduce heat and simmer for 50 minutes.
6. Pull out from the heat, add lemon juice and blend the soup.
7. Heat again over low heat for 4-5 minutes.
8. Serve topped with parsley sprigs.

Nutrition: 241Calories 21g Fat 4g Protein

134. Roasted Root Vegetable Soup

Preparation Time: 10 minutes

Cooking Time: 35 minutes

Servings: 6

Ingredients:

- 2 parsnips, peeled and sliced
- 2 carrots, peeled and sliced
- 2 sweet potatoes, peeled and sliced
- 1 teaspoon chopped fresh rosemary
- 1 teaspoon chopped fresh thyme
- 1 teaspoon sea salt
- ½ teaspoon freshly ground black pepper
- 2 tablespoons extra-virgin olive oil
- 4 cups low-sodium vegetable soup
- ½ cup grated Parmesan cheese, for garnish (optional)

Directions:

1. Preheat the oven to 400ºF (205ºC). Line a baking sheet with aluminum foil.
2. Combine the parsnips, carrots, and sweet potatoes in a large bowl, then sprinkle with rosemary, thyme, salt, and pepper, and drizzle with olive oil. Toss to coat the vegetables well.
3. Arrange the vegetables on the baking sheet, then roast in the preheated oven for 30 minutes or until lightly browned and soft. Flip the vegetables halfway through the roasting.
4. Pour the roasted vegetables with vegetable broth in a food processor, then pulse until creamy and smooth.
5. Pour the puréed vegetables in a saucepan, then warm over low heat until heated through.
6. Spoon the soup in a large serving bowl, then scatter with Parmesan cheese. Serve immediately.
7. Tip: If you don't have vegetable soup, just use the same water to replace it.

Nutrition:

calories: 192 fat: 5.7g Protein: 4.8g carbs: 31.5g fiber: 5.7g Sodium: 797mg

135. Super Mushroom and Red Wine Soup

Preparation Time: 40 minutes

Cooking Time: 35 minutes

Servings: 6

Ingredients:

- 2 ounces (57 g) dried morels
- 2 ounces (57 g) dried porcini
- 1 tablespoon extra-virgin olive oil
- 8 ounces (227 g) button mushrooms, chopped
- 8 ounces (227 g) portobello mushrooms, chopped
- 3 shallots, finely chopped
- 2 cloves garlic, minced
- 1 teaspoon finely chopped fresh thyme
- Sea salt and freshly ground pepper, to taste

- 1/3 cup dry red wine
- 4 cups low-sodium chicken broth
- 1/2 cup heavy cream
- 1 small bunch flat-leaf parsley, chopped

Directions:

1. Put the dried mushrooms in a large bowl and pour in enough water to submerge the mushrooms. Soak for 30 minutes and drain.
2. Heat the olive oil in a stockpot over medium-high heat until shimmering.
3. Add the mushrooms and shallots to the pot and sauté for 10 minutes or until the mushrooms are tender.
4. Add the garlic and sauté for an additional 1 minute or until fragrant. Sprinkle with thyme, salt, and pepper.
5. Pour in the dry red wine and chicken broth. Bring to a boil over high heat.
6. Reduce the heat to low. Simmer for 20 minutes.
7. After simmering, pour half of the soup in a food processor, then pulse until creamy and smooth.
8. Pour the puréed soup back to the pot, then mix in the cream and heat over low heat until heated through.
9. Pour the soup in a large serving bowl and spread with chopped parsley before serving.
10. Tip: If you don't have dry red wine, you can use white wine to replace it, such as sherry.

Nutrition:

calories: 139 fat: 7.4g Protein: 7.1g carbs: 14.4g fiber: 2.8g Sodium: 94mg

136. Smoked Ham Split Pea Soup

Preparation Time: 10 minutes

Cooking Time: 1 Hour

Servings: 8

Ingredients:

- 2 tablespoons olive oil
- 4 oz. smoked ham, diced
- 1 sweet onion, chopped

- 1 jalapeno pepper, chopped
- 2 red bell peppers, cored and diced
- 2 garlic cloves, chopped
- 2 carrots, diced
- 1 parsnip, diced
- 2 tomatoes, peeled and diced
- 2 cups vegetable stock
- 6 cups water
- ½ cup split peas
- Salt and pepper to taste
- 1 lemon, juiced
- Crème fraiche for serving

Directions:

1. Heat the oil in a soup pot and stir in the ham. Cook for 5 minutes then add the rest of the ingredients.
2. Season with salt and pepper and cook on low heat for 30 minutes.
3. Serve the soup warm, topped with crème Fraiche.

Nutrition: Calories:139 Fat:5.1g Protein:6.7g Carbohydrates:18.0g

137. Mushroom Spinach Soup

Preparation Time: 25 mins

Cooking Time: 10 minutes

Servings: 4

Ingredients

- 1 cup spinach, cleaned and chopped
- 1 cup mushrooms, chopped
- 1 onion
- 6 garlic cloves
- ½ teaspoon red chili powder
- Salt and black pepper, to taste
- 3 tablespoons buttermilk
- 1 teaspoon almond flour
- 2 cups chicken broth
- 3 tablespoons butter
- ¼ cup fresh cream for garnish

Directions

1. Heat butter in a pan and add onions and garlic.
2. Sauté for about 3 minutes and add spinach, salt and red chili powder.
3. Sauté for about 4 minutes and add mushrooms.

4. Transfer into a blender and blend to make a puree.
5. Return to the pan and add buttermilk and almond flour for the creamy texture.
6. Mix well and simmer for about 2 minutes.
7. Garnish with fresh cream and serve hot.

Nutrition: Calories: 160 Carbs: 7g Fats: 13.3g Proteins: 4.7g Sodium: 462mg Sugar: 2.7g

138. Delicata Squash Soup

Preparation Time: 45mins

Cooking Time: 20 minutes

Servings: 5

Ingredients

- 1 ½ cups beef bone broth
- 1 small onion, peeled and grated.
- ½ teaspoon sea salt
- ¼ teaspoon poultry seasoning
- 2 small Delicata Squash, chopped
- 2 garlic cloves, minced
- 2 tablespoons olive oil
- ¼ teaspoon black pepper
- 1 small lemon, juiced
- 5 tablespoons sour cream

Directions

1. Put Delicata Squash and water in a medium pan and bring to a boil.
2. Reduce the heat and cook for about 20 minutes.
3. Drain and set aside.
4. Put olive oil, onions, garlic and poultry seasoning in a small sauce pan.
5. Cook for about 2 minutes and add broth.
6. Allow it to simmer for 5 minutes and remove from heat.
7. Whisk in the lemon juice and transfer the mixture to a blender.
8. Pulse until smooth and top with sour cream.

Nutrition: Calories: 109 Carbs: 4.9g Fats: 8.5g Proteins: 3g Sodium: 279mg Sugar: 2.4g

139. Cod Potato Soup

Preparation Time: 10 minutes

Cooking Time: 1 Hour

Servings: 8

Ingredients:

- 2 tablespoons olive oil
- 2 shallots, chopped
- 1 celery stalk, sliced
- 1 carrot, sliced
- 1 red bell pepper, cored and diced
- 2 garlic cloves, chopped
- 1 ½ pounds potatoes, peeled and cubed
- 1 cup diced tomatoes
- 1 bay leaf
- 1 thyme sprig
- ½ teaspoon dried marjoram
- 2 cups chicken stock
- 6 cups water
- Salt and pepper to taste
- 4 cod fillets, cubed
- 2 tablespoons lemon juice

Directions:

1. Heat the oil in a soup pot and stir in the shallots, celery, carrot, bell pepper and garlic.
2. Cook for 5 minutes then stir in the potatoes, tomatoes, bay leaf, thyme, marjoram, stock and water.
3. Season with salt and pepper and cook on low heat for 20 minutes.
4. Add the cod fillets and lemon juice and continue cooking for 5 additional minutes.
5. Serve the soup warm and fresh.

Nutrition: Calories:108 Fat:3.9g Protein:2.2g Carbohydrates:17.1g

140. Keto French Onion Soup

Preparation Time: 40 mins

Cooking Time: 35 minutes

Servings: 6

Ingredients

- 5 tablespoons butter
- 500 g brown onion medium
- 4 drops liquid stevia

- 4 tablespoons olive oil
- 3 cups beef stock

Directions

1. Put the butter and olive oil in a large pot over medium-low heat and add onions and salt.
2. Cook for about 5 minutes and stir in stevia.
3. Cook for another 5 minutes and add beef stock.
4. Reduce the heat to low and simmer for about 25 minutes.
5. Dish out into soup bowls and serve hot.

Nutrition: Calories: 198 Carbs: 6g Fats: 20.6g Proteins: 2.9g Sodium: 883mg Sugar: 1.7g

141. Minestrone Soup

Preparation Time: 10 minutes

Cooking Time: 1 hour

Servings: 4

Ingredients:

- 1 small white onion
- 4 cloves garlic
- 1/2 cup carrots
- 1 medium zucchini
- 1 medium yellow squash
- 2 tablespoons minced fresh parsley
- 1/4 cup celery sliced
- 3 tablespoons olive oil
- 2 x 15 oz. cans cannellini beans
- 2 x 15 oz. can red kidney beans
- 1 x 14.5 oz. can fire-roasted diced tomatoes, drained
- 4 cups vegetable stock
- 2 cups of water
- 1 1/2 teaspoons oregano
- 1/2 teaspoon basil
- 1/4 teaspoon thyme
- 1 teaspoon salt
- 1/2 teaspoon pepper
- 3/4 cup small pasta shells
- 4 cups fresh baby spinach
- 1/4 cup Parmesan or Romano cheese

Directions:

1. Grab a stockpot and place over medium heat. Add the oil, onions, garlic, carrots, zucchini, squash, parsley, and celery. Cook for five minutes

until the veggies are getting soft.

2. Pour in the stock, water, beans, tomatoes, herbs, and salt and pepper. Stir well. Decrease heat, cover, and simmer for 30 minutes.
3. Add the pasta and spinach, stir well, then cover and cook for 20 minutes until the pasta is cooked through. Stir through the cheese, then serve and enjoy.

Nutrition: 34 calories 26.3 g protein 30.3 g fat

142. Chicken Wild Rice Soup

Preparation Time: 10 minutes

Cooking Time: 15 minutes

Servings: 6

Ingredients:

- 2/3 cup wild rice, uncooked
- 1 tablespoon onion, chopped finely
- 1 tablespoon fresh parsley, chopped
- 1 cup carrots, chopped
- 8-ounces chicken breast, cooked
- 2 tablespoon butter
- 1/4 cup all-purpose white flour
- 5 cups low-sodium chicken broth
- 1 tablespoon slivered almonds

Directions:

1. Start by adding rice and 2 cups broth along with ½ cup water to a cooking pot. Cook the chicken until the rice is al dente and set it aside. Add butter to a saucepan and melt it.
2. Stir in onion and sauté until soft then add the flour and the remaining broth.
3. Stir it and then cook for it 1 minute. Then add the chicken, cooked rice, and carrots—Cook for 5 minutes on simmer. Garnish with almonds. Serve fresh.

Nutrition: 287 calories 21g protein 35g fat

143. Classic Chicken Soup

Preparation Time: 10 minutes

Cooking Time: 25 minutes

Servings: 2

Ingredients:

- 1 1/2 cups low-sodium vegetable broth
- 1 cup of water
- 1/4 teaspoon poultry seasoning
- 1/4 teaspoon black pepper
- 1 cup chicken strips
- 1/4 cup carrot
- 2-ounces egg noodles, uncooked

Directions:

1. Gather all the ingredients into a slow cooker and toss it. Cook soup on high heat for 25 minutes.
2. Serve warm.

Nutrition: 103 calories 8g protein 11g fat

144. Cucumber Soup

Preparation Time: 10 minutes

Cooking Time: 0 minute

Servings: 4

Ingredients:

- 2 medium cucumbers
- 1/3 cup sweet white onion
- 1 green onion
- 1/4 cup fresh mint
- 2 tablespoons fresh dill
- 2 tablespoons lemon juice
- 2/3 cup water
- 1/2 cup half and half cream
- 1/3 cup sour cream
- 1/2 teaspoon pepper
- Fresh dill sprigs for garnish

Directions:

1. Situate all of the ingredients into a food processor and toss. Puree the mixture and refrigerate for 2 hours. Garnish with dill sprigs. Enjoy fresh.

Nutrition: 77 calories 2g protein 6g fats

145. Squash and Turmeric Soup

Preparation Time: 10 minutes

Cooking Time: 30 minutes

Servings: 4

Ingredients:

- 4 cups low-sodium vegetable broth
- 2 medium zucchini squash
- 2 medium yellow crookneck squash
- 1 small onion
- 1/2 cup frozen green peas
- 2 tablespoons olive oil
- 1/2 cup plain nonfat Greek yogurt
- 2 teaspoon turmeric

Directions:

1. Warm the broth in a saucepan on medium heat. Toss in onion, squash, and zucchini. Let it simmer for approximately 25 minutes then add oil and green peas.
2. Cook for another 5 minutes then allow it to cool. Puree the soup using a handheld blender then add Greek yogurt and turmeric. Refrigerate it overnight and serve fresh.

Nutrition: 100 calories 4g protein 10g fat

146. Leek, Potato, and Carrot Soup

Preparation Time: 15 minutes

Cooking Time: 25 minutes

Servings: 4

Ingredients:

- 1 - leek
- ¾ - cup diced and boiled potatoes
- ¾ - cup diced and boiled carrots
- 1 - garlic clove
- 1 - tablespoon oil
- Crushed pepper to taste
- 3 - cups low sodium chicken stock
- Chopped parsley for garnish
- 1 - bay leaf
- ¼ - teaspoon ground cumin

Directions:

1. Trim off and take away a portion of the coarse inexperienced portions of the leek, at that factor reduce daintily and flush altogether in virus water. Channel properly. Warm the oil in an extensively based pot. Include the leek and garlic, and sear over low warmth for two-3 minutes, till sensitive.
2. Include the inventory, inlet leaf, cumin, and pepper. Heat the mixture, mix constantly. Include the bubbled potatoes and carrots and stew for 10-15minutes. Modify the flavoring, eliminate the inlet leaf, and serve sprinkled generously with slashed parsley.
3. To make a pureed soup, make the soup in a blender or nourishment processor until smooth Come again to the pan. Include ½ field milk. Bring to bubble and stew for 2-3minutes

Nutrition: 315 calories 8g fat 15g protein

147. Kale Chicken Soup

Preparation Time: 12 minutes.

Cooking Time: 18 minutes.

Servings: 6.

Ingredients:

- 1 Tablespoon Olive Oil.
- 3 Cups Kale, Chopped.
- 1 Cup Carrot, Minced.
- 2 Cloves Garlic, Minced.
- 8 Cups Chicken Broth, Low Sodium.
- Sea Salt & Black Pepper to Taste.
- ¾ Cup Patina Pasta, Uncooked.
- 2 Cups Chicken, Cooked & Shredded.
- 3 Tablespoons Parmesan Cheese, Grated.

Directions:

1. Start by getting out a stockpot over medium heat and heat your oil. Add in your garlic, cooking for half a minute. Stir frequently and add in the kale

and carrots. Cook for an additional five minutes, and make sure to stir so it doesn't burn.

2. Add in salt, pepper, and broth, turning the heat to high. Boil before adding in your pasta.
3. Set the heat to medium then cook for extra ten minutes. Your pasta should be cooked all the way through, but make sure to stir occasionally so it doesn't stick to the bottom. Add in the chicken, and cook for two minutes.
4. Ladle the soup and serve topped with cheese.

Nutrition: Calories: 187 Protein: 15g Fat: 5g

Chapter 7. Salads & Sides

148. Mediterranean Tortellini Salad

Preparation Time: 30 minutes

Cooking Time: 12 minutes

Servings: 6

Ingredients:

- 500g tortellini
- 300g dried tomatoes
- 2 onions
- 3 tbsp olive oil
- 3 tbsp white wine vinegar
- 1 teaspoon thyme
- salt and pepper
- 200g rocket

Directions:

1. Cook the tortellini, drain and set aside.
2. Chop the onions and sauté them in olive oil with thyme. Add the chopped sun-dried tomatoes and fry for about 2 minutes. Then add the tortellini and remove the pan from the heat.
3. Season to taste with salt, pepper and white wine vinegar. Finally, add the tomatoes and rocket. Finished! Serve and enjoy.

Nutrition: Calories: 343 Carbohydrates: 45.03g Protein: 12.35g Fat: 12.93g

149. Mediterranean Salad With Parsnips And Peppers

Preparation Time: 15 minutes

Cooking Time: 1 hour

Servings: 2

Ingredients:

- 2 parsnips
- 1 bell pepper
- 1 clove of garlic
- 50g dried tomatoes
- 1 tbsp balsamic vinegar
- Basil and chili flakes
- salt and pepper
- olive oil

Directions:

1. Peel the parsnips, cut them into thin slices, and cook in a saucepan with a little water for about 5 minutes.
2. Clean, core and dice the peppers.
3. Heat olive oil in a pan and fry the chopped peppers and parsnip slices.
4. Peel and chop the garlic and add to the vegetables in the pan—season to taste with chili flakes, basil, pepper and salt. As soon as the pepper cubes and the parsnip slices are golden browns, put all the ingredients in a bowl and mix the whole thing with the balsamic vinegar.
5. Finished! Serve and enjoy.

Nutrition: Calories: 32 Carbohydrates: 7.01g Protein: 1.21g Fat: 0.17g

150. Fried Mushroom Salad

Preparation Time: 30 minutes

Cooking Time: 0 minutes

Servings: 4

Ingredients:

- 1 zucchini
- 125g mushrooms
- 1 bell pepper
- 2 tomatoes
- 200g feta cheese
- 1 small onion
- Lemon juice and olive oil
- Balsamic vinegar
- salt and pepper

Directions:

1. Cut everything into small pieces
2. Fry the zucchini, bell pepper and mushrooms in a pan.
3. Put everything in a bowl and season with balsamic vinegar, olive oil, lemon juice, a pinch of sugar, as well as salt, pepper and garlic.

Nutrition: Calories: 255 Carbohydrates: 32.72g Protein: 11.34g Fat: 11.19g

151. Mediterranean Chickpea Salad

Preparation Time: 15 minutes

Cooking Time: 15 minutes

Servings: 4

Ingredients:

- 265g chickpeas
- 200g feta cheese
- 1 onion
- 1 bell pepper
- ½ cucumber
- 2 tbsp olives
- 2 tbsp parsley
- salt and pepper

For the dressing

- 100ml olive oil
- 50ml white wine vinegar
- 1 tbsp lime juice
- 1 tsp chili flakes
- salt and pepper

Directions:

1. Drain the chickpeas, wash them and place them in a large bowl. Cut the cucumber into slices. Core and chop the olives. Dice the paprika and feta, chop the onion. Chop the parsley.
2. Combine all ingredients except for the dressing in a bowl.
3. For the dressing: mix olive oil, white wine vinegar, lime juice, chili flakes, salt and pepper.
4. Add the dressing to the other ingredients and mix everything well. Finished! Serve and enjoy.

Nutrition: Calories: 419 Carbohydrates: 51.19g Protein: 21.88g Fat: 15.37g

152. Mediterranean Tuna Salad

Preparation Time: 20 minutes

Cooking Time: 0 minutes

Servings: 4

Ingredients:

- 1 clove of garlic
- 4 tomatoes
- 2 onions
- 200g feta cheese
- 1 cucumber
- 3 tbsp olive oil

- 1 tin of tuna
- 1 teaspoon rosemary
- 2 tablespoons balsamic vinegar
- salt and pepper

Directions:

1. Wash and dice tomatoes and cucumbers. Peel and chop the garlic and onions. Crumble the feta. Drain the tuna.
2. Put the garlic, tomatoes, onions, and cucumber in a bowl, season with rosemary and basil, and add a little olive oil.
3. Add the tuna and feta cheese. Season to taste with salt, pepper and balsamic vinegar. Finished! Serve and enjoy.

Nutrition: Calories: 285 Carbohydrates: 15.81g Protein: 9.35g Fat: 21.2g

153. Mediterranean Egg Broccoli Salad

Preparation Time: 40 minutes

Cooking Time: 15 minutues

Servings: 4

Ingredients:

- 5 eggs
- 800g broccoli
- 200g mushrooms
- 2 tbsp pine nuts
- 50g dried tomatoes
- 250g yogurt
- 2 tbsp olive oil
- ½ onion
- 10 basil leaves
- salt and pepper

Direction

1. Hard boil eggs. Clean the broccoli and cut off the florets. Peel and cut the broccoli stalks. Cut the dried tomatoes into strips. Peel and chop the onion and garlic. Clean the mushrooms and cut them into slices.
2. Cook the broccoli in boiling salted water for about 12 minutes. Drain the water and let it cool down.
3. Roast pine nuts in a pan and then set aside.
4. Mix yogurt with olive oil, add onion and garlic and season

everything with salt and pepper for the dressing.

5. Mix the broccoli, mushrooms and tomato strips. Fold in the dressing and let everything steep for about 15 minutes.
6. Peel the eggs, cut eighths and fold into the salad. Refine the salad with roasted pine nuts and fresh basil and serve. Good Appetite!

Nutrition: Calories: 463 Carbohydrates: 49.74g Protein: 29.22g Fat: 20.65g

154. Mediterranean Salad With Baked Camembert

Preparation Time: 30 minutes

Cooking Time: 15 minutes

Servings: 4

Ingredients:

- 800g asparagus
- 200g rocket
- 200g cherry tomatoes
- 100g olives
- 3 tbsp balsamic vinegar
- 4 mini camembert
- 2 tablespoons cranberries
- 5 tbsp olive oil
- 1 teaspoon mustard
- salt and pepper

Directions:

1. Clean and peel the asparagus and cut off the woody ends— Cook in boiling salted water for about 10 minutes. Then drain and drain.
2. Thoroughly clean the rocket and spin dry. Wash and quarter the tomatoes.
3. For the dressing: mix the balsamic vinegar, 3 tbsp olive oil, salt, mustard and pepper in a bowl.
4. Bake the Camembert in a preheated oven at 200 ° C. Then take it out, let it cool and cover with a few cranberries.
5. Arrange the rocket with asparagus, tomatoes and olives on a plate. Drizzle with the salad sauce and add the melted camembert with cranberries. Finished! Serve and enjoy.

Nutrition: Calories: 277
Carbohydrates: 21.02g Protein: 5.46g
Fat: 21.13g

155. Tomato and Avocado Salad

Preparation Time: 10 minutes

Cooking Time: 0 minutes

Servings: 4

Ingredients:

- 1-pound cherry tomatoes
- 2 avocados
- 1 sweet onion, chopped
- 2 tablespoons lemon juice
- 1 and ½ tablespoons olive oil
- Handful basil, chopped

Directions:

1. Mix the tomatoes with the avocados and the rest of the ingredients in a serving bowl, toss and serve right away.

Nutrition: 148 Calories 7.8g Fat 5.5g Protein

156. Arugula Salad

Preparation Time: 5 minutes

Cooking Time: 0 minutes

Servings: 4

Ingredients:

- Arugula leaves (4 cups)
- Cherry tomatoes (1 cup)
- Pine nuts (.25 cup)
- Rice vinegar (1 tbsp.)
- Olive/grapeseed oil (2 tbsp.)
- Grated parmesan cheese (.25 cup)
- Black pepper & salt (as desired)
- Large sliced avocado (1)

Directions:

1. Peel and slice the avocado. Rinse and dry the arugula leaves, grate the cheese, and slice the cherry tomatoes into halves.
2. Combine the arugula, pine nuts, tomatoes, oil, vinegar, salt, pepper, and cheese.
3. Toss the salad to mix and portion it onto plates with the avocado slices to serve.

Nutrition: 257 Calories 23g Fats 6.1g Protein

157. Chickpea Salad

Preparation Time: 15 minutes

Cooking Time: 0 minutes

Servings: 4

Ingredients:

- Cooked chickpeas (15 oz.)
- Diced Roma tomato (1)
- Diced green medium bell pepper (half of 1)
- Fresh parsley (1 tbsp.)
- Small white onion (1)
- Minced garlic (.5 tsp.)
- Lemon (1 juiced)

Directions:

1. Chop the tomato, green pepper, and onion. Mince the garlic. Combine each of the fixings into a salad bowl and toss well.
2. Cover the salad to chill for at least 15 minutes in the fridge. Serve when ready.

Nutrition: 163 Calories 7g Fats 4g Protein

158. Chopped Israeli Mediterranean Pasta Salad

Preparation Time: 15 minutes

Cooking Time: 2 minutes

Servings: 8

Ingredients:

- Small bow tie or other small pasta (.5 lb.)
- 1/3 cup Cucumber
- 1/3 cup Radish
- 1/3 cup Tomato
- 1/3 cup Yellow bell pepper
- 1/3 cup Orange bell pepper
- 1/3 cup Black olives
- 1/3 cup Green olives
- 1/3 cup Red onions
- 1/3 cup Pepperoncini
- 1/3 cup Feta cheese
- 1/3 cup Fresh thyme leaves
- Dried oregano (1 tsp.)

Dressing:

- 0.25 cup + more, olive oil
- juice of 1 lemon

Directions:

1. Slice the green olives into halves. Dice the feta and pepperoncini. Finely dice the remainder of the veggies.
2. Prepare a pot of water with the salt, and simmer the pasta until it's al dente (checking at two minutes under the listed time). Rinse and drain in cold water.
3. Combine a small amount of oil with the pasta. Add the salt, pepper, oregano, thyme, and veggies. Pour in the rest of the oil, lemon juice, mix and fold in the grated feta.
4. Pop it into the fridge within two hours, best if overnight. Taste test and adjust the seasonings to your liking; add fresh thyme.

Nutrition: 65 Calories 5.6g Fats 0.8g Protein

159. Pork and Greens Salad

Preparation Time: 10 minutes

Cooking Time: 15 minutes

Servings: 4

Ingredients:

- 1-pound pork chops
- 8 ounces white mushrooms, sliced
- ½ cup Italian dressing
- 6 cups mixed salad greens
- 6 ounces jarred artichoke hearts, drained
- Salt and black pepper to the taste
- ½ cup basil, chopped
- 1 tablespoon olive oil

Directions:

1. Heat a pan with the oil over medium-high heat, add the pork, and brown for 5 minutes.
2. Add the mushrooms, stir, and sauté for 5 minutes more.
3. Add the dressing, artichokes, salad greens, salt, pepper, and basil, cook for 4-5 minutes, divide everything into bowls and serve.

Nutrition: 235 Calories 6g Fat 11g Protein

160. Mediterranean Duck Breast Salad

Preparation Time: 10 minutes

Cooking Time: 20 minutes

Servings: 4

Ingredients:

- 3 tablespoons white wine vinegar
- 2 tablespoons sugar
- 2 oranges, peeled and cut into segments
- 1 teaspoon orange zest, grated
- 1 tablespoon lemon juice
- 1 teaspoon lemon zest, grated
- 3 tablespoons shallot, minced
- 2 duck breasts
- 1 head of frisée, torn
- 2 small lettuce heads
- 2 tablespoons chives

Directions:

1. Heat a small saucepan over medium-high heat, add vinegar and sugar, stir and boil for 5 minutes and take off the heat.
2. Add orange zest, lemon zest, and lemon juice, stir, and leave aside for a few minutes. Add shallot, salt, and pepper to taste the oil, whisk well and leave aside for now.
3. Pat dry the duck pieces, score the skin, trim, and season with salt and pepper. Heat a pan over medium-high heat for 1 minute, arrange duck breast pieces skin side down, brown for 8 minutes, reduce heat to medium and cook for 4 more minutes.
4. Flip pieces, cook for 3 minutes, transfer to a cutting board, and cover them with foil. Put frisée and lettuce in a bowl, stir and divide between plates.
5. Slice duck, arrange on top, add orange segments, sprinkle chives, and drizzle the vinaigrette.

Nutrition: 320 Calories 4g Fat 14g Protein

161. Creamy Chicken Salad

Preparation Time: 10 minutes

Cooking Time: 0 minute

Servings: 6

Ingredients:

- 20 ounces chicken meat
- ½ cup pecans, chopped
- 1 cup green grapes
- ½ cup celery, chopped
- 2 ounces canned mandarin oranges, drained
- For the creamy cucumber salad dressing:
- 1 cup Greek yogurt cucumber, chopped garlic clove
- 1 teaspoon lemon juice

Directions:

1. In a bowl, mix cucumber with salt, pepper to taste, lemon juice, garlic, and yogurt, and stir very well.
2. In a salad bowl, mix chicken meat with grapes, pecans, oranges, and celery.
3. Add cucumber salad dressing, toss to coat, and keep in the fridge until you serve it.

Nutrition: 200 Calories 3g Fat 8g Protein

162. Chicken and Cabbage Salad

Preparation Time: 10 minutes

Cooking Time: 6 minutes

Servings: 4

Ingredients:

- 3 medium chicken breasts
- 4 ounces green cabbage
- 5 tablespoon extra-virgin olive oil
- Salt and black pepper to taste
- 2 tablespoons sherry vinegar tablespoon chives
- ¼ cup feta cheese, crumbled
- ¼ cup barbeque sauce
- Bacon slices, cooked and crumbled

Directions:

1. Mix 4 tablespoons oil with vinegar, salt, and pepper to taste and stir well in a bowl.
2. Add the shredded cabbage, toss to coat, and leave aside for now.
3. Season chicken with salt and pepper, heat a pan with

remaining oil over medium-high heat, add chicken, cook for 6 minutes, take off heat, transfer to a bowl and mix well with barbeque sauce.
4. Arrange salad on serving plates, add chicken strips, sprinkle cheese, chives, and crumbled bacon, and serve right away.

Nutrition: 200 Calories 15g Fat 33g Protein

163. Roasted Broccoli Salad

Preparation Time: 9 minutes

Cooking Time: 17 minutes

Servings: 4

Ingredients:

- 1 lb. broccoli
- 3 tablespoons olive oil, divided
- 1-pint cherry tomatoes
- 1 ½ teaspoon honey
- 3 cups cubed bread, whole grain
- 1 tablespoon balsamic vinegar
- ½ teaspoon black pepper
- ¼ teaspoon sea salt, fine
- grated parmesan for serving

Directions:

1. Set the oven to 450, and then place a rimmed baking sheet.
2. Drizzle your broccoli with a tablespoon of oil, and toss to coat.
3. Take out from the oven, and spoon the broccoli. Leave oil at the bottom of the bowl, add in your tomatoes, toss to coat, and then mix tomatoes with a tablespoon of honey. place on the same baking sheet.
4. Roast for fifteen minutes, and stir halfway through your cooking time.
5. Add in your bread, and then roast for three more minutes.
6. Whisk two tablespoons of oil, vinegar, and remaining honey. Season. Pour this over your broccoli mix to serve.

Nutrition: 226 Calories 7g Protein 12g Fat

164. Tomato Salad

Preparation Time: 22 minutes

Cooking Time: 0 minute

Servings: 4

Ingredients:

- 1 cucumber, sliced
- ¼ cup sun-dried tomatoes, chopped
- 1 lb. tomatoes, cubed
- ½ cup black olives
- 1 red onion, sliced
- 1 tablespoon balsamic vinegar
- ¼ cup parsley, fresh & chopped
- 2 tablespoons olive oil

Directions:

1. Get out a bowl and combine all your vegetables. to make your dressing, mix all your seasoning, olive oil, and vinegar.
2. Toss with your salad and serve fresh.

Nutrition: 126 Calories 2.1g Protein 9.2g Fat

165. Feta Beet Salad

Preparation Time: 16 minutes

Cooking Time: 0 minute

Servings: 4

Ingredients:

- 6 Red Beets, Cooked & Peeled
- 3 Ounces Feta Cheese, Cubed
- 2 Tablespoons Olive Oil
- 2 Tablespoons Balsamic Vinegar

Directions:

Combine everything, and then serve.

Nutrition: 230 Calories 7.3g Protein 12g Fat

166. Chicken and Quinoa Salad

Preparation Time: 10 minutes

Cooking Time: 20 minutes

Servings: 2

Ingredients:

- 2 tablespoons olive oil
- 2 ounces quinoa
- 2 ounces cherry tomatoes, cut in quarters

- 3 ounces sweet corn
- Lime juice from 1 lime
- Lime zest from 1 lime, grated
- 2 spring onions, chopped
- Small red chili pepper, chopped
- 1 Avocado
- 2 ounces chicken meat

Directions:

1. Fill water in a pan, bring to a boil over medium-high heat, add quinoa, stir, and cook for 12 minutes.
2. Meanwhile, put corn in a pan, heat over medium-high heat, cook for 5 minutes, and leave aside for now.
3. Drain quinoa, transfer to a bowl, add tomatoes, corn, coriander, onions, chili, lime zest, olive oil, and salt and black pepper to taste and toss.
4. In another bowl, mix avocado with lime juice and stir well.
5. Add this to quinoa salad and chicken, toss to coat and serve.

Nutrition: 320 Calories 4g Fat 7g Protein

167. Melon Salad

Preparation Time: 20 minutes

Cooking Time: 0 minutes

Servings: 6

Ingredients:

- ¼ teaspoon sea salt
- ¼ teaspoon black pepper
- 1 tablespoon balsamic vinegar
- 1 cantaloupe
- 12 watermelons
- 2 cups mozzarella balls, fresh
- 1/3 cup basil, fresh & torn
- 2 tablespoons olive oil

Directions:

1. Spoon out balls of cantaloupe, then situate them in a colander over the bowl.
2. Using a melon baller to cut the watermelon as well
3. Drain fruits for ten minutes, then chill the juice.
4. Wipe the bowl dry, and then place your fruit in it.
5. Mix in basil, oil, vinegar, mozzarella, and tomatoes before seasoning.

6. Gently mix and serve.

Nutrition: 218 Calories 10g Protein 13g Fat

168. Bean and Toasted Pita Salad

Preparation Time: 15 minutes

Cooking Time: 10 minutes

Servings: 4

Ingredients:

- 3 tbsp chopped fresh mint
- 3 tbsp chopped fresh parsley
- 1 cup crumbled feta cheese
- 1 cup sliced romaine lettuce
- ½ cucumber, peeled and sliced
- 1 cup diced plum tomatoes
- 2 cups cooked pinto beans, well-drained and slightly warmed
- Pepper to taste
- 3 tbsp extra virgin olive oil
- 2 tbsp ground toasted cumin seeds
- 2 tbsp fresh lemon juice
- 1/8 tsp salt
- 2 cloves garlic, peeled
- 2 6-inch whole-wheat pita bread, cut or torn into bite-sized pieces

Directions:

1. In a large baking sheet, spread torn pita bread and bake in a preheated 400oF oven for 6 minutes.
2. With the back of a knife, mash garlic and salt until paste-like. Add into a medium bowl.
3. Whisk in ground cumin and lemon juice. In a steady and slow stream, pour oil as you whisk continuously—season with pepper.
4. In a large salad bowl, mix cucumber, tomatoes, and beans. Pour in dressing, toss to coat well.
5. Add mint, parsley, feta, lettuce, and toasted pita, toss to mix again, and serve.

Nutrition: Calories: 427 Carbohydrates: 47.3g Protein: 17.7g Fat: 20.4g

169. Salad With Pine Nuts And Mozzarella

Preparation Time: 20 minutes

Cooking Time: 0 minutes

Servings: 2

Ingredients:

- 300g mini mozzarella
- 100g cocktail tomatoes
- 40g pine nuts
- 80g rocket
- 150g mixed salad
- 2 teaspoons of olive oil
- 2 teaspoons of red wine vinegar
- 2 teaspoons of balsamic vinegar
- 4 tbsp olive oil
- 1 teaspoon mustard
- 1 tbsp yogurt
- salt and pepper

Directions:

1. Drain the mozzarella. Thoroughly clean and spin lettuce and rocket. Quarter the cherry tomatoes and put everything in a salad bowl.
2. For the dressing: Mix the red wine vinegar, balsamic vinegar, olive oil, mustard and yogurt together. Season with salt and pepper and mix everything with the salad.
3. Then add the pine nuts. Finished! Serve and enjoy.

Nutrition: Calories: 1324 Carbohydrates: 43.69g Protein: 21.88g Fat: 120.18g

170. Mediterranean Salad With Feta

Preparation Time: 15 minutes

Cooking Time: 0 minutes

Servings: 2

Ingredients:

- 200g feta cheese
- 200g cocktail tomatoes
- 50g almond slivers
- 100g mixed salad
- 2 tbsp red wine vinegar
- 1 tbsp raspberry vinegar
- 1 tbsp green pesto
- 3 tbsp olive oil
- 1 teaspoon mustard

- salt and pepper

Directions:

1. Drain and dice the feta. Clean the lettuce and spin dry. Quarter the cherry tomatoes and place everything in a salad bowl.
2. Mix red wine vinegar, raspberry vinegar, olive oil, mustard and pesto. Season with salt and pepper and pour over the salad.
3. Finally, add the almond slivers. Finished! Serve and enjoy.

Nutrition: Calories: 959

Carbohydrates: 15.44g Protein: 21.45g Fat: 91.88g

171. Tomato And Cucumber Salad With Feta

Preparation Time: 10 minutes

Cooking Time: 0 minutes

Servings: 4

Ingredients:

- 2 tomatoes
- ½ cucumber
- ½ bunch of spring onions
- 200g feta
- 6 tbsp olive oil
- 3 tbsp balsamic vinegar
- salt and pepper

Directions:

1. Thoroughly clean the tomatoes and cucumber. Eight tomatoes. Cut the cucumber into thin slices. Cut the spring onion into thin rings. Chop the herbs. Dice the feta.
2. Put all ingredients in a salad bowl. Add oil and balsamic vinegar, season with salt and pepper and mix well. Done! Serve and enjoy.

Nutrition: Calories: 341

Carbohydrates: 8.28g Protein: 8.-6g Fat: 31.09g

172. Mediterranean Salad With Peppers And Tomatoes

Preparation Time: 35 minutes

Cooking Time: 30 minutes

Servings: 2

Ingredients:

- 1 eggplant
- 1 zucchini
- 1 bell pepper
- 4 tomatoes
- 1 onion
- 4 sprigs of rosemary
- 6 sprigs of thyme
- 4 stalks of sage
- 3 tbsp olive oil
- 3 tbsp balsamic vinegar
- salt and pepper

Directions:

1. Quarter tomatoes. Cut the remaining vegetables into bite-sized pieces, halve the onion and chop it into small pieces. Line a baking sheet with parchment paper, place the vegetables on top, drizzle with olive oil and mix well.
2. Season with salt and pepper. Scatter the herbs over the vegetables. Put the vegetables in the oven and bake at 200 degrees for about 30 minutes.
3. Remove and transfer to a large bowl and mix with olive oil with balsamic vinegar—season with salt and pepper.
4. Let it draw covered. When the salad is still lukewarm, add the tomato quarters and mix well.
5. Serve the salad lukewarm.

Nutrition: Calories: 355

Carbohydrates: 39.43g Protein: 6.51g

Fat: 21.43g

173. Mediterranean Potato Salad With Beans

Preparation Time: 180 minutes

Cooking Time: 15 minutes

Servings: 4

Ingredients:

- 500g potatoes
- 300g green beans
- 1 tbsp rosemary
- 8 sun-dried tomatoes
- 40g bacon
- 3 tbsp red wine vinegar
- 200g olives
- 1 egg yolk
- salt and pepper

Directions:

1. Wash green beans, break into short pieces, boil in salted water for about 10 minutes, and then drain in a colander. Collect some boiled bean water.
2. Drain the tomatoes and cut them into small pieces. Collect some tomato oil. Chop the rosemary and cut the bacon into thin strips—Fry bacon with chopped rosemary in olive oil and tomato oil in a pan. Pour in the vinegar and the bean water and add the tomato pieces. Heat the potatoes and beans, let them steep and wait until they have cooled down. Then pour off using a sieve and collect the vinaigrette. Mix the potato salad with the olives.
3. Whisk the vinaigrette with egg yolk and then heat gently, constantly stirring, until the sauce thickens. Season with salt and pepper and pour over the salad. Let it steep for an hour. Finished! Serve and enjoy.

Nutrition: Calories: 237 Carbohydrates: 29.02g Protein: 5.81g Fat: 12.26g

174. Orzo Olive Salad

Preparation Time: 180 minutes

Cooking Time: 10 minutes

Servings: 4

Ingredients:

- 250g orzo
- 100g cocktail tomatoes
- 100g olives
- onion
- ½ bunch of parsley
- 250g feta cheese
- For the dressing
- 1 lemon, squeezed
- salt and pepper
- 30ml olive oil
- 2 cloves of garlic

Directions:

1. Cook the pasta for about 10 minutes according to the instructions on the packet.

Wash and halve cocktail tomatoes, core the olives, peel and chop the onion, crumble the feta.
2. For the dressing: lemon juice, olive oil, garlic, salt and pepper mixture.
3. Mix the Orzo with the dressing and finally add the remaining ingredients. Finished. Serve and enjoy.

Nutrition: Calories: 302 Carbohydrates: 25.76g Protein: 13.3g Fat: 17.63g

175. Mushroom Arugula Salad

Preparation Time: 25 minutes

Cooking Time: 0 minutes

Servings: 4

Ingredients:

- 500g mushrooms
- 200g sheep cheese
- 75g rocket
- 60g pine nuts
- 3 tbsp olive oil
- salt and pepper

Directions:

1. Wash the mushrooms and cut them into thin slices. Clean the rocket and cut it into small pieces. Dice the sheep's cheese.
2. Put everything in a salad bowl with olive oil and balsamic vinegar. Season to taste with salt and pepper.
3. Toast the pine nuts in a pan until they are golden brown.
4. Add the pine nuts to the salad. Finished! Serve and enjoy.

Nutrition: Calories: 710 Carbohydrates: 101.65g Protein: 22.4g Fat: 32.27g

176. Italian Bread Salad

Preparation Time: 60 minutes

Cooking Time: 30 minutes

Servings: 4

Ingredients:

- 2 ciabatta
- 5 tomatoes
- ½ cucumber
- 1 bunch of parsley
- 2 tbsp olive oil

- ½ bunch of rosemary
- 2 cloves of garlic
- salt and pepper

Directions:

1. Preheat oven to 220 degrees. Dice the ciabatta, spread on a baking sheet with baking paper and drizzle with olive oil. Toast the bread cubes in the oven, remove them and let them cool down.
2. Wash and dice tomatoes and cucumbers.
3. For the dressing: finely chop the parsley and rosemary. Peel and squeeze the garlic and mix with salt, pepper, olive oil and herbs.
4. Add the dressing to the diced tomatoes and cucumber.
5. Let it steep in the refrigerator for about 30 minutes.
6. Fold the bread cubes into the salad.
7. Finished! Serve and enjoy.

Nutrition: Calories: 97 Carbohydrates: 8.13g Protein: 1.76g Fat: 7.14g

177. Mediterranean Beef Salad

Preparation Time: 5 minutes

Cooking Time: 15 minutes

Servings: 4-5

Ingredients:

- 8 oz quality roast beef, thinly sliced
- 1 avocado, peeled and diced
- 2 tomatoes, diced
- 1 cucumber, peeled and diced
- 1 yellow pepper, sliced
- 2 carrots, shredded
- 1 cup black olives, pitted and halved
- 2-3 fresh basil leaves, torn
- 2-3 fresh oregano leaves
- 1 tbsp balsamic vinegar
- 4 tbsp extra virgin olive oil
- salt and black pepper, to taste

Directions:

1. Combine the avocado and all vegetables in a large salad bowl. Add in basil and oregano leaves.

2. Season with salt and pepper, drizzle with balsamic vinegar and olive oil and toss to combine. Top with roast beef and serve.

Nutrition: calories: 318 fat: 6.47g Protein: 10.04g carbs: 14.32g fiber: 5.8g Sodium: 385mg

178. Ground Beef Salad with Creamy Avocado Dressing

Preparation Time: 5 minutes

Cooking Time: 5 minutes

Servings: 4-5

Ingredients:

- 1 green lettuce, cut in stripes
- 2-3 green onions, finely cut
- 1 garlic clove, crushed
- ½ cup black olives pitted and halved
- 4-5 radishes, sliced
- 8 oz ground beef
- 2 tbsp extra virgin olive oil
- 1/2 tsp ground cumin
- 1/2 tsp dried oregano
- 1 tsp paprika
- salt and pepper, to taste

For the dressing:

- 1 avocado, peeled and cut
- 1 tbsp extra virgin olive oil
- 4 tbsp lemon juice
- 2 garlic cloves, cut
- 1 tbsp water
- 1/2 tsp salt

Directions:

1. Blend the dressing ingredients until smooth.
2. Heat olive oil in a medium saucepan and gently cook the ground beef and the seasonings, stirring, for 5-6 minutes, or until cooked through.
3. Place lettuce, cooked beef and all other salad ingredients in a bowl. Toss well to combine. Drizzle with dressing and serve.

Nutrition: calories: 328 fat: 24.87g Protein: 9.7g carbs: 19.46g fiber:8.4g sodium: 536mg

179. Tuna Salad with Lettuce and Chickpeas

Preparation Time: 5 minutes

Cooking Time: 0 minutes

Servings: 4

Ingredients:

- 1 head green lettuce, washed cut in thin strips
- 1 cup chopped watercress
- 1 cucumber, peeled and chopped
- 1 tomato, diced
- 1 can tuna, drained and broken into small chunks
- 1/2 cup chickpeas from a can
- 7-8 radishes, sliced
- 3-4 spring onions, chopped
- juice of the half lemon
- 3 tbsp extra virgin olive oil

Directions:

Mix all the vegetables in a large bowl. Add the tuna and the chickpeas and season with lemon juice, oil and salt to taste.

Nutrition: calories: 329 fat: 7.49g

Protein: 19.7g carbs: 51.1g fiber:16.6g

sodium: 358mg

180. Sweet Potato Puree

Preparation Time: 10 minutes

Cooking Time: 15 minutes

Servings: 6

Ingredients:

- 2 pounds sweet potatoes, peeled
- 1 ½ cups water
- 5 Medjool dates, pitted and chopped

Directions:

1. Place all ingredients in a pot.
2. Close the lid and allow to boil for 15 minutes until the potatoes are soft.
3. Drain the potatoes and place them in a food processor together with the dates.
4. Pulse until smooth.
5. Place in individual containers.
6. Put a label and store it in the fridge.

7. Allow thawing at room temperature before heating in the microwave oven.

Nutrition: Calories per serving: 619; Carbs: 97.8g; Protein: 4.8g; Fat: 24.3g; Fiber: 14.7g

181. Chickpea & Lentil Salad

Preparation Time: 10 minutes

Cooking Time: 3 Hours And 50 minutes

Servings: 4

Ingredients:

- 1 1/2 cups dried chickpeas, rinsed and drained
- 1 cup green lentils
- 1 teaspoon herbs de Provence
- 2 cups vegetable broth
- 12 oz. cherry tomatoes, sliced in half

Directions:

1. Combine the chickpeas, 2 cups water and 1 tablespoon olive oil in the pot.
2. Mix well.
3. Cook at high heat for 38 minutes.
4. Drain the chickpeas and set them aside.
5. Add the lentils, vegetable broth and seasoning.
6. Slow cook for 3 hours.
7. Toss the lentils, tomatoes and chickpeas in a salad bowl.

Nutrition: (Per Serving): Calories 508 ;Total Fat 8.4g ;Saturated Fat 1.1g ;Cholesterol 0mg ;Sodium 432mg ;Total Carbohydrate 78.3g ;Dietary Fiber 30g ;Total Sugars 11.8g ;Protein 31.9g ;Potassium 1419mg

182. Mashed Fava Beans

Preparation Time: 15 minutes

Cooking Time: 10 minutes

Servings: 4

Ingredients:

- 3 pounds fava beans, removed from the pods but unpeeled
- ¼ cup water
- ½ teaspoon salt
- ¼ cup extra-virgin olive oil

- 3 garlic cloves, chopped
- 1 tablespoon finely chopped fresh rosemary
- ¼ teaspoon freshly ground black pepper

Directions:

1. Bring a large pot of water to a boil over high heat and cook the beans for 3 minutes. Drain the beans and rinse under cold running water to cool.
2. Peel the outer skin off the beans. The inner bean should pop out easily. You are going to be mashing the beans so that you can be messy during this step.
3. Put the beans in a food processor, add the water and salt, and puree.
4. In a skillet, heat the olive oil over low heat. Add the fava bean puree, garlic, rosemary, and pepper. Stir to combine and cook for about 5 minutes, until most of the water evaporates.

Nutrition: Calories: 423; Total Fat: 16g; Saturated Fat: 2g; Protein: 27g; Total Carbohydrates: 61g; Fiber: 26g; Sugar: 31g; Cholesterol: 0mg

183. Spicy Borlotti Beans

Preparation Time: 10 minutes, plus overnight to soak

Cooking Time: 1 hour 30 minutes

Serving 8

Ingredients:

- 1-pound dried borlotti beans, soaked overnight, drained and rinsed
- 1 teaspoon salt, divided
- 2 tablespoons extra-virgin olive oil
- 1 large onion, chopped
- ½ green bell pepper, seeded and chopped
- 1 (14.5-ounce) can diced tomatoes, undrained
- 3 garlic cloves, minced
- 1 (1-inch) piece fresh red chile, seeded and minced
- ¼ teaspoon freshly ground black pepper

- ¼ teaspoon red pepper flakes

Directions:

1. Put the beans in a large soup pot, cover with water, and add ½ teaspoon of salt. Bring to a boil over medium-high heat, then reduce the heat to low and simmer for 1 to 1½ hours, until the beans soften. Drain.
2. In a large skillet, heat the olive oil over medium heat. Cook the onion and bell pepper for about 10 minutes until softened.
3. Add the beans, tomatoes and their juices, garlic, chile, remaining ½ teaspoon of salt, black pepper, and red pepper flakes. Bring to a boil, then reduce the heat and simmer for 10 minutes.

Nutrition: Calories: 240; Total Fat: 4g; Saturated Fat: 1g; Protein: 13g; Total Carbohydrates: 39g; Fiber: 13g; Sugar: 3g; Cholesterol: 0mg

184. Vegetable Stew

Preparation Time: 10 minutes

Cooking Time: 45 minutes

Servings: 4

Ingredients:

- 1-pound potatoes, peeled and cut into bite-sized pieces
- 2 tablespoons coconut oil, unsalted
- 3 tablespoons olive oil
- 2 cups vegetable broth
- 2 carrots, peeled and chopped
- 3 celery stalks, chopped
- 2 onions, peeled and chopped
- 1 zucchini, cut into ½ inch thick slices
- 1 tablespoon paprika
- 1 tablespoon salt
- 1 teaspoon black pepper
- A handful of fresh celery leaves

Directions:

1. Warm oil on Sauté mode
2. Stir-fry onions for 3-4 minutes
3. Add celery, zucchini, carrots, and ¼ cup broth
4. Cook for 10 minutes more and keep stirring continuously
5. Stir in potatoes, cayenne pepper, bay leaves, remaining

broth, celery leaves, salt and pepper
6. Close the lid
7. Cook at Meat/Stew for 30 minutes on High
8. Quick-release the pressure
9. Serve and enjoy!

Nutrition Calories: 331 Fat: 14g Carbohydrates: 44g Protein: 17g

185. Quick Spinach Focaccia

Preparation Time: 10 minutes

Cooking Time: 25 minutes

Servings: 12

Ingredients:

- 10 eggs
- 2 cups spinach, chopped
- ¼ tsp garlic powder
- ¼ tsp onion powder
- ½ tsp dried basil
- 1 ½ cups parmesan cheese, grated
- Salt

Directions:

1. Preheat the oven to 400 F. Grease muffin tin and set aside.
2. In a large bowl, whisk eggs with basil, garlic powder, onion powder, and salt.
3. Add cheese and spinach and stir well.
4. Pour egg mixture into the prepared muffin tin and bake for 15 minutes.
5. Serve and enjoy.

Nutrition: 110 Calories 7g Fat 9g Protein

186. Sumptuous Greek Vegetable Salad

Preparation Time: 20 minutes

Cooking Time: 0 minutes

Servings: 6

Ingredients:

Salad:

- 1 (15-ounce / 425-g) can chickpeas, drained and rinsed

- 1 (14-ounce / 397-g) can artichoke hearts, drained and halved
- 1 head Bibb lettuce, chopped (about 2½ cups)
- 1 cucumber, peeled, deseeded and chopped (about 1½ cups)
- 1½ cups grape tomatoes halved
- ¼ cup chopped basil leaves
- ½ cup sliced black olives
- ½ cup cubed feta cheese

Dressing:

- 1 tablespoon freshly squeezed lemon juice (from about ½ small lemon)
- ¼ teaspoon freshly ground black pepper
- 1 tablespoon chopped fresh oregano
- 2 tablespoons extra-virgin olive oil
- 1 tablespoon red wine vinegar
- 1 teaspoon honey

Directions:

1. Combine the ingredients for the salad in a large salad bowl, then toss to combine well.
2. Combine the ingredients for the dressing in a small bowl, then stir to mix well.
3. Dressing the salad and serve immediately.
4. Tip: You can use ½ head romaine lettuce or other fresh leaves to replace the Bibb lettuce.

Nutrition: calories: 165 fat: 8.1g Protein: 7.2g carbs: 17.9g fiber: 7.0g Sodium: 337mg

187. Brussels Sprout and Apple Slaw

Preparation Time: 15 minutes

Cooking Time: 0 minutes

Servings: 4

Ingredients:

Salad:

- 1-pound (454 g) Brussels sprouts, stem ends removed and sliced thinly
- 1 apple, cored and sliced thinly
- ½ red onion, sliced thinly

Dressing:

- 1 teaspoon Dijon mustard
- 2 teaspoons apple cider vinegar
- 1 tablespoon raw honey
- 1 cup plain coconut yogurt
- 1 teaspoon sea salt

For Garnish:

- ½ cup pomegranate seeds
- ½ cup chopped toasted hazelnuts

Directions:

1. Combine the ingredients for the salad in a large salad bowl, then toss to combine well.
2. Combine the ingredients for the dressing in a small bowl, then stir to mix well.
3. Dressing the salad. Let sit for 30 minutes, then serve with pomegranate seeds and toasted hazelnuts on top.
4. Tip: If you don't like pomegranate seeds, you can replace them with sunflower seeds, pumpkin seeds, or chia seeds.

Nutrition: calories: 248 fat: 11.2g Protein: 12.7g carbs: 29.9g fiber: 8.0g Sodium: 645mg

188. Peas And Tubetti With Pancetta

Preparation Time: 5 minutes

Cooking Time: 10 minutes

Serving 4

Ingredients:

- Salt to taste
- 1-pound tubetti
- 3 tablespoons extra-virgin olive oil
- ½ cup diced pancetta
- 2 scallions, thinly sliced
- 12 ounces frozen peas
- ¼ cup water
- ¼ cup finely grated Parmesan cheese

Directions:

1. Bring a large pot of water to a boil over high heat. Once boiling, salt the water to your liking, stir, and return to a boil. Add the tubetti and cook according to package directions until al dente. Drain, reserving about ¼ cup of the cooking water.
2. In a large skillet, heat the olive oil over medium heat. Cook the pancetta for 2 minutes, then add the scallions and cook for another 2 minutes, until the pancetta is thoroughly cooked.
3. Add the peas and water. Cover and cook for 5 minutes, stirring occasionally.
4. Add the cooked pasta and toss to combine. Add the reserved pasta water a little at a time as needed.
5. Sprinkle with Parmesan cheese.

Nutrition: calories: 661; Total Fat: 20g; Saturated Fat: 5g; Protein: 22g; Total Carbohydrates: 98g; Fiber: 8g; Sugar: 8g; Cholesterol: 11mg

189. Asparagus with Feta

Preparation Time: 10 minutes

Cooking Time: 5 minutes

Servings: 4

Ingredients:

- 1 cup feta cheese, cubed
- 1-pound asparagus spears end trimmed
- 1 tablespoon olive oil
- 1 cup of water
- 1 lemon
- Salt and freshly ground black pepper, to taste

Directions:

1. Add water into a pot and set trivet over the water
2. Place steamer basket on the trivet
3. Place the asparagus into the steamer basket
4. Close the lid
5. Cook for 1 minute on high pressure
6. Release the pressure quickly

7. Take a bowl and add olive oil to it
8. Toss in asparagus until well-coated
9. Season with pepper and salt
10. Serve with feta cheese and lemon
11. Enjoy!

Nutrition: Calories: 170 Fat: 18g Carbohydrates: 2g Protein: 3g

190. Rosemary Sweet Potato Medallions

Preparation Time: 10 minutes

Cooking Time: 18 minutes

Servings: 4

Ingredients:

- 4 sweet potatoes
- 2 tablespoons coconut oil
- 1 cup of water
- 1 tablespoon rosemary
- 1 teaspoon garlic powder
- Salt, to taste

Directions:

1. Add water and place steamer rack over the water
2. Using a fork, prick sweet potatoes all over
3. Then set on a steamer rack
4. Close the lid and cook for 12 minutes on High pressure
5. Release the pressure quickly
6. Cut the sweet potatoes into ½ inch
7. Melt the coconut oil on Sauté mode
8. Add in the medallions
9. Cook each side for 2 to 3 minutes until browned
10. Season with salt and garlic powder
11. Add rosemary on top
12. Serve and enjoy!

Nutrition: Calories: 291 Fat: 10g Carbohydrates: 30g Protein: 5g

191. Artichoke with Garlic Mayo

Prep Time: 10 minutes

Cook Time: 12 minutes

Servings: 4

Ingredients:

- 2 large artichokes

- ½ cup mayonnaise
- 2 cups of water
- 2 garlic cloves, smashed
- 1 lime juice
- Salt and black pepper, to taste

Directions:

1. Using a serrated knife, trim about 1 inch from the artichoke's top
2. Take a top, add water and set trivet over
3. Place the artichoke on the trivet
4. Close the lid and cook for 12 minutes on High pressure
5. Release the pressure quickly
6. Mix the mayonnaise with garlic and lime juice
7. Season with salt and pepper
8. Serve with garlic mayo and enjoy!

Nutrition: Calories: 413 Fat: 21g Carbohydrates: 40g Protein: 12g

192. Steamed Artichoke with Lemon Aioli

Prep Time: 10 minutes

Cook Time: 10 minutes

Servings: 4

Ingredients:

- 4 artichokes, trimmed
- 1 lemon, halved
- 1 teaspoon lemon zest
- 1 tablespoon lemon juice
- 3 cloves garlic, crushed
- ½ cup mayonnaise
- 1 cup of water
- 1 handful parsley, chopped
- Salt, to taste

Directions:

1. Cut the artichoke's ends, rub with lemon
2. Add water into the pot
3. Set steamer basket on top
4. Add artichoke into your basket and point this upward
5. Then sprinkle with salt
6. Close the lid and cook for 10 minutes on High pressure
7. Release the pressure quickly
8. Take a mixing bowl and add lemon juice, garlic, mayonnaise, and lemon zest
9. Season with salt

10. Serve with parsley on top and enjoy!

Nutrition: Calories: 63 Fat: 0g Carbohydrates: 15g Protein: 4g

193. Herby-Garlic Potatoes

Prep Time: 10 minutes

Cook Time: 15 minutes

Servings: 4

Ingredients:

- 1 ½ pounds of potatoes
- 3 tablespoons coconut oil
- ½ cup vegetable broth
- 2 tablespoons fresh rosemary, chopped
- 3 cloves garlic, thinly chopped
- ½ teaspoon fresh thyme, chopped
- ½ teaspoon fresh parsley, chopped
- ¼ teaspoon black pepper, ground

Directions:

1. Take a small knife and pierce each potato to ensure there are no blowouts
2. Then place under pressure
3. Melt coconut oil on Sauté mode
4. Add in potatoes, rosemary, thyme, garlic, parsley and pepper
5. Cook for 10 minutes
6. Take a bowl and mix miso paste and vegetable stock
7. Stir in the mixture in the pot.
8. Then close the lid and cook for 5 minutes on high heat.
9. Serve with parsley on top and enjoy!

Nutrition: Calories: 389 Fat: 14g Carbohydrates: 51g Protein: 16g

194. Lentils with Spinach and Garlic Chips

Preparation Time: 5 minutes

Cooking Time: 30 minutes

Servings: 6

Ingredients

- 2 tablespoons extra-virgin olive oil
- 4 garlic cloves, sliced thin
- Salt and pepper to taste
- 1 onion, chopped fine

- 1 teaspoon ground coriander
- 1 teaspoon ground cumin
- 2½ cups water
- 1 cup green or brown lentils, picked over and rinsed
- 8 ounces curly-leaf spinach, stemmed and chopped coarsely
- 1 tablespoon red wine vinegar

Directions

1. Cook oil and garlic in a large saucepan over medium-low heat, often stirring, until garlic turns crisp and golden but not brown, about 5 minutes.
2. Transfer garlic to a paper towel-lined plate using a slotted spoon and season lightly with salt; set aside. A
3. dd onion and ½ teaspoon salt to oil left in saucepan and cook over medium heat until softened and lightly browned, 5 to 7 minutes. Stir in coriander and cumin and cook until fragrant, about 30 seconds. Stir in water and lentils and bring to simmer.
4. Reduce heat to low, cover, and simmer gently, occasionally stirring, until lentils are primarily tender but still intact, 45 to 55 minutes.
5. Stir in spinach, 1 handful at a time.
6. Cook, uncovered, occasionally stirring, until spinach is wilted and lentils are completely tender about 8 minutes.
7. Stir in vinegar and season with salt and pepper to taste. 5. Transfer to serving dish, sprinkle with toasted garlic and serve.

Nutrition: Calories: 58 Total Fat: 2.42g, Carbs: 7.71g, Protein: 3.05g

195. Artichoke and Arugula Salad

Preparation Time: 10 minutes

Cooking Time: 0 minutes

Servings: 6

Ingredients:

Salad:

- 6 canned oil-packed artichoke hearts, sliced
- 6 cups baby arugula leaves
- 6 fresh olives, pitted and chopped
- 1 cup cherry tomatoes, sliced in half

Dressing:

- 1 teaspoon Dijon mustard
- 2 tablespoons balsamic vinegar
- 1 clove garlic, minced
- 2 tablespoons extra-virgin olive oil

For Garnish:

- 4 fresh basil leaves, thinly sliced

Directions:

1. Mix the ingredients for the salad in a large salad bowl, then toss to combine well.
2. Mix the ingredients for the dressing in a small bowl, then stir to mix well.
3. Dressing the salad, then serve with basil leaves on top.
4. Tip: If you don't like canned food and are good at dealing with or dealing with fresh artichokes, you can use the same amount of fresh artichoke to replace the canned artichoke hearts.

Nutrition Per Serving

calories: 134 fat: 12.1g Protein: 1.6g carbs: 6.2g fiber: 3.0gsodium: 65mg

196. Spiced Lentil Salad with Winter Squash

Preparation Time: 5 minutes

Cooking Time: 60 minutes

Serving 6

Ingredients

- Salt and pepper to taste
- 1 cup black lentils, picked over and rinsed
- 1-pound butternut squash, peeled, seeded, and cut into ½-inch pieces (3 cups)
- 5 tablespoons extra-virgin olive oil
- 2 tablespoons balsamic vinegar

- 1 garlic clove, minced
- 1/2 teaspoon ground coriander
- 1/4 teaspoon ground cumin
- 1/4 teaspoon ground ginger
- 1/8 teaspoon ground cinnamon
- 1 teaspoon Dijon mustard
- 1/2 cup fresh parsley leaves
- 1/4 cup finely chopped red onion
- 1 tablespoon raw pepitas, toasted

Directions:

1. Dissolve 1 teaspoon salt in 4 cups warm water (about 110 degrees) in a bowl. Add lentils and soak at room temperature for 1 hour.
2. Drain well. Meanwhile, adjust oven racks to middle and lowest positions and heat oven to 450 degrees. Toss squash with 1 tablespoon oil, 1½ teaspoons vinegar, ¼ teaspoon salt, and ¼ teaspoon pepper.
3. Arrange squash in a single layer in a rimmed baking sheet and roast on the lower rack until well browned and tender, 20 to 25 minutes, stirring halfway through roasting. Let cool slightly. Reduce oven temperature to 325 degrees.
4. Cook 1 tablespoon oil, garlic, coriander, cumin, ginger, and cinnamon in a medium oven-safe saucepan over medium heat until fragrant, about 1 minute. Stir in 4 cups water and lentils.
5. Cover, transfer saucepan to the upper rack in the oven and cook until lentils are tender but remain intact for 40 to 60 minutes.
6. Drain lentils well.
7. Whisk remaining 3 tablespoons oil, remaining 1½ tablespoons vinegar, and mustard together in a large bowl.
8. Add squash, lentils, parsley, and onion and toss to combine. Season with salt and pepper to taste.
9. Transfer to a serving platter and sprinkle with pepitas.

Serve warm or at room temperature.

Nutrition: Calories: 114 Total Fat: 5.91g, Carbs: 14.79g, Protein: 2.61g

197. Rosemary Scent Cauliflower Bundles

Preparation Time: 10 minutes

Cooking Time: 30 minutes

Servings: 4

Ingredients:

- 1/3 cup of almond flour
- 4 cups of riced cauliflower
- 1/3 cup of reduced-fat, shredded mozzarella or cheddar cheese
- 2 eggs
- 2 tablespoons of fresh rosemary, finely chopped
- ½ teaspoon of salt

Directions:

1. Preheat your oven to 400°F
2. Combine all the listed ingredients in a medium-sized bowl
3. Scoop cauliflower mixture into 12 evenly-sized rolls/biscuits onto a lightly greased and foil-lined baking sheet.
4. Bake until it turns golden brown, which should be achieved in about 30 minutes.

Nutrition: 254 Calories 24g Protein 8g Fat

198. Barley, Parsley, and Pea Salad

Preparation Time: 10 minutes

Cooking Time: 10 minutes

Servings: 4

Ingredients:

- 2 cups water
- 1 cup quick-cooking barley
- 1 small bunch flat-leaf parsley, chopped (about 1 to 1½ cups)
- 2 cups sugar snap pea pods
- Juice of 1 lemon
- ½ small red onion, diced
- 2 tablespoons extra-virgin olive oil
- Sea salt and freshly ground pepper, to taste

Directions:

1. Pour the water into a saucepan. Bring to a boil. Add the barley to the saucepan, then put the lid on.
2. Reduce the heat to low. Simmer the barley for 10 minutes or until the liquid is absorbed, then sit for 5 minutes.
3. Open the lid, then transfer the barley to a colander and rinse under cold running water.
4. Pour the barley into a large salad bowl and add the remaining ingredients. Toss to combine well.
5. Serve immediately.
6. Tip: If you have enough time, you can use pearl barley to replace the quick-cooking barley, and it may cost 15 more minutes to simmer the barley.

Nutrition Per Serving

calories: 152 fat: 7.4g Protein: 3.7g carbs: 19.3g fiber: 4.7gsodium: 20mg

199. Cheesy Peach and Walnut Salad

Preparation Time: 10 minutes

Cooking Time: 0 minutes

Servings: 1

Ingredients:

- 1 ripe peach, pitted and sliced
- 1/4 cup chopped walnuts, toasted
- 1/4 cup shredded Parmesan cheese
- 1 teaspoon raw honey
- Zest of 1 lemon
- 1 tablespoon chopped fresh mint

Directions:

1. Combine the peach, walnut, and cheese in a medium bowl, then drizzle with honey. Spread the lemon zest and mint on top. Toss to combine everything well.
2. Serve immediately.
3. Tip: You can serve this salad as breakfast, serve it with plain almond yogurt and toss with

cubed whole wheat bread if desired.

Nutrition Per Serving

calories: 373 fat: 26.4g Protein: 12.9g carbs: 27.0g fiber: 4.7g Sodium: 453mg

200. Delicious Feta with Fresh Spinach

Preparation Time: 10 minutes

Cooking Time: 0 minutes

Servings: 6

Ingredients:

- 6 cups fresh baby spinach, chopped
- ¼ cup scallions, white and green parts, chopped
- 1 (16-ounce) package orzo pasta, cooked according to package directions, rinsed, drained, and cooled
- 3/4 cup crumbled feta cheese
- 1/4 cup halved Kalamata olives
- 1/2 cup red wine vinegar
- 1/4 cup extra-virgin olive oil
- 1½ teaspoons freshly squeezed lemon juice
- Sea salt
- Freshly ground black pepper

Directions:

1. In a large bowl, combine the spinach, scallions, and cooled orzo.
2. Sprinkle with the feta and olives.
3. In a small bowl, whisk the vinegar, olive oil, and lemon juice. Season with sea salt and pepper.
4. Add the dressing to the salad and gently toss to combine. Refrigerate until serving.

Nutrition: 255 Calories 8g Protein 8g Fat

201. Celeriac Mix with Cauliflower

Preparation Time: 10 minutes

Cooking Time: 12 minutes

Servings: 6

Ingredients:

- 1 head cauliflower
- 1 small celery root
- ¼ cup butter

- 1 tablespoon. chopped rosemary
- 1 tablespoon. chopped thyme
- 1 cup cream cheese

Directions:

1. Skin the celery root and cut it into small pieces.
2. Cut the cauliflower into similar-sized pieces and combine.
3. Toast the herbs in the butter in a large pan until they become fragrant.
4. Add the cauliflower and celery root and stir to combine.
5. Season and cook at medium-high until whatever moisture in the vegetables releases itself, then cover and cook on low for 10-12 minutes.
6. Once the vegetables are soft, remove them from the heat and place them in the blender.
7. Make it smooth, then put the cream cheese and puree again.
8. Season and serve.

Nutrition: 225 Calories 20g Fat 5g Protein

202. Lentil Salad with Olives, Mint, and Feta

Preparation Time: 5 minutes

Cooking Time: 60 minutes

Servings: 4 To 6

Ingredients

- Salt and pepper to taste
- 1 cup lentils, picked over and rinsed
- 5 garlic cloves, lightly crushed and peeled
- 1 bay leaf
- 5 tablespoons extra-virgin olive oil
- 3 tablespoons white wine vinegar
- ½ cup pitted kalamata olives, chopped coarsely
- ½ cup chopped fresh mint
- 1 large shallot, minced
- 1-ounce feta cheese, crumbled (¼ cup)

Directions

1. Dissolve 1 teaspoon salt in 4 cups warm water (about 110 degrees) in bowl.

2. Add lentils and soak at room temperature for 1 hour. Drain well. Adjust oven rack to middle position and heat oven to 325 degrees.
3. In a medium oven-safe saucepan, combine lentils, 4 cups water, garlic, bay leaf, and ½ teaspoon salt.
4. Cover, transfer saucepan to the oven and cook until lentils are tender but remain intact 40 to 60 minutes.
5. Drain lentils well, discarding garlic and bay leaf.
6. In a large bowl, whisk vinegar and oil together. A
7. dd lentils, olives, mint, and shallot and toss to combine. Season with salt and pepper to taste. Transfer to a serving dish and sprinkle with feta. Serve warm or at room temperature.

Nutrition: Calories: 120 Total Fat: 8.76g, Carbs: 5.38g, Protein: 5.58g

Chapter 8. Vegetables

203. Stewed Okra

Preparation Time: 5 minutes

Cooking Time: 25 minutes

Servings: 4

Ingredients:

- 4 cloves garlic, finely chopped
- 1 pound fresh or frozen okra, cleaned
- 1 (15-ounce) can plain tomato sauce
- 2 cups water
- ½ cup fresh cilantro, finely chopped

Direction

1. In a big pot at medium heat, stir and cook ¼ cup of olive oil, 1 onion, garlic, and salt for 1 minute.
2. Stir in the okra and cook for 3 minutes.
3. Add the tomato sauce, water, cilantro, and black pepper; stir, cover, and let cook for 15 minutes, stirring occasionally.
4. Serve warm.

Nutrition: 201 Calories 4g Protein 18g Carbohydrates

204. Sweet Veggie-Stuffed Peppers

Preparation Time: 20 minutes

Cooking Time: 30 minutes

Servings: 6

Ingredients:

- 6 large bell peppers, different colors
- 3 cloves garlic, minced
- 1 carrot, chopped
- 1 (16-ounce) can garbanzo beans
- 3 cups cooked rice

Direction

1. Preheat the oven to 350°F.
2. Make sure to choose peppers that can stand upright. Cut off the pepper cap and remove the

seeds, reserving the cap for later. Stand the peppers in a baking dish.

3. In a skillet over medium heat, cook up olive oil, 1 onion, garlic, and carrots for 3 minutes.
4. Stir in the garbanzo beans. Cook for another 3 minutes.
5. Take out the pan from the heat and spoon the cooked ingredients into a large bowl.
6. Add the rice, salt, and pepper; toss to combine.
7. Stuff each pepper to the top and then put the pepper caps back on.
8. Wrap the baking dish using aluminum foil and bake for 25 minutes.
9. Pull out the foil and bake for 6 minutes.
10. Serve warm.

Nutrition: 301 Calories 8g Protein 50g Carbohydrates

205. Brussels Sprouts Chips

Preparation Time: 20 minutes

Cooking Time: 20 minutes

Servings: 3

Ingredients:

- ½ pounds Brussels sprouts, sliced thinly
- 4 tablespoons olive oil
- 2 tablespoons mozzarella cheese, grated
- 1 teaspoon garlic powder
- Salt and pepper to taste

Directions:

1. Preheat the oven to 400F.
2. In a bowl, combine all ingredients.
3. Toss to coat the ingredients
4. Place in a baking sheet and bake for 20 minutes or until golden brown.
5. Place in individual containers.
6. Put a label and store it in the fridge.
7. Allow warming at room temperature before heating in the microwave oven.

Nutrition: Calories per serving:227; Carbs: 5.1g; Protein:15.2 g; Fat: 20.5g; Fiber:3.1 g

Potassium 950mg

206. Balsamic Roasted Carrots and Baby Onions

Preparation Time: 50 minutes

Cooking Time: 26 minutes

Servings: 4

Ingredients:

- 2 bunches baby carrots, scrubbed, ends trimmed
- 10 small onions, peeled, halved
- 4 tbsp. 100% pure maple syrup (unprocessed)
- 1 tsp thyme
- 1 tbsp. extra virgin olive oil

Directions:

1. Preheat oven to 350F. Line a baking tray with baking paper.
2. Place the carrots, onion, thyme, and oil in a large bowl and toss until well coated. Spread carrots and onion, in a single layer, on the baking tray. Roast for 25 minutes or until tender.
3. Sprinkle over the maple syrup and vinegar and toss to coat. Roast for 25-30 minutes more or until vegetables is tender and caramelized. Season well and serve.

Nutrition: 401 calories 49g fat 20g protein

207. Lentil and Tomato Collard Wraps

Preparation Time: 15 minutes

Cooking Time: 0 minutes

Servings: 4

Ingredients:

- 2 cups cooked lentils
- 5 Roma tomatoes, diced
- 1/2 cup crumbled feta cheese
- 10 large fresh basil leaves, thinly sliced
- 1/4 cup extra-virgin olive oil
- 1 tablespoon balsamic vinegar
- 2 garlic cloves, minced
- 1/2 teaspoon raw honey
- 1/2 teaspoon salt

- 1/4 teaspoon freshly ground black pepper
- 4 large collard leaves, stems removed

Directions:

1. Combine the lentils, tomatoes, cheese, basil leaves, olive oil, vinegar, garlic, honey, salt, and black pepper in a large bowl and stir until well blended.
2. Lay the collard leaves on a flat work surface. Spoon the equal-sized amounts of the lentil mixture onto the edges of the leaves. Roll them up and slice them in half to serve.
3. Tip: If you want to make the collard leaves easier to wrap, you can steam them for 1 to 2 minutes before wrapping.

Nutrition: calories: 318 fat: 17.6g Protein: 13.2g carbs: 27.5g fiber: 9.9g Sodium: 475mg

208. Wedding of Broccoli and Tomatoes

Preparation Time: 7 minutes

Cooking Time: 2 minutes

Servings: 3

Ingredients:

- 1 head broccoli, cut into florets, then blanched
- ¼ cup tomatoes, diced
- Salt and pepper to taste
- Chopped parsley for garnish

Directions:

1. Place all ingredients in a bowl.
2. Toss to coat all ingredients.
3. Serve.

Nutrition: 52 Calories 1.1g Protein 0.1g Fat

209. Zucchini Fettuccine with Mexican Taco

Preparation Time: 9 minutes

Cooking Time: 20 minutes

Servings: 6

Ingredients:

- 1 tablespoon olive oil
- 1-pound lean ground turkey
- 1 clove garlic, minced
- ½ small onion, chopped
- 1 tablespoon chili powder
- ¼ teaspoon garlic powder
- ¼ teaspoon onion powder
- ¼ teaspoon dried oregano
- 1 ½ teaspoon ground cumin
- ¼ cup water
- ¼ cup diced tomatoes
- 2 large zucchinis, spiralized
- ½ cup shredded cheddar cheese

Directions:

1. Place oil in a pot and heat over medium flame.
2. Sauté the turkey for 2 minutes before adding the garlic and onions. Stir for another minute.
3. Season with chili powder, garlic powder, onion powder, oregano, and ground cumin. Sauté for another minute before adding the water and tomatoes.
4. Close the lid and allow to simmer for 7 minutes.
5. Add in the zucchini and cheese and allow to cook for 3 more minutes.

Nutrition: 145 Calories 15g Protein 2.1g Fat

210. Grilled Eggplant Rolls

Preparation Time: 30 minutes

Cooking Time: 10 minutes

Servings: 5

Ingredients:

- 2 large eggplants
- 4 ounces goat cheese
- 1 cup ricotta
- ¼ cup fresh basil, finely chopped

Directions:

1. Slice the tops of the eggplants off and cut the eggplants lengthwise into ¼-inch-thick slices. Sprinkle the slices with the salt and place the eggplant in a colander for 15 to 20 minutes.

2. In a large bowl, combine the goat cheese, ricotta, basil, and pepper.
3. Preheat a grill, grill pan, or lightly oiled skillet on medium heat. Pat the eggplant slices dry using a paper towel and lightly spray with olive oil spray. Place the eggplant on the grill, grill pan, or skillet and cook for 3 minutes on each side.
4. Take out the eggplant from the heat and let cool for 5 minutes.
5. To roll, lay one eggplant slice flat, place a tablespoon of the cheese mixture at the base of the slice, and roll-up. Serve immediately or chill until serving.

Nutrition: 255 Calories 15g Protein 19g Carbohydrates

211. Easy And Healthy Baked Vegetables

Preparation Time: 5 minutes

Cooking Time: 1 Hour And 15 minutes

Servings: 6

Ingredients:

- 2 lbs. Brussels sprouts, trimmed
- 3 lbs. Butternut Squash, peeled, seeded and cut into the same size as sprouts
- 1 lb Pork breakfast sausage
- 1 tbsp fat from the fried sausage

Directions:

1. Grease a 9x13 inch baking pan and preheat the oven to 350F.
2. On medium-high fire, place a large nonstick saucepan and cook sausage. Break up sausages and cook until browned.
3. In a greased pan, mix browned sausage, squash, sprouts, sea salt and fat. Toss to mix well. Pop into the oven and cook for an hour.
4. Remove from oven and serve warm.

Nutrition: Calories per **Servings:** 364; Carbs: 41.2g; Protein: 19.0g; Fat: 16.5g

Calories 11g Fat 3.6g Protein

212. Rosemary Scent Cauliflower Bundles

Preparation Time: 10 minutes

Cooking Time: 30 minutes

Servings: 4

Ingredients:

- 1/3 cup of almond flour
- 4 cups of riced cauliflower
- 1/3 cup of reduced-fat, shredded mozzarella or cheddar cheese
- 2 eggs
- 2 tablespoons of fresh rosemary, finely chopped
- ½ teaspoon of salt

Directions:

1. Preheat your oven to 400°F
2. Combine all the listed ingredients in a medium-sized bowl
3. Scoop cauliflower mixture into 12 evenly-sized rolls/biscuits onto a lightly greased and foil-lined baking sheet.
4. Bake until it turns golden brown, which should be achieved in about 30 minutes.

Nutrition: 254 Calories 24g Protein 8g Fat

213. Triumph of Cucumbers and Avocados

Preparation Time: 10 minutes

Cooking Time: 15 minutes

Servings: 4

Ingredients:

- 12 oz cherry tomatoes, cut in half
- 5 small cucumbers, chopped
- 3 small avocados, chopped
- ½ tsp ground black pepper
- 2 tbsp olive oil
- 2 tbsp fresh lemon juice
- ¼ cup fresh cilantro, chopped
- 1 tsp sea salt

Directions:

1. Add cherry tomatoes, cucumbers, avocados, and cilantro into the large mixing bowl and mix well.

2. Mix olive oil, lemon juice, black pepper, and salt and pour over salad.
3. Toss well and serve immediately.

Nutrition: 442 Calories 37g Fat 6.2g Protein

214. Crispy Zucchini Fritters

Preparation Time: 15 minutes

Cooking Time: 20 minutes

Servings: 6

Ingredients:

- 2 large green zucchinis
- 1 cup flour
- 1 large egg, beaten
- ½ cup water
- 1 teaspoon baking powder

Direction

1. Grate the zucchini into a large bowl.
2. Add the 2 tbsp. Of parsley, 3 garlic cloves, salt, flour, egg, water, and baking powder to the bowl and stir to combine.
3. In a large pot or fryer over medium heat, heat oil to 365°F.
4. Drop the fritter batter into 3 cups of vegetable oil. Turn the fritters over using a slotted spoon and fry until they are golden brown, about 2 to 3 minutes.
5. Strain fritters from the oil and place them on a plate lined with paper towels.
6. Serve warm with Creamy Tzatziki or Creamy Traditional Hummus as a dip.

Nutrition: 446 Calories 5g Protein 19g Carbohydrates

215. Cheesy Spinach Pies

Preparation Time: 20 minutes

Cooking Time: 40 minutes

Servings: 5

Ingredients:

- 2 tablespoons extra-virgin olive oil
- 3 (1-pound) bags of baby spinach, washed
- 1 cup feta cheese

- 1 large egg, beaten
- Puff pastry sheets

Direction

1. Preheat the oven to 375°F.
2. Using a big skillet over medium heat, cook the olive oil, 1 onion, and 2 garlic cloves for 3 minutes.
3. Add the spinach to the skillet one bag at a time, letting it wilt in between each bag. Toss using tongs. Cook for 4 minutes. Once cooked, strain any extra liquid from the pan.
4. Mix feta cheese, egg, and cooked spinach.
5. Lay the puff pastry flat on a counter. Cut the pastry into 3-inch squares.
6. Place a tablespoon of the spinach mixture in the center of a puff-pastry square. Turn over one corner of the square to the diagonal corner, forming a triangle. Crimp the edges of the pie by pressing down with the tines of a fork to seal them together. Repeat until all squares are filled.
7. Situate the pies on a parchment-lined baking sheet and bake for 25 to 30 minutes or until golden brown. Serve warm or at room temperature.

Nutrition: 503 Calories 16g Protein 38g Carbohydrates

216. Vegetable and Red Lentil Stew

Preparation Time: 10 minutes

Cooking Time: 35 minutes

Servings: 6

Ingredients:

- 1 tablespoon extra-virgin olive oil
- 2 onions, peeled and finely diced
- 6½ cups water
- 2 zucchinis, finely diced
- 4 celery stalks, finely diced
- 3 cups red lentils
- 1 teaspoon dried oregano
- 1 teaspoon salt, plus more as needed

Directions:

1. Heat the olive oil in a large pot over medium heat.
2. Add the onions and sauté for about 5 minutes, stirring constantly or softening the onions.
3. Stir in the water, zucchini, celery, lentils, oregano, and salt and bring the mixture to a boil.
4. Reduce the heat to low and let simmer covered for 30 minutes, stirring occasionally, or until the lentils are tender.
5. Taste and adjust the seasoning as needed.
6. Tip: You can try this recipe with different lentils such as brown and green lentils, but they need additional cooking time, about 20 minutes.

Nutrition: calories: 387 fat: 4.4g protein: 24.0g carbs: 63.7g fiber: 11.7g sodium: 418mg

217. Mozzarella Eggplants

Preparation Time: 20 minutes

Cooking Time: 40 minutes

Servings: 4

Ingredients:

- 2 large eggplants
- 3 tomatoes
- 4 Mozzarella balls
- 1 tablespoon olive oil
- 1 teaspoon salt

Directions:

1. Trim the eggplants and make the cross cuts to get the Hasselback eggplants.
2. Sprinkle the vegetables with salt.
3. After this, slice the tomatoes and Mozzarella balls.
4. Fill the eggplant cuts with Mozzarella and tomatoes and sprinkle with olive oil.
5. Then wrap every eggplant in foil.
6. Bake the vegetables for 40 minutes at 375F.
7. Discard the foil from the eggplants and cut them into 4 servings (1/2 part of eggplant = 1 serving).

Nutrition: Per Serving calories 195, fat 11.2, fiber 10.8, carbs 19.7, protein 8.5

218. Sautéed Green Beans with Tomatoes

Preparation Time: 10 minutes

Cooking Time: 20 minutes

Servings: 4

Ingredients:

- 1/4 cup extra-virgin olive oil
- 1 large onion, chopped
- 4 cloves garlic, finely chopped
- 1 pound (454 g) green beans, fresh or frozen, cut into 2-inch pieces
- 1½ teaspoons salt, divided
- 1 can diced tomatoes
- 1/2 teaspoon freshly ground black pepper

Directions:

1. Heat the olive oil in a large skillet over medium heat.
2. Add the onion and garlic and sauté for 1 minute until fragrant.
3. Stir in the green beans and sauté for 3 minutes. Sprinkle with ½ teaspoon of salt.
4. Add the tomatoes, remaining salt, and pepper and stir to mix well. Cook for an additional 12 minutes, stirring occasionally, or until the green beans are crisp and tender.
5. Remove from the heat and serve warm.
6. Tips: To add more flavors to this meal, top the green beans with a sprinkle of toasted pine nuts or almonds before serving. For a spicy kick, you can sprinkle with ½ teaspoon red pepper flakes.

Nutrition: calories: 219 fat: 13.9g Protein: 4.0g carbs: 17.7g fiber: 6.2g Sodium: 843mg

219. Simple Baked Okra

Preparation Time: 20 minutes

Cooking Time: 10 minutes

Servings: 2

Ingredients:

- 8 oz okra, chopped
- ½ teaspoon ground black pepper
- ½ teaspoon salt
- 1 tablespoon olive oil

Directions:

1. Line the baking tray with foil.
2. Place the okra in the tray in one layer.
3. Sprinkle the vegetables with ground black pepper and salt Mix up generously.
4. Then drizzle the okra with olive oil.
5. Roast the vegetables in the preheated to 375F oven for 10 minutes.
6. Stir the okra with the help of a spatula every 3 minutes.

Nutrition: Per Serving calories 107, fat 7.2, fiber 3.8, carbs 8.8, protein 2.3

220. Baked Tomatoes and Chickpeas

Preparation Time: 15 minutes

Cooking Time: 40 to 45 minutes

Servings: 4

Ingredients:

- 1 tablespoon extra-virgin olive oil
- ½ medium onion, chopped
- 3 garlic cloves, chopped
- ¼ teaspoon ground cumin
- 2 teaspoons smoked paprika
- 2 (15-ounce / 425-g) cans chickpeas, drained and rinsed
- 4 cups halved cherry tomatoes
- ½ cup plain Greek yogurt, for serving
- 1 cup crumbled feta cheese, for serving

Directions:

1. Preheat the oven to 425ºF (220ºC).
2. Heat the olive oil in an ovenproof skillet over medium heat.
3. Add the onion and garlic and sauté for about 5 minutes, stirring occasionally, or until tender and fragrant.
4. Add the paprika and cumin and cook for 2 minutes. Stir in the

chickpeas and tomatoes and allow to simmer for 5 to 10 minutes.
5. Transfer the skillet to the preheated oven and roast for 25 to 30 minutes, or until the mixture bubbles and thickens.
6. Remove from the oven and serve topped with yogurt and crumbled feta cheese.
7. Tips: If you want to make it a vegan dish, you can skip the plain Greek yogurt and feta cheese topping. To add more flavors to this dish, serve chickpeas and tomatoes over cauliflower rice or quinoa.

Nutrition: calories: 411 fat: 14.9g Protein: 20.2g carbs: 50.7g fiber: 13.3g Sodium: 443mg

221. Vegetarian Chili

Preparation Time: 15 minutes

Cooking Time: 1 hour 10 minutes

Servings: 8

Ingredients:

- 2 tablespoons extra-virgin olive oil
- 2 medium onions, finely chopped
- 1 medium leek, finely chopped
- 1 fresh red chile, seeded and minced
- 4 garlic cloves, minced
- 2 tablespoons ground cumin
- 2 tablespoons ground coriander
- 2 tablespoons smoked paprika
- 2 tablespoons dried oregano
- 1 teaspoon ground cinnamon
- 1/4 teaspoon ground nutmeg
- 2 tablespoons tomato paste
- 2 tablespoons water
- 6 cups vegetable broth
- 1 cup green lentils
- 1 cup red lentils
- 2 (15-ounce) cans of red kidney beans, rinsed and drained
- 2 (15-ounce) cans of black beans, rinsed and drained
- 2 (14.5-ounce) cans chopped tomatoes, undrained
- 1 teaspoon salt

Directions:

1. In a large soup pot, heat the olive oil over medium heat. Add the onions and cook for about 4 minutes until they start to soften. Add the leek, chile, and garlic and cook for about 1 minute, until fragrant.
2. Add the cumin, coriander, paprika, oregano, cinnamon, and nutmeg and cook for another minute, stirring to wake up the spices.
3. Stir in the tomato paste and water. Cook for about 2 minutes until warmed through.
4. Add the broth, lentils, kidney beans, black beans, tomatoes and juices, and salt. Bring the pot to a boil, then reduce to a simmer and cook for 1 hour, stirring every 15 minutes or so.

INGREDIENT TIP: If you crave more heat in your chili, you can leave the seeds in the chile.

Nutrition: calories: 430; Total Fat: 6g; Saturated Fat: 1g; Protein: 25g; Total Carbohydrates: 74g; Fiber: 20g; Sugar: 7g; Cholesterol: 0mg

222. Mediterranean Veggie Bowl

Preparation Time: 10 minutes

Cooking Time: 20 minutes

Servings: 4

Ingredients:

- 1 cup quinoa, rinsed
- 1½ teaspoons salt, divided
- 2 cups cherry tomatoes, cut in half
- 1 large bell pepper, cucumber
- 1 cup Kalamata olives

Direction

1. Using medium pot over medium heat, boil 2 cups of water. Add the bulgur (or quinoa) and 1 teaspoon of salt. Close and cook for 18 minutes.
2. To arrange the veggies in your 4 bowls, visually divide each bowl into 5 sections. Place the cooked bulgur in one section. Follow with the tomatoes, bell pepper, cucumbers, and olives.

3. Scourge ½ cup of lemon juice, olive oil, remaining ½ teaspoon salt, and black pepper.
4. Evenly spoon the dressing over the 4 bowls.
5. Serve.

Nutrition: 772 Calories 6g Protein 41g Carbohydrates

223. Spanish Green Beans

Preparation Time: 10 minutes

Cooking Time: 20 minutes

Servings: 4

Ingredients:

- 1 large onion, chopped
- 4 cloves garlic, finely chopped
- 1-pound green beans, fresh or frozen, trimmed
- 1 (15-ounce) can diced tomatoes

Direction

1. In a massive pot over medium heat, cook olive oil, onion, and garlic; cook for 1 minute.
2. Cut the green beans into 2-inch pieces.
3. Add the green beans and 1 teaspoon of salt to the pot and toss everything together; cook for 3 minutes.
4. Add the diced tomatoes, remaining ½ teaspoon of salt, and black pepper to the pot; continue to cook for another 12 minutes, stirring occasionally.
5. Serve warm.

Nutrition: 200 Calories 4g Protein 18g Carbohydrates

224. Roasted Cauliflower and Tomatoes

Preparation Time: 5 minutes

Cooking Time: 25 minutes

Servings: 4

Ingredients:

- 4 cups cauliflower, cut into 1-inch pieces
- 6 tablespoons extra-virgin olive oil, divided
- 4 cups cherry tomatoes

- ½ teaspoon freshly ground black pepper
- ½ cup grated Parmesan cheese

Direction

1. Preheat the oven to 425°F.
2. Add the cauliflower, 3 tablespoons of olive oil, and ½ teaspoon of salt to a large bowl and toss to coat evenly. Fill onto a baking sheet and arrange the cauliflower out in an even layer.
3. Add the tomatoes, remaining 3 tablespoons of olive oil, and ½ teaspoon of salt in another large bowl, and toss to coat evenly. Pour onto a different baking sheet.
4. Put the sheet of cauliflower and the sheet of tomatoes in the oven to roast for 17 to 20 minutes until the cauliflower is lightly browned and the tomatoes are plump.
5. Using a spatula, spoon the cauliflower into a serving dish, and top with tomatoes, black pepper, and Parmesan cheese. Serve warm.

Nutrition: 294 Calories 9g Protein 13g Carbohydrates

225. Roasted Acorn Squash

Preparation Time: 10 minutes

Cooking Time: 35 minutes

Servings: 6

Ingredients:

- 2 acorn squash, medium to large
- 2 tablespoons extra-virgin olive oil
- 5 tablespoons unsalted butter
- ¼ cup chopped sage leaves
- 2 tablespoons fresh thyme leaves

Direction

1. Preheat the oven to 400°F.
2. Cut the acorn squash in half lengthwise. Scoop out the seeds and cut them horizontally into ¾-inch-thick slices.
3. Drizzle the squash with the olive oil, sprinkle with salt, and

toss together to coat in a large bowl.

4. Lay the acorn squash flat on a baking sheet.
5. Situate the baking sheet in the oven and bake the squash for 20 minutes. Flip squash over with a spatula and bake for another 15 minutes.
6. Cook the butter in a medium saucepan over medium heat.
7. Sprinkle the sage and thyme into the melted butter and let them cook for 30 seconds.
8. Transfer the cooked squash slices to a plate. Spoon the butter/herb mixture over the squash—season with salt and black pepper. Serve warm.

Nutrition: 188 Calories 1g Protein 16g Carbohydrates

226. Sautéed Garlic Spinach

Preparation Time: 5 minutes

Cooking Time: 10 minutes

Servings: 4

Ingredients:

- 1/4 cup extra-virgin olive oil
- 1 large onion, thinly sliced
- 3 cloves garlic, minced
- 6 bags of baby spinach, washed
- 1 lemon, cut into wedges

Directions

1. Cook the olive oil, onion, and garlic in a large skillet for 2 minutes over medium heat.
2. Add one bag of spinach and ½ teaspoon of salt. Cover the skillet and let the spinach wilt for 30 seconds—repeat (omitting the salt), adding 1 bag of spinach at a time.
3. When all is added, open and cook for 3 minutes, letting some of the moisture evaporate.
4. Serve warm with lemon juice over the top.

Nutrition: 301 Calories 17g Protein 29g Carbohydrates

227. Garlicky Sautéed Zucchini with Mint

Preparation Time: 5 minutes

Cooking Time: 10 minutes

Servings: 4

Ingredients:

- 3 large green zucchinis
- 3 tablespoons extra-virgin olive oil
- 1 large onion, chopped
- 3 cloves garlic, minced
- 1 teaspoon dried mint

Direction

1. Cut the zucchini into ½-inch cubes.
2. Using a large skillet, place over medium heat, cook the olive oil, onions, and garlic for 3 minutes, stirring constantly.
3. Add the zucchini and salt to the skillet and toss to combine onions and garlic, cooking for 5 minutes.
4. Add the mint to the skillet, tossing to combine. Cook for another 2 minutes. Serve warm.

Nutrition: 147 Calories 4g Protein 12g Carbohydrates

228. Baked Bean and Rice Casserole

Preparation Time: 8 minutes

Cooking Time: 22 minutes

Servings: 4

Ingredients:

- 1 can red beans, rinsed
- 1 cup water
- 2/3 cup rice
- 2 onions, chopped
- 1 tsp dried mint

Directions:

1. Cook olive oil in an ovenproof casserole dish and gently sauté the chopped onions for 1-2 minutes. Stir in the rice and cook, constantly stirring, for another minute.
2. Rinse the beans and add them to the casserole. Stir in a cup of water and the mint and bake in a preheated 350 F oven for 20 minutes.

Nutrition: 405 calories 49g fat 12g protein

229. Okra and Tomato Casserole

Preparation Time: 25 minutes

Cooking Time: 26 minutes

Servings: 4

Ingredients:

- lb. okra, trimmed
- 1 tomato, cut into wedges
- 1 garlic cloves, chopped
- 1 cup fresh parsley leaves, finely cut
- 1 tbsp. extra virgin olive oil

Directions:

1. In a deep ovenproof baking dish, combine okra, sliced tomatoes, olive oil and garlic.
2. Toss to combine and bake in a preheated to 350 degrees F oven for 45 minutes. Drizzle with parsley and serve.

Nutrition: 304 calories 48g fat 13g protein

230. Spicy Baked Feta with Tomatoes

Preparation Time: 15 minutes

Cooking Time: 22 minutes

Servings: 4

Ingredients:

- 1block. feta cheese, cut into slices
- 2 ripe tomatoes, sliced
- 1 onion, sliced
- 1/2 tbsp. hot paprika
- 1 tbsp. extra virgin olive oil

Directions:

1. Let the oven heat to 430F.
2. In an ovenproof baking dish, assemble the slices of tomatoes and onions overlapping slightly but not too much. Dust with olive oil.
3. Bake for 5 minutes, then put the feta slices on the uppermost of the vegetables. Dust with hot paprika. Bake for 15 minutes more.
4. Serve.

Nutrition: 303 calories 46g fat 12g protein

231. Black-Eyed Peas With Mint

Preparation Time: 10 minutes

Cooking Time: 10 minutes

Servings: 8

Ingredients:

- 4 (15-ounce) cans black-eyed peas, undrained
- 1 cup baby spinach
- 1 cup chopped fresh mint
- 1/2 red onion, finely chopped
- 1 carrot, grated
- 3 scallions, thinly sliced
- 1/2 cup extra-virgin olive oil
- 3 tablespoons white wine vinegar
- 1 teaspoon salt
- 1/2 teaspoon freshly ground black pepper

Directions:

1. In a large saucepan, bring the black-eyed peas and their liquid to a boil over medium heat. Cook for about 5 minutes until heated through. Drain.
2. Return the beans to the saucepan and stir in the spinach, mint, red onion, carrot, and scallions. Heat until warmed through.
3. In a small bowl, whisk together the olive oil, vinegar, salt, and pepper. Pour the mixture over the beans and stir to combine.

MAKE-AHEAD TIP: This dish can also be eaten cold and will keep in an airtight container in the refrigerator for up to 3 days.

Nutrition: calories: 304; Total Fat: 14g; Saturated Fat: 2g; Protein: 12g; Total Carbohydrates: 33g; Fiber: 13g; Sugar: 1g; Cholesterol: 0mg

Chapter 9. Poultry & Meat Recipes

232. Garlic Caper Beef Roast

Preparation Time: 10 minutes

Cooking Time: 40 minutes

Servings: 4

Ingredients:

- 2 lbs. beef roast, cubed
- 1 tbsp fresh parsley, chopped
- 1 tbsp garlic, minced
- 1/2 tsp dried rosemary
- 1 onion, chopped
- 1 tbsp olive oil
- 1 tbsp capers, chopped
- 1 cup chicken stock
- 1/2 tsp ground cumin
- Salt
- Pepper

Directions:

1. Add oil into the pot.
2. Add garlic and onion and sauté for 5 minutes.
3. Add meat and cook until brown.
4. Add remaining ingredients and stir well.
5. Seal pot with lid and cook on high for 30 minutes.
6. Once done, allow to release pressure naturally. Remove lid.
7. Stir well and serve.

Nutrition: Calories 470 Fat 17.9 g Carbohydrates 3.9 g Sugar 1.4 g Protein 69.5 g Cholesterol 203 mg

233. Cauliflower Tomato Beef

Preparation Time: 10 minutes

Cooking Time: 25 minutes

Servings: 2

Ingredients:

- 1/2 lb beef stew meat, chopped
- 1 tsp paprika
- 1 celery stalk, chopped
- 1 tbsp balsamic vinegar
- 1/4 cup grape tomatoes, chopped
- 1 onion, chopped
- 1/4 cup cauliflower, chopped

- 1 tbsp olive oil
- Pepper
- Salt

Directions:

1. Add oil into the pot.
2. Add meat and sauté for 5 minutes.
3. Add remaining ingredients and stir well.
4. Seal pot with lid and cook on high for 20 minutes.
5. Once the meat is cooked, remove the lid.
6. Stir and serve.

Nutrition: Calories 306 Fat 14.3 g Carbohydrates 7.6 g Sugar 3.5 g Protein 35.7 g Cholesterol 101 mg

234. Dinner Party Brisket

Preparation Time: 15 minutes

Cooking Time: 11 hours 5 minutes

Servings: 8

Ingredients:

- 1 fresh beef brisket, trimmed
- 3 tsp. dried Italian seasoning, crushed and divided
- 1 can diced tomatoes with basil, garlic and oregano with juice
- 1/2 C. olives, pitted
- 1 tsp. lemon peel, grated finely
- Pinch salt and freshly ground black pepper to taste
- 1/2 C. low-sodium beef broth
- 2 medium fennel bulbs, trimmed, cored and cut into wedges
- 2 tbsp. all-purpose flour
- 1/4 C. cold water

Directions:

1. Season the brisket with 1 tsp of Italian seasoning.
2. Add the remaining Italian seasoning, tomatoes with juice, olives, lemon peel, salt, black pepper, and broth in a bowl and mix well.
3. In a slow cooker, place the brisket and top with fennel, followed by the tomato mixture.
4. Set the slow cooker on "Low" and cook, covered for about 10-11 hours.

5. Uncover the slow cooker and with a slotted spoon, transfer the brisket and vegetables onto a platter.
6. With a piece of foil, cover the meat to keep warm.
7. Skim off the fat from the top of the cooking liquid.
8. In a small pan, add about 2 C. of the cooking liquid over medium heat.
9. In a small bowl, dissolve the flour in water.
10. In the pan of cooking liquid, add the flour mixture, stirring continuously.
11. Cook for about 2-3 minutes or until the desired thickness of the sauce, stirring continuously.
12. Cut the brisket into desired-sized slices and serve with the topping of gravy.

Nutrition:

Calories per serving: 367; Carbohydrates: 8.g; Protein: 53.3g; Fat: 12.3g; Sugar: 1.5g; Sodium: 266mg; Fiber: 2.8g

235. Sunday Dinner Brisket

Preparation Time: 10 minutes

Cooking Time: 8 hours 10 minutes

Servings: 6

Ingredients:

- 2 1/2 lb. beef brisket, trimmed
- Salt and freshly ground black pepper, to taste
- 2 tsp. olive oil
- 2 medium onions, chopped
- 2 large garlic cloves, sliced
- 1 tbsp. Herbs de Provence
- 1 (15-oz.) can diced tomatoes, drained
- 2 tsp. Dijon mustard
- 1 C. dry red wine

Directions:

1. Season the brisket with salt and black pepper evenly.
2. In a non-stick skillet, heat the oil over medium heat and cook the brisket for about 4-5 minutes per side.
3. Transfer the brisket into a slow cooker.

4. Add the remaining ingredients and stir to combine.
5. Set the slow cooker on "Low" and cook, covered for about 8 hours.
6. Uncover the slow cooker and with a slotted spoon, transfer the brisket onto a platter.
7. Cut the brisket into desired sized slices and serve with the topping of the pan sauce.

Nutrition:

Calories per serving: 427; Carbohydrates: 7.7g; Protein: 58.5g; Fat: 193.6g; Sugar: 3.7g; Sodium: 178mg; Fiber: 1.7g

236. Moist Shredded Beef

Preparation Time: 10 minutes

Cooking Time: 20 minutes

Servings: 8

Ingredients:

- 2 lbs. beef chuck roast, cut into chunks
- 1/2 tbsp dried red pepper
- 1 tbsp Italian seasoning
- 1 tbsp garlic, minced
- 2 tbsp vinegar
- 14 oz can fire-roasted tomatoes
- 1/2 cup bell pepper, chopped
- 1/2 cup carrots, chopped
- 1 cup onion, chopped
- 1 tsp salt

Directions:

1. Add all ingredients into the pot.
2. Seal pot with lid and cook on high for 20 minutes.
3. Once the meat is cooked, remove the lid.
4. Shred the meat using a fork.
5. Stir well and serve.

Nutrition: Calories 456 Fat 32.7 g Carbohydrates 7.7 g Sugar 4.1 g Protein 31 g Cholesterol 118 mg

237. Hearty Beef Ragu

Preparation Time: 10 minutes

Cooking Time: 50 minutes

Servings: 4

Ingredients:

- 1 1/2 lbs. beef steak, diced
- 1 1/2 cup beef stock

- 1 tbsp coconut amino
- 14 oz can tomato, chopped
- 1/2 tsp ground cinnamon
- 1 tsp dried oregano
- 1 tsp dried thyme
- 1 tsp dried basil
- 1 tsp paprika
- 1 bay leaf
- 1 tbsp garlic, chopped
- 1/2 tsp cayenne pepper
- 1 celery stick, diced
- 1 carrot, diced
- 1 onion, diced
- 2 tbsp olive oil
- 1/4 tsp pepper
- 1 1/2 tsp sea salt

Directions:

1. Add oil into the pot.
2. Add celery, carrots, onion, and salt and sauté for 5 minutes.
3. Add meat and remaining ingredients and stir everything well.
4. Seal pot with lid and cook on high for 30 minutes.
5. Once the meat is cooked, remove the lid.
6. Shred meat using a fork. Set pot on sauté mode and cook for 10 minutes. Stir every 2-3 minutes.
7. Serve and enjoy.

Nutrition: Calories 435 Fat 18.1 g Carbohydrates 12.3 g Sugar 5.5 g Protein 54.4 g Cholesterol 152 mg

238. Dill Beef Brisket

Preparation Time: 10 minutes

Cooking Time: 50 minutes

Servings: 4

Ingredients:

- 2 1/2 lbs. beef brisket, cut into cubes
- 2 1/2 cups beef stock
- 2 tbsp dill, chopped
- 1 celery stalk, chopped
- 1 onion, sliced
- 1 tbsp garlic, minced
- Pepper
- Salt

Directions:

1. Add all ingredients into a pot and stir well.

2. Seal pot with lid and cook on high heat for 50 minutes.
3. Once cooked, remove the lid.
4. Serve and enjoy.

Nutrition: Calories 556 Fat 18.1 g Carbohydrates 4.3 g Sugar 1.3 g Protein 88.5 g Cholesterol 253 mg

239. Tasty Beef Stew

Preparation Time: 10 minutes

Cooking Time: 30 minutes

Servings: 4

Ingredients:

- 2 1/2 lbs. beef roast, cut into chunks
- 1 cup beef broth
- 1/2 cup balsamic vinegar
- 1 tbsp honey
- 1/2 tsp red pepper flakes
- 1 tbsp garlic, minced
- Pepper
- Salt

Directions:

1. Add all ingredients into the pot and stir well.
2. Seal pot with lid and cook on high for 30 minutes.
3. Once the meat is cooked, remove the lid.
4. Stir well and serve.

Nutrition: Calories 562 Fat 18.1 g Carbohydrates 5.7 g Sugar 4.6 g Protein 87.4 g Cholesterol 253 mg Meatloaf **Preparation Time:** 10 minutes **Cooking Time:** 35 minutes **Servings:** 6

240. Italian Style Ground Beef

Preparation Time: 10 minutes

Cooking Time: 20 minutes

Servings: 4

Ingredients:

- 2 lbs. ground beef
- 2 eggs, lightly beaten
- 1/4 tsp dried basil
- 3 tbsp olive oil
- 1/2 tsp dried sage
- 1 1/2 tsp dried parsley
- 1 tsp oregano
- 2 tsp thyme
- 1 tsp rosemary

- Pepper
- Salt

Directions:

1. Pour 1 1/2 cups of water into the pot, then place the trivet in the pot.
2. Spray loaf pan with cooking spray.
3. Add all ingredients into the mixing bowl and mix until well combined.
4. Transfer the meat mixture into the prepared loaf pan and place the loaf pan on top of the trivet in the pot.
5. Seal pot with lid and cook on high for 35 minutes.
6. Once the meat is cooked, remove the lid.
7. Serve and enjoy.

Nutrition: Calories 365 Fat 18 g Carbohydrates 0.7 g Sugar 0.1 g Protein 47.8 g Cholesterol 190 mg

241. Spicy Beef Chili Verde

Preparation Time: 10 minutes

Cooking Time: 23 minutes

Servings: 2

Ingredients:

- 1/2 lb beef stew meat, cut into cubes
- 1/4 tsp chili powder
- 1 tbsp olive oil
- 1 cup chicken broth
- 1 Serrano pepper, chopped
- 1 tsp garlic, minced
- 1 small onion, chopped
- 1/4 cup grape tomatoes, chopped
- 1/4 cup tomatillos, chopped
- Pepper
- Salt

Directions:

1. Add oil into the pot.
2. Add garlic and onion and sauté for 3 minutes.
3. Add remaining ingredients and stir well.
4. Seal pot with lid and cook on high for 20 minutes.
5. Once the meat is cooked, remove the lid.
6. Stir well and serve.

Nutrition: Calories 317 Fat 15.1 g Carbohydrates 6.4 g Sugar 2.6 g Protein 37.8 g Cholesterol 101 mg

242. Carrot Mushroom Beef Roast

Preparation Time: 10 minutes

Cooking Time: 40 minutes

Servings: 4

Ingredients:

- 1 1/2 lbs. beef roast
- 1 tsp paprika
- 1/4 tsp dried rosemary
- 1 tsp garlic, minced
- 1/2 lb mushrooms, sliced
- 1/2 cup chicken stock
- 2 carrots, sliced
- Pepper
- Salt

Directions:

1. Add all ingredients into the pot and stir well.
2. Seal pot with lid and cook on high for 40 minutes.
3. Once the meat is cooked, remove the lid.
4. Slice and serve.

Nutrition: Calories 345 Fat 10.9 g Carbohydrates 5.6 g Sugar 2.6 g Protein 53.8 g Cholesterol 152 mg

243. Italian Beef Roast

Preparation Time: 10 minutes

Cooking Time: 50 minutes

Servings: 6

Ingredients:

- 2 1/2 lbs. beef roast, cut into chunks
- 1 cup chicken broth
- 1 cup red wine
- 2 tbsp Italian seasoning
- 2 tbsp olive oil
- 1 bell pepper, chopped
- 2 celery stalks, chopped
- 1 tsp garlic, minced
- 1 onion, sliced
- Pepper
- Salt

Directions:

1. Add oil into the pot.
2. Add the meat into the pot and sauté until brown.
3. Add onion, bell pepper, and celery, and sauté for 5 minutes.

4. Add remaining ingredients and stir well.
5. Seal pot with lid and cook on high for 40 minutes.
6. Once the meat is cooked, remove the lid.
7. Stir well and serve.

Nutrition: Calories 460 Fat 18.2 g Carbohydrates 5.3 g Sugar 2.7 g Protein 58.7 g Cholesterol 172 mg

244. Thyme Beef Round Roast

Preparation Time: 10 minutes

Cooking Time: 55 minutes

Servings: 8

Ingredients:

- 4 lbs. beef bottom round roast, cut into pieces
- 2 tbsp honey
- 5 fresh thyme sprigs
- 2 cups red wine
- 1 lb carrots, cut into chunks
- 2 cups chicken broth
- 6 garlic cloves, smashed
- 1 onion, diced
- 1/4 cup olive oil
- 2 lbs. potatoes, peeled and cut into chunks
- Pepper
- Salt

Directions:

1. Add all ingredients except carrots and potatoes into the pot.
2. Seal pot with lid and cook on high for 45 minutes.
3. It was once done. Remove lid.
4. Add carrots and potatoes and stir well.
5. Seal pot again with lid and cook on high for 10 minutes.
6. Once the meat is cooked, remove the lid.
7. Stir well and serve.

Nutrition: Calories 648 Fat 21.7 g Carbohydrates 33.3 g Sugar 9.7 g Protein 67.1 g Cholesterol 200 mg

245. Jalapeno Beef Chili

Preparation Time: 10 minutes

Cooking Time: 40 minutes

Servings: 8

Ingredients:

- 1 lb ground beef
- 1 tsp garlic powder
- 1 jalapeno pepper, chopped
- 1 tbsp ground cumin
- 1 tbsp chili powder
- 1 lb ground pork
- 4 tomatillos, chopped
- 1/2 onion, chopped
- 5 oz tomato paste
- Pepper
- Salt

Directions:

1. Add oil into the pot.
2. Add beef and pork and cook until brown.
3. Add remaining ingredients and stir well.
4. Seal pot with lid and cook on high for 35 minutes.
5. Once the meat is cooked, remove the lid.
6. Stir well and serve.

Nutrition: Calories 217 Fat 6.1 g Carbohydrates 6.2 g Sugar 2.7 g Protein 33.4 g Cholesterol 92 mg

246. Bean Beef Chili

Preparation Time: 10 minutes

Cooking Time: 40 minutes

Servings: 4

Ingredients:

- 1 lb ground beef
- 1/2 onion, diced
- 1 tsp chili powder
- 1 tsp garlic, chopped
- 14 oz can black beans, rinsed and drained
- 14 oz can red beans, rinsed and drained
- 1/2 jalapeno pepper, minced
- 1/2 bell pepper, chopped
- 1 cup chicken broth
- Pepper
- Salt

Directions:

1. Add the meat into the pot and sauté until brown.
2. Add remaining ingredients and stir well.
3. Seal pot with lid and cook on high for 35 minutes.

4. Once the meat is cooked, remove the lid.
5. Stir well and serve.

Nutrition: Calories 409 Fat 8.3 g Carbohydrates 36.3 g Sugar 4.2 g Protein 46.6 g Cholesterol 101 mg

247. Fall-Apart Tender Beef

Preparation Time: 10 minutes

Cooking Time: 11 hours

Servings: 12

Ingredients:

- 4 lb. boneless beef chuck roast, trimmed
- 2 large onions, sliced into thin strips
- 4 celery stalks, sliced
- 4 garlic cloves, minced
- 1 1/2 C. catsup
- 1 C. BBQ sauce
- 1/4 C. molasses
- 1/4 C. apple cider vinegar
- 2 tbsp. prepared yellow mustard
- 1/4 tsp. red chili powder
- Fresh ground black pepper, to taste

Directions:

1. In a slow cooker, place all the ingredients and stir to combine.
2. Set the slow cooker on "Low" and cook, covered for about 8-10 hours.
3. Uncover the slow cooker and with 2 forks, shred the meat.
4. Stir the meat with pan sauce.
5. Set the slow cooker on "Low" and cook, covered for about 1 hour.
6. Serve hot.

Nutrition:

Calories per serving: 454; Carbohydrates: 43.4g; Protein: 48.3g; Fat: 10g; Sugar: 35.5g; Sodium: 1000mg; Fiber: 1.2g

248. Beef and Cabbage Roast

Preparation Time: 10 minutes.

Cooking Time: 7 hours on low + 1 hour on low.

Servings: 10

Ingredients:

- 1 red onion, quartered
- 2 garlic cloves, minced
- 2-3 stocks celery, diced (approximately 1 cup)
- 4-6 dry pimento berries
- 2 bay leaves
- 5.5 pounds beef brisket (two pieces)
- 1 teaspoon chili powder
- 1 teaspoon ground cumin
- 2 cups broth, beef + 2 cups hot water
- Salt and pepper to taste
- 1 medium cabbage (approximately 2.2 pounds), cut in half, then quartered

Directions:

1. Add all ingredients, except cabbage, to a pot in order of the list.
2. Cover, cook on low for 7 hours.
3. Uncover, add the cabbage on top of the stew.
4. Re-cover, cook for 1 additional hour.

Nutrition per serving: net Carb 8g; Protein: 42g; Fat: 40g

249. Rustic Lamb Shanks

Preparation Time: 15 minutes

Cooking Time: 4 1/4 hours

Servings: 6

Ingredients:

- 6 lamb shanks, frenched
- 1/4 C. flour
- 3 tbsp. olive oil, divided
- 2 onions, sliced
- 4 garlic cloves, sliced thinly
- 1 (14-oz.) can marinated artichoke hearts
- 3/4 C. Kalamata olives, pitted
- 2 tbsp. lemon rind, grated
- 1 tbsp. fresh oregano, chopped
- Salt and freshly ground black pepper, to taste
- 1/2 C. white wine
- 2 1/2 C. chicken broth

Directions:

1. In a large plastic bag, place the lamb shanks and flour.
2. Seal the bag and shake to coat.

3. In a pan, heat 2 tbsp. Of the oil and sear the lamb shanks in 2 batches for about 4-5 minutes or browned completely.
4. With a slotted spoon, transfer the shanks onto a platter.
5. Heat the remaining oil over medium heat in the same pan and sauté the onions and garlic for about 4-5 minutes.
6. Remove from the heat.
7. In a slow cooker, place the lamb shanks and onion mixture.
8. Top with the remaining ingredients and stir to combine.
9. Set the slow cooker on "High" and cook, covered for about 4 hours.
10. Serve hot.

Nutrition:

Calories per serving: 710; Carbohydrates: 17.9g; Protein: 85.1g; Fat: 20.4g; Sugar: 2.8g; Sodium: 772mg; Fiber: 5.g

250. Holiday Feast Lamb Shanks

Preparation Time: 15 minutes

Cooking Time: 8 hours 5 minutes

Servings: 4

Ingredients:

- 4 lamb shanks
- Salt and freshly ground black pepper, to taste
- 1 tbsp. olive oil
- 1 lb. baby potatoes, halved
- 1 C. Kalamata olives
- 1 (3-oz.) jar sun-dried tomatoes
- 1 C. chicken broth
- 3 tbsp. fresh lemon juice
- 2 1/2 tsp. dried oregano
- 1 tsp. dried rosemary
- 1 tsp. dried basil
- 1 tsp. onion powder

Directions:

1. Season the lamb shanks with salt and black pepper evenly.
2. In a large heavy-bottomed skillet, heat the olive oil over medium-high heat and sear the lamb shanks for about 4-5

minutes or browned completely.
3. Remove from the heat.
4. Place the potatoes, olives, sun-dried tomatoes, salt, black place the lamb on top and sprinkle with dried herbs and onion powder.
5. Set on "Low" and cook, covered for about 8 hours.
6. Serve hot.

Nutrition:

Calories per serving: 696; Carbohydrates: 22.5g; Protein: 83.5g; Fat: 28.6g; Sugar: 2.5g; Sodium: 749mg; Fiber: 4.7g

251. Succulent Leg of Lamb

Preparation Time: 15 minutes

Cooking Time: 4 hours 8 minutes

Servings: 8

Ingredients:

- 1 (3-lb.) boneless leg of lamb, trimmed
- Salt and freshly ground black pepper, to taste
- 5 tbsp. extra-virgin olive oil, divided
- 6 garlic cloves, sliced thinly
- 2 tbsp. fresh lemon juice
- 6 garlic cloves, minced
- 2 tsp. fresh thyme
- 2 tsp. dried rosemary
- 1 tsp. dried oregano
- 3/4 tsp. sweet paprika
- 1 lb. pearl onions, peeled
- 1 C. dry red wine
- 1/2 C. low-sodium beef broth

Directions:

1. Season the leg of lamb with salt and black pepper generously.
2. Set aside at room temperature for up to 1 hour.
3. In a large skillet, heat 2 tbsp. of the oil over medium heat and sear the lamb for about 7-8 minutes or browned completely.
4. Remove from the heat and set aside to cool slightly.
5. With a sharp knife, cut slits into the lamb on both sides.
6. Insert 1 garlic slice in each slit.

7. Add the remaining oil, lemon juice, minced garlic, herbs, and paprika in a small bowl and mix well.
8. Coat the leg of lamb with the oil mixture evenly.
9. In a slow cooker, place the pearl onions, wine and broth.
10. Arrange the leg of lamb on top.
11. Set the slow cooker on "High" and cook, covered for about 3-4 hours.
12. Uncover the slow cooker and with 2 tongs, transfer the leg of lamb onto a serving platter.
13. Top with pan juices and serve.

Nutrition:

Calories per serving: 450; Carbohydrates: 7.6g; Protein: 48.8g; Fat: 21.4g; Sugar: 2.8g; Sodium: 182mg; Fiber: 1.7g

252. Melt-in-Mouth Lamb Shoulder

Preparation Time: 10 minutes

Cooking Time: 5 hours 10 minutes

Servings: 8

Ingredients:

- 3 1/4 lb. bone-in lamb shoulder, trimmed
- 2 brown onions, sliced thinly
- 5-6 garlic cloves
- 1/4 C. beef broth
- 1/4 C. olive oil
- 1 tbsp. dried thyme
- Salt and freshly ground black pepper, to taste

Directions:

1. Heat a large cast-iron skillet over medium-high heat and sear the lamb shoulder for about 4-5 minutes per side.
2. Remove from the heat.
3. In a slow cooker, place the onion slices and garlic evenly and arrange the lamb shoulder on top.
4. Place the remaining ingredients on top.
5. Set the slow cooker on "High" and cook, covered for about 4-5 hours.
6. Uncover the slow cooker and with a slotted spoon, transfer

the lamb shoulder onto a platter.

7. Cut the lamb shoulder into desired-sized slices and serve with the topping of the pan sauce.

Nutrition:

Calories per serving: 413; Carbohydrates: 3.4g; Protein: 52.3g; Fat: 19.9g; Sugar: 1.2g; Sodium: 185mg; Fiber: 0.8g

253. Greek Spiced Pork Souvlaki

Preparation Time: 10 minutes

Cooking Time: 8 hours

Servings: 5

Ingredients:

- 1/4 C. olive oil
- 1/4 C. fresh lemon juice
- 2 tbsp. red wine vinegar
- 1 tbsp. dried oregano
- 1 tbsp. dried mint
- 1 tbsp. za'atar
- 1 tbsp. garlic powder
- 1 tsp. chili flakes
- Salt, to taste
- 2 lb. boneless pork shoulder, cubed

Directions:

1. In a medium bowl, add all the ingredients except for pork shoulder and mix well.
2. In the bottom of a slow cooker, place the pork shoulder and top with oil mixture.
3. Set the slow cooker on "Low" and cook, covered for about 8 hours.
4. Uncover the slow cooker and with 2 forks, shred the meat.
5. With a spoon, mix the meat with pan juices and serve.

Nutrition:

Calories per serving: 359; Carbohydrates: 2.2g; Protein: 55.7g; Fat: 16.7g; Sugar: 0.7g; Sodium: 138mg; Fiber: 0.7g

254. Lovely Smelling Pork Loin

Preparation Time: 10 minutes

Cooking Time: 8 hours

Servings: 8

Ingredients:

- 2 tbsp. olive oil
- 3/4 C. chicken broth
- 1/2 tbsp. paprika
- 1/2 tbsp. garlic powder
- 2¼ tsp. dried sage
- 1 tsp. dried basil
- 1 tsp. dried oregano
- 1/4 tsp. dried marjoram
- 1/4 tsp. dried rosemary
- 1/4 tsp. dried thyme
- 2½ lb. boneless pork loin, trimmed

Directions:

1. In a medium bowl, add all the ingredients except for pork loin and mix well.
2. In the bottom of a slow cooker, place the pork loin and top with oil mixture.
3. Set the slow cooker on "Low" and cook, covered for about 7-8 hours.
4. Uncover the slow cooker and with 2 forks, shred the meat.
5. With a spoon, mix the meat with pan juices and serve.

Nutrition:

Calories per serving: 242; Carbohydrates: 1.2g; Protein: 37.8g; Fat: 8.8g; Sugar: 0.3g; Sodium: 13mg; Fiber: 0.5g

255. Elegant Pork Loin

Preparation Time: 15 minutes

Cooking Time: 6 hours 5 minutes

Servings: 8

Ingredients:

- 1 (3-lb.) boneless pork loin roast, trimmed
- 4 tsp. Greek seasoning
- 2 fennel bulbs, trimmed and sliced
- 4 plum tomatoes, chopped
- 1/3 C. plus 2 tbsp. low-sodium chicken broth, divided
- Salt and freshly ground black pepper, to taste
- 2 tbsp. cornstarch
- 1½ tsp. Worcestershire sauce
- ¼ C. black olives, pitted and chopped

Directions:

1. Rub the pork loin with 1 tsp. Of the Greek seasoning evenly.
2. In the bottom of a slow cooker, place the fennel slices and top with pork loin.
3. Arrange the tomatoes around the pork.
4. Top with 1/3 C. of the broth, followed by remaining Greek seasoning, salt and black pepper.
5. Set the slow cooker on "Low" and cook, covered for about 6 hours.
6. Meanwhile, in a small bowl, dissolve the cornstarch in the remaining broth and Worcestershire sauce.
7. Uncover the slow cooker and with a slotted spoon, transfer the pork onto a platter.
8. With a piece, cover the pork to keep warm.
9. Through a strainer, strain the cooking liquid into a small pan.
10. Place the pan over medium-high heat and bring to a boil.
11. Add the cornstarch mixture, beating continuously until well combined.
12. Cook for about 1 minute, stirring continuously.
13. Remove from the heat and pour the sauce over pork.
14. Garnish with olives and serve.

Nutrition:

Calories per serving: 295; Carbohydrates: 10.5g; Protein: 46.2g; Fat: 6.7g; Sugar: 2.7g; Sodium: 283mg; Fiber: 2.6g

256. Zero-Fussing Pork Meal

Preparation Time: 20 minutes

Cooking Time: 6 hours

Servings: 4

Ingredients:

- 1 lb. lean pork, cut into bite-sized cubes
- 2 potatoes, peeled and quartered
- 1 lb. fresh green beans
- 2 carrots, peeled and sliced thinly

- 2 celery stalks, sliced thinly
- 1 large onion, chopped
- 3 fresh tomatoes, grated
- ½ C. extra-virgin olive oil
- 1 tsp. dried thyme
- Salt and freshly ground black pepper, to taste

Directions:

1. In a pot, place all the ingredients and stir to combine.
2. Set on "High" and cook, covered for about 6 hours.
3. Serve hot.

Nutrition:

Calories per serving: 533; Carbohydrates: 35.3g; Protein: 35.1g; Fat: 29.7g; Sugar: 8.4g; Sodium: 151mg; Fiber: 9.3g

257. Grilled Steak

Preparation Time: 10 minutes

Cooking Time: 20 minutes

Servings: 2

Ingredients

- 2 steaks
- 1 c. spinach, chopped
- 1 tbsp. olive oil
- 2 tbsps. red onions, diced
- 2 tbsps. feta cheese, crumbled
- 2 tbsps. panko breadcrumbs
- 1 tbsp. diced sun-dried tomato
- Salt and pepper

Directions:

1. Preheat grill to medium-high heat.
2. Use a skillet to sauté the onions in olive oil for 5 minutes.
3. Add the remaining ingredients, except the steaks, and stir for 2 minutes. Take off the stove and let sit.
4. Grill the steaks to the desired doneness.
5. Top each steak with the spinach mix. Cook in the broiler until the top turns brown.

Nutritional: Calories 531 Total Fat 33.2 g Sat. fat 12.2 g Carbs 37.8 g Fiber 1.6 g Sugars 0.9 g Protein 22.7 g Sodium 582 mg

258. Spicy Roasted Leg of Lamb

Preparation Time: 30 minutes

Cooking Time: 2 hours

Servings: 4

Ingredients

for the Lamb:

- 1 lb./450 g. leg of lamb, bone-in
- Salt and pepper
- 3 tbsps. olive oil
- 5 sliced garlic cloves
- 2 c. water
- 4 cubed potatoes
- 1 onion, chopped
- 1 tsp. garlic powder

For the Lamb Spice Rub:

- 15 peeled garlic cloves
- 3 tbsps. oregano
- 2 tbsps. mint
- 1 tbsp. paprika
- ½ c. olive oil
- ¼ c. lemon juice

Directions:

1. Allow the lamb to rest for 1 hour at room temperature.
2. While you wait, put all of the spice rub ingredients in a food processor and blend. Refrigerate the rub.
3. Make a few cuts in the lamb using a knife—season with salt and pepper.
4. Place on a roasting pan.
5. Heat the broiler and broil for 5 minutes on each side, so the whole thing is seared.
6. Place the lamb on the counter and set the oven temperature to 375°F/190°C.
7. Let the lamb cool, fill the cuts with the garlic slices and cover with the spice rub.
8. To the roasting pan, set in 2 cups of water.
9. Sprinkle the potatoes and onions with garlic powder, salt, and pepper. Arrange them around the leg of lamb.
10. Add oil to the top of lamb and vegetables.
11. Use aluminum foil to cover the roasting pan and place it back in the oven.
12. Roast the lamb for 1 hour.

13. Discard the foil and roast for 15 more minutes.
14. Let the leg of lamb sit for 20 minutes before serving.

Nutritional: Calories 504 Total Fat 19.9 g Sat. fat 4.8 g Carbs 45.2 g Fiber 8.5 g Sugars 4.6 g Protein 37.6 g Sodium 111mg

259. Dijon & Herb Pork Tenderloin

Preparation Time: 1hr

Cooking Time: 30 minutes

Servings: 6

Ingredients

- ½ c. freshly chopped Italian parsley leaves,
- 3 tbsps. fresh rosemary leaves, chopped
- 3 tbsps. fresh thyme leaves, chopped
- 3 tbsps. Dijon mustard
- 1 tbsp. extra-virgin olive oil
- 4 garlic cloves, minced
- ½ tsp. Sea salt
- ¼ tsp. freshly ground black pepper
- 1½ lbs./680 g. pork tenderloin

Directions:

1. Preheat the oven to 400°F/204°C.
2. In a blender or food processor, combine the parsley, rosemary, thyme, mustard, olive oil, garlic, sea salt, and pepper. Process for about 30 seconds until smooth.
3. Spread the mixture evenly over the pork and place it on a rimmed baking sheet.
4. Bake for about 20 minutes or until the meat reaches an internal temperature of 140°F/60°C.
5. Allow resting for 10 minutes before slicing and serving.

Nutritional: Calories 393 Total Fat 12 g Sat. fat 4 g Carbs 5 g Fiber 3 g Sugars 1 g Protein 74 g Sodium 617 mg

260. Grilled Lamb Gyro Burger

Preparation Time: 15 minutes

Cooking Time: 12 minutes

Servings: 2

Ingredient :

- 4 oz./115 g. lean ground lamb
- 4 naan flatbread or pita
- 2 tbsps. olive oil
- 2 tbsps. tzatziki sauce
- 1 red onion, thinly sliced
- 1 tomato, sliced
- 1 bunch lettuce, separated

Directions:

1. Grill meat for 10 minutes.
2. Toast naan bread and drizzle with olive oil.
3. Top two of the halves of naan bread with meat and the rest ingredients.
4. Cover with other halves and enjoy!

Nutritional: Calories 470Total fat 28 g Sat. fat 11 g Carbs 44 g Fiber 0.7 g Sugars 5 g Protein 20 g

Sodium 236 mg

261. Pork Loin & Orzo

Preparation Time: 20 minutes

Cooking Time: 30 minutes

Servings: 4

Ingredients:

- 1 lb./450 g. pork tenderloin
- 1 tsp. coarsely ground pepper
- 1 tsp. kosher salt
- 2 tbsps. olive oil
- 1 c. uncooked orzo pasta
- Water as needed
- 2 c. spinach
- 1 c. cherry tomatoes
- ¾ c. crumbled feta cheese

Directions:

1. Coat the pork loin with kosher salt and black pepper and massage it into the meat. Then cut the meat into one-inch cubes.
2. Heat the olive oil in a cast-iron skillet over medium heat until sizzling hot. Cook the pork for about 8 minutes until there's no pink left.
3. Cook the orzo in water according to package directions (adding a pinch of salt to the water).

4. Stir in the spinach and tomatoes and add the cooked pork.
5. Top with feta and serve.

Nutritional: Calories 372 Total Fat 11 g Sat. fat 4 g Carbs 34 g Fiber 3 g Sugars 2 g Protein 31 g Sodium 306 mg

262. Lamb Chops

Preparation Time: 10 minutes

Cooking Time: 20 minutes

Servings: 4

Ingredients:

- 4 oz./115 g. trimmed lamb rib chops
- 4 tbsps. olive oil
- 1 tbsp. Kosher salt
- ½ tsp. black pepper
- 3 tbsps. Balsamic vinegar
- Non-stick cooking spray

Directions:

1. Mix one tablespoon of oil with the rind and juice into a Ziploc-type bag. Add the chops and coat well. Marinate at room temperature for ten minutes.
2. Remove it from the bag and season with pepper and salt.
3. Using the med-high heat setting, coat a pan with the spray. Add the lamb and cook two minutes per side until it's the way you like it.
4. Using a saucepan, pour in the vinegar (med-high) and cook until it's syrupy or about three minutes.
5. Drizzle the vinegar and the rest of the oil (1 teaspoon) over the lamb.
6. Serve with your favorite sides.

Nutritional: Calories 226 Total Fat 17.55 g Sat. fat 7.6 g Carbs 0 g Fiber 0 g Sugars 0 g Protein 15.86 g Sodium 281mg

263. Roasted Lamb with Vegetables

Preparation Time: 20 minutes

Cooking Time: 1 hour

Servings: 4

Ingredients:

- 1 lb./450 g. lamb leg shanks

- ½ tbsp. dried Italian seasoning
- ¼ tsp. salt
- ¼ tsp. black pepper
- 2 tbsps. olive oil
- 1 cloves garlic
- 1 onion
- 2 carrots
- 1 potato
- 2 apples
- 2 rosemary sprigs

Directions:

1. Season the lamb shanks with Italian seasoning, salt, and fresh ground black pepper.
2. Preheat oven to 370°F/190°C.
3. Place lamb into the greased baking dish, cover with foil and bake it for 40 minutes.
4. Meanwhile, in a medium heat pan, sauté the garlic and onion in olive oil.
5. Add the carrots and potatoes, and sauté for another 3-5 minutes.
6. Transfer vegetables to the baking dish around the lamb and add the apples.
7. Bake the lamb with vegetables for another 20 minutes without foil until golden brown outside and tender inside.
8. Garnish with fresh rosemary.

Nutritional: Calories 65 Total Fat 29.4 g Sat. fat 3 g Carbs 33.6 g Fiber 7 g Sugars 2 g Protein 58.8 g

Sodium 473 mg

264. Pan-Fried Pork Chops with Orange Sauce

Preparation Time: 10 minutes

Cooking Time: 20 minutes

Servings: 8

Ingredients:

- 2 lbs./900 g. lean pork chops
- ¾ tsp. salt
- ½ tsp. black pepper
- 2 tbsp. olive oil
- 1 clove garlic
- ½ c. orange juice
- 1 orange

Directions:

1. Apply black pepper and salt to the pork chops.
2. In a medium heat pan, sauté the garlic in olive oil.
3. Add the pork chops and sear them on both sides until tender and golden brown. Remove fried pork chops from the pan and set them aside.
4. In the same pan, pour the orange juice. Let it simmer for 4 minutes until the sauce thickens.
5. On a serving plate, place the pork chops with orange sauce and orange wedges.

Nutritional: Calories 250 Total Fat 15.7 g Sat. fat 4.8 g Carbs 5.5 g Fiber 0.2 g Sugars 0.1 g Protein 20.5 g Sodium 411 mg

265. Beef Spicy Salsa Braised Ribs

Preparation Time: 30 minutes

Cooking Time: 4 hours

Servings: 12

Ingredients:

- 6 lbs./2.7 kg. beef ribs
- 4 diced tomatoes
- 2 chopped jalapenos
- 2 chopped shallots
- 1 c. chopped parsley
- ½ c. chopped cilantro
- 3 tbsps. Olive oil
- 2 tbsps. Balsamic vinegar
- 1 tsp. Worcestershire sauce
- Salt and pepper

Directions:

1. Combine all the ingredients except the beef ribs.
2. Set in the ribs and cover with aluminum foil.
3. Cook in the preheated oven at 300F/150C for 3 1/3 hours.
4. Serve the ribs warm.

Nutritional: Calories 228 Total Fat 13.6 g Sat. fat 6 g Carbs 4.3 g Fiber 0.2 g Sugars 2 g Protein 12 g

Sodium 934.6 mg

266. Chargrilled Mediterranean Beef Lasagna

Preparation Time: 25 minutes

Cooking Time: 55 minutes

Servings: 4

Ingredients

- 1 tbsp butter
- 1 tbsp sunflower oil
- 100 g frozen diced onion
- 2 cloves of garlic
- 500 g frozen ground beef
- 3 tbsp tomato paste
- 400 g diced tomatoes
- 100 ml of water hot
- 1 cube of beef stock
- 1 bay leaf
- 1 teaspoon of frozen basil
- 1 teaspoon of frozen oregano
- 80 g cheddar cheese
- 1 tbsp butter (for the sauce)
- 50 g cheddar cheese and Grana Padang (for the top)
- Dried lasagna sheets
- 500 g frozen grilled Mediterranean vegetables

Directions

1. Preheat the oven to 180 C and lightly grease a 1.2-liter frying pan.
2. Heat oil and butter in a large skillet or saucepan over medium heat and gently fry the onions until they thaw and soften.
3. Add the ground beef and season with salt and pepper. Fry until completely brown.
4. Stir in the tomato paste and cook for a few more minutes. Add the canned tomatoes, herbs, stock cube, and hot water mix well, reduce the temperature and simmer over medium heat for about 10 minutes.
5. For the sauce, heat the butter in a medium saucepan until it starts to bubble slightly. Stir in the flour and cook, constantly stirring, for one minute.
6. Remove from heat, whisk in milk until combined, and return to heat, occasionally stirring while the mixture

thickens. When the mixture has thickened, remove from heat and stir in 80 grams of the cheddar cheese. Put aside.

7. Before assembling, place a spoonful of sauce on the bottom of an oven dish. Finish with a layer of dried lasagna sheets. Spoon the remaining beef mixture over the pasta and drizzle with some Grana Padano cheese.
8. Add another layer of lasagna sheet and top with the frozen grilled Mediterranean vegetables. Finish with more lasagna sheets. Spoon the cheese sauce over it until the last layer of pasta is completely covered.
9. Sprinkle with the remaining cheddar and Grana Padang and bake in a preheated 190 C oven for 35-40 minutes, or until the top is golden and bubbly.

Nutrition: Calories 1623 Total Fat 164.72 g Sat. fat 118.76 g Carbs 11.8 g Fiber 2 g Sugars 4.74 g Protein 35.29 g Sodium 553 mg

267. Beef Cacciatore (Italy)

Preparation Time: 20 minutes

Cooking Time: 35 minutes

Servings: 4

Ingredients

- 1-pound beef, thinly sliced
- 1/4 cup extra virgin olive oil
- 1 onion, chopped
- 2 red peppers, chopped
- 1 orange bell pepper, chopped
- pepper and salt to taste
- 1 cup of tomato sauce
- Your choice of pasta (regular or gluten-free), cooked or prepared rice as desired

Directions

1. Add olive oil to a pan, heat over medium heat, and then add meat and brown well. Add onions and sauté for 1 minute. Add peppers and cook for 2 minutes. Add tomato sauce and salt and pepper to taste.
2. Bring to boil. Cover and cook until meat is tendered, about 40 minutes.

3. Remove most of the sauce with the peppers (leave the meat in the pan) and puree in a food processor. Add back to the pan and simmer for an additional 5 minutes, stirring constantly.
4. Serve with the pasta of your choice (you can also use gluten-free pasta or rice.

Nutrition: Calories 303 Total Fat 12.65 g Sat. fat 118.76 g Carbs 20.19 g Fiber 5.2 g Sugars 10.7 g Protein 26.2 g Sodium 1131 mg

268. Green Curry Beef

Preparation Time: 10 mins

Cooking Time: 40 mins

Servings: 3

Ingredients

- 1 tbsp. olive oil
- ½ mug chopped parsley
- 1 mug cilantro leaves
- 1 white onion, chopped
- 1 Thai green chili, chopped
- 2 cloves garlic, thinly sliced
- ¼ tsp. Turmeric
- ½ tsp. ground cumin
- 2 tbsp. Lime juice
- ¼ tsp. sea salt
- Black pepper
- 16 ounces beef top round, cut into pieces
- 1 can light coconut milk
- ¼ tsp. turmeric
- ½ tsp. ground cumin
- ¼ tsp. sea salt

Directions

1. Green curry paste:
2. In a blender or blender, combine olive oil, parsley, cilantro, onion, chili pepper, garlic, turmeric, cumin, lime juice, sea salt, and pepper; process until very smooth.
3. Combine beef and green curry paste in a container; toss to coat.
4. Refrigerate for at least 30 mins.
5. When ready, flame a large skillet over medium to high flame and add beef with the green curry sauce.
6. Lower flame and stir for about 10 mins or until the meat is browned on the outside.

7. Stir in coconut milk and cook for about 30 mins or until the sauce is thick.
8. Serve immediately.

Nutrition: Calories 298 Total Fat 10.6 g Sat. fat 0.32 g Carbs 2.83 g Fiber 0.6 g Sugars 0.31 g Protein 45.56 g Sodium 510 mg

269. Mediterranean Beef Pitas

Preparation Time: 10 mins

Cooking Time: 5 mins

Servings: 4

Ingredients

- 1 pound ground beef
- Freshly ground black pepper
- Sea salt
- 1 ½ tsp. dried oregano
- 2 tbsp. olive oil, divided
- ¼ red onion, sliced
- 3/4 mug store-bought hummus
- 2 tbsp. Flat-parsley
- 4 pitas
- 4 lemon wedges

Directions

1. Form beef into 16 patties; season with ¼ teaspoon ground pepper, ½ teaspoon sea salt, and oregano.
2. Add 1 tbsp of olive oil in a skillet set over medium heat; cook the beef patties for about 2 mins per side or until lightly browned. To serve, top pitas with the beef patties, hummus, parsley, and onion and drizzle with the remaining olive oil; garnish with lemon wedges.

Nutrition: Calories 435 Total Fat 25.96 g Sat. fat 0.32 g Carbs 19.14 g Fiber 2.4 g Sugars 1.5 g Protein 31.64 g Sodium 202 mg

270. Cumin Lamb Mix

Preparation Time: 10 minutes

Cooking Time: 10 minutes

Servings: 2

Ingredients:

- 2 lamb chops (3.5 oz each)
- 1 tablespoon olive oil
- 1 teaspoon ground cumin

- ½ teaspoon salt

Directions:

1. Rub the lamb chops with ground cumin and salt.
2. Then sprinkle them with olive oil.
3. Let the meat marinate for 10 minutes.
4. After this, preheat the skillet well.
5. Place the lamb chops in the skillet and roast them for 10 minutes. Flip the meat on another side from time to time to avoid burning.

Nutrition: calories 384, fat 33.2, fiber 0.1, carbs 0.5, protein 19.2

271. Herb-Roasted Lamb Leg

Preparation Time: 14 minutes

Cooking Time: 2 hours

Servings: 4

Ingredients:

- (6-lb) boneless leg of lamb, trimmed
- cups fresh spinach leaves
- 1/3 cup water
- 1 Tbsp. Italian seasoning
- 1 Tbsp. extra virgin olive oil

Directions:

1. Combine spinach, Italian seasoning and olive oil in a food processor. Process until finely chopped.
2. Thoroughly cover the top and sides of the lamb with this mixture.
3. Situate in the bottom of a big roasting pan. Pour water and cook, covered, at 300 F for approximately two hours or until cooked through.
4. Uncover and cook for 10 minutes more.

Nutrition: 309 calories 41g fat 12g protein

272. Spring Lamb Stew

Preparation Time: 34 minutes

Cooking Time: 13 minutes

Servings: 4

Ingredients:

- lb. lamb, cubed
- 1 lb. white mushrooms, chopped
- 4 cups fresh spring onions, chopped
- 1 tbsp. extra virgin olive oil
- 1 tbsp. Italian seasoning

Directions:

1. Heat olive oil in a deep casserole. Gently brown lamb pieces for 2-3 minutes. Cook the mushrooms for 2 minutes.
2. Stir in Italian seasoning, cover, and cook for an hour or until tender. Add in spring onions and simmer for 10 minutes more.
3. Uncover and cook until almost all the liquid evaporates.

Nutrition: 309 calories 41g fat 10g protein

273. Pork and Mushroom Crock Pot

Preparation Time: 1 hour

Cooking Time: 8 hours

Servings: 4

Ingredients:

- 2 lbs. pork tenderloin, sliced
- 1 can chopped white button mushrooms
- 1 can cream of mushroom soup
- 1 cup sour cream
- salt and black pepper, to taste

Directions:

1. Spray the slow cooker with nonstick spray.
2. Combine all ingredients into the slow cooker.
3. Cook on low for 8 hours, covered.

Nutrition: 311 calories 51g fat 18g protein

274. Buttery Herb Lamb Chops

Preparation Time: 10 minutes

Cooking Time: 10 minutes

Servings: .

Ingredients:

- 8 Lamb Chops
- 1 Tablespoon Olive Oil

- 1 Tablespoon Butter
- Sea Salt & Black Pepper to Taste
- 4 Ounces Herb Butter.
- 1 Lemon, Cut into Wedges

Directions:

1. Season well the chops, then prep a pan.
2. Heat butter in a pan at medium-high heat and then fry your chops for four minutes per side.
3. Arrange on a serving plate with herb butter on each one. Serve with a lemon wedge.

Nutrition: Calories: 729. Protein: 43g Fat: 62g

275. Special Chops

Preparation Time: 12 minutes.

Cooking Time: 12 minutes

Servings: 2.

Ingredients:

- 2 Lamb Chops.
- Minced Shallots 2 Tablespoons.
- Balsamic Vinegar, 2 Tablespoons.
- Chicken Broth, 2 Tablespoons.
- Basil, ¼ Teaspoon.
- Rosemary, 1 Teaspoon.
- Thyme, ¼ Teaspoon.
- Salt and Pepper as Needed.
- Extra Virgin Olive Oil, 1 Tablespoon.
- Greek Yogurt, 2 Tablespoons.

Directions:

1. Take a mixing bowl and mix all herbs and yogurt with seasoning.
2. Rub this mixture into the chops thoroughly. Leave them for a few minutes.
3. Heat a skillet over medium heat and cook both sides of the chops well.
4. When tender, brown the shallots on the skillet and add the vinegar and broth.
5. Top the chops with the warm sauce of broth and serve on a platter.

Nutrition: Calories: 255 Fat: 13.9g Protein: 14.6g

276. Rib Roast

Preparation Time: 10 minutes

Cooking Time: 80 minutes

Servings: 2

Ingredients:

- Rib Roast, 4 Pounds.
- Salt and Pepper to Taste.
- Garlic, 1 Clove, Minced.
- Extra Virgin Olive Oil, 1 Teaspoon.
- Thyme, ¼ Teaspoon.

Directions:

1. Arrange the Meat in The Roasting Pan.
2. Take A Small Bowl, And Mix the Rest of The Ingredients.
3. Apply the Mixture to The Meat. Leave for One Hour.
4. Bake That At 500F for 25 minutes.
5. Then, Bake Again At 325F for 80 minutes.

Serve warm.

Nutrition: Calories: 562 Fat: 48g Protein: 29.6g

277. Spicy Lamb Rounds

Preparation Time: 10 minutes

Cooking Time: 12 minutes

Servings: 2

Ingredients:

- Ground Lamb, 1 Pound.
- Garlic, 1 Tablespoon, Chopped.
- Mint Leaves, 1 Tablespoon, Chopped.
- Oregano, 1 Tablespoon, Chopped.
- Cilantro, 1 Tablespoon, Chopped.
- Red Pepper, ½ Teaspoon.
- Ground Cumin, ½ Teaspoon.
- Salt and Pepper, ½ Teaspoon Each.
- Feta Cheese, 4 Ounces.
- Extra Virgin Olive Oil as Needed.
- Greek Yogurt, 2 Tablespoons.

Directions:

1. Heat a grill pan over medium heat.

2. Meanwhile, coat the lamb with the yogurt, spices, seasoning, and herbs in a bowl.
3. Stir the rest of the ingredients, excluding the feta cheese.
4. Brush the grill pan with cooking oil.
5. Shape the lamb meat into small round cutlets or patties.
6. Grill them, and serve with cheese on top.

Nutrition: Calories: 478 Fat: 22.4g Protein: 29.4g

278. Prime BBQ

Preparation Time: 35 minutes

Cooking Time: 85 minutes

Servings: 2

Ingredients:

- Ribs of Your Choice, 2 Pounds.
- Garlic, 1 Teaspoon, Minced.
- Pepper to Taste.
- Salt as Needed.

Directions:

1. Take a large pot and apply salt, pepper, and garlic well to the ribs.
2. Boil the ribs in boiling water.
3. When tender, bake them at 325f for 15 minutes.
4. Cover them in aluminum foil and place a warm coal piece on the foil.
5. Let the ribs absorb the coal smell and taste for one hour.
6. Bake the ribs again.
7. Serve warm.

Nutrition: Calories: 441 Fat: 22.2g Protein: 33.3g

279. Pork And Chestnuts Mix

Preparation Time: 30 minutes

Cooking Time: 0 minutes

Servings: 6

Ingredients:

- 1 and ½ cups brown rice, already cooked
- 2 cups pork roast, already cooked and shredded

- 3 ounces water chestnuts, drained and sliced
- ½ cup sour cream
- A pinch of salt and white pepper

Directions:

1. In a bowl, mix the rice with the roast and the other ingredients, toss and keep in the fridge for 2 hours before serving.

Nutrition: calories 294, fat 17, fiber 8, carbs 16, protein 23.5

280. Steak with Olives and Mushrooms

Preparation Time: 20 minutes

Cooking Time: 9 minutes

Servings: 6

Ingredients:

- lb. boneless beef sirloin steak
- 1 large onion, sliced
- 5-6 white button mushrooms
- 1/2 cup green olives, coarsely chopped
- 4 tbsp. extra virgin olive oil

Directions:

2. Heat olive oil in a heavy-bottomed skillet over medium-high heat. Brown the steaks on both sides, then put them aside.
3. Gently sauté the onion in the same skillet, for 2-3 minutes, stirring rarely. Sauté in the mushrooms and olives.
4. Return the steaks to the skillet, cover, cook for 5-6 minutes and serve.

Nutrition: 299 calories 56g fat 16g protein

281. Greek Pork

Preparation Time: 10 minutes

Cooking Time: 1 Hour And 10 minutes

Servings: 8

Ingredients:

- 3 lb. pork roast, sliced into cubes
- 1/4 cup chicken broth
- 1/4 cup lemon juice
- 2 teaspoons dried oregano
- 2 teaspoons garlic powder

Directions:

1. Put the pork in the Pot.
2. In a bowl, mix all the remaining ingredients.
3. Pour the mixture over the pork.
4. Toss to coat evenly.
5. Secure the pot.
6. Once the meat is cooked, remove the lid.
7. Serve.

Nutrition: (Per Serving): Calories 478 ;Total Fat 21.6g ;Saturated Fat 7.9g ;Cholesterol 195mg ;Sodium 161mg ;Total Carbohydrate 1.2g ;Dietary Fiber 0.3g ;Total Sugars 0.5g ;Protein 65.1g ;

282. Rosemary Pork Chops

Preparation Time: 30 minutes

Cooking Time: 35 minutes

Servings: 4

Ingredients:

- 4 pork loin chops, boneless
- Salt and black pepper to the taste
- 4 garlic cloves, minced
- 1 tablespoon rosemary, chopped
- 1 tablespoon olive oil

Directions:

1. In a roasting pan, combine the pork chops with the rest of the ingredients, toss, and bake at 425 degrees F for 10 minutes.
2. Reduce the heat to 350 degrees F and cook the chops for 25 minutes more.
3. Divide the chops between plates and serve with a side salad.

Nutrition: calories 161, fat 5, fiber 1, carbs 1, protein 25

283. Pork Rind Salmon Cakes

Preparation Time: 10 minutes

Cooking Time: 10 minutes

Servings: 2

Ingredients

- 6 ounces canned Alaska wild salmon, drained

- 2 tablespoons crushed pork rinds
- 1 egg, lightly beaten
- 1 tablespoon ghee
- ½ tablespoon Dijon mustard

Directions:

1. In a medium bowl, incorporate salmon, pork rinds, egg, and 1½ tablespoons of mayonnaise, and season with pink Himalayan salt and pepper.
2. With the salmon mixture, form patties the size of hockey pucks or smaller. Keep patting the cakes until they keep together.
3. Position the medium skillet over medium-high heat, melt the ghee. When the ghee sizzles, place the salmon patties in the pan. Cook for 6 minutes on both sides. Transfer the cakes to a paper towel-lined plate.
4. In a small bowl, mix the remaining 1½ tablespoons of mayonnaise and the mustard.
5. Serve the salmon cakes with the mayo-mustard dipping sauce.

Nutrition: 362 Calories 31g Fat 24g Protein

284. Worcestershire Pork Chops

Preparation Time: 15 minutes

Cooking Time: 15 minutes

Servings: 3

Ingredients:

- 2 tablespoons Worcestershire sauce
- 8 oz pork loin chops
- 1 tablespoon lemon juice
- 1 teaspoon olive oil

Directions:

1. Mix up together Worcestershire sauce, lemon juice, and olive oil.
2. Brush the pork loin chops with the sauce mixture from each side.
3. Preheat the grill to 395F.

4. Place the pork chops in the grill and cook them for 5 minutes.
5. Then flip the pork chops on another side and brush with the remaining sauce mixture.
6. Grill the meat for 7-8 minutes more.

Nutrition per **Servings**: calories 267, fat 20.4, fiber 0, carbs 2.1, protein 17

285. Pork With Green Beans & Potatoes

Preparation Time: 1 hour 30 minutes

Cooking Time: 45 minutes

Servings: 6

Ingredients:

- 1 lb. lean pork, sliced into cubes
- 1 onion, chopped
- 2 carrots, sliced thinly
- 2 cups canned crushed tomatoes
- 2 potatoes, cubed

Directions:

1. Add ½ cup of olive oil to a pot.
2. Cook the pork for 5 minutes, stirring frequently.
3. Add the rest of the ingredients.
4. Mix well.
5. Seal the pot.
6. Once the meat is cooked, remove the lid.
7. Serve.

Nutrition: (Per Serving): Calories 428 ;Total Fat 24.4g ;Saturated Fat 5.2g ;Cholesterol 60mg ;Sodium 249mg ;Total Carbohydrate 27.6g ;Dietary Fiber 8.2g ;Total Sugars 8.6g ;Protein 26.7g ;Potassium 926mg

286. Chicken with Peas

Preparation Time: 5 minutes

Cooking Time: 30 minutes

Servings: 4

Ingredients:

Four chicken fillets

- 1 tsp. cayenne pepper
- 1 tsp. salt
- 1 tbsp. mayonnaise
- 1 cup green peas
- ¼ cup of water
- One carrot, peeled, chopped

Directions:

1. Sprinkle the chicken fillet with cayenne pepper and salt.
2. Line the baking tray using foil and place chicken fillets in it.
3. Then brush the chicken with mayonnaise.
4. Add carrot and green peas.
5. Then add water and cover the ingredients with foil.
6. Bake the chicken for 30 minutes at 355F.

Nutrition: Calories 329 Fat 12.3 Fiber 2.3 Carbs 7.9 Protein 44.4

287. Chicken Wrap

Preparation Time: 10 minutes

Cooking Time: 0 minutes

Servings: 2

Ingredients:

- Two whole wheat tortilla flatbreads
- Six chicken breast slices, skinless, boneless, cooked, and shredded
- A handful of baby spinach
- Two provolone cheese slices
- Four tomato slices
- Ten kalamata olives, pitted and sliced
- One red onion, sliced
- 2 tbsp. roasted peppers, chopped

Directions:

1. Arrange the tortillas on a working surface, and divide the chicken and the other ingredients on each.
2. Roll the tortillas and serve them right away.

Nutrition: Calories 190 Fat 6.8 g Fiber 3.5 g Carbs 15.1 g Protein 6.6 g

288. Almond Chicken Bites

Preparation Time: 5 minutes

Cooking Time: 5 minutes

Servings: 8

Ingredients:

- 1-pound chicken fillet
- 1 tbsp. potato starch
- ½ tsp. salt
- 1 tsp. paprika

- 2 tbsp. wheat flour, whole grain
- One egg, beaten
- 1 tbsp. almond butter

Directions:

1. Chop the chicken fillet on the small pieces and place it in the bowl.
2. Add egg, salt, and potato starch. Mix up the chicken.
3. Then mix up wheat flour and paprika.
4. Then coat every chicken piece in a wheat flour mixture.
5. Place almond butter in the skillet and heat it.
6. Add chicken popcorn and roast it for 5 minutes over medium heat.
7. Dry the chicken popcorn with the help of a paper towel.

Nutrition: Calories 141 Fat 5.9 g Fiber 0.4 g Carbs 3.3 g Protein 17.8 g

289. Garlic Chicken and Endives

Preparation Time: 5 minutes

Cooking Time: 15 minutes

Servings: 4

Ingredients:

- 1-pound chicken breasts, skinless, boneless, and cubed
- Two endives, sliced
- 2 tbsp. olive oil
- Four garlic cloves, minced
- ½ cup chicken stock
- 2 tbsp. parmesan, grated
- 1 tbsp. parsley, chopped
- Salt and black pepper to the taste

Directions:

1. Heat a pan with the oil over medium-high heat, add the chicken and cook for 5 minutes.
2. The endives, garlic, stock, salt, and pepper, stir, bring to a simmer and cook over medium-high heat for 10 minutes.
3. Add the parmesan and the parsley, toss gently, divide everything between plates and serve.

Nutrition: Calories 280 Fat 9.2g Fiber 10.8g Carbs 21.6g Protein 33.8g

290. Butter Chicken Thighs

Preparation Time: 5 minutes

Cooking Time: 30 minutes

Servings: 4

- Ingredients:
- 1 tsp. fennel seeds
- One garlic clove, peeled
- 1 tbsp. butter
- 1 tsp. Coconut oil
- ¼ tsp. Thyme
- ½ tsp. salt
- 1 oz. fennel bulb, chopped
- 1 oz. shallot, chopped
- Four chicken thighs, skinless, boneless
- 1 tsp. ground black pepper

Directions:

1. Rub the chicken thighs with ground black pepper.
2. In the skillet, mix up together butter and coconut oil.
3. Add fennel seeds, garlic clove, thyme, salt, and shallot.
4. Roast the mixture for 1 minute.
5. Then add fennel bulb and chicken thighs.
6. Roast the chicken thighs for 2 minutes from each side over high heat.
7. Then transfer the skillet with chicken in the oven and cook the meal for 20 minutes at 360F.

Nutrition: Calories 324 Fat 14.9g Fiber 0.6g Carbs 2.6g Protein 42.7g

291. Chicken and Olives Salsa

Preparation Time: 10 minutes

Cooking Time: 25 minutes

Servings: 4

Ingredients:

- 2 tbsp. avocado oil
- Four chicken breast halves, skinless and boneless
- Salt and black pepper to the taste
- 1 tbsp. sweet paprika
- One red onion, chopped
- 1 tbsp. balsamic vinegar
- 2 tbsp. parsley, chopped

- One avocado, peeled, pitted, and cubed
- 2 tbsp. black olives, pitted and chopped

Directions:

1. Heat and set your grill over medium-high heat, add the chicken brushed with half of the oil and seasoned with paprika, salt, and pepper, cook for 7 minutes on each side, and divide between plates.
2. Meanwhile, mix the onion with the rest of the ingredients and the remaining oil in a bowl, toss, add on top of the chicken, and serve.

Nutrition: Calories 289 Fat 12.4g Fiber 9.1g Carbs 23.8g Protein 14.3g

292. Chili Chicken Mix

Preparation Time: 10 minutes

Cooking Time: 18 minutes

Servings: 4

Ingredients:

- 2 pounds chicken thighs, skinless and boneless
- 2 tbsp. olive oil
- 2 cups yellow onion, chopped
- 1 tsp. onion powder
- 1 tsp. smoked paprika
- 1 tsp. Chili pepper
- ½ tsp. coriander seeds, ground
- 2 tsp. oregano, dried
- 2 tsp. parsley flakes
- 30 ounces canned tomatoes, chopped
- ½ cup black olives pitted and halved

Directions:

1. Add the oil to a pot, heat it, add the onion, onion powder, and the rest of the ingredients except the tomatoes, olives, and the chicken, stir, and sauté for 10 minutes.
2. Add the chicken, tomatoes, and olives, put the lid on, and cook on high heat.
3. Once the meat is cooked, remove the lid.

4. Split the mix into bowls and serve.

Nutrition: Calories 153 Fat 8 Fiber 2 Carbs 9 Protein 12

293. Duck and Orange Warm Salad

Preparation Time: 10 minutes

Cooking Time: 25 minutes

Servings: 4

Ingredients:

- 2 tbsp. balsamic vinegar
- Two oranges, peeled and cut into segments
- 1 tsp. orange zest, grated
- 1 tbsp. orange juice
- Three shallots, minced
- 2 tbsp. olive oil
- Salt and black pepper to the taste
- Two duck breasts, boneless and skin scored
- 2 cups baby arugula
- 2 tbsp. chives, chopped

Directions:

1. Heat a pan with the oil over medium-high heat, add the duck breasts skin side down, and brown for 5 minutes.
2. Flip the duck, add the shallot and the other ingredients except for the arugula, orange, and chives, and cook for 15 minutes more.
3. Transfer the duck breasts to a cutting board, cool down, cut into strips, and put in a salad bowl.
4. Add the remaining ingredients, toss, and serve warm.

Nutrition: Calories 304 Fat 15.4 Fiber 12.6 Carbs 25.1 Protein 36.4

294. Turmeric Baked Chicken Breast

Preparation Time: 5 minutes

Cooking Time: 40 minutes

Servings: 2

Ingredients:

- 8 oz. chicken breast, skinless, boneless

- 2 tbsp. capers
- 1 tsp. Olive oil
- ½ tsp. Paprika
- ½ tsp. Ground turmeric
- ½ tsp. Salt
- ½ tsp. minced garlic

Directions:

1. Make the lengthwise cut in the chicken breast.
2. Rub the chicken with olive oil, paprika, capers, ground turmeric, salt, and minced garlic.
3. Then fill the chicken cut with capers and secure it with toothpicks.
4. Bake the chicken breast for 40 minutes at 350F.
5. Remove the toothpicks from the chicken breast and slice it.

Nutrition: Calories 156 Fat 5.4 Fiber 0.6 Carbs 1.3 Protein 24.4

295. Chicken Tacos

Preparation Time: 10 minutes

Cooking Time: 20 minutes

Servings: 4

Ingredients:

- Two bread tortillas
- 1 tsp. butter
- 2 tsp. olive oil
- 1 tsp. Taco seasoning
- 6 oz. chicken breast, skinless, boneless, sliced
- 1/3 cup Cheddar cheese, shredded
- One bell pepper, cut on the wedges

Directions:

1. Pour 1 tsp. Of olive oil in the skillet and add chicken.
2. Sprinkle the meat with Taco seasoning and mix up well.
3. Roast chicken for 10 minutes over medium heat. Stir it from time to time.
4. Then transfer the cooked chicken to the plate.
5. Add remaining olive oil to the skillet.
6. Then add bell pepper and roast it for 5 minutes. Stir it all the time.
7. Mix up together bell pepper with chicken.

8. Toss butter in the skillet and melt it.
9. Put one tortilla in the skillet.
10. Put Cheddar cheese on the tortilla and flatten it.
11. Then add a chicken-pepper mixture and cover it with the second tortilla.
12. Roast the quesadilla for 2 minutes from each side.
13. Cut the cooked meal on the halves and transfer it to the serving plates.

Nutrition: Calories 194 Fat 8.3 g Fiber 0.6 g Carbs 16.4g Protein 13.2 g

296. Chicken and Butter Sauce

Preparation Time: 5 minutes

Cooking Time: 30 minutes

Servings: 5

Ingredients:

- 1-pound chicken fillet
- 1/3 cup butter, softened
- 1 tbsp. rosemary
- ½ tsp. thyme
- 1 tsp. salt
- ½ lemon

Directions:

1. Churn together thyme, salt, and rosemary.
2. Chop the chicken fillet roughly and mix it up with churned butter mixture.
3. Place the prepared chicken in the baking dish.
4. Squeeze the lemon over the chicken.
5. Chop the squeezed lemon and add it to the baking dish.
6. Cover the chicken with foil and bake it for 20 minutes at 365F.
7. Then discard the foil and bake the chicken for 10 minutes more.

Nutrition: Calories 285 Fat 19.1 Fiber 0.5 Carbs 1 Protein 26.5

297. Spicy Mustard Chicken

Preparation Time: 32 minutes

Cooking Time: 36 minutes

Servings: 4

Ingredients:

- 4 chicken breasts
- 2 garlic cloves, crushed
- 1/3 cup chicken broth
- 3 tbsp. Dijon mustard
- ½ tsp chili powder

Directions:

1. In a small bowl, mix the mustard, chicken broth, garlic and chili. Marinate the chicken for 30 minutes.
2. Bake in a preheated to 375 F oven for 35 minutes.

Nutrition: 302 calories 18g fat 49g protein

298. Walnut and Oregano Crusted Chicken

Preparation Time: 36 minutes

Cooking Time: 13 minutes

Servings: 4

Ingredients:

- 4 skinless, boneless chicken breasts
- 10-12 fresh oregano leaves
- 1/2 cup walnuts, chopped
- 2 garlic cloves, chopped
- 2 eggs, beaten

Directions:

1. Blend the garlic, oregano, and walnuts in a food processor until a rough crumb is formed. Place this mixture on a plate.
2. Whisk eggs in a deep bowl. Soak each chicken breast in the beaten egg, then roll it in the walnut mixture. Place coated chicken on a baking tray and bake at 375 F for 13 minutes on each side.

Nutrition: 304 calories 54g fat 14g protein

299. Coriander and Coconut Chicken

Preparation Time: 10 minutes

Cooking Time: 30 minutes

Servings: 4

Ingredients:

- 2 pounds chicken thighs, skinless, boneless, and cubed
- 2 tbsp. olive oil

- Salt and black pepper to the taste
- 3 tbsp. coconut flesh, shredded
- One and ½ tsp. orange extract
- 1 tbsp. ginger, grated
- ¼ cup orange juice
- 2 tbsp. coriander, chopped
- 1 cup chicken stock
- ¼ tsp. red pepper flakes

Directions:

1. Heat a pan with the oil over medium-high heat, add the chicken, and brown for 4 minutes on each side.
2. Add salt, pepper, and the rest of the ingredients, bring to a simmer and cook over medium heat for 20 minutes.
3. Divide the mix between plates and serve hot.

Nutrition: Calories 297, Fat 14.4g Fiber 9.6g Carbs 22g Protein 25g

300. Chicken Pilaf

Preparation Time: 10 minutes

Cooking Time: 30 minutes

Servings: 4

Ingredients:

- 4 tbsp. avocado oil
- 2 pounds chicken breasts, skinless, boneless, and cubed
- ½ cup yellow onion, chopped
- Four garlic cloves, minced
- 8 ounces brown rice
- 4 cups chicken stock
- ½ cup kalamata olives pitted
- ½ cup tomatoes, cubed
- 6 ounces baby spinach
- ½ cup feta cheese, crumbled
- A pinch of salt and black pepper
- 1 tbsp. marjoram, chopped
- 1 tbsp. basil, chopped
- Juice of ½ lemon
- ¼ cup pine nuts, toasted

Directions:

1. Heat a pot with 1 tbsp. Avocado oil set over medium-high heat, add the chicken, salt, and pepper, brown for 5 minutes on each side, and transfer to a bowl.
2. Heat the pot again with the rest of the avocado oil over medium

heat, add the onion and garlic and sauté for 3 minutes.
3. Add the rice, the rest of the ingredients except the pine nuts, return the chicken, toss, bring it to a simmer and cook over medium heat for 20 minutes.
4. Divide the mix between plates, top each serving with some pine nuts and serve.

Nutrition: Calories 283 Fat 12.5g Fiber 8.2g Carbs 21.5 g Protein 13.4 g

301. Chicken and Black Beans

Preparation Time: 10 minutes

Cooking Time: 20 minutes

Servings: 4

Ingredients:

- 12 oz. chicken breast, skinless, boneless, chopped
- 1 tbsp. taco seasoning
- 1 tbsp. nut oil
- ½ tsp. cayenne pepper
- ½ tsp. salt
- ½ tsp. garlic, chopped
- ½ red onion, sliced
- 1/3 cup black beans, canned, rinsed
- ½ cup Mozzarella, shredded

Directions:

1. Rub the chopped chicken breast with taco seasoning, salt, and cayenne pepper.
2. Place the chicken in the skillet, add nut oil and roast it for 10 minutes over medium heat. Mix up the chicken pieces from time to time to avoid burning.
3. After this, transfer the chicken to the plate.
4. Add sliced onion and then garlic to the skillet. Roast the vegetables for 5 minutes. Stir them constantly. Then add black beans and stir well—Cook the ingredients for 2 minutes more.
5. Add the chopped chicken and mix up well. Top the meal with Mozzarella cheese.
6. Close the lid and cook the meal for 3 minutes.

Nutrition: Calories 209 Fat 6.4 Fiber 2.8 Carbs 13.7, 22.7

302. Coconut Chicken

Preparation Time: 10 minutes

Cooking Time: 5 minutes

Servings: 4

Ingredients:

- 6 oz. chicken fillet
- ¼ cup of sparkling water
- One egg
- 3 tbsp. coconut flakes
- 1 tbsp. coconut oil
- 1 tsp. Greek Seasoning

Directions:

1. Cut the chicken fillet into small pieces (nuggets).
2. Then crack the egg in the bowl and whisk it.
3. Mix up together egg and sparkling water.
4. Add Greek seasoning and stir gently.
5. Dip the chicken nuggets in the egg mixture and then coat in the coconut flakes.
6. Melt the coconut oil in the skillet and heat it until it is shimmering.
7. Then add prepared chicken nuggets.
8. Roast them for 1 minute from each or until they are light brown.
9. Dry the cooked chicken nuggets with the paper towels help and transfer them to the serving plates.

Nutrition: Calories 141 Fat 8.9 Fiber 0.3 Carbs 1 Protein 13.9

303. Ginger Chicken Drumsticks

Preparation Time: 10 minutes

Cooking Time: 30 minutes

Servings: 4

Ingredients:

Four chicken drumsticks

- One apple, grated
- 1 tbsp. curry paste
- 4 tbsp. milk
- 1 tsp. coconut oil
- 1 tsp. chili flakes

- ½ tsp. minced ginger

Directions:

1. Mix up together grated apple, curry paste, milk, chili flakes, and minced garlic.
2. Put coconut oil in the skillet and melt it.
3. Add apple mixture and stir well.
4. Then add chicken drumsticks and mix up well.
5. Roast the chicken for 2 minutes from each side.
6. Then preheat the oven to 360F.
7. Place the skillet with chicken drumsticks in the oven and bake for 25 minutes.

Nutrition: Calories 150 Fat 6.4g Fiber 1.4g Carbs 9.7g Protein 13.5 g

304. Parmesan Chicken

Preparation Time: 10 minutes

Cooking Time: 30 minutes

Servings: 3

Ingredients:

- 1-pound chicken breast, skinless, boneless
- 2 oz. Parmesan, grated
- 1 tsp. Dried oregano
- ½ tsp. dried cilantro
- 1 tbsp. Panko bread crumbs
- One egg, beaten
- 1 tsp. turmeric

Directions:

1. Cut the chicken breast into three servings.
2. Then combine Parmesan, oregano, cilantro, bread crumbs, and turmeric.
3. Dip the chicken servings in the beaten egg carefully.
4. Then coat every chicken piece in the cheese-bread crumbs mixture.
5. Line the baking tray using baking paper.
6. Arrange the chicken pieces in the tray.
7. Bake the chicken for 30 minutes at 365F.

Nutrition: Calories 267 Fat 9.5 Fiber 0.5 Carbs 3.2 Protein 40.4

305. Grilled Chicken With Lemon And Fennel

Preparation Time: 25 minutes

Cooking Time: 25 minutes

Servings: 4

Ingredients:

- 2 cups chicken fillets
- 1 large fennel bulb
- 2 garlic cloves
- 1 jar green olives
- 1 lemon

Directions:

1. Pre-heat your grill to medium-high
2. Crush garlic cloves
3. Take a bowl and add olive oil and season with salt and pepper
4. Coat chicken skewers with the marinade
5. Transfer them under grill and grill for 20 minutes, making sure to turn them halfway through until golden
6. Zest half of the lemon and cut the other half into quarters
7. Cut the fennel bulb into similarly sized segments
8. Brush olive oil all over the garlic clove segments and cook for 3-5 minutes
9. Chop them and add them to the bowl with the marinade
10. Add lemon zest and olives
11. Once the meat is read, serve with the vegetable mix

Nutrition: 649 Calories 16g Fat 33g Carbohydrates

306. Chicken and Onion Casserole

Preparation Time: 16 minutes

Cooking Time: 47 minutes

Servings: 4

Ingredients:

- 4 chicken breasts
- 4-5 large onions, sliced
- 2 leeks, cut
- 4 tbsp. extra virgin olive oil
- 1 tsp thyme

Directions:

1. Cook olive oil in a large, deep frying pan over medium-high heat. Brown chicken, turning, for 2-3 minutes on each side or until golden. Set aside in a casserole dish.
2. Cut the onions and leeks and add them on and around the chicken; add in olives, thyme, salt and black pepper to taste. Cover it using aluminum foil and bake at 375 F for 35 minutes, or until the chicken is cooked through. Open then situate back to the oven for 6 minutes.

Nutrition: 309 calories 59g fat 18g protein

307. Slow-Cooked Pot Roast

Preparation Time: 1 hour

Cooking Time: 9 hours

Servings: 4

Ingredients:

- 2 lb. pot roast
- 1-2 garlic cloves, crushed
- 3 small onions, finely cut
- 1/2 cup chicken broth
- 1 tbsp. Italian seasoning

Directions:

1. Spray the slow cooker with nonstick spray.
2. Place the roast in the slow cooker.
3. In a bowl, incorporate chicken broth, garlic, onions and Italian seasoning. Spread this sauce over the meat.
4. Cover and cook on low for 9 hours.

Nutrition: 315 calories 50g fat 19g protein

308. Chicken Quesadilla

Preparation Time: 5 minutes

Cooking Time: 5 minutes

Servings: 2

Ingredients:

- low-carbohydrate tortillas
- ½ cup shredded Mexican blend cheese
- 2 ounces shredded chicken

- 1 teaspoon Tajin seasoning salt
- 2 tablespoons sour cream

Direction

1. In a big skillet at medium-high heat, cook olive oil. Add a tortilla, then layer on top ¼ cup of cheese, the chicken, the Tajin seasoning, and the remaining ¼ cup of cheese. Top with the second tortilla.
2. Peek under the edge of the bottom tortilla to monitor how it is browning. Once the bottom tortilla gets golden and the cheese begins to melt, after about 2 minutes, flip the quesadilla over. The second side will cook faster, about 1 minute.
3. Once the second tortilla is crispy and golden, transfer the quesadilla to a cutting board and let sit for 2 minutes. Cut the quesadilla into 4 wedges using a pizza cutter or chef's knife.
4. Transfer half the quesadilla to each of the two plates. Pour 1 tablespoon of sour cream into each dish, and serve hot.

Nutrition: 414 Calories 28g Fat 17g Fiber

309. Quinoa Chicken Fingers

Preparation Time: 10 minutes

Cooking Time: 10 minutes

Servings: 6

- **Ingredients:**
- 2 lbs./900 g. sliced chicken breasts
- 2 egg whites
- 1 ½ c. quinoa, cooked
- ½ c. breadcrumbs
- 2 tbsps. olive oil
- Salt, black pepper, paprika

Directions:

1. Season chicken with salt, pepper, and paprika.
2. Dip the chicken in the broken egg mix, then coat with quinoa and breadcrumbs.
3. Cook the chicken in oil for 5 minutes on each side.

Nutritional: Calories 770 Total Fat 44g Sat. fat 6g Carbs 55g Fiber 6g Sugar 2g Protein 38g Sodium 545mg

310. Garlic-Parmesan Chicken Wings

Preparation Time: 10 minutes

Cooking Time: 3 hours

Servings: 2

Ingredients:

- 8 tablespoons (1 stick) butter
- 2 garlic cloves, minced
- 1 tablespoon dried Italian seasoning
- ¼ cup grated Parmesan cheese, plus ½ cup
- 1-pound chicken wings

Directions:

1. With the crock insert in place, preheat the slow cooker to high—cover baking sheet with a silicone baking mat.
2. Put the butter, garlic, Italian seasoning, and ¼ cup of Parmesan cheese in the slow cooker and season with pink Himalayan salt and pepper. Heat the butter, and stir the ingredients until well mixed.
3. Add the chicken wings and stir until coated with the butter mixture.
4. Cover the slow cooker and cook for 2 hours and 45 minutes.
5. Preheat the broiler.
6. Transfer the wings to the prepared baking sheet, sprinkle the remaining ½ cup of Parmesan cheese over the wings, and cook under the broiler until crispy, about 5 minutes.
7. Serve hot.

Nutrition: 738 Calories 66g Fat 39g Protein

311. Chicken Breasts With Stuffing

Preparation Time: 15 minutes

Cooking Time: 37 minutes

Servings: 8

Ingredients:

- ¼ cup crumbled feta cheese

- 1 large bell pepper, halved and seeded
- 1 tbsp minced fresh basil
- 2 tbsp finely chopped, pitted Kalamata olives
- 8 pcs of 6-oz boneless and skinless chicken breasts

Directions:

1. In a greased baking sheet, place bell pepper with the skin facing up and pop into a preheated broiler on high. Broil until blackened around 15 minutes. Remove from broiler and place right away into a re-sealable bag, seal, and leave for 15 minutes.
2. After, peel bell pepper and mince—Preheat grill to medium-high fire.
3. In a medium bowl, mix well basil, olives, cheese and bell pepper.
4. Form a pocket on each chicken breast by creating a slit through the thickest portion; add 2 tbsp bell pepper mixture and seal with a wooden pick. (At this point, you can stop and freeze chicken and just thaw when needed for grilling already)
5. Season chicken breasts with pepper and salt.
6. Grill for six minutes per side, remove from grill, cover loosely with foil, and let stand for 10 minutes before serving.

Nutrition: Calories per **Servings:** 201.1; Carbs: 1.8g; Protein: 35.2g; Fat: 5.9g

312. Turkey Sausage, Fresh Herbs & Feta

Preparation Time: 20 minutes

Cooking Time: 40 minutes

Servings: 6

Ingredients:

- 1 onion, sliced thinly
- 1 smoked turkey sausage, sliced into rounds
- 1 cup white rice
- 4 tablespoons fresh herbs, chopped (parsley, basil)
- 4 oz. feta cheese, crumbled

Directions:

1. Add 1 tablespoon olive oil to the pot.
2. Cook the onion and sausage for 5 minutes.
3. Season with a bit of salt and pepper.
4. Add the rice and stir.
5. Add 2 cups chicken stock.
6. Stir well.
7. Seal the pot.
8. Once cooked, remove the lid.
9. Serve.
10. Add the herbs and top with the feta cheese.

Nutrition: Calories 179 ;Total Fat 4.9g ;Saturated Fat 3.1g ;Cholesterol 19mg ;Sodium 230mg ;Total Carbohydrate 27.6g ;Dietary Fiber 1.1g ;Total Sugars 1.6g ;Protein 5.6g ;Potassium 108mg

313. Chicken With Spanish Rice

Preparation Time: 15 minutes

Cooking Time: 40 minutes

Servings: 12

Ingredients:

- 6 chicken breast fillets, sliced into cubes
- 4 cloves garlic, minced
- 1 onion, chopped
- 4 cups brown rice
- 28 oz. canned diced tomatoes with green chili

Directions:

1. Season the chicken with salt and pepper.
2. Pour 1 tablespoon of oil into the pot.
3. Saute and brown the chicken and set aside.
4. Add the garlic, onion and rice.
5. Cook for 2 minutes.
6. Add the canned tomatoes with green chili and 4 ½ cups of water.
7. Seal the pot.
8. Once the meat is cooked, remove the lid.
9. Serve.
10. Fluff the rice and top with the chicken.

Nutrition: Calories 383 ;Total Fat 7.2g ;Saturated Fat 1.8g ;Cholesterol 65mg ;Sodium 331mg ;Total Carbohydrate 51.8g ;Dietary Fiber 2.4g ;Total Sugars 0.4g ;Protein 26.5g ;Potassium 435mg

314. Italian Chicken

Preparation Time: 10 minutes

Cooking Time: 30 minutes

Servings: 6

Ingredients:

- 1 carrot, chopped
- 1/2 lb. mushrooms
- 8 chicken thighs
- 1 cup tomato sauce
- 3 cloves garlic, crushed

Directions:

1. Season the chicken with salt and pepper.
2. Cover and marinate for 30 minutes.
3. Add 1 tablespoon of ghee to a pot.
4. Cook the carrots and mushrooms until soft.
5. Add the tomato sauce and garlic.
6. Add the chicken, tomatoes and olives.
7. Cook and mix well.
8. Seal the pot.
9. Once the meat is cooked, remove the lid.
10. Serve.

Nutrition: Calories 425 ;Total Fat 16.9g ;Saturated Fat 5.3g ;Cholesterol 179mg ;Sodium 395mg ;Total Carbohydrate 7.5g ;Dietary Fiber 2.1g ;Total Sugars 4.5g ;Protein 58.9g ;Potassium 929mg

315. Turkey Meatloaf

Preparation Time: 15 minutes

Cooking Time: 50 minutes

Servings: 6

Ingredients:

- 1/2 cup bread crumbs
- 1/4 cup onion, chopped
- 1 lb. lean ground turkey
- 1/4 cup sun-dried tomatoes, diced
- 1/2 cup feta cheese, crumbled

Directions:

1. Mix all the ingredients in a bowl.
2. Form a loaf and cover with foil.
3. Pour 1 cup of water into the pot.
4. Add the steamer basket inside.
5. Place the wrapped turkey mixture on top of the basket.
6. Cover the pot.
7. Once the meat is cooked, remove the cover.
8. Serve.

Nutrition: Calories 226 ;Total Fat 11g ;Saturated Fat 4.5g ;Cholesterol 78mg ;Sodium 330mg ;Total Carbohydrate 10.2g ;Dietary Fiber 0.9g ;Total Sugars 1.5g ;Protein 21.7g ;Potassium 424mg

316. Chicken And Tzaziki Pitas

Preparation Time: 10 minutes

Cooking Time: 0 minutes

Servings: 8

Ingredients:

- 4 pita bread
- 10 oz chicken fillet, grilled
- 1 cup lettuce, chopped
- 8 teaspoons tzatziki sauce

Directions:

1. Cut every pita bread on the halves to get 8 pita pockets.
2. Then fill every pita pocket with chopped lettuce and sprinkle greens with tzatziki sauce.
3. Chop chicken fillet and add it in the pita pockets too.

Nutrition: calories 106, fat 3.8, fiber 0.2, carbs 6.1, protein 11

317. Lime Chicken With Black Beans

Preparation Time: 15 minutes

Cooking Time: 30 minutes

Servings: 8

Ingredients:

- 8 chicken thighs (boneless and skinless)
- 3 tablespoons lime juice
- 1 cup black beans
- 1 cup canned tomatoes
- 4 teaspoons garlic powder

Directions:

1. Marinate the chicken in a mixture of lime juice and garlic powder.
2. Add the chicken to the pot.
3. Pour the tomatoes on top of the chicken.
4. Seal the pot.
5. Cook at high heat for 10 minutes.
6. Stir in the black beans.
7. Simmer until black beans are cooked.

Nutrition: Calories 370 ;Total Fat 11.2g ;Saturated Fat 3.1g ;Cholesterol 130mg ;Sodium 128mg ;Total Carbohydrate 17.5g ;Dietary Fiber 4.1g ;Total Sugars 1.5g ;Protein 47.9g ;Potassium 790mg

318. Lemon Chicken Mix

Preparation Time: 10 minutes

Cooking Time: 10 minutes

Servings: 2

Ingredients:

- 8 oz chicken breast, skinless, boneless
- 1 teaspoon Cajun seasoning
- 1 teaspoon balsamic vinegar
- 1 teaspoon olive oil
- 1 teaspoon lemon juice

Directions:

1. Cut the chicken breast on the halves and sprinkle with Cajun seasoning.
2. Then sprinkle the poultry with olive oil and lemon juice.
3. Then sprinkle the chicken breast with balsamic vinegar.
4. Preheat the grill to 385F.
5. Grill the chicken breast halves for 5 minutes from each side.
6. Slice Cajun chicken and place it on the serving plate.

Nutrition: calories 150, fat 5.2, fiber 0, carbs 0.1, protein 24.1

319. Chicken Shawarma

Preparation Time: 15 minutes

Cooking Time: 30 minutes

Servings: 8

Ingredients:

- 2 lb. chicken breast, sliced into strips
- 1 teaspoon paprika
- 1 teaspoon ground cumin
- 1/4 teaspoon granulated garlic
- 1/2 teaspoon turmeric
- 1/4 teaspoon ground allspice

Directions:

1. Season the chicken with spices and a little salt and pepper.
2. Pour 1 cup chicken broth into the pot.
3. Cover the pot.
4. Cook for 15 minutes.
5. Once the meat is cooked, remove the lid.
6. Serve.

Nutrition: Calories 132 ;Total Fat 3g ;Saturated Fat 0g ;Cholesterol 73mg ;Sodium 58mg ;Total Carbohydrate 0.5g ;Dietary Fiber 0.2g ;Total Sugars 0.1g ;Protein 24.2g ;Potassium 435mg

320. Braised Chicken Thighs with Kalamata Olives

Preparation Time: 10 minutes

Cooking Time: 40 minutes

Servings: 4

Ingredients:

- 4 chicken thighs, skin on
- 2 tablespoons ghee
- ½ cup chicken broth
- lemon, ½ sliced and ½ juiced
- ½ cup pitted Kalamata olives

Directions:

1. Preheat the oven to 375 degrees F.
2. Dry the chicken thighs using paper towels, and season with pink Himalayan salt and pepper.
3. In a medium oven-safe skillet or high-sided baking dish over medium-high heat, melt the ghee. When the ghee has melted and is hot, add the chicken thighs, skin-side

down, and leave them for 8 minutes.

4. Cook the other side for 2 minutes. Around the chicken thighs, pour in the chicken broth, and add the lemon slices, lemon juice, and olives.
5. Bake for 30 minutes. Add the butter to the broth mixture.
6. Divide the chicken and olives between two plates and serve.

Nutrition: 567 Calories 47g Fat 33g Protein

321. Buttery Garlic Chicken

Preparation Time: 5 minutes

Cooking Time: 40 minutes

Servings: 2

Ingredients:

- 2 tablespoons ghee, melted
- 2 boneless skinless chicken breasts
- tablespoon dried Italian seasoning
- 4 tablespoons butter
- ¼ cup grated Parmesan cheese

Directions:

1. Preheat the oven to 375°F. Select a baking dish that fits both chicken breasts and coat it with ghee.
2. Pat-dry the chicken breasts. Season with pink Himalayan salt, pepper, and Italian seasoning. Place the chicken in the baking dish.
3. Using medium skillet at medium heat, melt the butter. Sauté minced garlic for about 5 minutes.
4. Remove the butter-garlic mixture from the heat, and pour it over the chicken breasts.
5. Roast in the oven for 30 to 35 minutes. Sprinkle some of the Parmesan cheese on top of each chicken breast. Let the chicken rest in the baking dish for 5 minutes.
6. Divide the chicken between two plates, spoon the butter sauce over the chicken, and serve.

Nutrition: 642 Calories 45g Fat 57g Protein

322. Honey Almond Chicken Tenders

Preparation Time: 10 minutes.

Cooking Time: 20 minutes

Servings: 4.

Ingredients:

- 1 Tablespoon Honey, Raw.
- 1 Tablespoon Dijon Mustard.
- 1 Cup Almonds.
- Sea Salt & Black Pepper to Taste.
- 1 Lb. Chicken Breast Tenders, Boneless & Skinless.

Directions:

1. Set oven to 425F, and then get out a baking sheet. Wrap it with parchment paper, and then put a cooking rack on it. Spray your cooling rack down with nonstick cooking spray.
2. Get out a bowl and combine your mustard and honey. Season with salt and pepper, and then add in your chicken. Make sure it's well coated and place it to the side.
3. Use a knife and chop your almonds. You can also use a food processor. You want them to be the same size as sunflower seeds roughly. Press your chicken into the almonds, and then lay it on your cooking rack.
4. Bake for fifteen to twenty minutes. Your chicken should be cooked all the way through.

Nutrition: Calories: 263. Protein: 31g Fat: 12g

323. Chicken and Mushrooms

Preparation Time: 20 minutes

Cooking Time: 7 minutes

Servings: 4

Ingredients:

- 4 chicken breasts, diced
- 2 lbs. mushrooms, chopped
- onion, chopped
- 4 tbsp. extra virgin olive oil
- salt and black, pepper to taste

Directions:

1. Heat olive oil in a deep-frying pan over medium-high heat. Brown chicken, stirring, for 2 minutes on each side, or until golden. Add the chopped onion, mushrooms, salt and black pepper, and stir to combine. Adjust heat, cover and simmer for 30 minutes. Uncover and simmer for 5 more minutes.

Nutrition: 290 calories 49g fat 9g protein

324. Blue Cheese and Mushroom Chicken

Preparation Time: 25 minutes

Cooking Time: 18 minutes

Servings: 4

Ingredients:

- 4 chicken breast halves
- 1 cup crumbled blue cheese
- 1 cup sour cream
- salt and black pepper, to taste
- 1/2 cup parsley, finely cut

Directions:

2. Prep the oven to 350 degrees F. Grease a casserole with nonstick spray. Place all ingredients into it, turn chicken to coat.
3. Bake for 22 minutes. Sprinkle with parsley and serve.

Nutrition: 287 calories 46g fat 10g protein

325. Lemon Chicken

Preparation Time: 10 minutes

Cooking Time: 20 minutes

Servings: 4

Ingredients:

- 1-pound chicken breast, skinless, boneless
- 3 tablespoons lemon juice
- 1 tablespoon olive oil
- 1 teaspoon ground black pepper

Directions:

1. Cut the chicken breast into 4 pieces.

2. Sprinkle every chicken piece with olive oil, lemon juice, and ground black pepper.
3. Then place them in the skillet.
4. Roast the chicken for 20 minutes over medium heat.
5. Flip the chicken pieces every 5 minutes.

Nutrition: calories 163, fat 6.5, fiber 0.2, carbs 0.6, protein 24.2

326. Greek Chicken Bites

Preparation Time: 10 minutes

Cooking Time: 20 minutes

Servings: 6

Ingredients:

- 1-pound chicken fillet
- 1 tablespoon Greek seasoning
- 1 teaspoon sesame oil
- ½ teaspoon salt
- 1 teaspoon balsamic vinegar

Directions:

1. Cut the chicken fingers on small tenders (fingers) and sprinkle them with Greek seasoning, salt, and balsamic vinegar. Mix up well with the help of the fingertips.
2. Then sprinkle chicken with sesame oil and shake gently.
3. Line the baking tray with parchment.
4. Place the marinated chicken fingers in the tray in one layer.
5. Bake the chicken fingers for 20 minutes at 355F. Flip them on another side after 10 minutes of cooking.

Nutrition: calories 154, fat 6.4, fiber 0, carbs 0.8, protein 22

327. Turkey Verde With Brown Rice

Preparation Time: 15 minutes

Cooking Time: 30 minutes

Servings: 5

Ingredients:

- 2/3 cup chicken broth
- 1 1/4 cup brown rice
- 1 1/2 lb. turkey tenderloins
- 1 onion, sliced
- 1/2 cup salsa verde

Directions:

1. Add the chicken broth and rice to the Pot.
2. Top with the turkey, onion and salsa.
3. Cover the pot.
4. Once the meat is cooked, remove the lid.
5. Serve.

Nutrition: Calories 336 ;Total Fat 3.3g ;Saturated Fat 0.3g ;Cholesterol 54mg ;Sodium 321mg ;Total Carbohydrate 39.4g ;Dietary Fiber 2.2g ;Total Sugars 1.4g ;Protein 38.5g ;Potassium 187mg

328. Lemon Garlic Chicken

Preparation Time: 30 minutes

Cooking Time: 1 Hour And 20 minutes

Servings: 6

Ingredients:

- 6 chicken breast fillets
- 3 tablespoons olive oil
- 1 tablespoon lemon juice
- 3 cloves garlic, crushed and minced
- 2 teaspoon dried parsley

Directions:

1. Marinate the chicken breast fillets in a mixture of olive oil, lemon juice, garlic, parsley, and a pinch of salt and pepper.
2. Let sit for 1 hour covered in the refrigerator.
3. Pour in the vegetable oil in a pan. Heat then put the chicken.
4. Cook, the chicken for 5 minutes per side or until fully cooked.

Nutrition: Calories 341 ;Total Fat 17.9g ;Saturated Fat 4g ;Cholesterol 130mg ;Sodium 127mg ;Total Carbohydrate 0.7g ;Dietary Fiber 0.1g ;Total Sugars 0.1g ;Protein 42.4g ;Potassium 368mg

329. Turkey With Basil & Tomatoes

Preparation Time: 10 minutes

Cooking Time: 20 minutes

Servings: 4

Ingredients:

- 4 turkey breast fillets
- 1 tablespoon olive oil

- 1/4 cup fresh basil, chopped
- 1 1/2 cups cherry tomatoes, sliced in half
- 1/4 cup olive tapenade

Directions:

1. Season the turkey fillets with salt.
2. Add the olive oil to the pot and heat it.
3. Cook the turkey until brown on both sides.
4. Stir in the basil, tomatoes and olive tapenade.
5. Cook for 3 minutes, stirring frequently.

Nutrition: Calories 188 ;Total Fat 5.1g ;Saturated Fat 1g ;Cholesterol 0mg ;Sodium 3mg ;Total Carbohydrate 2.8g ;Dietary Fiber 1.6g ;Total Sugars 1.9g ;Protein 33.2g ;Potassium 164mg

330. Honey Balsamic Chicken

Preparation time 20 minutes

Cooking Time: 1 Hour

Servings: 10

Ingredients:

- 1/4 cup honey
- 1/2 cup balsamic vinegar
- 1/4 cup soy sauce
- 2 cloves garlic minced
- 10 chicken drumsticks

Directions:

1. Mix the honey, vinegar, soy sauce and garlic in a bowl.
2. Marinate the chicken in the sauce for 30 minutes.
3. Cover the pot.
4. Set it to manual.
5. Cook at high pressure for 10 minutes.
6. Release the pressure quickly.
7. Choose the sauté button to thicken the sauce.

Nutrition: Calories 184 ;Total Fat 4.4g ;Saturated Fat 1.2g ;Cholesterol 67mg ;Sodium 662mg ;Total Carbohydrate 13g ;Dietary Fiber 0.1g ;Total Sugars 11.9g ;Protein 21.9g ;Potassium 202mg

331. Mediterranean Chicken

Preparation Time: 10 minutes

Cooking Time: 20 minutes

Servings: 6

Ingredients:

- 2 lb. chicken breast fillet, sliced into strips
- Wine mixture (1/4 cup white wine mixed with 3 tablespoons red wine)
- 2 tablespoons light brown sugar
- 1 1/2 teaspoons dried oregano
- 6 garlic cloves, chopped

Directions:

1. Pour the wine mixture into the pot.
2. Stir in the rest of the ingredients.
3. Toss the chicken to coat evenly.
4. Seal the pot.
5. Put under high heat.
6. Cook for 10 minutes.
7. Serve.

Nutrition: Calories 304 ;Total Fat 11.3g ;Saturated Fat 3.1g ;Cholesterol 135mg ;Sodium 131mg ;Total Carbohydrate 4.2g ;Dietary Fiber 0.2g ;Total Sugars 3g ;Protein 44g ;Potassium 390mg

332. Turkey Lasagna

Preparation Time: 15 minutes

Cooking Time: 30 minutes

Servings: 4

Ingredients:

- 4 tortillas
- 1 1/4 cup salsa
- 1/2 can refried beans
- 1 1/2 cups cooked turkey
- 1 1/4 cup cheddar cheese, shredded

Directions:

1. Spray a small pan with oil.
2. Spread the refried beans on each tortilla.
3. Place the first tortilla inside the pan.
4. Add layers of the turkey, salsa and cheese.

5. Place another tortilla and repeat the layers.
6. Pour 1 cup of water into the pot.
7. Place the layers on top of a steamer basket.
8. Place the basket inside the Pot.
9. Once the meat is cooked, remove the lid.
10. Serve.

Nutrition: Calories 335 ;Total Fat 15.5g ;Saturated Fat 8.6g ;Cholesterol 79mg ;Sodium 849mg ;Total Carbohydrate 21.1g ;Dietary Fiber 4.5g ;Total Sugars 3g ;Protein 28.5g ;Potassium 561mg

333. Whole Roasted Chicken

Preparation Time: 10 minutes

Cooking Time: 8 hours on low

Servings: 6

Ingredients:

- 1 whole chicken (approximately 5.5 pounds)
- 4 garlic cloves
- 6 small onions
- 1 Tablespoon olive oil for rubbing
- 2 teaspoons salt
- 2 teaspoons sweet paprika
- 1 teaspoon Cayenne pepper
- 1 teaspoon onion powder
- 1 teaspoon ground thyme
- 2 teaspoons fresh ground black pepper
- 4 Tablespoons butter, cut into cubes

Directions:

1. Mix all dry ingredients well.
2. Stuff the chicken belly with garlic and onions.
3. On the bottom of the pot, place four balls of aluminum foil.
4. Set the chicken on top of the balls. Rub it generously with olive oil.
5. Cover the chicken with seasoning, drop in butter pieces.
6. Cover, cook on low heat for 8 hours.

Nutrition per serving: net Carb 6g; Protein 15g; Fat 40g

334. Turkey and Cranberry Sauce

Preparation Time: 10 minutes

Cooking Time: 50 minutes

Servings: 4

Ingredients

- 1 cup chicken stock
- 2 tablespoons avocado oil
- ½ cup cranberry sauce
- 1 big turkey breast, skinless, boneless, and sliced
- 1 yellow onion, roughly chopped
- Salt and black pepper to the taste

Directions

1. Heat a pan with the avocado oil over medium-high heat, add the onion and sauté for 5 minutes.
2. Add the turkey and brown for 5 minutes more.
3. Add the rest of the ingredients, toss, introduce in the oven at 350 degrees F and cook for 40 minutes

Nutrition: Calories 382, Fat 12.6, Fiber 9.6, Carbs 26.6, Protein 17.6

335. Sage Turkey Mix

Preparation Time: 10 minutes

Cooking Time: 40 minutes

Servings: 4

Ingredients

- 1 big turkey breast, skinless, boneless, and roughly cubed
- Juice of 1 lemon
- 2 tablespoons avocado oil
- 1 red onion, chopped
- 2 tablespoons sage, chopped
- 1 garlic clove, minced
- 1 cup chicken stock

Directions

1. Heat a pan with the avocado oil over medium-high heat, add the turkey, and brown for 3 minutes on each side.
2. Add the rest of the ingredients, bring to a simmer and cook over medium heat for 35 minutes.
3. Divide the mix between plates and serve with a side dish.

Nutrition: Calories 382, Fat 12.6, Fiber 9.6, Carbs 16.6, Protein 33.2

336. Turkey and Asparagus Mix

Preparation Time: 10 minutes

Cooking Time: 30 minutes

Servings: 4

Ingredients

- 1 bunch asparagus, trimmed and halved
- 1 big turkey breast, skinless, boneless and cut into strips
- 1 teaspoon basil, dried
- 2 tablespoons olive oil
- A pinch of salt and black pepper
- ½ cup tomato sauce
- 1 tablespoon chives, chopped

Directions

1. Heat a pan with the oil over medium-high heat, add the turkey, and brown for 4 minutes.
2. Add the asparagus and the rest of the ingredients except the chives, bring to a simmer and cook over medium heat for 25 minutes.
3. Add the chives, divide the mix between plates, and serve.

Nutrition: Calories 337, Fat 21.2, Fiber 10.2, Carbs 21.4, Protein 17.6

337. Herbed Almond Turkey

Preparation Time: 10 minutes

Cooking Time: 40 minutes

Servings: 4

Ingredients

- 1 big turkey breast, skinless, boneless, and cubed
- 1 tablespoon olive oil
- ½ cup chicken stock
- 1 tablespoon basil, chopped
- 1 tablespoon rosemary, chopped
- 1 tablespoon oregano, chopped
- 1 tablespoon parsley, chopped
- 3 garlic cloves, minced
- ½ cup almonds, toasted and chopped
- 3 cups tomatoes, chopped

Directions

1. Heat up a pan with the oil over medium-high heat, add the turkey and the garlic, and brown for 5 minutes.
2. Add the stock and the rest of the ingredients, bring to a simmer over medium heat and cook for 35 minutes.
3. Divide the mix between plates and serve.

Nutrition: Calories 297, Fat 11.2, Fiber 9.2, Carbs 19.4, Protein 23.6

338. Yogurt Chicken Breasts

Preparation Time: 10 minutes

Cooking Time: 10 minutes

Servings: 4

Ingredients:

Yogurt Sauce:

- ½ cup plain Greek yogurt
- 2 tablespoons water
- Pinch saffron (3 or 4 threads)
- 3 garlic cloves, minced
- ½ onion, chopped
- 2 tablespoons chopped fresh cilantro
- Juice of ½ lemon
- ½ teaspoon salt
- 1 pound (454 g) boneless, skinless chicken breasts, cut into 2-inch strips
- 1 tablespoon extra-virgin olive oil

Directions:

1. Make the yogurt sauce: Place the yogurt, water, saffron, garlic, onion, cilantro, lemon juice, and salt in a blender, and pulse until thoroughly mixed.
2. Transfer the yogurt sauce to a large bowl, along with the chicken strips. Toss to coat well.
3. Cover with plastic wrap and marinate in the refrigerator for at least 1 hour, or up to overnight.
4. When ready to cook, heat the olive oil in a large skillet over medium heat.
5. Add the chicken strips to the skillet, discarding any excess

marinade. Cook each side for 5 minutes or until cooked through.
6. Let the chicken cool for 5 minutes before serving.

Tips: If the saffron isn't available, you can use ½ teaspoon of turmeric to replace it. To make this a complete meal, serve it with your favorite salad or cooked brown rice.

Nutrition: calories: 154 fat: 4.8g protein: 26.3g carbs: 2.9g fiber: 0g sodium: 500mg

339. Coconut Chicken Tenders

Preparation Time: 10 minutes

Cooking Time: 15 to 20 minutes

Servings: 6

Ingredients:

- 4 chicken breasts, each cut lengthwise into 3 strips
- ½ teaspoon salt
- ¼ teaspoon freshly ground black pepper
- ½ cup coconut flour
- 2 eggs
- 2 tablespoons unsweetened plain almond milk
- 1 cup unsweetened coconut flakes

Directions:

1. Preheat the oven to 400ºF (205ºC). Line a baking sheet with parchment paper.
2. On a clean work surface, season the chicken with salt and pepper.
3. In a small bowl, add the coconut flour. In a separate bowl, whisk the eggs with almond milk until smooth. Place the coconut flakes on a plate.
4. One at a time, roll the chicken strips in the coconut flour, then dredge them in the egg mixture, shaking off any excess, and finally in the coconut flakes to coat.
5. Arrange the coated chicken pieces on the baking sheet. Bake in the preheated oven for 15 to 20 minutes, flipping the chicken halfway through, or

until the chicken is golden brown and cooked through.
6. Remove from the oven and serve on plates.

Tip: The chicken tenders can be served with anything you like. They taste great with a small potato with a green salad.

Nutrition: calories: 215 fat: 12.6g Protein: 20.2g carbs: 8.9g fiber: 6.1g Sodium: 345mg

340. Chicken Skewers with Peanut Sauce

Preparation Time: 70 minutes

Cooking Time: 15 minutes

Servings: 2

Ingredients:

- 1-pound boneless skinless chicken breast, cut into chunks
- 3 tablespoons soy sauce (or coconut amino), divided
- ½ teaspoon plus ¼ teaspoon Sriracha sauce
- 3 teaspoons toasted sesame oil, divided
- 2 tablespoons peanut butter

Directions:

1. In a large zip-top bag, mix chicken chunks with 2 tablespoons of soy sauce, ½ tsp. of Sriracha sauce and 2 tsp. Of sesame oil. Cover and marinate for an hour or so in the refrigerator or up to overnight.
2. If you are using wood 8-inch skewers, soak them in water for 30 minutes before using them.
3. Preheat your grill pan or grill to low. Oil the grill pan with ghee.
4. Shred the chicken chunks onto the skewers.
5. Cook the skewers at low heat for 13 minutes, flipping halfway through.
6. Stir the peanut dipping sauce. Stir together the remaining 1 tablespoon of soy sauce, ¼ teaspoon of Sriracha sauce, 1 teaspoon of sesame oil, and the peanut butter. Season well.
7. Serve with peanut sauce.

Nutrition: 586 Calories 29g Fat 75g Protein

Chapter 10. Fish & Seafood

341. Shrimp and Lemon Sauce

Preparation Time: 10 minutes

Cooking Time: 15 minutes

Servings: 4

Ingredients:

- 1-pound shrimp, peeled and deveined
- 1/3 cup lemon juice
- 4 egg yolks
- 2 tablespoons olive oil
- 1 cup chicken stock
- Salt and black pepper to the taste
- 1 cup black olives, pitted and halved
- 1 tablespoon thyme, chopped

Directions:

1. In a bowl, mix the lemon juice with the egg yolks and whisk well.
2. Heat a pan with the oil over medium heat, add the shrimp, cook for 2 minutes on each side, and transfer to a plate.
3. Heat a pan with the stock over medium heat, add some of this over the egg yolks and lemon juice mix and whisk well.
4. Add this over the rest of the stock, also add salt and pepper, whisk well and simmer for 2 minutes.
5. Add the shrimp and the rest of the ingredients, toss and serve right away.

Nutrition: calories 237, fat 15.3, fiber 4.6, carbs 15.4, protein 7.6

342. Shrimp and Beans Salad

Preparation Time: 10 minutes

Cooking Time: 4 minutes

Servings: 4

Ingredients:

- 1-pound shrimp, peeled and deveined

- 30 ounces canned cannellini beans, drained and rinsed
- 2 tablespoons olive oil
- 1 cup cherry tomatoes, halved
- 1 teaspoon lemon zest, grated
- ½ cup red onion, chopped
- A pinch of salt and black pepper
- For the dressing:
- 3 tablespoons red wine vinegar
- 2 garlic cloves, minced
- ½ cup olive oil

Directions:

1. Heat a pan with 2 tablespoons oil over medium-high heat, add the shrimp and cook for 2 minutes on each side.
2. In a salad bowl, combine the shrimp with the beans and the rest of the ingredients except for the dressing and toss.
3. In a separate bowl, combine the vinegar with ½ cup oil and the garlic and whisk well.
4. Pour over the salad, toss and serve right away.

Nutrition: calories 207, fat 12.3, fiber 6.6, carbs 15.4, protein 8.7

343. Pecan Salmon Fillets

Preparation Time: 10 minutes

Cooking Time: 15 minutes

Servings: 6

Ingredients:

- 3 tablespoons olive oil
- 3 tablespoons mustard
- 5 teaspoons honey
- 1 cup pecans, chopped
- 6 salmon fillets, boneless
- 1 tablespoon lemon juice
- 3 teaspoons parsley, chopped
- Salt and pepper to the taste

Directions:

1. In a bowl, mix the oil with the mustard and honey and whisk well.
2. Put the pecans and the parsley in another bowl.
3. Season the salmon fillets with salt and pepper, arrange them on a baking sheet lined with parchment paper, brush with the honey and mustard mix, and top with the pecans mix.

4. Introduce in the oven at 400 degrees F, bake for 15 minutes, divide between plates, drizzle the lemon juice on top and serve.

Nutrition: calories 282, fat 15.5, fiber 8.5, carbs 20.9, protein 16.8

344. Salmon and Broccoli

Preparation Time: 10 minutes

Cooking Time: 20 minutes

Servings: 4

Ingredients:

- 2 tablespoons balsamic vinegar
- 1 broccoli head, florets separated
- 4 pieces salmon fillets, skinless
- 1 big red onion, roughly chopped
- 1 tablespoon olive oil
- Sea salt and black pepper to the taste

Directions:

1. In a baking dish, combine the salmon with the broccoli and the rest of the ingredients, introduce in the oven and bake at 390 degrees F for 20 minutes.
2. Divide the mix between plates and serve.

Nutrition: calories 302, fat 15.5, fiber 8.5, carbs 18.9, protein 19.8

345. Dijon Fish Fillets

Preparation Time: 15 minutes

Cooking Time: 3 minutes

Servings: 2

Ingredients:

- 2 white fish fillets
- 1 tbsp Dijon mustard
- 1 cup of water
- Pepper
- Salt

Directions:

1. Pour water into the pot and place the trivet in the pot.
2. Brush fish fillets with mustard and season with pepper and salt and place on top of the trivet.

3. Cover the pot with a lid and cook on high heat for 3 minutes.
4. Once the fish is cooked, remove the lid.
5. Serve and enjoy.

Nutrition: Calories 270 Fat 11.9 g Carbohydrates 0.5 g Sugar 0.1 g Protein 38 g Cholesterol 119 mg

346. Marinated Tuna Steak

Preparation Time: 6 minutes

Cooking Time: 18 minutes

Servings: 4

Ingredients:

- Olive oil (2 tbsp.)
- Orange juice (.25 cup)
- Soy sauce (.25 cup)
- Lemon juice (1 tbsp.)
- Fresh parsley (2 tbsp.)
- Garlic clove (1)
- Ground black pepper (.5 tsp.)
- Fresh oregano (.5 tsp.)
- Tuna steaks (4 - 4 oz. Steaks)

Directions:

1. Mince the garlic and chop the oregano and parsley.
2. Mix the pepper, oregano, garlic, parsley, lemon juice, soy sauce, olive oil, and orange juice in a glass container.
3. Warm the grill using the high heat setting. Grease the grate with oil.
4. Add to tuna steaks and cook for five to six minutes. Turn and baste with the marinated sauce.
5. Cook another five minutes or until it's the way you like it. Discard the remaining marinade.

Nutrition: Calories: 200 Protein: 27.4g Fat: 7.9g

347. Garlic and Shrimp Pasta

Preparation Time: 4 minutes

Cooking Time: 16 minutes

Servings: 4

Ingredients:

- 6 ounces whole-wheat spaghetti
- 12 ounces raw shrimp, peeled and deveined, cut into 1-inch pieces
- 1 bunch asparagus, trimmed
- 1 large bell pepper, thinly sliced
- 1 cup fresh peas
- 3 garlic cloves, chopped
- 1 and ¼ teaspoons kosher salt
- ½ and ½ cups non-fat plain yogurt
- 3 tablespoon lemon juice
- 1 tablespoon extra-virgin olive oil
- ½ teaspoon fresh ground black pepper
- ¼ cup pine nuts, toasted

Directions:

1. Take a large-sized pot and bring water to a boil
2. Add your spaghetti and cook them for about minutes less than the directed package instruction
3. Add shrimp, bell pepper, asparagus and cook for about 2-4 minutes until the shrimp are tender
4. Drain the pasta and the contents well
5. Take a large bowl and mash garlic until a paste form
6. Whisk in yogurt, parsley, oil, pepper and lemon juice into the garlic paste
7. Add pasta mixture and toss well
8. Serve by sprinkling some pine nuts!

Nutrition: Calories: 406 Fat: 22g Protein: 26g

348. Paprika Butter Shrimps

Preparation Time: 6 minutes

Cooking Time: 31 minutes

Servings: 2

Ingredients:

- ¼ tablespoon smoked paprika
- 1/8 cup sour cream
- ½ pound tiger shrimps
- 1/8 cup butter
- Salt and black pepper, to taste

Directions:

1. Prep the oven to 390F and grease a baking dish.
2. Mix all the ingredients in a large bowl and transfer them into the baking dish.
3. Situate in the oven and bake for about 15 minutes.
4. Place paprika shrimp in a dish and set aside to cool for meal prepping. Divide it into 2 containers and cover the lid. Refrigerate for 1-2 days and reheat in microwave before serving.

Nutrition: Calories: 330 Protein: 32.6g Fat: 21.5g

349. Mediterranean Avocado Salmon Salad

Preparation Time: 6 minutes

Cooking Time: 10 minutes

Servings: 4

Ingredients:

- 1 lb. skinless salmon fillets
- Marinade/Dressing:
- 3 tbsp. olive oil
- 2 tbsp. lemon juice fresh, squeezed
- 1 tbsp. red wine vinegar, optional
- 1 tbsp. fresh chopped parsley
- 2 tsp garlic minced
- 1 tsp dried oregano
- 1 tsp salt
- Cracked pepper, to taste
- Salad:
- 4 cups Romaine (or Cos) lettuce leaves
- 1 large cucumber
- 2 Roma tomatoes
- 1 red onion
- 1 avocado
- 1/2 cup feta cheese
- 1/3 cup pitted Kalamata olives

Directions:

1. Scourge the olive oil, lemon juice, red wine vinegar, chopped parsley, garlic minced, oregano, salt and pepper
2. Fill out half of the marinade into a large, shallow dish, refrigerate the remaining marinade to use as the dressing

3. Coat the salmon in the rest of the marinade
4. Place a skillet pan or grill over medium-high, add 1 tbsp oil and sear salmon on both sides until crispy and cooked through
5. Allow the salmon to cool
6. Distribute the salmon among the containers, store in the fridge for 2-3 days
7. to Serve: Prep the salad by putting the romaine lettuce, cucumber, Roma tomatoes, red onion, avocado, feta cheese, and olives in a bowl. Reheat the salmon in the microwave for 30seconds to 1 minute or until heated through.
8. Slice the salmon and arrange over salad. Drizzle the salad with the remaining untouched dressing, serve with lemon wedges.

Nutrition: Calories:411 Fat: 27g Protein: 28g

350. Tuna with Vegetable Mix

Preparation Time: 8 minutes

Cooking Time: 16 minutes

Servings: 4

Ingredients:

- ¼ cup extra-virgin olive oil, divided
- 1 tablespoon rice vinegar
- 1 teaspoon kosher salt, divided
- ¾ teaspoon Dijon mustard
- ¾ teaspoon honey
- 4 ounces baby gold beets, thinly sliced
- 4 ounces fennel bulb, trimmed and thinly sliced
- 4 ounces baby turnips, thinly sliced
- 6 ounces Granny Smith apple, very thinly sliced
- 2 teaspoons sesame seeds, toasted
- 6 ounces tuna steaks
- ½ teaspoon black pepper
- 1 tablespoon fennel fronds, torn

Directions:

1. Scourge 2 tablespoons of oil, ½ a teaspoon of salt, honey, vinegar, and mustard.
2. Give the mixture a nice mix.
3. Add fennel, beets, apple, and turnips; mix and toss until everything is evenly coated.
4. Sprinkle with sesame seeds and toss well.
5. Using a cast-iron skillet, heat 2 tablespoons of oil over high heat.
6. Carefully season the tuna with ½ a teaspoon of salt and pepper
7. Situate the tuna in the skillet and cook for 4 minutes, giving 1 ½ minutes per side.
8. Remove the tuna and slice it up.
9. Place in containers with the vegetable mix.
10. Serve with the fennel mix, and enjoy!

Nutrition: Calories: 443 Fat: 17.1g Protein: 16.5g

351. Salmon and Peach Pan

Preparation Time: 10 minutes

Cooking Time: 11 minutes

Servings: 4

Ingredients:

- 1 tablespoon balsamic vinegar
- 1 teaspoon thyme, chopped
- 1 tablespoon ginger, grated
- 2 tablespoons olive oil
- Sea salt and black pepper to the taste
- 3 peaches, cut into medium wedges
- 4 salmon fillets, boneless

Directions:

1. Heat a pan with the oil over medium-high heat, add the salmon and cook for 3 minutes on each side.
2. Add the vinegar, the peaches and the rest of the ingredients, cook for 5 minutes more, divide everything between plates and serve.

Nutrition: calories 293, fat 17.1, fiber 4.1, carbs 26.4, protein 24.5

352. Tarragon Cod Fillets

Preparation Time: 10 minutes

Cooking Time: 12 minutes

Servings: 4

Ingredients:

- 4 cod fillets, boneless
- ¼ cup capers, drained
- 1 tablespoon tarragon, chopped
- Sea salt and black pepper to the taste
- 2 tablespoons olive oil
- 2 tablespoons parsley, chopped
- 1 tablespoon olive oil
- 1 tablespoon lemon juice

Directions:

1. Heat a pan with the oil over medium-high heat, add the fish and cook for 3 minutes on each side.
2. Add the rest of the ingredients, cook everything for 7 minutes more, divide between plates and serve.

Nutrition: calories 162, fat 9.6, fiber 4.3, carbs 12.4, protein 16.5

353. Salmon and Radish Mix

Preparation Time: 10 minutes

Cooking Time: 15 minutes

Servings: 4

Ingredients:

- 2 tablespoons olive oil
- 1 tablespoon balsamic vinegar
- 1 and ½ cup chicken stock
- 4 salmon fillets, boneless
- 2 garlic cloves, minced
- 1 tablespoon ginger, grated
- 1 cup radishes, grated
- ¼ cup scallions, chopped

Directions:

1. Heat a pan with the oil over medium-high heat, add the salmon, cook for 4 minutes on each side and divide between plates
2. Add the vinegar and the rest of the ingredients to the pan, toss gently, cook for 10 minutes, add the salmon and serve.

Nutrition: calories 274, fat 14.5, fiber 3.5, carbs 8.5, protein 22.3

354. Smoked Salmon and Watercress Salad

Preparation Time: 5 minutes

Cooking Time: 0 minutes

Servings: 4

Ingredients:

- 2 bunches watercress
- 1-pound smoked salmon, skinless, boneless and flaked
- 2 teaspoons mustard
- ¼ cup lemon juice
- ½ cup Greek yogurt
- Salt and black pepper to the taste
- 1 big cucumber, sliced
- 2 tablespoons chives, chopped

Directions:

1. In a salad bowl, combine the salmon with the watercress and the rest of the ingredients, toss and serve right away.

Nutrition: calories 244, fat 16.7, fiber 4.5, carbs 22.5, protein 15.6

355. Salmon and Corn Salad

Preparation Time: 5 minutes

Cooking Time: 0 minutes

Servings: 4

Ingredients:

- ½ cup pecans, chopped
- 2 cups baby arugula
- 1 cup corn
- ¼ pound smoked salmon, skinless, boneless and cut into small chunks
- 2 tablespoons olive oil
- 2 tablespoon lemon juice
- Sea salt and black pepper to the taste

Directions:

1. In a salad bowl, combine the salmon with the corn and the rest of the ingredients, toss and serve right away.

Nutrition: calories 284, fat 18.4, fiber 5.4, carbs 22.6, protein 17.4

356. Cod and Mushrooms Mix

Preparation Time: 10 minutes

Cooking Time: 25 minutes

Servings: 4

Ingredients:

- 2 cod fillets, boneless
- 4 tablespoons olive oil
- 4 ounces mushrooms, sliced
- Sea salt and black pepper to the taste
- 12 cherry tomatoes, halved
- 8 ounces lettuce leaves, torn
- 1 avocado, pitted, peeled and cubed
- 1 red chili pepper, chopped
- 1 tablespoon cilantro, chopped
- 2 tablespoons balsamic vinegar
- 1-ounce feta cheese, crumbled

Directions:

1. Put the fish in a roasting pan, brush it with 2 tablespoons oil, sprinkle salt and pepper all over and broil under medium-high heat for 15 minutes. Meanwhile, heat a pan with the rest of the oil over medium heat, add the mushrooms, stir and sauté for 5 minutes.
2. Add the rest of the ingredients, toss, cook for 5 minutes more and divide between plates.
3. Top with the fish and serve right away.

Nutrition: calories 257, fat 10, fiber 3.1, carbs 24.3, protein 19.4

357. Sesame Shrimp Mix

Preparation Time: 10 minutes

Cooking Time: 0 minutes

Servings: 4

Ingredients:

- 2 tablespoon lime juice
- 3 tablespoons teriyaki sauce
- 2 tablespoons olive oil
- 8 cups baby spinach
- 14 ounces shrimp, cooked, peeled and deveined
- 1 cup cucumber, sliced
- 1 cup radish, sliced
- ¼ cup cilantro, chopped
- 2 teaspoons sesame seeds, toasted

Directions:

1. In a bowl, mix the shrimp with the lime juice, spinach and the rest of the ingredients, toss and serve cold.

Nutrition: calories 177, fat 9, fiber 7.1, carbs 14.3, protein 9.4

358. Fish and Orzo

Preparation Time: 10 minutes

Cooking Time: 35 minutes

Servings: 4

Ingredients:

- 1 teaspoon garlic, minced
- 1 teaspoon red pepper, crushed
- 2 shallots, chopped
- 1 tablespoon olive oil
- 1 teaspoon anchovy paste
- 1 tablespoon oregano, chopped
- 2 tablespoons black olives, pitted and chopped
- 2 tablespoons capers, drained
- 15 ounces canned tomatoes, crushed
- A pinch of salt and black pepper
- 4 cod fillets, boneless
- 1-ounce feta cheese, crumbled
- 1 tablespoons parsley, chopped
- 3 cups chicken stock
- 1 cup orzo pasta
- Zest of 1 lemon, grated

Directions:

1. Heat a pan with the oil over medium heat, add the garlic, red pepper and the shallots and sauté for 5 minutes.
2. Add the anchovy paste, oregano, black olives, capers, tomatoes, salt and pepper, stir and cook for 5 minutes more.
3. Add the cod fillets, sprinkle the cheese and the parsley on top, introduce in the oven and bake at 375 degrees F for 15 minutes more.
4. Meanwhile, put the stock in a pot, bring to a boil over medium heat, add the orzo and the lemon zest, bring to a simmer, cook for 10 minutes, fluff with a fork, and divide between plates.
5. Top each serving with the fish mix and serve.

Nutrition: calories 402, fat 21, fiber 8, carbs 21, protein 31

359. Baked Sea Bass

Preparation Time: 10 minutes

Cooking Time: 12 minutes

Servings: 4

Ingredients:

- 4 sea bass fillets, boneless
- Salt and black pepper to the taste
- 2 cups potato chips, crushed
- 1 tablespoon mayonnaise

Directions:

1. Season the fish fillets with salt and pepper, brush with the mayonnaise, and dredge each in the potato chips.
2. Arrange the fillets on a baking sheet lined with parchment paper and bake at 400 degrees F for 12 minutes.
3. Divide the fish between plates and serve with a side salad.

Nutrition: calories 228, fat 8.6, fiber 0.6, carbs 9.3, protein 25

360. Fish and Tomato Sauce

Preparation Time: 10 minutes

Cooking Time: 30 minutes

Servings: 4

Ingredients:

- 4 cod fillets, boneless
- 2 garlic cloves, minced
- 2 cups cherry tomatoes, halved
- 1 cup chicken stock
- A pinch of salt and black pepper
- ¼ cup basil, chopped

Directions:

1. Put the tomatoes, garlic, salt and pepper in a pan, heat up over medium heat and cook for 5 minutes.
2. Add the fish and the rest of the ingredients, bring to a simmer, cover the pan and cook for 25 minutes.
3. Divide the mix between plates and serve.

Nutrition: calories 180, fat 1.9, fiber 1.4, carbs 5.3, protein 33.8

361. Halibut and Quinoa Mix

Preparation Time: 10 minutes

Cooking Time: 12 minutes

Servings: 4

Ingredients:

- 4 halibut fillets, boneless
- 2 tablespoons olive oil
- 1 teaspoon rosemary, dried
- 2 teaspoons cumin, ground
- 1 tablespoons coriander, ground
- 2 teaspoons cinnamon powder
- 2 teaspoons oregano, dried
- A pinch of salt and black pepper
- 2 cups quinoa, cooked
- 1 cup cherry tomatoes, halved
- 1 avocado, peeled, pitted and sliced
- 1 cucumber, cubed
- ½ cup black olives, pitted and sliced
- Juice of 1 lemon

Directions:

1. In a bowl, combine the fish with the rosemary, cumin, coriander, cinnamon, oregano, salt and pepper and toss.
2. Heat a pan with the oil over medium heat, add the fish, and sear for 2 minutes on each side.
3. Introduce the pan in the oven and bake the fish at 425 degrees F for 7 minutes.
4. Meanwhile, mix the quinoa with the remaining ingredients in a bowl, toss, and divide between plates.
5. Add the fish next to the quinoa mix and serve right away.

Nutrition: calories 364, fat 15.4, fiber 11.2, carbs 56.4, protein 24.5

362. Lemon and Dates Barramundi

Preparation Time: 10 minutes

Cooking Time: 12 minutes

Servings: 2

Ingredients:

- 2 barramundi fillets, boneless

- 1 shallot, sliced
- 4 lemon slices
- Juice of ½ lemon
- Zest of 1 lemon, grated
- 2 tablespoons olive oil
- 6 ounces baby spinach
- ¼ cup almonds, chopped
- 4 dates, pitted and chopped
- ¼ cup parsley, chopped
- Salt and black pepper to the taste

Directions:

1. Season the fish with salt and pepper and arrange on 2 parchment paper pieces.
2. Top the fish with the lemon slices, drizzle the lemon juice, and then top with the other ingredients except for the oil.
3. Drizzle 1 tablespoon oil over each fish mix, wrap the parchment paper around the fish shaping into packets and arrange them on a baking sheet.
4. Bake at 400 degrees F for 12 minutes cool the mix a bit, unfold, divide everything between plates and serve.

Nutrition: calories 232, fat 16.5, fiber 11.1, carbs 24.8, protein 6.5

363. Catfish Fillets and Rice

Preparation Time: 10 minutes

Cooking Time: 55 minutes

Servings: 2

Ingredients:

- 2 catfish fillets, boneless
- 2 tablespoons Italian seasoning
- 2 tablespoons olive oil

For the rice:

- 1 cup brown rice
- 2 tablespoons olive oil
- 1 and ½ cups water
- ½ cup green bell pepper, chopped
- 2 garlic cloves, minced
- ½ cup white onion, chopped
- 2 teaspoons Cajun seasoning
- ½ teaspoon garlic powder
- Salt and black pepper to the taste

Directions:

1. Heat a pot with 2 tablespoons of oil over medium heat, add the onion, garlic, garlic powder, salt and pepper and sauté for 5 minutes.
2. Add the rice, water, bell pepper and the seasoning, bring to a simmer and cook over medium heat for 40 minutes.
3. Heat a pan with 2 tablespoons oil over medium heat, add the fish and the Italian seasoning, and cook for 5 minutes on each side.
4. Divide the rice between plates, add the fish on top and serve.

Nutrition: calories 261, fat 17.6, fiber 12.2, carbs 24.8, protein 12.5

364. Halibut Pan

Preparation Time: 10 minutes

Cooking Time: 20 minutes

Servings: 4

Ingredients:

- 4 halibut fillets, boneless
- 1 red bell pepper, chopped
- 2 tablespoons olive oil
- 1 yellow onion, chopped
- 4 garlic cloves, minced
- ½ cup chicken stock
- 1 teaspoon basil, dried
- ½ cup cherry tomatoes halved
- 1/3 cup kalamata olives, pitted and halved
- Salt and black pepper to the taste

Directions:

1. Heat a pan with the oil over medium heat, add the fish, cook for 5 minutes on each side and divide between plates.
2. Add the onion, bell pepper, garlic and tomatoes to the pan, stir and sauté for 3 minutes.
3. Add salt, pepper and the rest of the ingredients, toss, cook for 3 minutes more, divide next to the fish and serve.

Nutrition: calories 253, fat 8, fiber 1, carbs 5, protein 28

365. Baked Shrimp Mix

Preparation Time: 10 minutes

Cooking Time: 32 minutes

Servings: 4

Ingredients:

- 4 gold potatoes, peeled and sliced
- 2 fennel bulbs, trimmed and cut into wedges
- 2 shallots, chopped
- 2 garlic cloves, minced
- 3 tablespoons olive oil
- 1/2 cup kalamata olives, pitted and halved
- 2 pounds shrimp, peeled and deveined
- 1 teaspoon lemon zest, grated
- 2 teaspoons oregano, dried
- 4 ounces feta cheese, crumbled
- 2 tablespoons parsley, chopped

Directions:

1. In a roasting pan, combine the potatoes with 2 tablespoons of oil, garlic and the rest of the ingredients except the shrimp; toss, introduce in the oven and bake at 450 degrees F for 25 minutes.
2. Add the shrimp, toss, bake for 7 minutes more, divide between plates and serve.

Nutrition: calories 341, fat 19, fiber 9, carbs 34, protein 10

366. Tuna Bowl with Kale

Preparation Time: 4 minutes

Cooking Time: 18 minutes

Servings: 6

Ingredients:

- 3 tablespoons extra virgin olive oil
- 1 ½ teaspoons minced garlic
- ¼ cup of capers
- 2 teaspoons sugar
- 15 ounce can have drained and rinsed great northern beans
- 1-pound chopped kale with the center ribs removed
- ½ teaspoon ground black pepper
- 1 cup chopped onion
- 2 ½ ounces of drained sliced olives
- ¼ teaspoon sea salt
- ¼ teaspoon crushed red pepper

- 6 ounces of tuna in olive oil, do not drain

Directions:

1. Place a large pot, like a stockpot, on your stove and turn the burner to high heat.
2. Fill the pot about 3-quarters of the way complete with water and let it come to a boil.
3. Cook the kale for 2 minutes.
4. Drain the kale and set it aside.
5. Set the heat to medium and place the empty pot back on the burner.
6. Add the oil and onion. Sauté for 3 to 4 minutes.
7. Combine the garlic into the oil mixture and sauté for another minute.
8. Add the capers, olives, and red pepper.
9. Cook the ingredients for another minute while stirring.
10. Pour in the sugar and stir while you toss in the kale. Mix all the ingredients thoroughly and ensure the kale is thoroughly coated.
11. Cover the pot and set the timer for 8 minutes.
12. Put off the heat and stir in the tuna, pepper, beans, salt, and any other herbs that will make this one of the best Mediterranean dishes you've ever made.

Nutrition: Calories: 265 Fats: 12g Protein: 16g

367. Greek Baked Cod

Preparation Time: 9 minutes

Cooking Time: 13 minutes

Servings: 4

Ingredients:

- 1 ½ lb. Cod fillet pieces (4–6 pieces)
- 5 garlic cloves, peeled and minced
- 1/4 cup chopped fresh parsley leaves
- Lemon Juice Mixture:
- 5 tbsp. fresh lemon juice
- 5 tbsp. extra virgin olive oil
- 2 tbsp. melted vegan butter

For Coating:

- 1/3 cup all-purpose flour
- 1 tsp ground coriander
- 3/4 tsp sweet Spanish paprika
- 3/4 tsp ground cumin
- 3/4 tsp salt
- 1/2 tsp black pepper

Directions:

1. Preheat oven to 400F
2. Scourge lemon juice, olive oil, and melted butter, set aside
3. In another shallow bowl, mix all-purpose flour, spices, salt and pepper, set next to the lemon bowl to create a station
4. Pat the fish fillet dry, then dip the fish in the lemon juice mixture then dip it in the flour mixture, brush off extra flour
5. In a cast-iron skillet over medium-high heat, add 2 tbsp olive oil
6. Once heated, add in the fish and sear on each side for color, but do not thoroughly cook; remove from heat
7. With the remaining lemon juice mixture, add the minced garlic and mix
8. Drizzle all over the fish fillets
9. Bake for 10 minutes, until it begins to flake easily with a fork
10. Allow the dish to cool completely
11. Distribute among the containers, store for 2-3 days
12. to Serve: Reheat in the microwave for 1-2 minutes or until heated through. Sprinkle chopped parsley. Enjoy!

Nutrition: Calories: 321 Fat: 18g Protein: 23g

368. Pistachio Sole Fish

Preparation Time: 4 minutes

Cooking Time: 11 minutes

Servings: 4

Ingredients:

- 4 (5 ounces boneless sole fillets
- Salt and pepper as needed
- ½ cup pistachios, finely chopped

- Zest of 1 lemon
- Juice of 1 lemon
- 1 teaspoon extra virgin olive oil

Directions:

1. Pre-heat your oven to 350 degrees Fahrenheit
2. Prep a baking sheet using parchment paper then keep side
3. Pat fish dry with kitchen towels and lightly season with salt and pepper
4. Take a small bowl and stir in pistachios and lemon zest
5. Place sol on the prepped sheet and press 2 tablespoons of pistachio mixture on top of each fillet
6. Rub fish with lemon juice and olive oil
7. Bake for 10 minutes until the top is golden and fish flakes with a fork
8. Serve and enjoy!
9. Meal Prep/Storage Options: Store in airtight containers in your fridge for 1-2 days.

Nutrition: Calories: 166 Fat: 6g Protein: 26g

369. Baked Tilapia

Preparation Time: 9 minutes

Cooking Time: 16 minutes

Servings: 4

Ingredients:

- 1 lb. tilapia fillets (about 8 fillets)
- 1 tsp olive oil
- 1 tbsp. vegan butter
- 2 shallots finely chopped
- 3 garlic cloves minced
- 1 1/2 tsp ground cumin
- 1 1/2 tsp paprika
- 1/4 cup capers
- 1/4 cup fresh dill finely chopped
- Juice from 1 lemon
- Salt & Pepper to taste

Directions:

1. Preheat oven to 375F
2. Prep a rimmed baking sheet using parchment paper or foil

3. Lightly mist with cooking spray, arrange the fish fillets evenly on a baking sheet
4. Mix the cumin, paprika, salt and pepper
5. Rub the fish fillets with the spice mixture
6. Scourge the melted butter, lemon juice, shallots, olive oil, and garlic, and brush evenly over fish fillets
7. Top with the capers
8. Bake for 13 minutes
9. Pull out from the oven and allow the dish to cool completely
10. Distribute among the containers, store for 2-3 days
11. to Serve: Reheat in the microwave for 1-2 minutes or until heated through. Top with fresh dill. Serve!

Nutrition: Calories: 410 Fat: 5g Protein: 21g

370. A Great Mediterranean Snapper

Preparation Time: 11 minutes

Cooking Time: 19 minutes

Servings: 2

Ingredients:

- 2 tablespoons extra virgin olive oil
- 1 medium onion, chopped
- 2 garlic cloves, minced
- 1 teaspoon oregano
- 1 can (14 ounces tomatoes, diced with juice
- ½ cup black olives, sliced
- 4 red snapper fillets (each 4 ounces
- Salt and pepper as needed
- Garnish
- ¼ cup feta cheese, crumbled
- ¼ cup parsley, minced

Directions:

1. Pre-heat your oven to a temperature of 425-degree Fahrenheit

2. Take a 13x9 inch baking dish and grease it up with non-stick cooking spray
3. Take a large-sized skillet and place it over medium heat
4. Add oil and heat it up
5. Add onion, oregano and garlic
6. Sauté for 2 minutes
7. Add diced tomatoes with juice alongside black olives
8. Bring the mix to a boil
9. Remove the heat
10. Place the fish on the prepped baking dish
11. Season both sides with salt and pepper
12. Spoon the tomato mix over the fish
13. Bake for 10 minutes
14. Remove the oven and sprinkle a bit of parsley and feta
15. Enjoy!

Nutrition: Calories: 269 Fat: 13g Protein: 27g

371. Mediterranean Snapper

Preparation Time: 9 minutes

Cooking Time: 13 minutes

Servings: 4

Ingredients:

- non-stick cooking spray
- 2 tablespoons extra virgin olive oil
- 1 medium onion, chopped
- 2 garlic cloves, minced
- 1 teaspoon oregano
- 1 14-ounce can dice tomatoes
- ½ cup black olives, sliced
- 4 4-ounce red snapper fillets
- Salt
- Pepper
- ¼ cup crumbled feta cheese
- ¼ cup fresh parsley, minced

Directions:

1. Preheat oven to 425 degrees Fahrenheit.
2. Brush a 13x9 baking dish with non-stick cooking spray.
3. Cook oil in a large skillet over medium heat.

4. Sauté onion, oregano, garlic for 2 minutes.
5. Add a can of tomatoes and olives, and bring mixture to a boil; remove from heat.
6. Season both sides of fillets with salt and pepper and place in the baking dish.
7. Ladle the tomato mixture evenly over the fish.
8. Bake for 11 minutes.
9. Pull out from the oven and sprinkle with parsley and feta.
10. Enjoy!

Nutrition: Calories: 257 Fat: 9g Protein: 31.3 g

372. Mediterranean Salmon

Preparation Time: 9 minutes

Cooking Time: 16 minutes

Servings: 4

Ingredients:

- ½ cup of olive oil
- ¼ cup balsamic vinegar
- 4 garlic cloves, pressed
- 4 pieces salmon fillets
- 1 tablespoon fresh cilantro, chopped
- 1 tablespoon fresh basil, chopped
- 1½ teaspoons garlic salt

Directions:

1. Combine olive oil and balsamic vinegar.
2. Add salmon fillets to a shallow baking dish.
3. Rub the garlic onto the fillets.
4. Pour vinegar and oil all over, making sure to turn them once to coat them.
5. Season with cilantro, garlic salt, and basil.
6. Keep aside and marinate for 13 minutes.
7. Preheat the broiler to your oven.
8. Place the baking dish with the salmon about 6 inches from the heat source.
9. Broil for 15 minutes until both sides are evenly browned and can be flaked with a fork.
10. Make sure to keep brushing with sauce from the pan.

11. Enjoy!

Nutrition: Calories: 459 Fat: 36.2g Protein: 34.8g

373. Heartthrob Mediterranean Tilapia

Preparation Time: 8 minutes

Cooking Time: 16 minutes

Servings: 4

Ingredients:

- 3 tbsp. Sun-dried tomatoes, packed in oil
- 1 tbsp. capers
- 2 tilapia fillets
- 1 tbsp. oil from sun-dried tomatoes
- 1 tbsp. lemon juice
- 2 tbsp. Kalamata olives, chopped and pitted

Directions:

1. Pre-heat your oven to 372-degree Fahrenheit
2. Take a small-sized bowl and add sun-dried tomatoes, olives, capers and stir well
3. Keep the mixture on the side
4. Take a baking sheet and transfer the tilapia fillets and arrange them side by side
5. Drizzle olive oil all over them
6. Drizzle lemon juice
7. Bake in your oven for 10-15 minutes
8. After 10 minutes, check the fish for a "Flaky" texture
9. Once appropriately cooked, top the fish with tomato mixture and serve!

Nutrition: Calories: 183 Fat: 8g Protein: 18.3g

374. Herbed Salmon With Mashed Potatoes

Preparation Time: 15 minutes

Cooking Time: 30 minutes

Servings: 4

Ingredients:

For the salmon:

- 2 tablespoons extra-virgin olive oil, plus more for brushing
- 1 salmon fillet (16 to 20 ounces)

- Salt to taste
- Freshly ground black pepper to taste
- 2 thyme sprigs
- 2 marjoram sprigs

For the potatoes:

- 2 russet potatoes, peeled and diced
- 3 to 4 tablespoons whole milk
- 1 tablespoon unsalted butter
- 2 teaspoon salt

For the sauce :

- ½ cup Dijon mustard
- 2 tablespoons freshly squeezed lemon juice
- 1 teaspoon extra-virgin olive oil
- 2 tablespoons chopped fresh dill
- 2 tablespoons chopped fresh basil

Directions:

1. to cook the salmon
2. Preheat the oven to 400°F. Line a rimmed baking sheet with parchment paper and brush it with olive oil.
3. Place the salmon, skin-side down, on the prepared baking sheet. Rub it with olive oil and season it lightly with salt and pepper. Top with the herb sprigs.
4. Bake for 20 to 30 minutes, until the salmon flakes easily with a fork.
5. Remove the herbs sprigs and discard.
6. to cook the potatoes
7. When the salmon is nearly done, bring a large pot of water to a boil over high heat. Add the potatoes and boil for 5 to 10 minutes, until soft. Drain and transfer to a bowl.
8. Use a hand mixer on low, beat the potatoes with 2 tablespoons of milk, butter, and salt. Add the remaining 1 or 2 tablespoons of milk, a little at a time, until you reach the desired consistency.
9. to make the sauce
10. Whisk together the mustard, lemon juice, olive oil, dill, and basil in a small bowl.

11. Spoon the sauce over the salmon and serve with the mashed potatoes.

Nutrition:

Calories: 432; Total Fat: 20g; Saturated Fat: 4g; Protein: 28g; Total Carbohydrates: 36g; Fiber: 4g; Sugar: 2g; Cholesterol: 72mg

375. Mediterranean Snapper With Olives And Feta

Preparation Time: 10 minutes

Cooking Time: 20 minutes

Servings: 4

Ingredients:

- 3 tablespoons extra-virgin olive oil, divided, plus more for brushing
- 4 snapper fillets (4 to 5 ounces each)
- ½ teaspoon salt
- ¼ teaspoon freshly ground black pepper
- 1 onion, chopped
- 2 garlic cloves, minced
- 1 teaspoon dried oregano
- (14.5-ounce) can diced tomatoes, undrained
- ½ cup chopped pitted kalamata olives
- ¼ cup crumbled feta cheese
- 2 tablespoons chopped fresh flat-leaf parsley

Directions:

1. Preheat the oven to 425°F. Brush a 3-quart (13 × 9 × 2 inches) baking dish lightly with olive oil.
2. Place the snapper in the prepared baking dish. Massage it gently with 2 tablespoons of olive oil, then sprinkle with salt and pepper.
3. In a large skillet, heat the remaining 1 tablespoon of olive oil over medium heat. Add the onion, garlic, and oregano and cook for about 3 minutes until the onion starts to soften.
4. Add the tomatoes and their juices and the olives and cook for 5 minutes to warm through and combine the flavors.

5. Spoon the tomato mixture over the fish.
6. Bake for 10 to 15 minutes until the fish is tender and flakes easily with a fork.
7. Serve with a sprinkling of crumbled feta cheese and chopped parsley.

Nutrition:

Calories: 278; Total Fat: 16g; Saturated Fat: 3g; Protein: 26g; Total Carbohydrates: 8g; Fiber: 3g; Sugar: 4g; Cholesterol: 50mg

376. Moroccan Cod

Preparation Time: 10 minutes

Cooking Time: 30 minutes

Servings: 4

Ingredients:

- 2 russet potatoes, peeled and cut into large chunks
- 2 carrots, cut into large chunks
- 2 tablespoons extra-virgin olive oil, divided
- 1½ teaspoons salt, divided
- cod fillets (6 ounces each)
- ½ teaspoon ground cumin
- ½ teaspoon paprika
- ¼ teaspoon ground turmeric
- 1 large red onion, cut into large chunks
- Chopped fresh flat-leaf parsley for garnish

Directions:

1. Preheat the oven to 425°F. Line a rimmed baking sheet with aluminum foil.
2. Toss the potatoes and carrots on the prepared baking sheet with 3 tablespoons of olive oil and 1 teaspoon of salt. Spread out in a single layer and roast for 15 minutes.
3. Meanwhile, rub the remaining 1 tablespoon of olive oil all over the cod. In a small bowl, combine the cumin, paprika, turmeric, and remaining ½ teaspoon of salt and sprinkle the mixture over the fish.
4. Remove the baking sheet from the oven and move the vegetables over to clear four spots for the fish. Add the fish and red onion and roast for 15

to 20 minutes, until the fish is fully cooked and flakes easily with a fork. Garnish with parsley.

Nutrition:

Calories: 444; Total Fat: 15g; Saturated Fat: 2g; Protein: 31g; Total Carbohydrates: 47g; Fiber:

6g; Sugar: 8g; Cholesterol: 80mg

377. Tuna Puttanesca

Preparation Time: 10 minutes

Cooking Time: 30 minutes

Servings: 4

Ingredients:

- 1 tablespoon extra-virgin olive oil, plus more for brushing
- 1 (6-ounce) can tomato paste
- ½ cup water
- 3 garlic cloves, minced, divided
- 1 teaspoon dried oregano
- ½ teaspoon salt
- ¼ teaspoon freshly ground black pepper
- 2 tuna steaks (1 inch thick)
- ½ cup pitted kalamata olives 2 tablespoons capers
- 1 teaspoon red pepper flakes
- 8 fresh basil leaves for garnish

Directions:

1. Preheat the oven to 350°F. Line a rimmed baking sheet with parchment paper and lightly brush with olive oil.
2. In a skillet, heat the olive oil over medium heat. Add the tomato paste and water and stir to combine. Bring the mixture to a boil, then reduce the heat to a simmer.
3. Add 1 minced garlic clove, oregano, salt, and black pepper. Simmer for 10 minutes, then remove the pan from the heat.
4. Halve the tuna steaks horizontally to create four ½-inch-thick steaks. Place the tuna steaks on the prepared baking sheet.
5. Spoon the tomato sauce over the tuna—cover with the olives, capers, remaining 2

minced garlic cloves, and red pepper flakes.

6. Bake for 20 minutes or until the tuna steaks are cooked to your preference. Garnish with fresh basil.

Nutrition:

Calories: 212; Total Fat: 10g; Saturated Fat: 2g; Protein: 22g; Total Carbohydrates: 10g; Fiber: 3g; Sugar: 5g; Cholesterol: 32mg

378. Fish En Papillote

Preparation Time: 10 minutes

Cooking Time: 30 minutes

Servings: 4

Ingredients:

- 3 tablespoons extra-virgin olive oil, divided
- ½ green bell pepper, seeded and chopped
- ½ cup chopped radicchio
- 1 scallion, thinly sliced 2 garlic cloves, minced
- 1 salmon fillet (20 ounces)
- ½ teaspoon salt
- ¼ teaspoon freshly ground black pepper
- 3 thyme sprigs, leaves picked
- 3 plum tomatoes, chopped
- 3 cups chopped beet greens

Directions:

1. Preheat the oven to 400°F.
2. In a skillet, heat 2 tablespoons of olive oil over medium heat. Cook the bell pepper, radicchio, scallion, and garlic for about 3 minutes, until the radicchio has just wilted. Remove from the heat.
3. Place the salmon on half of a large sheet of parchment paper. Brush it with the remaining 1 tablespoon of olive oil and sprinkle with salt and pepper. Top with fresh thyme leaves. Spoon the sautéed vegetables over the top of the fish. Add the tomatoes on top.
4. Fold the other half of the parchment paper over the fish to enclose it. To seal, start at one end and firmly fold the

paper along the edges in small pleats to create a half-moon-shaped packet.

5. Place the packet on a rimmed baking sheet and bake for 25 minutes.
6. Meanwhile, in a skillet, heat ¼ inch water over medium-high heat. Add the beet greens and cook for about 10 minutes, until wilted and tender. Drain.
7. Remove the baking sheet from the oven. Be careful when opening the parchment packet because hot steam will be released. Serve the fish on a bed of beet greens, topped with the vegetables from the package.

Nutrition:

Calories: 313; Total Fat: 19g; Saturated Fat: 3g; Protein: 29g; Total Carbohydrates: 5g; Fiber: 2g; Sugar: 2g; Cholesterol: 78mg

379. Baked Fish Fingers

Preparation Time: 20 minutes

Cooking Time: 10 minutes

Servings: 4

Ingredients:

For the fish fingers

- Nonstick cooking spray
- 1-pound cod fillets
- 1 teaspoon salt
- ½ teaspoon freshly ground black pepper
- 1 cup all-purpose flour
- 1 teaspoon paprika
- 2 large eggs
- ¼ cup whole milk
- 1 cup bread crumbs

For the dipping sauce

- 1 cup low-fat plain Greek yogurt
- 2 tablespoons extra-virgin olive oil
- 2 tablespoons freshly squeezed lemon juice
- 1 garlic clove, minced
- 1 teaspoon minced fresh dill
- ½ teaspoon salt
- ¼ teaspoon freshly ground black pepper

Directions:

1. Make the fish fingers

2. Preheat the oven to 450°F. Line a rimmed baking sheet with parchment paper and coat with nonstick cooking spray.
3. Slice the cod into 1-inch-wide strips. You should get about 20 fish fingers. Season the fingers with salt and pepper.
4. Set up an assembly line with three shallow bowls. Mix the flour and paprika in the first bowl, beat together the eggs and milk in the second bowl, and put the bread crumbs in the third bowl.
5. Dredge a fish stick in the flour, dip it in the egg mixture, and roll it in the bread crumbs to coat it thoroughly. Place on the prepared baking sheet and repeat with the remaining fish fingers.
6. Bake for about 10 minutes until the fish is cooked through.
7. to make the dipping sauce
8. Stir together the yogurt, olive oil, lemon juice, garlic, dill, salt, and pepper in a small bowl. Serve with the fish fingers.

Nutrition:

Calories: 463; Total Fat: 13g; Saturated Fat: 3g; Protein: 34g; Total Carbohydrates: 50g; Fiber: 2g; Sugar: 7g; Cholesterol: 147mg

380. Shrimp Scampi

Preparation Time: 10 minutes

Cooking Time: 10 minutes

Servings: 4

Ingredients:

- 3 tablespoons extra-virgin olive oil, divided
- 4 garlic cloves, minced, divided
- 1 teaspoon salt
- ½ teaspoon freshly ground black pepper
- 1-pound large shrimp, peeled and deveined
- 1 shallot, chopped
- ¼ cup dry white wine
- 1 tablespoon freshly squeezed lemon juice
- ¼ teaspoon red pepper flakes
- 2 tablespoons unsalted butter

- ¼ cup chopped arugula

Directions:

1. In a large bowl, whisk together 1 tablespoon of olive oil, half the garlic, salt, and black pepper. Add the shrimp and toss to coat.
2. In a large skillet, heat the remaining 2 tablespoons of olive oil over medium heat. Add the shrimp and cook for 2 minutes.
3. Add the shallot, wine, lemon juice, remaining garlic, and red pepper flakes. Toss to coat the shrimp and cook until heated through and the liquid reduces by half.
4. Add the butter and arugula to the pan. Cook, stirring, until the butter melts and the arugula is wilted.

Nutrition:

Calories: 292; Total Fat: 22g; Saturated Fat: 9g; Protein: 16g; Total Carbohydrates: 3g; Fiber: 0g; Sugar: 0g; Cholesterol: 173mg

381. Mussels And Clams In White Wine

Preparation Time: 10 minutes

Cooking Time: 10 minutes

Servings: 4

Ingredients:

- 2 tablespoons extra-virgin olive oil
- 1 shallot, minced
- 2 garlic cloves, minced
- 1 cup dry white wine
- ½ teaspoon red pepper flakes
- 1-pound clams, scrubbed
- 1-pound mussels, scrubbed and debearded
- ¼ cup chopped arugula

Directions:

1. In a large, deep skillet, heat the olive oil over low heat. Cook the shallot for about 5 minutes until it starts to soften. Add the garlic and cook for 1 minute.
2. Stir in the white wine and red pepper flakes and cook for 1 minute to allow the alcohol to evaporate.

3. Increase the heat to medium and add the clams and mussels. Cover and steam for 3 to 5 minutes until the shellfish have opened. Discard any that do not open. If you need more liquid to cook them, add some water.
4. Remove the shellfish from the pan and top with the sauce from the pan and chopped arugula.

VARIATION TIP: You can enjoy this dish as is or serve it over linguine if you like.

Nutrition: Calories: 152; Total Fat: 8g; Saturated Fat: 1g; Protein: 7g; Total Carbohydrates: 4g; Fiber: 0g; Sugar: 1g; Cholesterol: 23mg

382. Shrimp Fra Diavolo

Preparation Time: 15 minutes

Cooking Time: 15 minutes

Servings: 4

Ingredients:

- 1 and ½ tablespoons extra-virgin olive oil
- 2 cups chopped onion
- 2 garlic cloves, minced
- (28-ounce) can whole peeled tomatoes, undrained
- 1/2 cup dry red wine
- 1 tablespoon dried oregano
- 1/2 teaspoon red pepper flakes
- 1/2 teaspoon salt, plus more for the pasta water
- 1/4 teaspoon freshly ground black pepper
- 1-pound linguine
- 1-pound large shrimp, peeled and deveined

Directions:

1. In a large skillet, heat the olive oil over medium heat. Add the onion and cook for about 3 minutes until it starts to soften. Add the garlic and cook for another minute.
2. Add the tomatoes and their juices, using a potato masher or spoon to break up the tomatoes in the pan.
3. Add the wine, oregano, red pepper flakes, salt, and black

pepper. Bring to a boil, then reduce to a simmer.

4. Meanwhile, bring a large pot of water to a boil over high heat. Once boiling, salt the water to your liking, stir, and return to a spot. Add the linguine and cook according to package directions until al dente.
5. Drain.
6. Add the shrimp to the simmering tomato sauce and cook for about 3 minutes, until opaque.
7. Serve the shrimp and sauce over the linguine.

Nutrition: Calories: 653; Total Fat: 10g; Saturated Fat: 2g; Protein: 33g; Total Carbohydrates: 101g; Fiber: 9g; Sugar: 12g; Cholesterol: 143mg

383. Sardine Pâté

Prep time: 10 minutes

Cooking Time: 20 minutes

Servings: 4

Ingredients:

- 2 (7-ounce) cans oil-packed sardines, drained
- 2 ounces cream cheese or mascarpone
- 1/4 cup shallot, minced
- 2 scallions, thinly sliced
- 1 tablespoon minced fresh chives
- 1 tablespoon freshly squeezed lemon juice
- Pinch cayenne pepper

Directions:

1. Put the sardines in a bowl. Remove any spines or tails. Using a fork, mash the sardines.
2. Add the cream cheese, shallot, scallions, chives, lemon juice, and cayenne and stir until well blended.

MAKE-AHEAD TIP: This mixture can be stored in an airtight container in the refrigerator for up to 2 days.

Nutrition: Calories: 243; Total Fat: 15g; Saturated Fat: 4g; Protein: 24g; Total

Carbohydrates: 1g; Fiber: 0g; Sugar: 1g; Cholesterol: 146mg

384. Mussels In Tomato Sauce With Pastina

Preparation Time: 10 minutes

Cooking Time: 20 minutes

Servings: 4

Ingredients:

- 1/4 cup extra-virgin olive oil
- 4 garlic cloves, sliced
- 1 cup dry white wine
- 1 (28-ounce) can whole peeled tomatoes, undrained
- 1 tablespoon dried oregano
- 1 teaspoon red pepper flakes
- 1 teaspoon salt
- 1/2 teaspoon freshly ground black pepper
- 2 pounds mussels, scrubbed and debearded
- 2 tablespoons pastina

Directions:

1. In a large, deep skillet, heat the olive oil over medium heat. Add the garlic and cook for 1 minute.
2. Add the white wine and bring to a boil.
3. Add the tomatoes and their juices, using a potato masher or spoon to break up the tomatoes in the pan.
4. Add the oregano, red pepper flakes, salt, and black pepper and stir to combine.
5. When the sauce starts to boil, add the mussels and cook for about 5 minutes until they all open. Discard any mussels that do not open.
6. Reduce the heat to low. Stir in the pastina and simmer for 7 to 8 minutes, until the pasta is cooked.
7. Ingredient Tip: Any small-shaped pasta will work in this dish. Orzo is a good alternative if you can't find pastina.

Nutrition: Calories: 256; Total Fat: 15g; Saturated Fat: 2g; Protein: 10g; Total Carbohydrates: 12g; Fiber: 4g; Sugar: 6g; Cholesterol: 18mg

385. Easy Fish And Papillote Recipe

Preparation Time 20 minutes

Cooking Time 25 minutes

Servings: 1-2

Ingredients

- 1 ¼ lb. cod fillet (2.5 cm thick) cut into 4 pieces
- Kosher salt and black pepper
- ½ tomato thinly sliced into 4 rounds
- ½ cored green pepper, thinly sliced into 4 rounds
- ½ lemon cut into thin rings
- A handful of pitted green olives optional

For the sauce

- ¼ cup of extra virgin olive oil I used Private Reserve Greek EVOO
- Juice of ½ lemon
- 1 shallot finely chopped
- 2 cloves of garlic finely chopped
- 1 teaspoon of oregano
- 1 tsp paprika powder
- ½ teaspoon of cumin

Directions

1. Heat the oven to 425 degrees F.
2. Season the fish on both sides with kosher salt and pepper.
3. Prepare the sauce. Place the olive oil, lemon juice, shallots, garlic, and herbs in a small mixing bowl or measuring cup and whisk to combine.
4. Prepare 4 large pieces of parchment paper (about 12 inches on each side). Fold the parchment paper pieces in the middle to mark two halves.
5. Assemble the bags. Place each fish fillet on the bottom half of a piece of parchment paper spoon 2 tablespoons of the prepared sauce over the fish. Add 1 slice of lemon, 1 slice of tomato, and 1 slice of bell pepper.
6. Fold the top half of the parchment paper over the fish and vegetables and fold and secure each piece of parchment

around the fish and vegetables to create a well-packed pouch.
7. Place the fish bags on a large baking tray. Bake on the center rack of your heated oven for 12 to 15 minutes or until the fish is cooked through and falls apart easily.
8. To serve, place the fish and vegetables in their closed parchment containers and place each bag on a serving platter.

Nutrition: Calories: 221.3kcal Carbohydrates: 4.9 g Protein: 26.1 g Fat: 11.7 g Saturated fat: 1.7 g Sodium: 370.9 mg Potassium: 700.5 mg Fiber: 1.4 g Sugar: 1.7 g

386. Calamari With Tomato Sauce

Preparation Time: 20 minutes

Cooking Time: 8 minutes

Servings: 4

Ingredients:

- 3 lbs. calamari
- 1/3 cup olive oil
- 1 tablespoon fresh oregano
- 1 teaspoon lemon juice
- 1 tablespoon garlic, minced
- ¼ teaspoon chopped fresh lemon peel
- ¼ teaspoon crushed red pepper
- ¼ cup vinegar

Sauce:

- 1 lb. fresh whole tomatoes
- 3 cloves garlic, minced
- 1 stalk of celery, chopped
- 1 tablespoon olive oil
- ½ green bell pepper
- Salt and pepper to taste
- ½ cup onion, chopped

Directions:

1. To make the sauce, mix all the sauce ingredients and add to blender.
2. Blend until the mixture is smooth. Clean the calamari and slice it into ½-inch rings.
3. Season calamari with vinegar, red pepper, lemon peel, garlic, lemon juice, and oregano. Add oil to the fryer. Add calamari

with its juice. Fry for about 6-minutes.

4. Stir once and fry for another 2-minutes. Serve with hot sauce.

Nutrition: Calories: 298, Total Fat: 11.3g, Carbs: 10.2g, Protein: 13.7g

387. Salmon & Eggs

Preparation Time: 10 minutes

Cooking Time: 10 minutes

Servings: 2

Ingredients:

- 2 eggs
- 1 lb. salmon, seasoned and cooked
- 1 cup celery, chopped
- 1 onion, chopped
- 1 tablespoon olive oil
- Salt and pepper to taste

Directions:

Whisk the eggs in a bowl. Add celery, onion, salt, and pepper. Add the oil to a baking tray and pour in the egg mixture. Place in the oven at 300°Fahrenheit. Let it cook for 10-minutes. When done, serve with cooked salmon.

Nutrition: Calories: 295, Total Fat: 10.8g, Carbs: 9.7g, Protein: 16.2g

388. Nacho-Crusted Shrimp

Preparation Time: 15 minutes

Cooking Time: 8 minutes

Servings: 8

Ingredients:

- 18 jumbo shrimps, peeled and deveined
- 1 egg, beaten
- 8-9-ounce nacho-flavored chips, crushed
- Salt and pepper to taste

Directions:

1. Prepare two shallow dishes, one with egg and one with crushed chips. Season with a pinch of salt and pepper. Dip shrimp in the egg and then coat in nacho crumbs. Heat oil in a pan. Arrange the shrimp in and cook for 8-minutes.

Nutrition: Calories: 298 , Total Fat: 10.2g, Carbs: 8.9g, Protein: 14.3g

389. Sriracha And Honey Tossed Calamari

Preparation Time: 45 minutes

Cooking Time: 13 minutes

Servings: 2

Ingredients:

- ½ lb. calamari tubes, about ¼ inch wide, rinsed and patted dry
- 1 cup club soda
- ½ cup honey
- Red pepper flakes to taste
- 1 cup almond flour
- Salt and black pepper to taste
- 2 tablespoons sriracha

Directions:

1. Cover calamari rings with club soda in a bowl.
2. Set aside for 10-minutes.
3. In another bowl, mix flour, salt, and black pepper. In a third bowl, combine honey, sriracha, and red pepper flakes.
4. Drain the calamari, pat dry, and cover with flour mixture. Grease your basket with cooking spray. Add calamari in one layer, leaving little space in between. Set temperature to 380°Fahrenheit and cook for 11-minutes.
5. Shake the basket a couple of times during the process.
6. Remove the calamari from the oven, cover with half of the honey sauce, and place inside the oven again. Cook for an additional 2-minutes.
7. When ready to serve, cover with remaining sauce.

Nutrition: Calories: 300, Total Fat: 9.6g, Carbs: 8.3g, Protein: 14.8g

390. Kataifi-Wrapped Shrimp With Lemon Garlic Butter

Preparation Time: 30 minutes

Cooking Time: 22 minutes

Servings: 5

Ingredients:

- 20 large green shrimps,
- peeled and deveined
- 7 tablespoons unsalted butter
- 12-ounces of kataifi pastry
- Wedges of lemon or lime
- Salt and pepper to taste
- 5 cloves of garlic, crushed
- 2 lemons, zested and juiced

Directions:

1. In a pan, over low heat, melt butter. Add the garlic and lemon zest, and sauté for about 2-minutes—season with salt, pepper and lemon juice.
2. Cover the shrimp with half of garlic butter sauce and set aside the remaining half of the sauce.
3. Preheat your oven to 360°Fahrenheit and cover the tray with a sheet of foil. Remove the pastry from the bag and tease out strands.
4. On the countertop lay 6-inch strands. Roll shrimp and butter into pastry. The shrimp tail should be exposed.
5. Repeat process for all shrimp. Place the shrimp into the oven for 10-minutes.
6. Flip shrimp over and place back into the oven for another 10-minutes.
7. Serve with a salad and lime or lemon wedges. Dip the shrimp into the remaining garlic butter sauce.

Nutrition: Calories: 301, Total Fat: 10.3g, Carbs: 9.5g, Protein: 15.4g

391. Fish Taco

Preparation Time: 25 minutes

Cooking Time: 8 minutes

Servings: 2

Ingredients:

- 1 ½ cups almond flour
- 1 can of beer
- 1 teaspoon baking powder
- 1 teaspoon sea salt
- ½ cup salsa
- 8-ounces fresh halibut, sliced into small strips
- Corn tortillas
- Cilantro, chopped

- Cholula sauce to taste
- 2 tablespoons olive oil
- 2 chili peppers, sliced

Avocado Cream:

- 1 large avocado
- ¾ cup buttermilk
- ½ lime juiced

Directions:

1. Make your batter by mixing baking powder, 1 cup of flour, beer, and salt. Stir well. Cover the halibut with the remaining ½ cup of flour and dip it into the batter to coat well. Preheat your oven to 390°Fahrenheit and grease basket with olive oil. Cook the fish for 8-minutes.
2. Mix the avocado cream ingredients in a blender until smooth. Place the corn tortillas on a plate and cover them with salsa. Set aside. Put the fish on top of tortillas and cover with avocado cream. Add Cholula sauce, sprinkle with cilantro and top with chili slices and serve.

Nutrition: Calories: 302, Total Fat: 9.2g, Carbs: 8.7g, Protein: 15.2g

392. Grilled Barramundi With Lemon Butter

Preparation Time: 10 minutes

Cooking Time: 40 minutes

Servings: 2

Ingredients:

- 1 lb. small potatoes
- 7-ounces barramundi fillets
- 1 teaspoon olive oil
- ¼ bunch of fresh thyme, chopped
- Green beans, cooked, optional

Lemon Butter Sauce:

- 1 scallion, chopped
- ½ cup thickened cream
- ½ cup white wine
- 1 bay leaf
- 10 black peppercorns
- 1 clove garlic, chopped
- 8-ounces unsalted butter
- 1 lemon, juiced

- Salt and pepper to taste

Directions:

1. Preheat your oven to 390°Fahrenheit for 5-minutes. In a bowl, add potatoes, salt, thyme and olive oil. Mix ingredients well. Put potatoes into the basket and cook for 20-minutes. Layer the fish fillets in a basket on top of potatoes— Cook for another 20-minutes. Prepare the sauce on top of the stove. Heat scallion and garlic over medium-high heat and add the peppercorns and bay leaf. Pour in the wine and reduce heat to low.
2. Add the thickened cream and stir to blend. Add the butter and whisk over low heat. When the butter has melted, add salt, pepper, and lemon juice. Strain the sauce to remove peppercorns and bay leaf. Place the fish and potatoes on a serving plate and add sauce and serve with green beans.

Nutrition: Calories: 302, Total Fat: 9.6g, Carbs: 8.3g, Protein: 15.8g

393. Cranberry Cod

Preparation Time: 5 minutes

Cooking Time: 20 minutes

Servings: 2

Ingredients:

- 3 filets cod
- 1 tablespoon olive oil
- 3 tablespoons cranberry jam

Directions:

Preheat your oven to 390°Fahrenheit. Brush the cod filets with olive oil. Spoon a tablespoon of cranberry jam on each filet—Cook for 20-minutes.

Nutrition: Calories: 289, Total Fat: 9.2g, Carbs: 8.3g, Protein: 14.3g

394. Cod Fish Teriyaki With Oysters, Mushrooms & Veggies

Preparation Time: 30 minutes

Cooking Time: 10 minutes

Servings: 2

Ingredients:

- 1 tablespoon olive oil
- 6 pieces mini king oyster mushrooms, thinly sliced
- 2 slices (1-inch) codfish
- 1 Napa cabbage leaf, sliced
- 1 clove garlic, chopped
- Salt to taste
- 1 green onion, minced
- Veggies, steamed of your choice

Teriyaki Sauce:

- 1 teaspoon liquid stevia
- 2 tablespoons mirin
- 2 tablespoons soy sauce

Directions:

1. Prepare teriyaki sauce by mixing all the ingredients in a bowl, then set aside. Grease the basket with oil.
2. Place the mushrooms, garlic, Napa cabbage leaf, and salt inside. Layer the fish on top. Preheat your oven to 360°Fahrenheit for 3-minutes.
3. Place the basket in the oven and cook for 5-minutes. Stir.
4. Pour the teriyaki sauce over ingredients in the basket. Cook for an additional 5-minutes. Serve with your choice of steamed veggies.

Nutrition: Calories: 297, Total Fat: 10.6g, Carbs: 9.2g, Protein: 14.2g

395. Salmon With Dill Sauce

Preparation Time: 20 minutes

Cooking Time: 23 minutes

Servings: 4

Ingredients:

- 1 ½ lb. of salmon
- 4 teaspoons olive oil
- Pinch of sea salt

Dill Sauce:

- ½ cup non-fat Greek yogurt
- ½ cup light sour cream
- 2 tablespoons dill, finely chopped
- Pinch of sea salt

Directions:

1. Cut salmon into four 6-ounce portions and drizzle 1 teaspoon of olive oil over each piece.
2. Season with sea salt. Place salmon in a heated pan with oil and cook for 23-minutes.
3. Make dill sauce. In a mixing bowl, mix sour cream, yogurt, chopped dill and sea salt.
4. Top cooked salmon with sauce and garnish with additional dill and serve.

Nutrition: Calories: 303, Total Fat: 10.2g, Carbs: 8.9g, Protein: 14.8g

396. Grilled Salmon With Capers & Dill

Preparation Time: 30 minutes

Cooking Time: 8 minutes

Servings: 2

Ingredients:

- 1 teaspoon capers, chopped
- 2 sprigs dill, chopped
- 1 lemon zest
- 1 tablespoon olive oil
- 4 slices lemon (optional)
- 11-ounce salmon fillet

Dressing:

- 5 capers, chopped
- 1 sprig dill, chopped
- 2 tablespoons plain yogurt
- Pinch of lemon zest
- Salt and black pepper to taste

Directions:

1. Mix dill, capers, lemon zest, olive oil and salt in a bowl. Cover the salmon with this mixture. Cook salmon in a heated pan with oil for 8-minutes.
2. Combine the dressing ingredients in another bowl.
3. When salmon is cooked, place on serving plate and drizzle dressing over it. Place lemon slices at the side of the plate and serve.

Nutrition: Calories: 300, Total Fat: 8.9g, Carbs: 7.3g, Protein: 16.2g

397. Black Cod With Grapes, Pecans, Fennel & Kale

Preparation Time: 1 hour

Cooking Time: 15 minutes

Servings: 2

Ingredients:

- 2 fillets black cod (8-ounces)
- 3 cups kale, minced
- 2 teaspoons white balsamic vinegar
- ½ cup pecans
- 1 cup grapes, halved
- 1 small bulb fennel, cut into inch-thick slices
- 4 tablespoons extra-virgin olive oil
- Salt and black pepper to taste

Directions:

1. Use salt and pepper to season your fish fillets. Drizzle with 1 teaspoon of olive oil.
2. Place the fish in the heated pan with oil with the skin side down and cook for 10-minutes. Take the fish out and cover it loosely with aluminum foil.
3. Combine fennel, pecans, and grapes. Pour 2 tablespoons of olive oil and season with salt and pepper. Cook for an additional 5-minutes.
4. In a bowl, combine minced kale and cooked grapes, fennel and pecans.
5. Cover ingredients with balsamic vinegar and the remaining 1 tablespoon of olive oil. Toss gently. Serve fish with sauce and enjoy!

Nutrition: Calories: 289, Total Fat: 9.2g, Carbs: 8.6g, Protein: 16.3g

398. Air-Fried Asian Style Fish

Preparation Time: 20 minutes

Cooking Time: 20 minutes

Servings: 2

Ingredients:

- 1 medium sea bass
- or halibut (12-ounces)
- 2 garlic cloves, minced

- 1 tablespoon olive oil
- 3 slices of ginger, julienned
- 2 tablespoons cooking wine
- 1 tomato, cut into quarters
- 1 lime, thinly cut
- 1 green onion, chopped
- 1 chili, diced

Directions:

1. Prepare ginger, garlic oil mixture: sauté ginger and garlic with oil until golden brown in a small saucepan over medium-heat on top of the stove.
2. Prepare fish: clean, rinse, and pat dry. Cut in half. Put the fish in a heated pan, then drizzle it with cooking wine.
3. Layer tomato and lime slices on top of fish. Cover with garlic ginger oil mixture.
4. Top with green onion and slices of chili. Cover with aluminum foil. Cook for 20-minutes.

Nutrition: Calories: 304, Total Fat: 9.2g, Carbs: 8.2g, Protein: 16.2g

399. Salmon With Creamy Zucchini

Preparation Time: 15 minutes

Cooking Time: 10 minutes

Servings: 2

Ingredients:

- 2 (6-ounce) salmon fillets, skin on
- Salt and pepper to taste
- 1 teaspoon olive oil
- Courgette:
- 2 large zucchinis, trimmed and spiralized
- 1 avocado, peeled and chopped
- A small handful of parsley, chopped
- ½ garlic clove, minced
- A small handful of cherry tomatoes halved
- A small handful of black olives, chopped
- 2 tablespoons pine nuts, toasted

Directions:

1. Brush salmon with olive oil and season with salt and pepper.
2. Cook salmon in a heated pan with oil and cook for 10-minutes.
3. Blend the avocado, garlic, and parsley in a food processor until smooth.
4. Toss in a bowl with zucchini, olives, and tomatoes.
5. Divide vegetables between two plates, top each portion with salmon fillet, sprinkle with pine nuts, and serve.

Nutrition: Calories: 302, Total Fat: 9.3g, Carbs: 7.8g, Protein: 15.7g

400. Cajun-Seasoned Lemon Salmon

Preparation Time: 20 minutes

Cooking Time: 7 minutes

Servings: 1

Ingredients:

- 1 salmon fillet
- 1 teaspoon Cajun seasoning
- 2 lemon wedges for serving
- 1 teaspoon liquid stevia
- ½ lemon, juiced

Directions:

1. Combine lemon juice and liquid stevia and coat salmon with this mixture.
2. Sprinkle Cajun seasoning all over salmon.
3. Place salmon on parchment paper in the oven and cook for 7-minutes. Serve with lemon wedges.

Nutrition: Calories: 287, Total Fat: 9.3g, Carbs: 8.4g, Protein: 15.3g

401. Salmon Croquettes

Preparation Time: 45 minutes

Cooking Time: 10 minutes

Servings: 4

Ingredients:

- 14-ounce tin of red salmon, drained
- 2 free-range eggs
- 5 tablespoons olive oil
- ½ cup breadcrumbs

- 2 tablespoons spring onions, chopped
- Salt and pepper to taste
- Pinch of herbs

Directions:

1. Add drained salmon into a bowl and mash well. Break in the egg, add herbs, spring onions, salt, pepper and mix well.
2. In another bowl, combine breadcrumbs and oil and mix well.
3. Take a spoon of the salmon mixture and shape it into a croquette shape in your hand.
4. Roll it in the breadcrumbs and fry it in a pan.
5. Serve.

Nutrition: Calories: 298, Total Fat: 8.9g, Carbs: 7.6g, Protein: 15.2g

402. Salmon Asparagus Sweet Potato Nicoise

Preparation Time 10 minutes

Cooking Time 15 minutes

Servings: 2

Ingredients

For the salad:

- 3 hard-boiled eggs
- 2 cups of fresh baby spinach
- 1 cup of seedless grapes
- Cut 2 scallions into 2-inch strips

For the sweet potatoes:

- 1 purple sweet potato peeled and thinly sliced into 1/8-inch-thick rounds
- 1 orange sweet potato peeled and thinly sliced into 1/8-inch-thick rounds
- 1 pinch of salt
- 1 teaspoon of olive oil

For the salmon and asparagus:

- 2 large salmon fillets - about 6 ounces each cut into 1-inch-thick strips
- 2 bunches of asparagus tips trimmed
- 1/2 teaspoon of salt
- 1/4 teaspoon freshly cracked black pepper
- 1/2 teaspoon Provencal herbs (or substitute dried oregano)

- 1 tablespoon of olive oil

For the dressing:

- Sweet Mustard Dill Sauce

Directions

1. Preheat the oven to 425 degrees F.
2. For the sweet potatoes:
3. Start with the sweet potatoes; mix them with a pinch of salt and olive oil and spread them in an even layer on a baking tray. When the oven is ready, roast the sweet potatoes until tender - about 15 minutes.
4. While the sweet potatoes are roasting, prepare the remaining salad
5. For the salmon and asparagus:
6. For the salmon and asparagus, place them in a single layer on a baking tray and sprinkle with salt, pepper, and Provencal herbs or dried oregano. Then divide the olive oil, drizzle the salmon with 1/2 tablespoon, toss the salmon pieces together, and put them back in a single layer on your baking sheet.
7. Drizzle the remaining 1/2 tablespoon of olive oil over the seasoned asparagus and mix well. Then divide the asparagus again in a single layer on the baking tray.
8. When the sweet potatoes are cooked, turn the oven to grill and grill the salmon and asparagus for 5-7 minutes (depending on the salmon's size and thickness) until the edges are golden and the salmon is cooked.

Nutrition: Calories 684 Calories from Fat 477 Fats 53g82% Saturated fat 10 g 63% Cholesterol 186 mg 62% Sodium 561 mg 24% Potassium 1195 mg 34%

403. Mediterranean Fish Packages

Preparation Time 10 minutes

Cooking Time 15 minutes

Servings: 12

Ingredients

- 4 tilapia fillets
- 1/2 cup wish-bone Robust Italian dressing
- 1 cup plum tomatoes (sliced ripe)
- 4 teaspoons capers (drained (optional))
- 1/2 cup of kalamata olives

Directions

1. Preheat the oven to 350 °.
2. Place the fillets in the center of four 12 x 18-inch pieces of heavy aluminum foil. Divide the vegetables evenly among the fillets and sprinkle with Wish-Bone® Robust Italian Dressing. Wrap the foil loosely around the fillet and vegetables and seal the edges airtight with a double fold. Arrange the packages on the jelly roll pan. Bake for 20 minutes or until fillets flake with a fork.

Nutrition: Calories: 68, Total Fat: 3.33g, Carbs: 1.74g, Protein: 7.9g

404. Mediterranean Style Fish Stew

Preparation Time 25 minutes

Cooking Time 55 minutes

Servings: 4

Ingredients

- 28 grams of San Marzano whole tomatoes
- 3 1/2 pounds of fresh cod
- 1 sweet onion (large, halved, and thinly sliced, about 2 cups)
- 2 cloves of garlic (peeled and broken, finely chopped)
- 1 teaspoon of dried oregano
- 1 teaspoon of salt (omit if salt-sensitive)
- 6 tablespoons of EVOO (divided between 4 and 2)
- 1 dash of pepper (to taste)
- 1 dash of red pepper flakes (optional)
- 12 green olives (large, with chili, halved)
- 12 Greek black olives (pitted, halved, Kalamata olives)
- pecorino Romano (grated as a topping, contrary to the old

belief that you should not use cheese with fish it is delicious)
- fresh parsley (finely chopped, for garnish, optional)

Directions

1. Crush the San Marzano tomatoes with your hands, reserve the liquid, and set aside.
2. Pat the fish dry with paper towels and cut them into 4–5-inch pieces.
3. In a large deep skillet, heat 2 tablespoons of EVOO over medium heat. Add half of the cod and cook for 3-4 minutes on each side. Remove from pan and set aside. Repeat with the second half of the fish, remove and set aside.
4. Heat the remaining EVOO over medium heat in the same skillet, add onions, oregano, zucchini, garlic, salt, and pepper until tender.
5. Add tomatoes and liquid to the pan. Bring to the boil.
6. Add the cod and bring back to the boil, spoon over the sauce. Reduce heat to low and leave uncovered until fish flake easily with a fork, about 5-7 minutes, no more.
7. Sprinkle with parsley and grated Pecorino Romano cheese.

Nutrition: Calories: 299, Total Fat: 2.95g, Carbs: 3.32g, Protein: 61.33g

405. Mediterranean Trout With Sautéed Vegetables

Preparation Time: 10 minutes

Cooking Time: 20 minutes

Servings: 4

Ingredients:

- 2 pounds (907 g) rainbow trout fillets
- Salt and ground white pepper, to taste
- 1 tablespoon olive oil
- 1-pound (454 g) asparagus
- 4 medium golden potatoes, thinly sliced
- 1 garlic clove, finely minced

- 1 scallion, thinly sliced, green and white parts separated
- 2 Roma tomatoes, chopped
- 1 large carrot, thinly sliced
- 8 pitted kalamata olives, chopped
- 1/4 cup ground cumin
- 2 tablespoons paprika
- 2 tablespoons dried parsley
- 1 tablespoon vegetable bouillon seasoning
- 1/2 cup dry white wine

Directions:

1. In a bowl, rub the rainbow trout fillets with salt and white pepper. Set aside.
2. Heat the olive oil in a large skillet over medium heat. Sauté the asparagus, golden potatoes, garlic, and the white parts of the scallion in the oil for about 5 minutes, stirring occasionally, or until the garlic is fragrant.
3. Toss in the tomatoes, carrot slices and olives, then continue to cook until the vegetables are tender but still crisp, about 5 to 7 minutes.
4. Add the cumin, paprika, parsley, vegetable bouillon seasoning, and salt. Stir to combine well. Top with the seasoned fillets and slowly pour in the white wine.
5. Turn the heat down to low, cover, and bring to a simmer for about 6 minutes, or until the flesh is opaque and it flakes apart easily.
6. Remove from the heat and sprinkle the scallion greens on top for garnish before serving.
7. TIP: If you don't want to cook the whole trout fillets at a time, you can cut them into uniform pieces, cover them with plastic wrap, and then put them in the freezer for the next meal.

Nutrition PER SERVING

Calories: 495 Total fat: 19.3g saturated fat: 5.2g total carbs: 41.2g fiber: 7.1g Protein: 40.2g Sugar: 8.1g Sodium: 732mg cholesterol: 110mg

406. Garlicky Branzino With Fresh Herbs

Preparation Time: 10 minutes

Cooking Time: 20 minutes

Servings: 2

Ingredients:

- 1½ pounds (680 g) branzino, scaled and gutted
- Salt and freshly ground black pepper, to taste
- 1 tablespoon olive oil
- 1 sliced lemon
- 3 minced garlic cloves
- ¼ cup chopped fresh herbs (any mixture of thyme, oregano, rosemary, and parsley)

Directions:

1. Preheat the oven to 425°F (220°C).
2. Arrange the branzino on a baking dish. Using a sharp knife, make 4 slits in the fish, about 1½ inches apart.
3. Generously brush the fish inside and out with salt and pepper, then drizzle with 1 tablespoon olive oil.
4. Place the lemon slices, garlic gloves, and fresh herbs into the cavity of the fish.
5. Roast the fish in the preheated oven for 15 to 20 minutes, or until the fish flakes easily with a fork and juices run clear.
6. Allow to cool for 5 minutes and remove the lemon slices before serving.
7. TIP: to make this a complete meal, serve it with sautéed mushroom and green beans as a side dish.

Nutrition PER SERVING

Calories: 290 Total fat: 12.3g total carbs: 2.2g fiber: 0g Protein: 42.3g Sugar: 0g Sodium: 150mg cholesterol: 92mg

407. Shrimp With Black Bean Pasta

Preparation Time: 10 minutes

Cooking Time: 15 minutes

Servings: 4

Ingredients:

- 1 package black bean pasta
- 4 tablespoons olive oil
- 3 garlic cloves, minced
- 1 onion, finely chopped
- 1 pound (454 g) fresh shrimp, peeled and deveined
- Salt and pepper, to taste
- ¾ cup low-sodium chicken broth
- ¼ cup basil, cut into strips

Directions:

1. Put the black bean pasta in a large pot of boiling water and cook for 6 minutes.
2. Remove the pasta from the heat. Drain and rinse with cold water, then set the pasta aside on a platter.
3. Heat the olive oil in a large skillet over medium heat. Add the garlic and onion, then cook for 3 minutes until the onion is translucent.
4. Add the shrimp and season with salt and pepper. Cook for 3 minutes, stirring occasionally, or until the shrimp is opaque. Pour in the chicken broth and let it simmer for 2 to 3 minutes until heated through.
5. Remove the shrimp from the heat to the platter of pasta. Pour the liquid over the pasta and garnish with basil, then serve.
6. TIP: If the black bean pasta is not available, you can try any of your favorite pasta with this recipe. And for a unique twist, the jumbo lump crab meat can be substituted for shrimp.

Nutrition PER SERVING

Calories: 670 Total fat: 19.2g saturated fat: 2.2g total carbs: 73.3g fiber: 31.2g Protein: 57.2g Sugar: 1.1g Sodium: 610mg cholesterol: 225mg

408. Spanish Style Salmon With Vegetables

Preparation Time: 10 minutes

Cooking Time: 20 minutes

Servings: 4

Ingredients:

- 2 small red onions, thinly sliced
- 1 cup shaved fennel bulbs
- 1 cup cherry tomatoes
- 15 green pimiento-stuffed olives
- 1 teaspoon cumin seeds
- ½ teaspoon smoked paprika
- Salt and freshly ground black pepper, to taste
- 4 (8-ounce / 227-g) salmon fillets
- ½ cup chicken broth, low-sodium
- 2 to 4 tablespoons olive oil
- 2 cups cooked couscous

Directions:

1. Preheat the oven to 375°F (190°C).
2. Arrange the red onions, fennel bulbs, cherry tomatoes, and olives on two baking sheets. Sprinkle with cumin seeds, paprika, salt, and pepper.
3. Place the salmon fillets on top of the vegetables and sprinkle with salt. Pour the chicken broth evenly over the two baking sheets and drizzle with olive oil.
4. Bake in the preheated oven for 18 to 20 minutes until the vegetables are tender and the fish is flaky, regularly checking to ensure they don't overcook.
5. Divide the cooked couscous among four serving plates and top with vegetables and fillets, then serve.

TIP: If you can't find the salmon fillets, you can use other fish of your choice, like swordfish. The leftovers can be stored for salmon patties.

Nutrition:

Calories: 480 Total fat: 18.3g saturated fat: 3.2g total carbs: 26.2g fiber: 3.1g Protein: 50.2g Sugar: 3.2g Sodium: 295mg cholesterol: 168mg

409. Quick Mussels With White Wine Sauce

Preparation Time: 5 minutes

Cooking Time: 10 minutes

Servings: 4

Ingredients:

- 2 pounds (907 g) small mussels
- 1 tablespoon olive oil
- 3 garlic cloves, sliced
- 1 cup thinly sliced red onion (about ½ medium onion)
- 2 (¼-inch-thick) lemon slices
- 1 cup dry white wine
- ¼ teaspoon kosher or sea salt
- ¼ teaspoon freshly ground black pepper
- Fresh lemon wedges, for garnish

Directions:

1. Put the small mussels in a colander in the sink and run them under cold water. Discard the open shells or damaged shells. Set the mussels aside in the colander.
2. In a large skillet, heat the olive oil over medium-high heat. Add the garlic and onion, cook for 3 to 4 minutes until tender, stirring occasionally.
3. Add the lemon slices, wine, salt, and pepper. Stir well and allow to simmer for 2 minutes.
4. Pour in the mussels and cook covered until the mussels open their shells, giving the pan a shake from time to time, about 3 minutes.
5. With a slotted spoon, transfer the mussels to a serving bowl. Be sure to discard any mussels that are still closed.
6. Pour the wine sauce over the mussels in the bowl and serve garnished with lemon wedges.

TIP: to make this a complete meal, you can serve it with garlic bread or lemony broth on the side.

Nutrition PER SERVING

Calories: 344 total fat: 16.3g saturated fat: 5.8g total carbs: 11.5g fiber: 0g protein: 36.4g sugar: 1.1g sodium: 1270mg phosphorus: 585mg potassium: 833mg cholesterol: 92mg

410. Breaded Fish

Preparation Time: 5 minutes

Cooking Time: 12 minutes

Servings: 4

Ingredients:

- 4 fish fillets
- 1 egg
- 5-ounces breadcrumbs
- 4 tablespoons olive oil

Directions:

1. In a bowl, mix oil and breadcrumbs. Whisk egg. Gently dip the fish into the egg and then into a crumb mixture. Heat oil in a pan. Fry the fish fillets.
2. Serve.

Nutrition per serving: Calories: 302, Total Fat: 10.4g, Carbs: 8.9g, Protein: 14.6g

411. Tilapia With Egg

Preparation Time: 30 minutes

Cooking Time: 15 minutes

Servings: 3

Ingredients:

- 2 egg yolks
- 4 wheat buns
- 1 lb. tilapia fillets, sliced
- 1 tablespoon nectar
- 1 tablespoon hot sauce
- 3 teaspoons of sweet pickle relish
- 2 tablespoons mayonnaise
- 1 tablespoon fish sauce

Directions:

1. Mix the fish sauce and egg yolks in a bowl. Add mayonnaise, sweet pickle relish, hot sauce, and nectar. Pour the mixture into a baking tray.
2. Place the tray inside the oven. Cook for 15 minutes at 300°Fahrenheit.

Nutrition per serving: Calories: 226, Total Fat: 8.8g, Carbs: 3.62g, Protein: 33.11g

412. Marinated Shrimp With Orange

Preparation Time: 10 minutes

Cooking Time: 10 minutes

Servings: 6

Ingredients:

- 1½ pounds (680 g) fresh raw shrimp, shells and tails removed
- 3 tablespoons olive oil, divided
- 1 large orange, zested and peeled
- 3 garlic cloves, minced
- 1 tablespoon chopped fresh thyme (about 6 sprigs)
- 1 tablespoon chopped fresh rosemary (about 3 sprigs)
- ¼ teaspoon kosher or sea salt
- ¼ teaspoon freshly ground black pepper

Directions:

1. Put the shrimp, 2 tablespoons olive oil, orange zest, garlic, thyme, rosemary, salt, and pepper in a zip-top plastic bag. Seal the bag and shake until the shrimp is coated thoroughly. Set aside to marinate for 5 minutes.
2. In a large skillet, heat 1 tablespoon olive oil over medium heat. Add the shrimp and cook for 2 to 3 minutes per side, or until the flesh is pink and opaque.
3. Meanwhile, slice the peeled orange into bite-sized wedges on your cutting board, then place them in a serving bowl.
4. Remove the shrimp from the pan to the bowl. Toss well. Serve immediately, or refrigerate to chill until you want to serve.

TIP: The orange zest can be replaced with lemon zest. You can use ¼ cup freshly chopped mint substituted for the thyme and rosemary in this recipe for a distinct combination.

Nutrition PER SERVING

Calories: 144 Total fat: 8.3g saturated fat: 1.1g total carbs: 3g fiber: 0.1g Protein: 23.4g Sugar: 1.8g Sodium: 1084mg Phosphorus: 227mg potassium: 137mg cholesterol: 286mg

413. Poached Salmon With Mustard Sauce

Preparation Time: 15 minutes

Cooking Time: 20 minutes

Servings: 2

Ingredients:

Mustard sauce:

- ¼ cup plain Greek yogurt
- 2 tablespoons Dijon mustard
- 1 ½ teaspoons dried tarragon
- Pinch salt
- Pinch freshly ground black pepper

Salmon:

- 10 ounces (284 g) salmon fillets
- 1 tablespoon olive oil
- Salt and freshly ground black pepper, to taste
- ½ fresh lemon, sliced
- ¼ cup dry white wine
- Juice of ½ lemon
- ¼ cup water

Directions:

1. Make the mustard sauce: In a bowl, mix the yogurt, Dijon mustard, tarragon, salt, and pepper until well combined. Set aside.
2. In a separate bowl, brush the salmon fillets with olive oil, salt, and pepper. Place the lemon slices on top of the fillets.
3. Add the white wine, lemon juice, and water to a skillet over medium-high heat. Bring them to a boil, then put in the salmon fillets.
4. Reduce the heat to medium and allow to simmer covered for 15 minutes, or until the fish is flaky.
5. Divide the salmon fillets between two serving plates. Pour the mustard sauce over the fillets, then serve warm.

TIP: You can try other fresh herbs of your choice, such as thyme, oregano, or rosemary.

Nutrition PER SERVING

Calories: 330 Total fat: 21.2g total carbs: 3.2g fiber: 0g Protein: 22.2g Sugar: 2.1g Sodium: 443mg cholesterol: 70mg

414. Grilled Halibut With Romesco Sauce

Preparation Time: 20 minutes

Cooking Time: 10 minutes

Servings: 2

Ingredients:

Romesco sauce:

- ½ cup jarred roasted piquillo peppers
- ¼ cup raw and unsalted almonds
- 2 tablespoons sun-dried tomatoes in olive oil with herbs
- ¼ teaspoon smoked paprika or more to taste
- 2 small garlic cloves
- ¼ cup olive oil
- 2 tablespoons red wine vinegar
- Pinch salt

Halibut:

- 2 (5-ounce / 142-g) halibut steaks
- 1 tablespoon olive oil for greasing the grill grates
- Salt and freshly ground black pepper, to taste

Directions:

1. Make the romesco sauce: In a food processor, put the piquillo peppers, almonds, tomatoes, paprika, garlic cloves, olive oil, vinegar, and salt. Pulse until all ingredients are combined into a smooth mixture. Transfer to a bowl and set aside.
2. Preheat the grill to medium-high heat. Lightly grease the grill grates with olive oil and set them aside.
3. In a separate bowl, rub the halibut steaks with olive oil, salt, and pepper.
4. Grill the halibut steaks on the preheated grill for about 10 minutes, flipping the steaks halfway through, or until the fish flakes easily with a fork and juices run clear.
5. Transfer the halibut steaks to two plates and pour over the romesco sauce. Serve hot.

TIP: You can store the remaining Romesco sauce in a sealed airtight container in the fridge for up to one week.

Nutrition PER SERVING

Calories: 266 Total fat: 13.2g total carbs: 3.2g fiber: 1.1g Protein: 31.2g Sugar: 1.1g Sodium: 107mg cholesterol: 0mg

415. Mackerel Niçoise Salad

Preparation Time: 10 minutes

Cooking Time: 20 minutes

Servings: 2

Ingredients:

Dressing:

- 4 tablespoons olive oil
- 3 tablespoons red wine vinegar
- 1 teaspoon Dijon mustard
- ¼ teaspoon salt
- Pinch freshly ground black pepper

Salad:

- 2 teaspoons salt
- 2 small red potatoes
- 1 cup green beans
- 2 cups baby greens
- 2 hard-boiled eggs, sliced
- ½ cup cherry tomatoes halved
- 1/3 cup Niçoise olives
- 2 (4-ounce / 113-g) cooked mackerel fillets

Directions:

1. Make the dressing: In a bowl, combine the olive oil, vinegar, mustard, salt, and pepper. Stir with a fork until mixed thoroughly and set aside.
2. Make the salad: Fill a large pot with 3 inches of cold water, and add the salt. Bring it to a boil, then add the red potatoes and cook until they can be pierced easily with the tip of a sharp knife but are still firm for about 12 minutes.
3. Remove the red potatoes from the heat to a colander. Blanch the green beans in the boiling water for 5 minutes or until they start to soften. Transfer the green beans to the colander of potatoes. Let them cool under running cold water. When cooked, drain and dry

with paper towels, slice the potatoes on a flat work surface.

4. Spread out the baby greens on two serving plates. Top each dish with the sliced potatoes, green beans, and hard-boiled eggs. Scatter the tomatoes and olives over them, then place the mackerel fillets on top of the salad.
5. To serve, pour the prepared dressing over the salad and toss well.

TIP: To save time, you can buy the canned mackerel fillets directly in the market. And you can try any of your favorite fish, like grilled salmon or canned tuna.

Nutrition PER SERVING

Calories: 660 total fat:47.3 g total carbs: 38.5g fiber: 7.2g Protein: 25.3g Sugar: 4.1g Sodium: 350mg cholesterol: 160mg

416. Browned Salmon Cakes

Preparation Time: 15 minutes

Cooking Time: 15 minutes

Servings: 4

Ingredients:

- 1-pound (454 g) salmon fillets, spine, bones, and skin removed
- ½ cup red onion, minced
- 1 large egg, whisked
- 2 tablespoons mayonnaise
- 1 ripe avocado, pitted, peeled, and mashed
- ½ cup almond flour
- 1 teaspoon garlic powder
- 1 to 2 teaspoons dried dill
- ½ teaspoon paprika
- 1 teaspoon salt
- ½ teaspoon freshly ground black pepper
- Zest and juice of 1 lemon
- ¼ cup olive oil

Directions:

1. Cut the salmon fillets into small pieces on a clean work surface and transfer them to a large bowl.
2. Add the minced red onion to the bowl and mash the salmon with a fork to break up any lumps. Add the whisked egg,

mayo, and mashed avocado. Stir to combine well and set aside.
3. Mix the almond flour, garlic powder, dill, paprika, salt, and pepper separately.
4. Pour the dry ingredients into the bowl of the salmon mixture, along with the lemon zest and juice. Mix well.
5. Make the salmon cakes: Scoop out equal-sized portions of the salmon mixture and shape them into patties with your palm, about 2 inches in diameter. Set aside on a plate for 15 minutes.
6. Heat the olive oil in a large skillet over medium heat. Add the salmon patties and fry for 2 to 3 minutes on each side until the edges are lightly browned. Reduce the heat to low and cook covered until the cakes are cooked through about 7 minutes.
7. Remove from the heat and serve on plates.

TIP: To add more flavors to this meal, serve it alongside the broccoli salad with toasted walnuts. It also tastes great paired with the garlic aioli.

Nutrition PER SERVING

Calories: 340 Total fat: 26.3g total carbs: 5.2g fiber: 1.1g Protein: 23.2g Sodium: 693mg

417. Shrimp Mojo de Ajo

Preparation Time: 10 minutes

Cooking Time: 40 minutes

Servings: 4

Ingredients

- 1/4 cup extra-virgin olive oil
- 10 garlic cloves, minced
- 1/8 teaspoon cayenne pepper, plus more as needed
- 8 ounces mushrooms, quartered
- 1-pound medium shrimp, peeled, deveined, and tails removed
- Juice of 1 lime
- 1/2 teaspoon sea salt
- 1/4 cup chopped fresh cilantro leaves

- 2 cups cooked brown rice

Directions

1. I am preparing the Ingredients. In a small saucepan over the lowest heat setting, bring the olive oil, garlic, and cayenne to a low simmer, so bubbles just barely break the surface of the oil. Simmer for 30 minutes, stirring occasionally. Strain the garlic from the oil and set it aside.
2. Cooking. Add the olive oil to a large skillet over medium-high heat and heat it until it shimmers. Add the mushrooms. Cook for about 5 minutes, stirring once or twice until browned. Add the shrimp, lime juice, and sea salt. Cook for about 4 minutes, occasionally stirring, until the shrimp are pink. Remove from the heat and stir in the cilantro and reserved garlic. Serve over the hot brown rice.

Nutrition PER SERVING

Calories: 315 Total fat: 7.57g total carbs: 47.24g fiber: 1.1g Protein: 21.47g Sodium: 1058mg

Chapter 11. Bread and Pizza Recipes

418. Rosemary-Walnut Loaf Bread

Preparation Time: 90 minutes

Cooking Time: 45 minutes

Servings: 8

Ingredients:

- ½ cup chopped walnuts
- 4 tbsp fresh, chopped rosemary
- 1 1/3 cups lukewarm carbonated water
- 1 tbsp honey
- ½ cup extra virgin olive oil
- 1 tsp apple cider vinegar
- 3 eggs
- 5 tsp instant dry yeast granules
- 1 tsp salt
- 1 tbsp xanthan gum
- ¼ cup buttermilk powder
- 1 cup white rice flour
- 1 cup tapioca starch
- 1 cup arrowroot starch
- 1 ¼ cups all-purpose Bob's Red Mill gluten-free flour mix

Directions for Cooking:

1. In a large mixing bowl, whisk healthy eggs. Add 1 cup warm water, honey, olive oil, and vinegar.
2. While beating continuously, add the rest of the ingredients except for rosemary and walnuts.
3. Continue beating. If the dough is too stiff, add a bit of warm water. The dough should be shaggy and thick.
4. Then add rosemary and walnuts continue kneading until evenly distributed.
5. Cover bowl of dough with a clean towel, place in a warm spot and let it rise for 30 minutes.
6. Fifteen minutes into rising time, preheat oven to 400oF.
7. Generously grease with olive oil a 2-quart Dutch oven and preheat inside the range without the lid.

8. Once the dough rises, remove the pot from the oven, and place the dough inside. With a wet spatula, spread the top of the dough evenly in the pot.
9. Brush bread tops with 2 tbsp of olive oil, cover Dutch oven, and bake for 35 to 45 minutes.
10. Once the bread is done, remove it from the oven. And gently remove bread from the pot.
11. Allow bread to cool at least ten minutes before slicing.
12. Serve and enjoy.

Nutrition:

Calories per **Servings:** 424; Carbs: 56.8g; Protein: 7.0g; Fat: 19.0g

419. Tasty Crabby Panini

Preparation Time: 20 minutes

Cooking Time: 10 minutes

Servings: 4

Ingredients:

- 1 tbsp Olive oil
- French bread split and sliced diagonally
- 1 lb. blue crab meat or shrimp or spiny lobster or stone crab
- ½ cup celery
- ¼ cup green onion chopped
- 1 tsp Worcestershire sauce
- 1 tsp lemon juice
- 1 tbsp Dijon mustard
- ½ cup light mayonnaise

Directions for Cooking:

1. In a medium bowl, mix the following thoroughly: celery, onion, Worcestershire, lemon juice, mustard and mayonnaise. Season with pepper and salt. Then gently add in the almonds and crabs.
2. Spread olive oil on sliced sides of bread and smear with crab mixture before covering with another bread slice.
3. Grill the sandwich in a Panini press until bread is crisped and ridged.

Nutrition:

Calories per **Servings:** 248; Carbs: 12.0g; Protein: 24.5g; Fat: 10.9g

420. Sardinian Flatbread

Preparation Time: 1 hour 15 minutes

Cooking Time: 15 minutes

Servings: 6

Ingredients:

- 1½ cups all-purpose flour, plus more for dusting
- 1½ cups semolina flour
- 1½ cups warm water
- 1 (¼-ounce) packet active dry yeast
- Pinch salt
- Extra-virgin olive oil for brushing

Directions:

1. Combine the flours, water, yeast, and salt in a large bowl and mix thoroughly to form a firm dough.
2. Turn out the dough onto a work surface and divide it into quarters. Set the dough pieces on a rimmed baking sheet, cover, and let rest for 1 hour.
3. Preheat the oven to 375°F. Lightly brush another rimmed baking sheet with olive oil.
4. Lightly flour a work surface and a rolling pin. Roll out one piece of dough until it is as thin as possible, then place it on the prepared baking sheet.
5. Bake for 2 minutes. Turn the flatbread over and bake for another 2 minutes, or until crisp.
6. Repeat with the remaining dough.

Nutrition PER SERVING:

Calories: 275; Total Fat: 2g; Saturated Fat: 0g; Protein: 9g; Total Carbohydrates: 55g; Fiber: 3g; Sugar: 0g; Cholesterol: 0mg

421. Focaccia (Italian Flatbread)

Preparation Time: 2 hours

Cooking Time: 30 minutes

Servings: 8

Ingredients:

- 2½ cups warm water, divided
- 2 teaspoons active dry yeast
- Pinch sugar
- 6 cups all-purpose flour, divided
- 5 tablespoons extra-virgin olive oil, divided
- 2 tablespoons coarse sea salt, divided
- 1 tablespoon chopped fresh rosemary

Directions:

1. Pour ½ cup of warm water into a large bowl and sprinkle on the yeast and sugar. Stir, then let rest for 1 minute. The yeast mixture should start to look foamy.
2. Add the remaining 2 cups of warm water, 2 cups of flour, 2 tablespoons of olive oil, and 1 tablespoon of sea salt. Stir until smooth.
3. Slowly add the remaining 4 cups of flour, using your hands to combine. If the dough is too sticky, add additional flour.
4. Turn out the dough onto a work surface and knead until you get a smooth, springy dough.
5. Brush a bowl with 1 tablespoon of olive oil. Place the dough in the bowl, cover with plastic wrap, and set aside in a warm place until the dough rises to double its size, about 1½ hours.
6. Preheat the oven to 425°F. Brush an 11-by-17-inch baking pan with 1 tablespoon of olive oil.
7. Press the dough into the prepared pan in an even layer, covering the entire surface. It may take a few minutes for the dough to cooperate. Cover the dough with a damp kitchen towel and let rise until doubled in size, about 30 minutes.
8. Press the dough with your fingers to add dimples all over. Brush with the remaining 2 tablespoons of olive oil, allowing it to pool in the dimples. Sprinkle with the

remaining 1 tablespoon of sea salt and the rosemary.

9. Place a baking pan filled with ice on the lowest oven shelf or on the oven floor to create steam. Place the baking pan on the rack above.
10. Bake for about 30 minutes, until golden.
11. Transfer the focaccia to a wire rack to cool, then cut into strips or squares.

VARIATION TIP: Feel free to experiment with toppings—you can add chopped tomatoes, onions, garlic, olives, or whatever you like.

Nutrition PER SERVING:

Calories: 419; Total Fat: 9g; Saturated Fat: 1g; Protein: 10g; Total Carbohydrates: 72g; Fiber: 3g; Sugar: 0g; Cholesterol: 0mg

422. Taralli (Pugliese Bread Knots)

Preparation Time: 45 minutes

Cooking Time: 25 minutes

Servings: 30 pieces

Ingredients:

- 2 cups all-purpose flour
- 1/2 teaspoon salt
- 1/2 cup dry white wine
- 1/3 cup extra-virgin olive oil
- 1/2 teaspoon freshly ground black pepper

Directions:

1. In a large bowl, combine the flour and salt. Add the wine and olive oil and mix with a fork until the mixture forms a rough dough.
2. Turn the dough onto a work surface and knead until smooth; sprinkle with the pepper as you work until it is all combined and the dough is soft.
3. Cover the dough with a kitchen towel and let it rest for 15 minutes.
4. Preheat the oven to 375°F. Line a rimmed baking sheet with parchment paper. Bring a large pot of water to a boil over high heat.

5. Roll a tablespoon of the dough into a rope about 4 inches long and ½ inch thick for each bread knot. Form a circle with the string, then crisscross the ends to form a knot shape and press the ends together to seal.
6. Drop a few knots at a time into the boiling water. When they float, after about 30 seconds, transfer them with a slotted spoon to a kitchen towel to dry.
7. Arrange the taralli on the prepared baking sheet in a single layer, ensuring they do not touch.
8. Bake for 25 minutes, or until golden.
9. Transfer to a rack to cool a bit before serving.

Nutrition PER SERVING (3 PIECES):

Calories: 164; Total Fat: 7g; Saturated Fat: 1g; Protein: 3g; Total Carbohydrates: 19g; Fiber: 1g; Sugar: 0g; Cholesterol: 0mg

423. Testaroli (Etruscan Pancakes)

Preparation Time: 5 minutes

Cooking Time: 15 minutes

Servings: 2

Ingredients:

- ½ cup whole wheat flour
- ½ cup all-purpose flour
- 1 cup warm water
- Salt
- 2 tablespoons extra-virgin olive oil

Directions:

1. In a bowl, whisk together the flours, water, and a pinch of salt until you get a thick batter. Let the mixture rest while you heat a cast-iron skillet over high heat. At the same time, fill a large pot with warm salted water.
2. Brush the skillet with about 1 teaspoon of olive oil, then pour about ¼ cup of the batter into the hot pan, just enough to cover the bottom. Cook for 1 to

2 minutes, until golden brown, flip, and cook the other side until golden.

3. Remove the pancake from the pan and cut the testaroli into 6 or 8 wedges like a pizza. Transfer the wedges to the pot of warm salted water and let them sit for 1 minute, then remove from the water.
4. Repeat with the remaining batter and oil.

COOKING TIP: If you want a drier pancake, you can skip the step of dunking the testaroli in warm water. They are just as tasty fresh out of the skillet.

Nutrition PER SERVING:

Calories: 335; Total Fat: 15g; Saturated Fat: 2g; Protein: 7g; Total Carbohydrates: 45g; Fiber: 4g; Sugar: 0g; Cholesterol: 0mg

424. Pesto Vegetable Bread

Preparation Time: 15 minutes

Cooking Time: 20 minutes

Servings: 4

Ingredients:

- 2 tablespoons extra-virgin olive oil, plus more for drizzling
- ½ eggplant, cut into cubes
- ½ fennel bulb, trimmed and sliced
- 1 red bell pepper, seeded and cut into strips
- 1 bunch broccoli rabe
- 1 loaf Focaccia
- 2 tablespoons Basil Pesto with Almond Butter or store-bought pesto
- ½ small onion, thinly sliced
- 4 radishes, sliced
- 1 teaspoon fresh thyme leaves
- ½ teaspoon salt
- 1 teaspoon minced garlic

Directions:

1. Preheat the oven to 350°F.
2. In a large skillet, heat the olive oil over medium heat. Add the eggplant, fennel, and bell pepper and cook for about 10 minutes until they start to soften.

3. Meanwhile, bring a large pot of water to a boil over high heat. Add the broccoli rabe and cook for 3 minutes. Drain, squeeze out any excess water and cut it into bite-size pieces.
4. Slice the focaccia in half horizontally all the way through and brush each cut side with the pesto. Arrange the eggplant, fennel, bell pepper, and broccoli rabe on the pesto. Top with the onion and radish slices and sprinkle with the thyme and salt.
5. Bake for 5 to 10 minutes, until the fresh ingredients start to warm.
6. Turn the oven to broil and toast for 1 minute.
7. Remove the bread from the oven. Sprinkle with the garlic and drizzle with a bit of olive oil. Cut into slices.

INGREDIENT TIP: Leftover roasted vegetables are ideal for this recipe.

Nutrition PER SERVING: Calories: 1,003; Total Fat: 30g; Saturated Fat: 4g; Protein: 24g; Total Carbohydrates: 158g; Fiber: 18g; Sugar: 6g; Cholesterol: 1mg

425. Tomato Bruschetta

Preparation Time: 10 minutes

Cooking Time: 4 minutes

Servings: 6

Ingredients:

- 1 baguette, sliced
- 3 large tomatoes, finely chopped
- 1 small onion, diced
- ¼ cup extra-virgin olive oil
- 4 garlic cloves, minced
- 1 teaspoon dried oregano
- 1 teaspoon salt
- ¼ teaspoon freshly ground black pepper
- Chopped fresh basil for garnish

Direction;

1. Preheat the oven to 350°F.
2. Place the baguette slices on a rimmed baking sheet. Toast for

2 minutes, turn them over and toast for another 2 minutes.

3. Combine the tomatoes, onion, olive oil, garlic, oregano, salt, and pepper in a large bowl and toss to mix thoroughly.
4. Arrange the toasted baguette slices on a serving plate and spoon the tomato mixture generously over each piece. Sprinkle with basil.

MAKE-AHEAD TIP: You can make the tomato mixture an hour ahead of time, cover it, and store it in the refrigerator.

Nutrition PER SERVING:

Calories: 206; Total Fat: 10g; Saturated Fat: 1g; Protein: 5g; Total Carbohydrates: 25g; Fiber: 2g; Sugar: 5g; Cholesterol: 0mg

426. White Bean Crostini

Preparation Time: 5 minutes

Cooking Time: 4 minutes

Serving 4

Ingredients:

- 1 baguette, sliced
- 1 (19-ounce) can cannellini beans, rinsed and drained
- 2 tablespoons extra-virgin olive oil, plus more for drizzling
- 1 garlic clove, peeled
- 1 teaspoon salt
- ½ teaspoon dried oregano
- ¼ teaspoon red pepper flakes
- ¼ teaspoon freshly ground black pepper

Directions:

1. Preheat the oven to 350°F.
2. Place the baguette slices on a rimmed baking sheet. Toast for 2 minutes, turn them over and toast for another 2 minutes.
3. Combine the beans, olive oil, garlic, salt, oregano, red pepper flakes, and black pepper and puree in a food processor or blender.
4. Spoon the bean mixture onto the toasted baguette slices and drizzle with extra-virgin olive oil.

Nutrition: PER SERVING:

Calories: 481; Total Fat: 11g; Saturated Fat: 2g; Protein: 17g; Total Carbohydrates: 79g; Fiber: 9g; Sugar: 4g; Cholesterol: 0mg

427. Pizza Bianca With Spinach

Preparation Time: 15 minutes

Cooking Time: 15 minutes

Servings: 4

Ingredients:

2 rounds Pizza Dough or 12-inch store-bought pizza crusts

2 tablespoons extra-virgin olive oil

2 garlic cloves, minced

2 cups frozen chopped spinach, thawed and drained

1 cup shredded provolone cheese

1 cup shredded mozzarella cheese

1 tablespoon dried oregano

Directions:

1. Preheat the oven to 450°F.
2. Brush the pizza crusts with olive oil and sprinkle with garlic and spinach.
3. Cover the pizzas with the cheeses and sprinkle with the oregano.
4. Bake for 10 to 15 minutes, until the cheese, is browned and bubbling.
5. Let rest for 1 minute before slicing.

Nutrition:

Calories: 586; Total Fat: 38g; Saturated Fat: 18g; Protein: 25g; Total Carbohydrates: 39g; Fiber: 5g; Sugar: 8g; Cholesterol: 77mg

428. Mashed Grape Tomato Pizzas

Preparation Time: 10 minutes

Cooking Time: 20 minutes

Servings: 6

Ingredients:

- 3 cups grape tomatoes, halved
- 1 teaspoon chopped fresh thyme leaves
- 2 garlic cloves, minced

- 1/4 teaspoon kosher salt
- 1/4 teaspoon freshly ground black pepper
- 1 tablespoon extra-virgin olive oil
- 3/4 cup shredded Parmesan cheese
- 6 whole-wheat pita bread

Directions:

1. Preheat the oven to 425ºF (220ºC).
2. Combine the tomatoes, thyme, garlic, salt, ground black pepper, and olive oil in a baking pan.
3. Roast in the preheated oven for 20 minutes. Remove the pan from the oven, mash the tomatoes with a spatula and stir to mix well halfway through the cooking time.
4. Meanwhile, divide and spread the cheese over each pita bread, then place the bread in a separate baking pan and roast in the oven for 5 minutes or until golden brown and the cheese melts.
5. Transfer the pita bread onto a large plate, then top with the roasted, mashed tomatoes. Serve immediately.

Tip: If you want a juicier pizza, you can replace the grape tomatoes with regular large tomatoes and chopped the tomatoes into chunks to make them easier for cooking.

Nutrition:

calories: 140 fat: 5.1g Protein: 6.2g carbs: 16.9g fiber: 2.0g Sodium: 466mg

429. Sumptuous Vegetable and Cheese Lavash Pizza

Preparation Time: 15 minutes

Cooking Time: 11 minutes

Servings 4

Ingredients:

- 2 (12 by 9-inch) lavash bread
- 2 tablespoons extra-virgin olive oil
- 10 ounces (284 g) frozen spinach, thawed and squeezed dry
- 1 cup shredded fontina cheese

- 1 tomato, cored and cut into ½-inch pieces
- ½ cup pitted large green olives, chopped
- ¼ teaspoon red pepper flakes
- 3 garlic cloves, minced
- ¼ teaspoon sea salt
- ¼ teaspoon ground black pepper
- ½ cup grated Parmesan cheese

Directions:

1. Preheat oven to 475ºF (246ºC).
2. Brush the lavash bread with olive oil, then place them on two baking sheets. Heat in the preheated oven for 4 minutes or until lightly browned. Flip the bread halfway through the cooking time.
3. Meanwhile, combine the spinach, fontina cheese, tomato pieces, olives, red pepper flakes, garlic, salt, and black pepper in a large bowl. Stir to mix well.
4. Remove the lavash bread from the oven and sit them on two large plates, spread them with the spinach mixture, then scatter with the Parmesan cheese on top.
5. Bake in the oven for 7 minutes or until the cheese melts and is well browned.
6. Slice and serve warm.

Tip: You can replace the tomato, spinach, and olives with broccoli, fennel and artichoke for a different lavash pizza.

Nutrition:

calories: 431 fat: 21.5g Protein: 20.0g carbs: 38.4g fiber: 2.5g Sodium: 854mg

430. Eggplant Pizza

Preparation Time: 40 minutes

Cooking Time: 50 minutes

Servings: 4

Ingredients:

- 1 large eggplant
- 1/3 Cup Olive oil
- Pepper to taste
- Salt to taste
- 2 cups cherry tomatoes – halved

- 1½ cups Shredded mozzarella cheese
- 1¼ cups Marinara sauce
- 1/2 cup Torn basil leaves

Directions:

1. Preheat your oven to 450°F.
2. Slice the eggplants into slices and arrange them on the baking sheet.
3. Cover each of the eggplant slices with olive oil.
4. Roast the eggplant slices until tender.
5. Spread two tbsp of the marinara sauce on each piece.
6. Add the cheese and arrange cherry tomato pieces on each.
7. Cook for about four minutes, removing when the cheese melts.

Nutrition: calories 466; fat 23.5 g; carbohydrates 44.5 g; Protein 20 g

431. BBQ Chicken Pizza

Preparation Time: 15 minutes

Cooking Time: 30 minutes

Servings: 4

Ingredients:

Dairy-Free Pizza Crust

- 6 tablespoons Parmesan cheese
- 6 large eggs
- 3 tablespoons psyllium husk powder
- Salt and black pepper, to taste
- 1½ teaspoons Italian seasoning

Toppings

- 6 oz. rotisserie chicken, shredded
- 4 oz. cheddar cheese
- 1 tablespoon mayonnaise
- 4 tablespoons tomato sauce
- 4 tablespoons BBQ sauce

Directions:

1. Warm the oven to 400 degrees F and grease a baking dish. Place all Pizza Crust ingredients in an immersion blender and blend until smooth.
2. Spread dough mixture onto the baking dish and transfer it to the oven. Bake for about 10 minutes and top with favorite

toppings. Bake for about 3 minutes and dish out.

Nutrition: Calories: 356 Carbs: 2.9g Fats: 24.5g Proteins: 24.5g

432. Caramelized Onion and Goat Cheese Pizza

Preparation Time: 1 hour & 15 minutes

Cooking Time: 30 minutes

Servings: 4

Ingredients:

For the crust:

- 2 cups flour
- 1 cup lukewarm water
- 1 pinch of sugar
- 1 tsp active dry yeast
- ¾ tsp salt
- 2 tbsp olive oil

For the topping:

- 2 tbsp butter
- 2 red onions, thinly sliced
- Salt and black pepper to taste
- 1 cup crumbled goat cheese
- 1 tbs almond milk
- 1 cup fresh curly endive, chopped

Directions:

1. Sift the flour and salt in a bowl and stir in yeast—mix lukewarm water, olive oil, and sugar in another bowl. Add the wet mixture to the dry mixture and whisk until you obtain a soft dough.
2. Place the dough on a lightly floured work surface and knead it thoroughly until elastic for 4-5 minutes. Transfer the dough to a greased bowl.
3. Cover with cling film and leave to rise for 50-60 minutes in a warm place until doubled in size. Roll out the dough to a thickness of around 12 inches.
4. Preheat the oven to 400 F. Line a pizza pan with parchment paper. Melt the butter in a large skillet and stir in the onions.
5. Reduce the heat to low, season the onions with salt, black pepper, and cook with frequent

stirring until caramelized, 15 to 20 minutes. Turn the heat.

6. In a medium bowl, mix the goat cheese with the almond milk and spread it on the crust. Top with the caramelized onions. Bake in the oven for 10 minutes and take out after. Top with the curly endive, slice, and serve warm.

Nutrition: Calories 317 Fats 20g Carbs 1g Protein 28g

433. Grilled Burgers with Mushrooms

Preparation Time: 10 minutes

Cooking Time: 10 minutes

Servings: 4

Ingredients:

- 2 Bibb lettuce, halved
- 4 slices red onion
- 4 slices tomato
- 4 whole wheat buns, toasted
- 2 tbsp olive oil
- ¼ tsp cayenne pepper, optional
- 1 garlic clove, minced
- 1 tbsp sugar
- ½ cup water
- 1/3 cup balsamic vinegar
- 4 large Portobello mushroom caps, around 5-inches in diameter

Directions for Cooking:

1. Remove stems from mushrooms and clean with a damp cloth. Transfer into a baking dish with gill-side up.
2. Mix thoroughly olive oil, cayenne pepper, garlic, sugar, water, and vinegar in a bowl. Pour over mushrooms and marinate mushrooms in the ref for at least an hour.
3. Once the one hour is nearly up, preheat the grill to medium-high fire and grease grill grate.
4. Grill mushrooms for five minutes per side or until tender. Baste mushrooms with the marinade, so it doesn't dry up.
5. To assemble, place ½ of bread bun on a plate, top with a slice of onion, mushroom, tomato and one lettuce leaf. Cover with

the other top half of the bun. Repeat process with remaining ingredients, serve and enjoy.

Nutrition:

Calories per **Servings:** 244.1; Carbs: 32g; Protein: 8.1g; Fat: 9.3g

434. Mediterranean Baba Ghanoush

Preparation Time: 5 minutes

Cooking Time: 25 minutes

Servings: 4

Ingredients:

- 1 bulb garlic
- 1 red bell pepper, halved and seeded
- 1 tbsp chopped fresh basil
- 1 tbsp olive oil
- 1 tsp black pepper
- 2 eggplants, sliced lengthwise
- 2 rounds of flatbread or pita
- Juice of 1 lemon

Directions for Cooking:

1. Grease grill grate with cooking sprays and preheat grill to medium-high.
2. Slice the tops of the garlic bulb and wrap in foil. Place in the more excellent portion of the grill and roast for at least 20 minutes.
3. Place bell pepper and eggplant slices on the hottest part of the grill.
4. Grill for at least two to three minutes on each side.
5. Once bulbs are done, peel off skins of roasted garlic and place peeled garlic into a food processor.
6. Add olive oil, pepper, basil, lemon juice, grilled red bell pepper and grilled eggplant.
7. Puree until smooth and transfer into a bowl.
8. Grill bread at least 30 seconds per side to warm.
9. Serve bread with the pureed dip and enjoy.

Nutrition:

Calories per **Servings:** 213.6; Carbs: 36.3g; Protein: 6.3g; Fat: 4.8g

435. Multi-Grain & Gluten-Free Dinner Rolls

Preparation Time: 30 minutes

Cooking Time: 20 minutes

Servings: 8

Ingredients:

- ½ tsp apple cider vinegar
- 3 tbsp olive oil
- 2 eggs
- 1 tsp baking powder
- 1 tsp salt
- 2 tsp xanthan gum
- ½ cup tapioca starch
- ¼ cup brown teff flour
- ¼ cup flax meal
- ¼ cup amaranth flour
- ¼ cup sorghum flour
- ¾ cup brown rice flour

Directions for Cooking:

1. Mix well water and honey in a small bowl and add yeast. Leave it for precisely 10 minutes.
2. In a large bowl, mix the following with a paddle mixer: baking powder, salt, xanthan gum, flax meal, sorghum flour, teff flour, tapioca starch, amaranth flour, and brown rice flour.
3. In a medium bowl, whisk healthy vinegar, olive oil, and eggs.
4. Into the bowl of dry ingredients, pour in vinegar and yeast mixture and mix well.
5. Grease a 12-muffin tin with cooking spray. Transfer dough evenly into 12 muffin tins and leave it for an hour to rise.
6. Then preheat oven to 375oF and bake dinner rolls until tops are golden brown, around 20 minutes.
7. Remove dinner rolls from the oven and muffin tins immediately and let them cool.
8. Best served when warm.

Nutrition:

Calories per **Servings:** 207; Carbs: 28.4g; Protein: 4.6g; Fat: 8.3g

436. Vegetarian Spinach-Olive Pizza

Preparation Time: 15 minutes

Cooking Time: 25 minutes

Servings: 4

Ingredients:

For the crust:

- ½ cup almond flour
- ¼ tsp salt
- 2 tbsp ground psyllium husk
- 1 tbsp olive oil
- 1 cup lukewarm water

For the topping:

- ½ cup tomato sauce
- ½ cup baby spinach
- 1 cup grated mozzarella cheese
- 1 tsp dried oregano
- 3 tbsp sliced black olives

Directions:

1. Preheat the oven to 400 F. Line a baking sheet with parchment paper. In a medium bowl, mix the almond flour, salt, psyllium powder, olive oil, and water until dough forms.
2. Spread the mixture on the pizza pan and bake in the oven until crusty, 10 minutes. When ready, remove the crust and spread the tomato sauce on top.
3. Add the spinach, mozzarella cheese, oregano, and olives. Bake until the cheese melts, 15 minutes. Take out of the oven, slice and serve warm.

Nutrition: Calories 95 Fats 4.3g Carbs 1.8g Protein 9.7g

437. Chicken Bacon Ranch Pizza

Preparation Time: 1 hour & 15 minutes

Cooking Time: 20 minutes

Servings: 4

Ingredients:

For the crust:

- 2 cups flour

- 1 cup lukewarm water
- 1 pinch of sugar
- 1 tsp active dry yeast
- ¾ tsp salt
- 2 tbsp olive oil

For the ranch sauce:

- 1 tbsp butter
- 2 garlic cloves, minced
- 1 tbsp cream cheese
- ¼ cup half and half
- 1 tbsp dry Ranch seasoning mix
- For the topping:
- 3 bacon slices, chopped
- 2 chicken breasts
- Salt and black pepper to taste
- 1 cup grated mozzarella cheese
- 6 fresh basil leaves

Directions:

1. Sift the flour and salt in a bowl and stir in yeast. Mix lukewarm water, olive oil, and sugar in another bowl. Add the wet mixture to the dry mixture and whisk until you obtain a soft dough.
2. Place the dough on a lightly floured work surface and knead it thoroughly until elastic for 4-5 minutes. Transfer the dough to a greased bowl.
3. Cover with cling film and leave to rise for 50-60 minutes in a warm place until doubled in size. Roll out the dough to a thickness of around 12 inches.
4. Preheat the oven to 400 F. Line a pizza pan with parchment paper. Mix the sauce's ingredients butter, garlic, cream cheese, half and half, and ranch mix in a bowl. Set aside.
5. Heat a grill pan over medium heat and cook the bacon until crispy and brown, 5 minutes. Transfer to a plate and set aside.
6. Season the chicken with salt, pepper and grill in the pan on both sides until golden brown, 10 minutes. Remove to a plate, allow cooling and cut into thin slices.

7. Spread the ranch sauce on the pizza crust, followed by the chicken and bacon, and then mozzarella cheese and basil. Bake for 5 minutes or until the cheese melts. Slice and serve warm.

Nutrition: Calories 528 Fats 27.8g Carbs 4.9g Protein 61.2g

438. Chicken Pizza

Preparation Time: 1 minute

Cooking Time: 10 minutes

Servings: 4

Ingredients:

- 2 flatbreads
- 1 tbsp. Greek vinaigrette
- ½ cup feta cheese, crumbled
- ¼ cup Parmesan cheese, grated
- ½ cup water-packed artichoke hearts, rinsed, drained and chopped
- ½ cup olives, pitted and sliced
- ½ cup cooked chicken breast strips, chopped
- 1/8 tsp. dried basil
- 1/8 tsp. dried oregano
- Pinch of ground black pepper
- 1 cup part-skim mozzarella cheese, shredded

Directions:

1. Preheat the oven to 400°F. Arrange the flatbreads onto a large ungreased baking sheet and coat each with vinaigrette.
2. Top with feta, followed by the Parmesan, veggies and chicken. Sprinkle with dried herbs and black pepper. Top with mozzarella cheese evenly.
3. Bake for about 8-10 minutes or until cheese is melted. Remove from the oven and set aside for about 1-2 minutes before slicing. Cut each flatbread into 2 pieces and serve.

Nutrition: Calories 393 Fat 22 g Carbs 20.6 g Protein 28.9 g

439. Shrimp Pizza

Preparation Time: 15 minutes

Cooking Time: 10 minutes

Servings: 1

Ingredients:

- 2 tbsp. spaghetti sauce
- 1 tbsp. pesto sauce
- 1 (6-inch) pita bread
- 2 tbsp. mozzarella cheese, shredded
- 5 cherry tomatoes, halved
- 1/8 cup bay shrimp
- Pinch of garlic powder
- Pinch of dried basil

Directions:

1. Preheat the oven to 325°F. Lightly grease a baking sheet. In a bowl, mix the spaghetti sauce and pesto. Spread the pesto mixture over the pita bread in a thin layer.
2. Top the pita bread with the cheese, followed by the tomatoes and shrimp. Sprinkle with garlic powder and basil.
3. Arrange the pita bread onto the prepared baking sheet and bake for about 7-10 minutes. Remove from the oven and set aside for about 3-5 minutes before slicing. Cut into desired-sized slices and serve.

Nutrition: Calories 482 Fat 18.9 g Carbs 44.5 g Protein 33.4 g

440. Veggie Pizza

Preparation Time: 20 minutes

Cooking Time: 12 minutes

Servings: 6

Ingredients:

- 1 (12-inch) prepared pizza crust
- ¼ tsp. Italian seasoning
- ¼ tsp. red pepper flakes, crushed
- 1 cup goat cheese, crumbled
- 1 (14-oz.) can quarter artichoke hearts
- 3 plum tomatoes, sliced into ¼-inch thick size
- 6 kalamata olives, pitted and sliced
- ¼ cup fresh basil, chopped

Directions:

1. Preheat the oven to 450°F. Grease a baking sheet. Sprinkle the pizza crust with Italian seasoning and red pepper flakes evenly.

2. Place the goat cheese over crust evenly, leaving about ½-inch of the sides. With the back of a spoon, gently press the cheese downwards.
3. Place the artichoke, tomato and olives on top of the cheese. Arrange the pizza crust onto the prepared baking sheet.
4. Bake for about 10-12 minutes or till cheese becomes bubbly. Remove from oven and sprinkle with the basil. Cut into equal-sized wedges and serve.

Nutrition: Calories 381 Fat 16.1 g Carbs 42.4 g Protein 19.4 g

441. Bread Machine Pizza Dough

Preparation Time: 15 minutes

Cooking Time: 24 minutes

Servings: 6

Ingredients:

- 1 cup of beer
- 2 tablespoons butter
- 2 tablespoons sugar
- 1 teaspoon of salt
- 2 1/2 cups of all-purpose flour
- 2 1/4 teaspoons of yeast

Directions:

1. Place beer, butter, sugar, salt, flour, and yeast in a bread maker in the order recommended by the manufacturer. Select the Paste setting and press Start.
2. Remove the dough from the bread maker once the cycle is complete. Roll or press the dough to cover a prepared pizza dish.
3. Brush lightly with olive oil. Cover and let stand for 15 minutes. Preheat the oven to 250 degrees (400 degrees F).
4. Spread the sauce and garnish on the dough. Bake until the crust is a bit brown and crispy on the outside, about 24 minutes.

Nutrition: Calories: 101 Carbs: 18g Fat: 2g Protein: 3g

442. Basil & Artichoke Pizza

Preparation Time: 1 hours & 15 minutes

Cooking Time: 24 minutes

Servings: 4

Ingredients:

- 1 cup canned passata
- 2 cups flour
- 1 cup lukewarm water
- 1 pinch of sugar
- 1 tsp active dry yeast
- ¾ tsp salt
- 2 tbsp olive oil
- 1 ½ cups frozen artichoke hearts
- ¼ cup grated Asiago cheese
- ½ onion, minced
- 3 garlic cloves, minced
- 1 tbsp dried oregano
- 1 cup sun-dried tomatoes, chopped
- ½ tsp red pepper flakes
- 5-6 basil leaves, torn

Directions:

1. Sift the flour and salt in a bowl and stir in yeast. Mix lukewarm water, olive oil, and sugar in another bowl. Add the wet mixture to the dry mixture and whisk until you obtain a soft dough.
2. Place the dough on a lightly floured work surface and knead it thoroughly until elastic for 4-5 minutes. Transfer the dough to a greased bowl.
3. Cover with cling film and leave to rise for 50-60 minutes in a warm place until doubled in size. Roll out the dough to a thickness of around 12 inches.
4. Preheat oven to 400 F. Warm oil in a saucepan over medium heat and sauté onion and garlic for 3-4 minutes. Mix in tomatoes and oregano and bring to a boil.
5. Decrease the heat and simmer for another 5 minutes. Transfer the pizza crust to a baking sheet. Spread the sauce

all over and top with artichoke hearts and sun-dried tomatoes.

6. Scatter the cheese and bake for 15 minutes until golden. Top with red pepper flakes and basil leaves and serve sliced.

Nutrition: Calories 254 Fat 9.5g Carbs 34.3g Protein 8g

443. Italian Mushroom Pizza

Preparation Time: 1 hour & 15 minutes

Cooking Time: 25 minutes

Servings: 4

Ingredients:

For the crust:

- 2 cups flour
- 1 cup lukewarm water
- 1 pinch of sugar
- 1 tsp active dry yeast
- ¾ tsp salt
- 2 tbsp olive oil

For the topping:

- 1 tsp olive oil
- 2 medium cremini mushrooms, sliced
- 1 garlic clove, minced
- ½ cup sugar-free tomato sauce
- 1 tsp sugar
- 1 bay leaf
- 1 tsp dried oregano
- 1tsp dried basil
- Salt and black pepper to taste
- ½ cup grated mozzarella cheese
- ½ cup grated Parmesan cheese
- 6 black olives, pitted and sliced

Directions:

1. Sift the flour and salt in a bowl and stir in yeast. Mix lukewarm water, olive oil, and sugar in another bowl. Add the wet mixture to the dry mixture and whisk until you obtain a soft dough.
2. Place the dough on a lightly floured work surface and knead it thoroughly until elastic for 4-5 minutes. Transfer the dough to a greased bowl.

3. Cover with cling film and leave to rise for 50-60 minutes in a warm place until doubled in size. Roll out the dough to a thickness of around 12 inches.
4. Preheat the oven to 400 F. Line a pizza pan with parchment paper. Heat the olive oil in a medium skillet and sauté the mushrooms until softened, 5 minutes. Stir in the garlic and cook until fragrant, 30 seconds.
5. Mix tomato sauce, sugar, bay leaf, oregano, basil, salt, and black pepper. Cook for 2 minutes and turn the heat off.
6. Spread the sauce on the crust, top with the mozzarella and Parmesan cheeses, and then the olives. Bake in the oven until the cheese melts, 15 minutes. Remove the pizza, slice, and serve warm.

Nutrition: Calories 203 Fats 8.6g Carbs 2.6g Protein 24.3g

444. Broccoli-Pepper Pizza

Preparation Time: 15 minutes

Cooking Time: 20 minutes

Servings: 4

Ingredients:

For the crust:

- ½ cup almond flour
- ¼ tsp salt
- 2 tbsp ground psyllium husk
- 1 tbsp olive oil
- 1 cup lukewarm water

For the topping:

- 1 tbsp olive oil
- 1 cup sliced fresh mushrooms
- 1 white onion, thinly sliced
- 3 cups broccoli florets
- 4 garlic cloves, minced
- ½ cup pizza sauce
- 4 tomatoes, sliced
- 1 ½ cup grated mozzarella cheese
- ½ cup grated Parmesan cheese

Directions:

1. Preheat the oven to 400 F. Line a baking sheet with parchment

paper. In a bowl, mix the almond flour, salt, psyllium powder, olive oil, and lukewarm water until dough forms.
2. Spread the mixture on the pizza pan and bake in the oven until crusty, 10 minutes. When ready, remove the crust and allow cooling.
3. Heat olive oil in a skillet and sauté the mushrooms, onion, garlic, and broccoli until softened, 5 minutes.
4. Spread the pizza sauce on the crust and top with the broccoli mixture, tomato, mozzarella and Parmesan cheeses. Bake for 5 minutes.

Nutrition: Calories 180 Fats 9g Carbs 3.6g Protein 17g

445. Mozzarella Bean Pizza

Preparation Time: 10 minutes

Cooking Time: 15 minutes

Servings: 6

Ingredients:

- 2 tbsp. cornmeal
- 1 cup mozzarella
- 1/3 cup barbecue sauce
- 1 Roma tomato, diced
- 1 cup black beans
- 1 cup corn kernels
- 1 medium whole-wheat pizza crust

Directions:

1. Preheat your oven to 400°F. Take a baking sheet, line it with parchment paper. Grease it with some avocado oil. Spread some cornmeal over the baking sheet.
2. In a bowl, mix the tomatoes, corn and beans. Place the pizza crust on the baking sheet.
3. Spread the sauce on top; add the topping, and top with the cheese and bake until the cheese melts and the crust edges are golden-brown for 12-15 minutes. Slice and serve warm.

Nutrition: Calories 223 Fat 14g Carbs 41g Protein 8g

446. Avocado Tomato Pizza

Preparation Time: 42 minutes

Cooking Time: 30 minutes

Servings: 4

Ingredients:

Pizza Crust:

- Two tbsp Olive oil
- Two cloves of garlic minced
- 1 1/4 cup Chickpea flour
- Sea salt and pepper
- 1 1/4 cup Coldwater
- One tsp any herbs of choice
- Soccer Pizza Toppings:
- Extra salt/pepper for seasoning
- 1 Roma tomato sliced
- One half of an avocado
- 2 ounces of gouda (sliced thin)
- 1/3 cup Tomato sauce
- Three tbsp Green onion (chopped)
- Red pepper flakes

Directions:

1. Preheat your oven to 350 F.
2. Place pan in the oven to warm.
3. Mix olive oil, water, flour, and herbs until smooth and chill for ten minutes.
4. Remove pan from oven after ten minutes, then add a tbsp of oil to the pan, moving it around to cover the bottom of the pan, then pour in your batter.
5. Set the oven temperature to 425F and put the pan back in the oven until the mixture has set.
6. Remove pan from oven and spread the tomato sauce on top, then sliced tomato and avocado.
7. Put the Gouda slices on top of the tomato and avocado.
8. Put back in the oven until the cheese melts.
9. Let it cool, then put the fresh green onion on the top.
10. Drizzle a bit of olive oil on top and enjoy.

Nutrition: calories 212; fat 11.3 g; carbohydrates 21.5 g; protein 6.2 g

447. Mediterranean Whole Wheat Pizza

Preparation Time: 5 minutes

Cooking Time: 25 minutes

Servings: 4

Ingredients:

- Whole-wheat pizza crust (1)
- Basil pesto (4 oz. jar)
- Artichoke hearts (.5 cup)
- Kalamata olives (2 tbsp.)
- Pepperoncini (2 tbsp. drained)
- Feta cheese (.25 cup)

Directions:

1. Program the oven to 450°F. Drain and pull the artichokes to pieces. Slice/chop the pepperoncini and olives.
2. Arrange the pizza crust onto a floured work surface and cover it using pesto. Arrange the artichoke, pepperoncini slices, and olives over the pizza. Lastly, crumble and add the feta.
3. Bake in the hot oven until the cheese has melted and it has a crispy crust for 10-12 minutes.

Nutrition: Calories: 277 Protein: 9.7 g Carbs: 24 g Fat: 18.6 g

448. Fruit Pizza

Preparation Time: 15 minutes

Cooking Time: 0 minutes

Servings: 4

Ingredients:

- 4 watermelon slices
- 1 oz blueberries
- 2 oz goat cheese, crumbled
- 1 teaspoon fresh parsley, chopped

Directions:

Put the watermelon slices on the plate in one layer. Then sprinkle them with blueberries, goat cheese, and fresh parsley.

Nutrition: Calories 69 Protein 4.4g Carbohydrates 1.4g Fat 5.1g

449. Artichoke Pizza

Preparation Time: 15 minutes

Cooking Time: 20 minutes

Servings: 4

Ingredients:

- 7 oz pizza crust
- 5 oz artichoke hearts, canned, drained, chopped
- 1 teaspoon fresh basil, chopped
- 1 tomato, sliced
- 1 cup Monterey Jack cheese, shredded

Directions:

1. Line the pizza mold with baking paper. Then put the pizza crust inside. Top it with sliced tomato, canned artichoke hearts, and basil.
2. Then top the pizza with Monterey Jack cheese and transfer it in the preheated to 365F oven. Cook the pizza for 20 minutes.

Nutrition: Calories 247 Protein 12.1g Carbohydrates 28.2g Fat 10.2g

450. 3-Cheese Pizza

Preparation Time: 15 minutes

Cooking Time: 10 minutes

Servings: 6

Ingredients:

- 1 pizza crust, cooked
- ½ cup Mozzarella, shredded
- ½ cup Cheddar cheese, shredded
- 2 oz Parmesan, grated
- ¼ cup tomato sauce
- 1 teaspoon Italian seasonings

Directions:

1. Put the pizza crust in the baking pan. Then brush it with tomato sauce and Italian seasonings.
2. After this, sprinkle the pizza with Mozzarella, Cheddar cheese, and Parmesan. Bake the pizza for 10 minutes at 375F.

Nutrition: Calories 106 Protein 7g Carbohydrates 6.3g Fat 6.1g

451. Chickpea Pizza

Preparation Time: 15 minutes

Cooking Time: 25 minutes

Servings: 6

Ingredients:

- 4 tablespoons marinara sauce
- 7 oz pizza dough
- 1 tomato, sliced
- 1 red onion, sliced
- 5 oz chickpeas, canned
- ½ cup Mozzarella cheese, shredded

Directions:

1. Roll up the pizza dough in the shape of pizza crust and transfer it to the pizza mold. Then brush the pizza crust with marinara sauce and sprinkle with sliced onion, tomato, and chickpeas.
2. Top the chickpeas with mozzarella cheese and bake the pizza for 25 minutes at 355F.

Nutrition: Calories 266 Protein 7.6g Carbohydrates 31.9g Fat 12.4g

452. Mushroom Pesto Pita Pizza

Preparation Time: 15 minutes

Cooking Time: 10 to 15 minutes

Servings: 4

Ingredients:

- 1/4 cup extra-virgin olive oil
- 12 large mushrooms, sliced
- 1 teaspoon salt
- 1/4 teaspoon red pepper flakes (optional)
- 4 whole-wheat pita bread
- 1/2 cup Pesto (here)
- 1/2 cup shredded Parmesan cheese

Directions:

1. Preheat the oven to 375°F.
2. Warm a medium skillet over high heat, then add the olive oil, mushrooms, salt, and red pepper flakes (if using). Sauté until the liquid from the mushrooms has evaporated, about 5 to 7 minutes.
3. Place the pita bread on a baking sheet. Spread the pesto over the

pitas and top with the mushrooms and Parmesan cheese.

4. Bake 10 to 15 minutes, or until the pizzas are lightly browned. Serve immediately.
5. This pizza can be made with gluten-free pita bread. To make it vegan, replace the pesto with a simple mixture of ½ cup olive oil, one garlic clove, 5 basil leaves, and ½ teaspoon salt puréed in a blender. Spread this over the pita instead of the pesto, and omit the Parmesan cheese. If you want to make your pita bread from scratch, check out the recipe for Pork Souvlaki with Tzatziki on Pita Bread here.

Nutrition: Calories: 474, Protein: 16g, Total Carbohydrates: 40g, Fiber: 6g, Total Fat: 31g, Saturated Fat: 7g, Cholesterol: 18mg, Sodium: 1247mg

453. Gluten-Free Zucchini and Walnut Pizza

Preparation Time: 20 minutes

Cooking Time: 20 minutes

Servings: 2

Ingredients:

For Crust:

- ¼ cup extra-virgin olive oil, plus 1 tablespoon to oil the pan
- 1 cup finely ground walnuts
- 2 cups shredded zucchini
- ¼ cup rice flour
- 1 egg
- 1 teaspoon salt
- ¼ teaspoon red pepper flakes (optional)
- ¼ teaspoon dried oregano

For The Pizza:

- ½ cup sun-dried tomatoes, chopped
- ½ cup crumbled feta cheese
- 1 tablespoon chopped fresh basil
- 1 garlic clove, minced

Directions:

MAKE THE CRUST

1. Preheat the oven to 375°F.
2. Brush a 9-inch pie plate with olive oil and set aside.
3. In a medium bowl, combine the walnuts, zucchini, rice flour, egg, olive oil, salt, red pepper flakes (if using), and oregano. Mix well.
4. Press the crust into the prepared pan and bake for about 15 to 20 minutes or until the crust is browned around the edges.
5. The cooked crust can be wrapped in plastic wrap and frozen for several months.

MAKE THE PIZZA

1. Top the baked crust with sun-dried tomatoes, feta cheese, basil, and garlic.
2. Return to the oven for 5 minutes to soften the feta.
3. Cut into wedges and serve.
4. Cooked pizza is best eaten right away. However, you can wrap leftovers in foil and refrigerate them for several days. Reheat in a hot oven or toaster oven for best results.
5. One cup of ground unsalted almonds or almond flour can be used in place of the ground walnuts. To make this pizza vegan, omit the feta and make an egg substitute by combining 1 tablespoon ground flaxseed with 3 tablespoons water and using this mixture instead of the egg.

Nutrition: Calories: 862, Protein: 27g, Total Carbohydrates: 36g, Fiber: 8g, Total Fat: 74g, Saturated Fat: 11g, Cholesterol: 107mg, Sodium: 1806mg

454. Cheesy Fig Pizzas with Garlic Oil

Preparation Time: 1 day 40 minutes

Cooking Time: 10 minutes

Servings: 2 pizzas

Ingredients:

- Dough:
- 1 cup almond flour

- 1 1/2 cups whole-wheat flour
- 3/4 teaspoon instant or rapid-rise yeast
- 2 teaspoons raw honey
- 1 1/4 cups ice water
- 2 tablespoons extra-virgin olive oil
- 1 3/4 teaspoons sea salt

Garlic Oil:

- 4 tablespoons extra-virgin olive oil, divided
- 1/2 teaspoon dried thyme
- 2 garlic cloves, minced
- 1/8 teaspoon sea salt
- 1/2 teaspoon freshly ground pepper

Topping:

- 1 cup fresh basil leaves
- 1 cup crumbled feta cheese
- 8 ounces (227 g) fresh figs, stemmed and quartered lengthwise
- 2 tablespoons raw honey

Directions:

Make the Dough:

1. Combine the flours, yeast, and honey in a food processor, pulse to combine well. Gently add water while pulsing. Let the dough sit for 10 minutes.
2. Mix the olive oil and salt in the dough and knead the dough until smooth. Wrap in plastic and refrigerate for at least 1 day.

Make the Garlic Oil:

1. Heat 2 tablespoons of olive oil in a nonstick skillet over medium-low heat until shimmering.
2. Add the thyme, garlic, salt, and pepper and sauté for 30 seconds or until fragrant. Set them aside until ready to use.

Make the pizzas:

1. Preheat the oven to 500ºF (260ºC). Grease two baking sheets with 2 tablespoons of olive oil.
2. Divide the dough in half and shape it into two balls. Press the balls into 13-inch rounds.

Sprinkle the games with a tough of flour if they are sticky.
3. Top the rounds with the garlic oil and basil leaves, then arrange the baking sheets. Scatter with feta cheese and figs.
4. Put the sheets in the preheated oven and bake for 9 minutes or until lightly browned. Rotate the pizza halfway through.
5. Remove the pizzas from the oven, then discard the bay leaves. Drizzle with honey. Let sit for 5 minutes and serve immediately.

Tip: You can replace the garlic oil with homemade pesto and top the pizzas with freshly chopped tomatoes, fried potatoes, and sautéed broccoli.

Nutrition:

calories: 1350 fat: 46.5g Protein: 27.5g carbs: 221.9g fiber: 23.7g Sodium: 2898mg

455. Hummus Pizza

Preparation Time: 15 minutes

Cooking Time: 20 minutes

Servings: 6

Ingredients:

- 6 oz pizza dough
- 5 oz hummus
- 3 oz Feta cheese, crumbled
- 1 tablespoon fresh parsley, chopped
- ½ cup black olives, sliced
- 3 sun-dried tomatoes, chopped
- 1 tablespoon avocado oil

Directions:

1. Roll up the pizza dough in the shape of the pizza crust. Then place it in pizza mold and brush with avocado oil.
2. Spread the pizza crust with hummus and sprinkle with parsley, black olives, and sun-dried tomatoes, and crumbled feta. Bake the pizza at 400F for 20 minutes.

Nutrition: Calories 237 Protein 6.2g Carbohydrates 19.2g Fat 15.6g

456. Pesto Pita Pizza

Preparation Time: 15 minutes

Cooking Time: 15 minutes

Servings: 4

Ingredients:

- 4 pita bread rounds
- 1/2 cup pesto
- 2 tomatoes, sliced
- 1 (4 oz) container crumbled feta cheese

Directions:

1. Preheat oven to 400 degrees. Arrange pita bread on a baking sheet. Bake in the preheated oven until pita is lightly toasted, about 4 minutes.
2. Spread pesto evenly over toasted pita bread and arrange tomato slices in a single layer. Top with feta cheese.
3. Continue baking until feta cheese is browned and pita bread is crisp, about 11 minutes more.

Nutrition: Calories: 540 Carbs: 49g Fat: 29g Protein: 25g

457. Veggie Pita Pizza

Preparation Time: 15 minutes

Cooking Time: 5 minutes

Servings: 1

Ingredients:

- 1 round pita bread
- 1 teaspoon of olive oil
- 3 tablespoons of pizza sauce
- 1/2 cup grated mozzarella cheese
- 1/4 cup sliced Cremini mushrooms
- 1/8 teaspoon salt with garlic

Directions:

1. Preheat the grill on medium heat. Spread a side of the pita with olive oil and pizza sauce. Garnish with cheese and mushrooms and season with garlic salt.
2. Lightly grease the grill. Place the pita pizza on the grill, cover, and cook until the cheese has completely melted, about 5 minutes.

Nutrition: Calories: 360 Carbs: 10g Fat: 10g Protein: 17g

458. Mini Pizzas with Arugula & Hummus

Preparation Time: 15 minutes

Cooking Time: 0 minutes

Servings: 1

Ingredients:

- 2 tablespoons hummus
- 1 naan bread
- 1 cup of arugula
- 1 date, pitted and chopped
- 2 teaspoons pumpkin seeds
- 1 teaspoon balsamic vinegar

Directions:

1. Spread the hummus on naan bread; garnish with arugula, date, and pumpkin seeds. Sprinkle balsamic vinegar on pizza. Serve.

Nutrition: Calories: 180 Carbs: 23g Fat: 6g Protein: 9g

459. Grilled Buffalo Chicken Pizza

Preparation Time: 12 hours & 15 minutes

Cooking Time: 35 minutes

Servings: 2

Ingredients:

- 1 boneless chicken fillet
- 2 pinches of steak herbs
- 2 tablespoons hot pepper sauce
- 2 pieces of naan tandoori bread
- 1 teaspoon of olive oil
- ½ cup of blue cheese dressing
- 2 tablespoons diced red onion
- 8 grams of grated cheddar cheese
- ½ cup of grated iceberg lettuce
- 1 Roma tomato, seeded and minced

Directions:

1. Season the chicken fillet with Montreal Steak Seasoning. 1/3 cup of hot pepper sauce into the bag. Close the bag and rub the hot sauce into the chicken.
2. Place the bag in the refrigerator and marinate for 12 hours. Preheat an outside grill over medium heat and lightly oil the grill.
3. Discard the marinade. Cook the chicken on the preheated grill

until it is no longer pink in the middle and the juice is clear, 5 to 7 minutes on each side.
4. An instant-read thermometer in the center must indicate at least 165° F (74° C). Put the chicken on a cutting board and let it sit for 5 to 10 minutes.
5. Cut the chilled chicken into bite-sized pieces. Mix chicken and remaining hot sauce in a bowl.
6. Brush every naan with olive oil; bake on the grill until golden brown and grilled on one side for 3 to 5 minutes.
7. Reduce the heat to low and medium and place the pieces of toasted bread on a baking sheet. Spread blue cheese vinaigrette on the grilled side of each naan.
8. Garnish each with diced chicken and red onion. Sprinkle with cheddar cheese.
9. Place the Naan on the grill and cook until the cheese has melted and the bottom is grilled and golden brown, another 5 to 10 minutes. Remove from the grill, cut into pieces and garnish with lettuce and tomato.

Nutrition: Calories: 250 Carbs: 26g Fat: 12g Protein: 10g

460. Portobello Mushroom Pizzas

Preparation Time: 15 minutes

Cooking Time: 10 minutes

Servings: 1

Ingredients:

- 2 2 ounces Portobello mushroom, stems removed and gills scraped out
- 1/4 cup Italian tomato sauce
- 4 ounces reduced-fat shredded mozzarella cheese
- 2 tablespoons shredded basil

Directions:

1. Preheat the broiler to medium-high heat.
2. Place the mushroom caps on a greased baking sheet lined with foil.

3. Broil for 4 minutes until tender.
4. Spread the tomato sauce into each and top with cheese and basil.
5. Broil for another 3 minutes.

Nutrition:

Calories per serving: 511; Protein: 47.7 g; Carbs: 92.8g; Fat: 1.3g Sugar: 6.4g

Chapter 12. Desserts

461. Blueberry Frozen Yogurt

Preparation Time: 10 minutes

Cooking Time: 30 minutes

Servings: 6

Ingredients:

- 1-pint blueberries, fresh
- 2/3 cup honey
- 1 small lemon, juiced and zested
- 2 cups yogurt, chilled

Directions for Cooking:

1. In a saucepan, combine the blueberries, honey, lemon juice, and zest.
2. Heat over medium heat and allow to simmer for 15 minutes while stirring constantly.
3. Once the liquid has reduced, transfer the fruits to a bowl and cool in the fridge for another 15 minutes.
4. Once chilled, mix with the chilled yogurt.

Nutrition:

Calories per serving: 233; Carbs:52.2 g; Protein:3.5 g; Fat: 2.9g

462. Delectable Strawberry Popsicle

Preparation Time: 5 minutes

Cooking Time: 10 minutes

Servings: 5

Ingredients:

- 2 ½ cups fresh strawberry
- ½ cup almond milk

Directions for Cooking:

1. Blend all ingredients until smooth.
2. Pour into the popsicle molds with sticks and freeze for at least 4 hours.
3. Serve chilled.

Nutrition: Calories per serving: 35; Carbs: 7.7g; Protein: 0.6g; Fat:0.5 g

463. Deliciously Cold Lychee Sorbet

Preparation Time: 0 minutes

Cooking Time: 5 minutes

Servings: 4

Ingredients:

- 2 cups fresh lychees, pitted and sliced
- 2 tablespoons honey
- Mint leaves for garnish

Directions for Cooking:

1. Place the lychee slices and honey in a food processor.
2. Pulse until smooth.
3. Pour in a container and place inside the fridge for at least two hours.
4. Scoop the sorbet and serve with mint leaves.

Nutrition: Calories per serving: 151; Carbs: 38.9g; Protein: 0.7g; Fat: 0.4

464. Easy Fruit Compote

Preparation Time: 5 minutes

Cooking Time: 15 minutes

Servings: 2

Ingredients:

- 1-pound fresh fruits of your choice
- 2 tablespoons maple syrup
- A dash of salt

Directions for Cooking:

1. Slice the fruits thinly and place them in a saucepan.
2. Add the honey and salt.
3. Heat the saucepan over medium-low heat and allow the fruits to simmer for 15 minutes or until the liquid has reduced.
4. Make sure that you constantly stir to prevent the fruits from sticking at the bottom of your pan and eventually burning.
5. Transfer in a lidded jar.
6. Allow cooling.
7. Serve with slices of whole wheat bread or vegan ice cream.

Nutrition: Calories per serving:218; Carbs: 56.8g; Protein: 0.9g; Fat: 0.2g

465. Apple Couscous Pudding

Preparation Time: 10 minutes

Cooking Time: 25 minutes

Servings: 4

Ingredients:

- ½ cup couscous
- ½ cups milk
- ¼ cup apple, cored and chopped
- 2 tbsps. stevia
- ½ tsp. rose water
- 1 tbsp. orange zest, grated

Directions:

1. Heat a pan with the milk over medium heat, add the couscous and the rest of the ingredients, whisk, simmer for 25 minutes, divide into bowls and serve.

Nutrition:

Calories 150, Fat: 4.5g, Fiber: 5.5g, Carbs: 7.5g, Protein: 4g

466. Ricotta Ramekins

Preparation Time: 10 minutes

Cooking Time: 1 hour

Servings: 4

Ingredients:

- 6 eggs, whisked
- ½ pounds ricotta cheese, soft
- ½ pound stevia
- 1 tsp. vanilla extract
- ½ tsp. baking powder

Cooking spray as needed

Directions:

1. Mix the eggs with the ricotta and the other ingredients except the cooking spray and whisk well in a bowl.
2. Grease 4 ramekins with the cooking spray, pour the ricotta cream in each and bake at 360F for 1 hour.
3. Serve cold.

Nutrition:

Calories 180, Fat: 5.3g, Fiber: 5.4g, Carbs: 11.5g, Protein: 4g

467. Papaya Cream

Preparation Time: 10 minutes

Cooking Time: 0 minutes

Servings: 2

Ingredients:

- 1 cup papaya, peeled and chopped
- 1 cup heavy cream
- 1 tbsp. stevia
- ½ tsp. vanilla extract

Directions:

1. In a blender, combine the cream with the papaya and the other ingredients, pulse well, divide into cups and serve cold.

Nutrition:

Calories 182, Fat: 3.1g, Fiber: 2.3g, Carbs: 3.5g, Protein: 2g

468. Orange Cake

Preparation Time: 20 minutes

Cooking Time: 60 minutes

Servings: 8

Ingredients:

- 4 oranges
- 1/3 cup water
- ½ cup Erythritol
- ½ tsp. ground cinnamon
- 4 eggs, beaten
- 3 tbsps. stevia powder
- 10 oz. Phyllo pastry
- ½ tsp. baking powder
- ½ cup Plain yogurt
- 3 tbsps. olive oil

Directions:

1. Squeeze the juice from 1 orange and pour it into the saucepan.
2. Add water, squeezed oranges, water, ground cinnamon, and Erythritol. Bring the liquid to a boil.
3. Simmer the liquid for 5 minutes over medium heat. When the time is over, cool it.
4. Grease the baking mold with 1 tbsp. Of olive oil. Chop the phyllo dough and place it in the baking mold.
5. Slice ½ of orange for decorating the cake. Slice it.

Squeeze juice from the remaining oranges.
6. Then mix up together, squeeze orange juice, Plain yogurt, baking powder, stevia powder, and eggs. Add remaining olive oil
7. Mix up the mixture with the help of the hand mixer.
8. Pour the liquid over the chopped Phyllo dough. Stir to distribute evenly.
9. Top the cake with sliced orange (that one which you leave for decorating).
10. Bake the dessert for 50 minutes at 370F.
11. Pour the baked cake with cooled orange juice syrup. Leave it for 10 minutes to let the cake soaks the syrup.
12. Cut it into servings.

Nutrition:

Calories 237, Fat: 4.4 g, Fiber: 1.4 g, Carbs: 36.9 g, Protein: 1.9 g

469. Orange Butterscotch Pudding

Preparation Time: 10 minutes

Cooking Time: 15 minutes

Servings: 4

Ingredients:

- 4 caramels
- 2 eggs, well-beaten
- 1/4 cup freshly squeezed orange juice
- 1/3 cup sugar
- 1 cupcake flour
- 1/2 teaspoon baking powder
- 1/4 cup milk
- 1 stick butter, melted
- 1/2 teaspoon vanilla essence

Sauce:

- 1/2 cup golden syrup
- 2 teaspoons cornflour
- 1 cup boiling water

Directions:

1. Melt the butter and milk in the microwave. Whisk in the eggs, vanilla, and sugar. After that, stir in the flour, baking powder, and orange juice.

2. Lastly, add the caramels and stir until everything is well combined and melted.
3. Divide between the four jars. Add 1 ½ cups of water and a metal trivet to the bottom of the pot. Lower the jars onto the trivet.
4. To make the sauce, whisk the boiling water, cornflour, and golden syrup until everything is well combined. Pour the sauce into each jar.
5. Secure the lid. Cook for 15 minutes under high heat. Once cooking is complete, carefully remove the cover. Enjoy!

Nutrition: Calories 565; Fat 25.9g; Carbohydrates 79.6g; Protein 6.4g; Sugars 51.5g

470. Recipe for Ruby Pears Delight

Preparation Time: 10 minutes

Cooking Time: 10 minutes

Servings: 4

Ingredients:

- 4 Pears
- Grape juice-26 oz.
- Currant jelly-11 oz.
- 4 garlic cloves
- Juice and zest of 1 lemon
- 4 peppercorns
- 2 rosemary springs
- 1/2 vanilla bean

Directions:

1. Pour the jelly and grape juice in your pot and mix with lemon zest and juice
2. In the mix, dip each pear and wrap them in a clean tin foil and place them orderly in the steamer basket of your pot.
3. Combine peppercorns, rosemary, garlic cloves and vanilla bean to the juice mixture,
4. Seal the lid and cook at high heat for 10 minutes.
5. Once cooked, carefully open the lid, bring out the pears, remove wrappers and arrange them on plates. Serve when

cold with toppings of cooking juice.

Nutrition: Calories: 145 Fat: 5.6 Fiber: 6 Carbs: 12 Protein: 12

471. Mixed Berry and Orange Compote

Preparation Time: 15 minutes

Cooking Time: 15 minutes

Servings: 4

Ingredients:

- 1/2-pound strawberries
- 1 tablespoon orange juice
- 1/4 teaspoon ground cloves
- 1/2 cup brown sugar
- 1 vanilla bean
- 1-pound blueberries
- 1/2-pound blackberries

Directions:

1. Place your berries in the inner pot. Add the sugar and let sit for 15 minutes. Add in the orange juice, ground cloves, and vanilla bean.
2. Secure the lid. Choose the "Manual" mode and cook for 2 minutes at high pressure. Once cooking is complete, use a natural pressure release for 10 minutes; carefully remove the lid.
3. As your compote cools, it will thicken. Bon appétit!

Nutrition: Calories 224; Fat 0.8g; Carbohydrates 56.3g; Protein 2.1g; Sugars 46.5g

472. Streuselkuchen with Peaches

Preparation Time: 10 minutes

Cooking Time: 20 minutes

Servings: 6

Ingredients

- 1 cup rolled oats
- 1 teaspoon vanilla extract
- 1/3 cup orange juice
- 4 tablespoons raisins
- 2 tablespoons honey
- 4 tablespoons butter
- 4 tablespoons all-purpose flour
- A pinch of grated nutmeg
- 1/2 teaspoon ground cardamom

- A pinch of salt
- 1 teaspoon ground cinnamon
- 6 peaches, pitted and chopped
- 1/3 cup brown sugar

Directions:

1. Place the peaches on the bottom of the inner pot. Sprinkle with cardamom, cinnamon and vanilla. Top with orange juice, honey, and raisins.
2. In a mixing bowl, whisk the butter, oats, flour, brown sugar, nutmeg, and salt. Drop by a spoonful on top of the peaches.
3. Secure the lid. Choose the "Manual" mode and cook for 8 minutes at high pressure. Once cooking is complete, use a natural pressure release for 10 minutes; carefully remove the lid. Bon appétit!

Nutrition: 329 Calories; 10g Fat; 56g Carbohydrates; 6.9g Protein; 31g Sugars

473. Black Tea Cake

Preparation Time: 10 minutes

Cooking Time: 35 minutes

Servings: 8

Ingredients:

- 6 tablespoons black tea powder
- 2 cups almond milk, warmed up
- 1 cup avocado oil
- 2 cups stevia
- 4 eggs
- 2 teaspoons vanilla extract
- 3 and ½ cups almond flour
- 1 teaspoon baking soda
- 3 teaspoons baking powder

Directions:

1. Combine the almond milk with the oil, stevia, and the rest of the ingredients in a bowl and whisk well.
2. Pour this into a cake pan lined with parchment paper, introduce it in the oven at 350° F and bake for 35 minutes.
3. Leave the cake to cool down, slice and serve.

Nutrition:

Calories 200; Fat 6.4 g; Fiber 4 g; Carbs 6.5 g; Protein 5.4 g

474. Zingy Blueberry Sauce

Preparation Time: 5 minutes

Cooking Time: 20 minutes

Servings: 10

Ingredients

- 1/4 cup fresh lemon juice
- 1-pound granulated sugar
- 1 tablespoon freshly grated lemon zest
- 1/2 teaspoon vanilla extract
- 2 pounds fresh blueberries

Directions:

1. Place the blueberries, sugar, and vanilla in the inner pot of your pot.
2. Secure the lid. Cook for 2 minutes at high heat. Once cooking is complete, carefully remove the lid.
3. Stir in the lemon zest and juice. Puree in a food processor; then, strain and push the mixture through a sieve before storing. Enjoy!

Nutrition: Calories 230; Fat 0.3g; Carbohydrates 59g; Protein 0.7g; Sugars 53.6g

475. Chocolate Almond Custard

Preparation Time: 10 minutes

Cooking Time: 15 minutes

Servings: 3

Ingredients

- 3 chocolate cookies, chunks
- A pinch of salt
- 1/4 teaspoon ground cardamom
- 3 tablespoons honey
- 1/4 teaspoon freshly grated nutmeg
- 2 tablespoons butter
- 3 tablespoons whole milk
- 1 cup almond flour
- 3 eggs
- 1 teaspoon pure vanilla extract

Directions:

1. In a mixing bowl, beat the eggs with butter. Now, add the milk and continue mixing until well combined.
2. Add the remaining ingredients in the order listed above. Divide the batter among 3 ramekins.
3. Add 1 cup of water and a metal trivet to the pot. Cover ramekins with foil and lower them onto the trivet.
4. Secure the lid and cook at high heat for 12 minutes. Once cooking is complete, carefully remove the lid.
5. Transfer the ramekins to a wire rack and allow them to cool slightly before serving. Enjoy!

Nutrition: Calories 304; Fat 18.9g; Carbohydrates 23.8g; Protein 10g; Sugars 21.1g

476. Honey Stewed Apples

Preparation Time: 5 minutes

Cooking Time: 5 minutes

Servings: 4

Ingredients

- 2 tablespoons honey
- 1 teaspoon ground cinnamon
- 1/2 teaspoon ground cloves
- 4 apples

Directions

1. Add all ingredients to the inner pot. Now, pour in 1/3 cup of water.
2. Secure the lid. Choose the "Manual" mode and cook for 2 minutes at high pressure. Once cooking is complete, use a quick pressure release; carefully remove the lid.
3. Serve in individual bowls. Bon appétit!

Nutrition: Calories 128; Fat 0.3g; Carbohydrates 34.3g; Protein 0.5g; Sugars 27.5g

477. Greek-Style Compote with Yogurt

Preparation Time: 5 minutes

Cooking Time: 15 minutes

Servings: 4

Ingredients:

- 1 cup Greek yogurt
- 1 cup pears
- 4 tablespoons honey
- 1 cup apples
- 1 vanilla bean
- 1 cinnamon stick
- 1/2 cup caster sugar
- 1 cup rhubarb
- 1 teaspoon ground ginger
- 1 cup plums

Directions:

1. Place the fruits, ginger, vanilla, cinnamon, and caster sugar in the inner pot of your pot.
2. Secure the lid and cook for 2 minutes at high heat. Once cooking is complete, carefully remove the lid.
3. Meanwhile, whisk the yogurt with the honey.
4. Serve your compote in individual bowls with a dollop of honeyed Greek yogurt. Enjoy!

Nutrition: Calories 304; Fat 0.3g; Carbohydrates 75.4g; Protein 5.1g; Sugars 69.2g

478. Butterscotch Lava Cakes

Preparation Time: 5 minutes

Cooking Time: 15 minutes

Servings: 6

Ingredients

- 7 tablespoons all-purpose flour
- A pinch of coarse salt
- 6 ounces butterscotch morsels
- 3/4 cup powdered sugar
- 1/2 teaspoon vanilla extract
- 3 eggs, whisked
- 1 stick butter

Directions

1. Add 1 ½ cups of water and a metal rack to the Pot. Line a standard-size muffin tin with muffin papers.
2. In a microwave-safe bowl, microwave butter and butterscotch morsels for about 40 seconds. Stir in the powdered sugar.

3. Add the remaining ingredients. Spoon the batter into the prepared muffin tin.
4. Secure the lid and cook at high heat for 10 minutes. Once cooking is complete, carefully remove the lid.
5. To remove, let it cool for 5 to 6 minutes. Run a small knife around the sides of each cake and serve. Enjoy!

Nutrition: Calories 393; Fat 21.1g; Carbohydrates 45.6g; Protein 5.6g; Sugars 35.4g

479. Vanilla Bread Pudding with Apricots

Preparation Time: 5 minutes

Cooking Time: 15 minutes

Servings: 6

Ingredients

- 2 tablespoons coconut oil
- 1 1/3 cups heavy cream
- 4 eggs, whisked
- 1/2 cup dried apricots, soaked and chopped
- 1 teaspoon cinnamon, ground
- 1/2 teaspoon star anise, ground
- A pinch of grated nutmeg
- A pinch of salt
- 1/2 cup granulated sugar
- 2 tablespoons molasses
- 2 cups milk
- 4 cups Italian bread, cubed
- 1 teaspoon vanilla paste

Directions

1. Add 1 ½ cups of water and a metal rack to the pot.
2. Grease a baking dish with a nonstick cooking spray. Throw the bread cubes into the prepared baking dish.
3. In a mixing bowl, thoroughly combine the remaining ingredients. Pour the mixture over the bread cubes. Cover with a piece of foil, making a foil sling.
4. Secure the lid and cook on high heat for 15 minutes. Once cooking is complete, carefully remove the lid. Enjoy!

Nutrition: Calories 410; Fat 24.3g; Carbohydrates 37.4g; Protein 11.5g; Sugars 25.6g

480. Green Tea and Vanilla Cream

Preparation Time: 2 hours

Cooking Time: 0 minutes

Servings: 4

Ingredients:

- 14 ounces almond milk, hot
- 2 tablespoons green tea powder
- 14 ounces heavy cream
- 3 tablespoons stevia
- 1 teaspoon vanilla extract
- 1 teaspoon gelatin powder

Directions:

1. In a bowl, combine the almond milk with the green tea powder and the rest of the ingredients, whisk well, cool down, divide into cups and keep in the fridge for 2 hours before serving.

Nutrition: Calories 120; Fat 3 g; Fiber 3 g; Carbs 7 g; Protein 4 g

481. Picositos Brownies

Preparation Time: 5 minutes

Cooking Time: 15 minutes;

Servings: 8

Ingredients:

- 3 cups brownies mix
- 2 eggs
- 1/3 cup of milk
- ½ teaspoon cayenne pepper
- 1 teaspoon cinnamon
- 1 teaspoon vanilla extract
- ¼ cup chocolate sprinkles
- Liquid candy to taste (decoration)
- Chocolate sauce to taste (decoration)
- Oil spray

Directions:

1. In a bowl, stir the following ingredients until a homogeneous mixture is obtained. Be sure to add them little by little, in the same order: mix for brownies, eggs, milk, cayenne pepper,

cinnamon, vanilla and chocolate sprinkles.
2. Preheat the skillet at medium-high temperature for 2 and a half minutes. Cover the pot with spray oil and reduce the temperature to low. Make sure the oil does not start to burn.
3. Add the previous mixture immediately, cover with the valve closed and cook for 15 minutes. Turn off the pot, remove the pan from the burner and let it sit for 3 minutes. Carefully invert the brownies on the Bamboo Cutting Board, slice them and serve with caramel or chocolate sauce.

Nutrition: Calories: 539 Carbohydrates: 54g Fat: 33g Protein: 8g Sugar: 29g Cholesterol: 115mg

482. Fruit Crepes

Preparation Time: 5 minutes

Cooking Time: 15 minutes

Servings: 4

Ingredients:
- Crepes:
- 1 cup wheat flour
- 2 eggs
- 1 ¼ cups of milk
- 1 teaspoon vanilla extract
- 2 tablespoons melted butter
- a pinch of salt
- Powdered sugar to taste (powdered sugar)
- Olive oil spray
- Filling
- 2 cups of strawberries, sliced
- ½ cup sour cream
- ¼ cup brown sugar
- 1 teaspoon vanilla extract

Directions:
1. In a bowl, combine the flour and eggs. Add the milk gradually. Then add the vanilla extract, butter, salt and icing sugar. Beat well until you get a homogeneous mixture.
2. In the other bowl, combine the filling ingredients well with the help of the Spatula.
3. Preheat the skillet at medium-high temperature for about 2

and a half minutes and immediately lower the temperature to low. Cover the pan with olive oil spray.

4. With the help of the spoon, add approximately 1/8 cup of the mixture to the pan. Tilt the pan slightly to allow the combination to spread evenly across the surface.
5. Cook the crepes for 40 to 45 seconds per side, or until lightly browned. Use the Silicone Spatula to flip them.
6. Repeat steps 4 and 5 with the remaining mixture. Add more spray oil, if necessary.
7. Fill the crepes and serve with syrup.

Nutrition: Calories: 101 Carbohydrates: 17g Fat: 1.4g Protein: 6g Sugar: 5g Cholesterol: 43.4mg

483. Crème Caramel

Preparation Time: 1 hour

Cooking Time: 1 hour

Servings: 12

Ingredients:

- 5 cups of whole milk
- 2 tsp vanilla extract
- 8 large egg yolks
- 4 large-sized eggs
- 2 cups sugar, divided
- ¼ cup 0f water

Directions:

1. Preheat the oven to 350°F
2. Heat the milk on medium heat until it is scalded.
3. Mix 1 cup of sugar and eggs in a bowl and add them to the eggs.
4. With a nonstick pan on high heat, boil the water and remaining sugar. Do not stir; instead, whirl the pan. When the sugar forms caramel, divide it into ramekins.
5. Divide the egg mixture into the ramekins and place them in a baking pan. Add water to the pan until it is half full. Bake for 30 minutes.
6. Remove the ramekins from the baking pan, cool, then refrigerate for at least 8 hours.
7. Serve.

Nutrition: Calories: 110kcal Carbs: 21g Fat: 1g Protein: 2g

484. Revani Syrup Cake

Preparation Time: 30 minutes

Cooking Time: 3 hours

Servings: 24

Ingredients:

- 1 tbsp. unsalted butter
- 2 tbsps. all-purpose flour
- 1 cup ground rusk or bread crumbs
- 1 cup fine semolina flour
- ¾ cup ground toasted almonds
- 3 tsp baking powder
- 16 large eggs
- 2 tbsps. vanilla extract
- 3 cups of sugar, divided
- 3 cups of water
- 5 (2-inch) strips lemon peel, pith removed
- 3 tbsps. fresh lemon juice
- 1 oz of brandy

Directions:

1. Preheat the oven to 350°F. Grease the baking pan with 1 Tbsp. Of butter and flour.
2. Mix the rusk, almonds, semolina, baking powder in a bowl.
3. In another bowl, mix the eggs, 1 cup of sugar, vanilla, and whisk with an electric mixer for about 5 minutes. Add the semolina mixture to the eggs and stir.
4. Pour the stirred batter into the greased baking pan and place it in the preheated oven.
5. The remaining sugar, lemon peels, and water make the syrup by boiling the mixture on medium heat. Add the lemon juice after 6 minutes, then cook for 3 minutes. Remove the lemon peels and set the syrup aside.
6. After the cake is made in the oven, spread the syrup over the cake.
7. Cut the cake as you please and serve.

Nutrition: Calories: 348kcal Carbs: 55g Fat: 9g Protein: 5g

485. Healthy & Quick Energy Bites

Preparation Time: 10 minutes

Cooking Time: 0 minutes

Servings: 20

Ingredients:

- 2 cups cashew nuts
- ¼ tsp cinnamon
- 1 tsp lemon zest
- 4 tbsp dates, chopped
- 1/3 cup unsweetened shredded coconut
- ¾ cup dried apricots

Directions:

1. Line baking tray with parchment paper and set aside.
2. Add all ingredients to a food processor and process until the mixture is crumbly and well combined.
3. Make small balls from the mixture and place them on a prepared baking tray.
4. Serve and enjoy.

Nutrition: Calories 100, Fat 7.5g, Carbohydrates 7.2g, Sugar 2.8g, Protein 2.4g, Cholesterol 0mg

486. Creamy Yogurt Banana Bowls

Preparation Time: 10 minutes

Cooking Time: 0 minutes

Servings: 4

Ingredients:

- 2 bananas, sliced
- ½ tsp ground nutmeg
- 3 tbsp flaxseed meal
- ¼ cup creamy peanut butter
- 4 cups Greek yogurt

Directions:

1. Divide Greek yogurt between 4 serving bowls and top with sliced bananas.
2. Add peanut butter in a microwave-safe bowl and microwave for 30 seconds.
3. Drizzle 1 tablespoon of melted peanut butter on each bowl on top of the sliced bananas.
4. Sprinkle cinnamon and flax meal on top and serve.

Nutrition: Calories 351, Fat 13.1g, Carbohydrates 35.6g, Sugar 26.1g, Protein 19.6g, Cholesterol 15mg

487. Chocolate Mousse

Preparation Time: 10 minutes

Cooking Time: 6 minutes

Servings: 5

Ingredients:

- 4 egg yolks
- ½ tsp vanilla
- ½ cup unsweetened almond milk
- 1 cup whipping cream
- ¼ cup cocoa powder
- ¼ cup water
- ½ cup Swerve
- 1/8 tsp salt

Directions:

1. Add egg yolks to a large bowl and whisk until well beaten.
2. In a saucepan, add swerve, cocoa powder, and water and whisk until well combined.
3. Add almond milk and cream to the saucepan and whisk until good mix.
4. Once saucepan mixtures are heated up, then turn off the heat.
5. Add vanilla and salt and stir well.
6. Add a tablespoon of chocolate mixture into the eggs and whisk until well combined.
7. Slowly pour the remaining chocolate into the eggs and whisk until well combined.
8. Pour batter into the ramekins.
9. Pour 1 ½ cups of water into the pot, then place a trivet in the pot.
10. Place ramekins on a trivet.
11. Seal pot with lid and cook for 6 minutes.
12. Open the lid.
13. Carefully remove ramekins from the spot and let them cool completely.
14. Serve and enjoy.

Nutrition: Calories 128, Fat 11.9g, Carbohydrates 4g, Sugar 0.2g, Protein 3.6g, Cholesterol 194mg

488. Carrot Spread

Preparation Time: 10 minutes

Cooking Time: 10 minutes

Servings: 4

Ingredients:

- ¼ cup veggie stock
- A pinch of salt and black pepper
- 1 teaspoon onion powder
- ½ teaspoon garlic powder
- ½ teaspoon oregano, dried
- 1 pound carrots, sliced
- ½ cup coconut cream

Directions:

1. In your pot, combine all the ingredients except the cream, put the lid on and cook on high heat for 10 minutes.
2. Once done, transfer the carrots mix to a food processor, add the cream, pulse well, divide into bowls and serve cold.

Nutrition: Calories 124, Fat 1g, Fiber 2g, Carbohydrates 5g, Protein 8g

489. Figs Pie

Preparation Time: 10 minutes

Cooking Time: 1 hour

Servings: 8

Ingredients:

- ½ cup stevia
- 6 figs, cut into quarters
- ½ teaspoon vanilla extract
- 1 cup almond flour
- 4 eggs, whisked

Directions:

1. Spread the figs on the bottom of a springform pan lined with parchment paper.
2. In a bowl, combine the other ingredients, whisk and pour over the figs,
3. Bake at 375° F for 1 hour, flip the pie upside down when it's done and serve.

Nutrition: Calories 200; Fat 4.4 g; Fiber 3 g; Carbs 7.6 g; Protein 8 g

490. Poached Apples with Greek Yogurt and Granola

Preparation Time: 5 minutes

Cooking Time: 15 minutes

Servings 4

Ingredients

- 4 medium-sized apples, peeled
- 1/2 cup brown sugar
- 1 vanilla bean
- 1 cinnamon stick
- 1/2 cup cranberry juice
- 1 cup water
- 1/2 cup 2% Greek yogurt
- 1/2 cup granola

Directions

1. Add the apples, brown sugar, water, cranberry juice, vanilla bean, and cinnamon stick to the pot.
2. Secure the lid and cook for 5 minutes on high heat. Once cooking is complete, carefully remove the lid. Reserve poached apples.
3. Let the sauce simmer until it has thickened.
4. Place the apples in serving bowls. Add the syrup and top each apple with granola and Greek yogurt. Enjoy!

Nutrition: 247 Calories; 3.1g Fat; 52.6g Carbohydrates; 3.5g Protein; 40g Sugars; 5.3g Fiber

491. Jasmine Rice Pudding with Cranberries

Preparation Time: 5 minutes

Cooking Time: 15 minutes

Servings 4

Ingredients

- 1 cup apple juice
- 1 heaping tablespoon honey
- 1/3 cup granulated sugar
- 1 ½ cups jasmine rice
- 1 cup water
- 1/4 teaspoon ground cinnamon
- 1/4 teaspoon ground cloves
- 1/3 teaspoon ground cardamom
- 1 teaspoon vanilla extract
- 3 eggs, well-beaten
- 1/2 cup cranberries

Directions

1. Thoroughly combine the apple juice, honey, sugar, jasmine rice, water, and spices in your pot.
2. Secure the lid and cook for 4 minutes at high heat. Once cooking is complete; carefully remove the lid.
3. Lower the heat and fold in the eggs. Cook until heated through.
4. Ladle into individual bowls and top with dried cranberries. Enjoy!

Nutrition: 402 Calories; 3.6g Fat; 81.1g Carbs; 8.9g Protein; 22.3g Sugars; 2.2g Fiber

492. Cherry Cream

Preparation Time: 2 hours

Cooking Time: 0 minutes

Servings: 4

Ingredients:

- 2 cups cherries, pitted and chopped
- 1 cup almond milk
- ½ cup whipping cream
- 3 eggs, whisked
- 1/3 cup stevia
- 1 teaspoon lemon juice
- ½ teaspoon vanilla extract

Directions:

1. In your food processor, combine the cherries with the milk and the rest of the ingredients, pulse well, divide into cups and keep in the fridge for 2 hours before serving.

Nutrition:

Calories 200; Fat 4.5 g; Fiber 3.3 g; Carbs 5.6 g; Protein 3.4 g

493. Healthy Avocado Chocolate Pudding

Preparation Time: 5 minutes

Cooking Time: 0 minutes

Servings: 4

Ingredients:

- 6 avocados, peeled, pitted, and cut into chunks

- ½ cup pure maple syrup, or more to taste
- ¾ cup unsweetened cocoa powder
- 2 teaspoons vanilla extract
- Fresh mint leaves, optional

Directions:

1. Mix the avocados, maple syrup, cocoa powder, and vanilla in a food processor until smooth.
2. Garnish with mint leaves, if desired.
3. Ingredient Tip: Avoid leftovers and eat it all! The avocado will oxidize and turn brown after just a few hours.

Nutrition: Calories: 578 Fat: 42g Carbohydrate: 58g Protein: 8g

494. Mexican Chocolate Mousse

Preparation Time: 15 minutes

Cooking Time: 0 minutes

Servings: 4

Ingredients:

- 8 ounces bittersweet or semisweet vegan chocolate
- 1¾ cups (about 1 pound) silken tofu
- ½ cup pure maple syrup
- 1 teaspoon vanilla
- 1½ teaspoons ground cinnamon

Directions:

1. Create a double boiler by bringing a medium pot filled halfway with water to a low simmer. Place a heatproof bowl above and make sure it is not touching the water. Add the chocolate to the bowl. Keep the pot over low heat and stir the chocolate until it is melted and silky smooth.
2. In a food processor, add all the ingredients. Blend until smooth.
3. Refrigerate before serving.
4. Substitution Tip: Substitute 1 teaspoon of chili powder for the ground cinnamon or add

both for an authentic Mexican chocolate experience.

Nutrition: Calories: 442 Fat: 18g Carbohydrate: 68g Protein: 12g

495. Chocolate Peanut Butter Cups

Preparation Time: 20 minutes

Cooking Time: 0 minutes

Servings: 8

Ingredients:

- 5 ounces vegan semisweet chocolate, divided
- ½ cup smooth peanut butter
- ½ teaspoon vanilla
- ¼ teaspoon salt

Directions:

1. Line a muffin tray with 9 mini or regular paper cupcake liners.
2. Place half the chocolate in a microwave-safe bowl and microwave on high for 25 seconds, then take it out and stir.
3. Place bowl back in the microwave and repeat the process of cooking for 25 seconds, stopping and stirring, until the chocolate has melted.
4. Spoon 1 to 1½ teaspoons of melted chocolate into each cup. Place in the refrigerator for 10 minutes until solid.
5. Stir the peanut butter, vanilla, and salt together in a bowl. Transfer the peanut butter mixture to a resealable plastic bag and seal it tightly. Cut one corner of the plastic bag, then squeeze the bag to pipe 2 to 3 teaspoons of peanut butter in the middle of each cup. Smooth with a small spoon.
6. Melt the remaining chocolate. Spoon 1 to 1½ teaspoon of chocolate into the top of each cup. Smooth with a small spoon.
7. Refrigerate until solid, 30 to 40 minutes. Peel off the liners and enjoy. Remove it from the refrigerator. Let it sit for 15 or a few minutes if you like softer chocolate.

8. Leftovers: Store leftovers in the refrigerator for up to 2 weeks or in the freezer for 1 month.

Nutrition: Calories: 177 Fat: 13g Carbohydrate: 15g Protein: 5g

496. Banana Ice Cream with Chocolate Sauce

Preparation Time: 10 minutes

Cooking Time: 0 minutes

Servings: 4

Ingredients:

- ½ cup raw unsalted cashews
- ¼ cup pure maple syrup
- 1 tablespoon unsweetened cocoa powder
- 1 teaspoon vanilla extract
- ¼ teaspoon salt
- ¼ cup water
- 6 ripe bananas, peeled and frozen

Directions:

1. Place cashews in a bowl and put water. Soak cashews for two hours or overnight. Drain and rinse.
2. Place the cashews, maple syrup, cocoa powder, vanilla, and salt in a food processor or blender. Blend, adding the water a couple of tablespoons at a time until you get a smooth consistency.
3. Transfer to an airtight container, then refrigerate. Bring to room temperature before using.
4. Place frozen bananas in the food processor. Process until you have smooth banana ice cream. Serve topped with chocolate sauce.
5. Ingredient Tip: The best way to freeze a banana is to start with ripe peeled bananas. Slice them into 2-inch chunks and arrange them in a single layer on a parchment-lined baking sheet. Pop them in the freezer. Once frozen, transfer to freezer-safe bags. Frozen bananas are also a delicious, healthy addition to smoothies. Individually freeze chunks of one banana, and

you'll always be ready to create an icy, rich, creamy smoothie.

Nutrition: Calories: 301 Fat: 8g Carbohydrate: 59g Protein: 5g

497. Raspberry Lime Sorbet

Preparation Time: 15 minutes, plus 5 hours or more to chill

Cooking Time: 0 minutes

Servings: 4

Ingredients:

- 3 pints fresh raspberries or 2 (10-ounce) bags frozen
- ½ cup fresh orange juice
- 4 tablespoons pure maple syrup
- 3 tablespoons fresh lime juice
- Dark chocolate curls, optional

Directions:

1. In a glass dish, combine the raspberries, orange juice, maple syrup, and lime juice. Stir well to mix. Cover then put in the freezer until frozen solid, about 5 hours.
2. Get it from the freezer and let it sit for 10 minutes. Crush chunks with a knife or large spoon and transfer the mixture to a food processor. Process this until smooth and creamy for 5 minutes. Serve immediately. The sorbet will freeze solid again but can be processed again until creamy just before serving.
3. To serve, place a scoop into an ice cream dish. Garnish with fresh raspberries and dark chocolate curls if using.
4. Preparation Tip: To make chocolate curls, use a vegetable peeler, and scrape the blade lengthwise across a piece of solid chocolate to create pretty, delicate rings. Refrigerate the curls until ready to use.

Nutrition: Calories: 191 Fat: 2g Carbohydrate: 46g Protein: 3g

498. Baked Apples with Dried Fruit

Preparation Time: 10 minutes

Cooking Time: 1 hour

Servings: 4

Ingredients:

- 4 large apples, cored to make a cavity
- 4 teaspoons raisins or cranberries
- 4 teaspoons pure maple syrup
- 1/2 teaspoon ground cinnamon
- 1/2 cup unsweetened apple juice or water

Directions:

1. Preheat the oven to 350°F.
2. Place apples in a baking pan that will hold them upright. Put the dried fruit into the cavities and drizzle with maple syrup. Sprinkle with cinnamon. Pour apple juice or water on the apples.
3. Cover loosely with foil and bake for 50 minutes to 1 hour, or until the apples are tender when pierced with a fork.
4. Serving Suggestion: Serve the apples topped with Vegan Whipped Cream.

Nutrition: Calories: 158 Fat: 1g Carbohydrate: 42g Protein: 1g

499. Hemp Seed Brittle

Preparation Time: 10 minutes

Cooking Time: 10 minutes

Servings: 6

Ingredients:

- ¼ cup hemp seeds
- 2½ tablespoons brown rice flour
- 3 tablespoons melted coconut oil
- 2½ tablespoons pure maple syrup
- Pinch salt

Directions:

1. Preheat the oven to 350°F. Line a baking sheet with parchment paper.

2. In a bowl, combine all ingredients, then mix well. Spread into an even layer on the baking sheet. Try to quickly, else edges will burn.
3. Bake for 10 minutes and make sure the brittle doesn't burn. Turn off the oven and leave it for 30 minutes to cool down.
4. When it's thoroughly cooled, break it into bite-size pieces with a sharp knife or your fingers.
5. Leftovers: Store leftovers in a sealed container at room temperature for 5 days or freeze for up to 1 month.

Nutrition: Calories: 151 Fat: 12g Carbohydrate: 9g Protein: 4g

500. Cardamom Date Bites

Preparation Time: 15 minutes, plus time to soak

Cooking Time: 15 minutes

Servings: 8

Ingredients:

- 1 cup pitted dates
- 3 cups old-fashioned rolled oats
- ¼ cup ground flaxseed
- 1 teaspoon ground cardamom
- 3 ripe bananas, mashed (about 1½ cups)

Directions:

1. Preheat the oven to 350°F. Line a baking sheet with parchment paper.
2. In a small bowl, place the dates and cover them with hot water. Let it sit until softened, 10 to 30 minutes, depending on the dates, and then drain. Purée in a food processor or blender. Set the date paste aside.
3. In the food processor, grind the oats and ground flaxseed until they resemble flour.
4. In a large bowl, mix the cardamom and mashed bananas. Stir in the ground oat-flaxseed mixture.
5. Form into walnut-size balls and flatten a little. Place on the baking sheet and form an indentation in the middle

using a ¼ teaspoon measuring spoon. Fill each indentation with about ½ teaspoon of date paste.

6. Bake for 15 minutes or until the bites are golden.

Nutrition: Calories: 82 Fat: 2g Carbohydrate: 16g Protein: 2g

Conclusion

Thank you for making it to the end. We hope that this book has provided you with the information and answers you are seeking regarding the Mediterranean diet. Our goal was to provide a thorough look at this diet and all the advantages and disadvantages it can bring to your life. As always, when making dietary changes, you should consult your physician first to ensure this is a healthy change for you to achieve your goals in regards to your health.

People who go to the Mediterranean can lose more weight, lower their risk factors of heart disease, and even preserve their bone mass and muscle mass later in life! By keeping your cells more active and healthy, you can slow down the process of aging that affects all of us over time. There can be a few disadvantages to the Mediterranean diet that people have to adjust to, but with the many health benefits, it's evident that the good outweighs the bad. Without the need to count calories or weigh your portion sizes, the ease of flexibility this diet provides makes it so appealing to many.

It's important to note that the Mediterranean diet isn't just about diet - it's a lifestyle change. You will be focusing on eating a diet with less red meat and more fresh fruits, vegetables, and seafood. Still, if you genuinely want to mimic the lifestyle of the Mediterranean, you have to incorporate physical activity into your routine. The people of this region naturally fit exercise into their daily lives, whether through walking, swimming, or boating. To gain the same health benefits, you should try and be more active in your life to gain those similar health benefits. Even if you aren't going to the gym, try making more conscious choices to burn calories and get your body moving. You could take a walk around the block, jog, bike, or spend some time gardening. Simply deciding to be more active allows you to expend calories and lose more weight.

To help you succeed, we have included many tips for weight loss and implementing the Mediterranean diet into your lifestyle long-term. You must know precisely what habits and foods you should be incorporating into your routine, like staying hydrated, having a diet full of fiber, and planning a mealtime schedule to avoid excess snacking. The more you can sustain a healthy diet, the less likely you will reach for the "forbidden" items like sugary snacks, processed foods, soda, or candy. You must remind yourself what you can eat on the Mediterranean diet versus what you cannot. You can include so many varieties of food in your meals like vegetables, whole grains, fish, seafood, beans, and even fruit! Some diets restrict fruit due to their natural sugars and net carbs, but the Mediterranean diet urges you to use fruit to satisfy your sweet tooth! You can even have a glass of your favorite wine if you are a wine drinker, but you must speak to your physician to ensure that you can drink alcohol with your individual health needs and condition.

We've included a 30-day sample meal plan to help you get started on your Mediterranean diet with easy and healthy recipes you can meal prep beforehand or make in a short amount of time. Not only that, we provide 500 recipes for breakfast, lunch, and dinner desserts, etc., so you aren't at a loss at what Mediterranean-friendly meal to make! With this knowledge, you can successfully implement this lifestyle into your busy life and gain all the benefits it can offer!

Finally, if you found this valuable book in any way, a review is always appreciated!

Measurement Conversion Table

US Dry Volume Measurements	
1/16 teaspoon	a dash
1/8 teaspoon	a pinch
3 teaspoons	1 tablespoon
¼ cup	4 tablespoons
1/3 cup	5 tablespoons + 1 teaspoons
½ cup	8 tablespoons
¾ cup	12 tablespoons
1 cup	16 tablespoons
1 pound	16 ounces

US Liquid Volume Measurements	
Eight fluid ounces	1 cup
1 pint = 2 cups	16 fluid ounces
1 quart = 2 pints	4 cups
1 gallon = 4 quarts	16 cups

Index of Recipes

Chapter 3.   Breakfast Recipes 14

1. Smoky Shrimp Chipotle 14
2. Low Carb Taco Bowls 15
3. Artichoke Frittatas 16
4. Chocolate Sweet Potato Pudding 16
5. Peanut Butter and Protein Pancake 17
6. Tex-Mex Tofu Breakfast Tacos .. 17
7. Mocha Oatmeal 18
8. Black and Blueberry Protein Smoothie 19
9. Barley Porridge 19
10. Ricotta Breakfast Casserole 20
11. Mango-Pear Smoothie 21
12. Strawberry-Rhubarb Smoothie 22
13. Pumpkin-Gingerbread Smoothie 22
14. Low Carb Sloppy Joes 23
15. Tex-Mex Seared Salmon 24
16. Tomato, Herb, and Goat Cheese Frittata 25
17. Prosciutto Breakfast Bruschetta 26
18. Prosciutto, Avocado, and Veggie Sandwiches 27
19. Chickpea and Hummus Patties in Pitas 28
20. Morning Creamy Iced Coffee ... 29
21. Versatile Sandwich Round 30
22. Tuna and Avocado Salad Sandwich 30
23. Protein Oatcakes 31
24. Polenta with Arugula, Figs, and Blue Cheese 32
25. Pumpkin Layers with Honey Granola 33
26. Shakshuka with Cilantro 33
27. Pumpkin Muffins 34
28. Cardamom-Cinnamon Overnight Oats 35
29. Vanilla Raspberry Overnight Oats 36
30. Toasted Sesame Ginger Chicken 36
31. Tender and Tasty Fish Tacos ... 37
32. Sausage Stuffed Mushrooms ... 38
33. Orange French Toast 39

34. Sweet Potato Toast 39
35. Cheesy Mini Frittatas 41
36. Savory Lentil Waffles 42
37. Baked Dandelion Toast 43
38. Spiced Almond Pancakes 44
39. Crustless Sun-Dried Tomato Quiche 45
40. Spinach Curry Pancakes with Apple, Raisins, And Chickpeas 46
41. Swiss Chard Gingerbread Pan with Egg, Onion, And Tomato 47
42. Cheesy Avocado Omelet 48
43. Bircher Muesli 49

Chapter 4.   Snacks And Appetizers   50

44. Mediterranean Mezze Dish 50
45. Marinated Feta and Artichokes 50
46. Citrus-Marinated Olives 51
47. Labneh and Veggie Parfaits 51
48. Mediterranean Nachos 52
49. Smoked Salmon and Avocado Summer Rolls 54
50. Healthy Lemon Bars 55
51. Mediterranean Baking Tray With Halloumi Pieces 56
52. Burrata Caprese Stack 57
53. Zucchini-Ricotta Fritters with Lemon-Garlic Aioli 58

54. Salmon-Stuffed Cucumbers 59
55. Goat Cheese–Mackerel Pâté 60
56. Baba Ghanoush 60
57. Taste of the Mediterranean Fat Bombs 61
58. Cream of Cauliflower Gazpacho 61
59. Passion Fruit and Spicy Couscous 62
60. Honey and Vanilla Custard Cups with Crunchy Filo Pastry 63
61. Citrus Cups 64
62. Bananas Foster 65
63. Cranberry Orange Cookies 66
64. Vinegar Beet Bites 66
65. Mediterranean White Bean Harissa Dip 67
66. Apple Chips with Maple Chocolate Tahini 68
67. Strawberry Caprese Skewers with Balsamic Glaze 69
68. Eggplant Dip 69
69. Veggie Fritters 70
70. Peppery Potatoes 70
71. Turkey Spheroids with Tzatziki Sauce 71
72. Cheesy Caprese Salad Skewers 72
73. Leafy Lacinato Tuscan Treat ... 73
74. Greek Guacamole Hybrid Hummus 73

75. Mediterranean-Style Trail Mix 74

76. Savory Mediterranean Spiced Popcorn 74

77. Hummus with Ground Lamb . 75

78. The Ultimate Mediterranean Appetizer Dish............................ 76

Chapter 5.   Pasta and Rice Recipes   77

79. Bean and Veggie Pasta.............. 77

80. Roasted Ratatouille Pasta 78

81. Lentil and Mushroom Pasta 79

82. Spinach Pesto Pasta 80

83. Authentic Pasta e Fagioli 81

84. Escarole And Cannellini Beans On Pasta 82

85. Simple Pesto Pasta 82

86. Meaty Baked Penne................... 83

87. Mediterranean Pasta with Tomato Sauce and Vegetables....... 84

88. Cheesy Spaghetti with Pine Nuts 85

89. Creamy Garlic-Parmesan Chicken Pasta 85

90. Roasted Pepper Pasta 86

91. Italian Chicken Pasta 87

92. Pesto Chicken Pasta................... 87

93. Fresh Sauce Pasta...................... 88

94. Three Sauces Lasagna 89

95. Penne In Tomato And Caper Sauce...................................90

96. Chicken Spinach and Artichoke Stuffed Spaghetti Squash 91

97. Angel Hair with Asparagus-Kale Pesto...................................92

98. Spicy Pasta Puttanesca 93

99. Roasted Vegetarian Lasagna....94

100. Artichoke Chicken Pasta........95

101. Spinach Beef Pasta 96

102. Asparagus Parmesan Pasta....97

103. Caramelized Onion Flatbread with Arugula..............................98

104. Quick Shrimp Fettuccine 99

105. Hearty Butternut Spinach, and Cheeses Lasagna 100

106. Minestrone Chickpeas and Macaroni Casserole 101

107. Roasted Butternut Squash and Zucchini with Penne 102

108. Small Pasta and Beans Pot .. 103

109. Garlic Shrimp Fettuccine.... 104

110. Broccoli and Carrot Pasta Salad.. 105

111. Mushroom and Vegetable Penne Pasta 106

112. Spaghetti With Garlic, Olive Oil, And Red Pepper..................... 107

113. Spaghetti With Anchovy Sauce 108

114. White Bean Alfredo Pasta ... 109
115. Penne Pasta with Tomato Sauce and Mizithra cheese 110
116. Delicious Chicken Pasta 111
117. Spaghetti Pesto Cake 111
118. Artichokes, Olives & Tuna Pasta 112
119. Broccoli Pesto Spaghetti 113
120. Spaghetti all'Olio 114
121. Quick Tomato Spaghetti 115
122. Easy Rice Pilaf 115
123. Baked Chicken Paella........... 116
124. Vegetable Rice Bake 118
125. Farro With Porcini Mushrooms 119
126. Sicilian Eggplant With Israeli Couscous 120
127. Polenta With Wild Greens .. 121
128. Baked Rice With Swordfish And Mussels 122
129. Cucumber Olive Rice 123
130. Chorizo-kidney Beans Quinoa Pilaf 124
131. Belly-filling Cajun Rice & Chicken 125

Chapter 6.   Soups 127
132. Spinach and Feta Cheese Soup 127
133. Moroccan Pumpkin Soup.... 127
134. Roasted Root Vegetable Soup 128
135. Super Mushroom and Red Wine Soup 129
136. Smoked Ham Split Pea Soup 130
137. Mushroom Spinach Soup 131
138. Delicata Squash Soup........... 132
139. Cod Potato Soup.................... 133
140. Keto French Onion Soup 133
141. Minestrone Soup 134
142. Chicken Wild Rice Soup....... 135
143. Classic Chicken Soup 136
144. Cucumber Soup 136
145. Squash and Turmeric Soup . 137
146. Leek, Potato, and Carrot Soup 137
147. Kale Chicken Soup................. 138

Chapter 7.   Salads & Sides 140
148. Mediterranean Tortellini Salad 140
149. Mediterranean Salad With Parsnips And Peppers................... 140
150. Fried Mushroom Salad......... 141
151. Mediterranean Chickpea Salad 142
152. Mediterranean Tuna Salad.. 142
153. Mediterranean Egg Broccoli Salad 143

154. Mediterranean Salad With Baked Camembert 144
155. Tomato and Avocado Salad 145
156. Arugula Salad 145
157. Chickpea Salad 146
158. Chopped Israeli Mediterranean Pasta Salad 146
159. Pork and Greens Salad 147
160. Mediterranean Duck Breast Salad 148
161. Creamy Chicken Salad 148
162. Chicken and Cabbage Salad. 149
163. Roasted Broccoli Salad 150
164. Tomato Salad 151
165. Feta Beet Salad 151
166. Chicken and Quinoa Salad .. 151
167. Melon Salad 152
168. Bean and Toasted Pita Salad 153
169. Salad With Pine Nuts And Mozzarella 154
170. Mediterranean Salad With Feta 154
171. Tomato And Cucumber Salad With Feta 155
172. Mediterranean Salad With Peppers And Tomatoes 155
173. Mediterranean Potato Salad With Beans 156
174. Orzo Olive Salad 157

175. Mushroom Arugula Salad ... 158
176. Italian Bread Salad 158
177. Mediterranean Beef Salad ... 159
178. Ground Beef Salad with Creamy Avocado Dressing 160
179. Tuna Salad with Lettuce and Chickpeas 161
180. Sweet Potato Puree 161
181. Chickpea & Lentil Salad 162
182. Mashed Fava Beans 162
183. Spicy Borlotti Beans 163
184. Vegetable Stew 164
185. Quick Spinach Focaccia 165
186. Sumptuous Greek Vegetable Salad 165
187. Brussels Sprout and Apple Slaw 166
188. Peas And Tubetti With Pancetta 167
189. Asparagus with Feta 168
190. Rosemary Sweet Potato Medallions 169
191. Artichoke with Garlic Mayo 169
192. Steamed Artichoke with Lemon Aioli 170
193. Herby-Garlic Potatoes 171
194. Lentils with Spinach and Garlic Chips 171
195. Artichoke and Arugula Salad 172

196. Spiced Lentil Salad with Winter Squash 173

197. Rosemary Scent Cauliflower Bundles 175

198. Barley, Parsley, and Pea Salad 175

199. Cheesy Peach and Walnut Salad 176

200. Delicious Feta with Fresh Spinach 177

201. Celeriac Mix with Cauliflower 177

202. Lentil Salad with Olives, Mint, and Feta 178

Chapter 8.   Vegetables 180

203. Stewed Okra 180

204. Sweet Veggie-Stuffed Peppers 180

205. Brussels Sprouts Chips 181

206. Balsamic Roasted Carrots and Baby Onions 182

207. Lentil and Tomato Collard Wraps 182

208. Wedding of Broccoli and Tomatoes 183

209. Zucchini Fettuccine with Mexican Taco 183

210. Grilled Eggplant Rolls.......... 184

211. Easy And Healthy Baked Vegetables 185

212. Rosemary Scent Cauliflower Bundles 186

213. Triumph of Cucumbers and Avocados 186

214. Crispy Zucchini Fritters....... 187

215. Cheesy Spinach Pies 187

216. Vegetable and Red Lentil Stew 188

217. Mozzarella Eggplants 189

218. Sautéed Green Beans with Tomatoes 190

219. Simple Baked Okra 190

220. Baked Tomatoes and Chickpeas 191

221. Vegetarian Chili 192

222. Mediterranean Veggie Bowl 193

223. Spanish Green Beans 194

224. Roasted Cauliflower and Tomatoes 194

225. Roasted Acorn Squash 195

226. Sautéed Garlic Spinach 196

227. Garlicky Sautéed Zucchini with Mint 196

228. Baked Bean and Rice Casserole 197

229. Okra and Tomato Casserole 198

230. Spicy Baked Feta with Tomatoes 198

231. Black-Eyed Peas With Mint . 199

Chapter 9. Poultry & Meat Recipes   200

232. Garlic Caper Beef Roast 200
233. Cauliflower Tomato Beef 200
234. Dinner Party Brisket 201
235. Sunday Dinner Brisket 202
236. Moist Shredded Beef 203
237. Hearty Beef Ragu 203
238. Dill Beef Brisket 204
239. Tasty Beef Stew 205
240. Italian Style Ground Beef 205
241. Spicy Beef Chili Verde 206
242. Carrot Mushroom Beef Roast 207
243. Italian Beef Roast 207
244. Thyme Beef Round Roast 208
245. Jalapeno Beef Chili 208
246. Bean Beef Chili 209
247. Fall-Apart Tender Beef 210
248. Beef and Cabbage Roast 210
249. Rustic Lamb Shanks 211
250. Holiday Feast Lamb Shanks 212
251. Succulent Leg of Lamb 213
252. Melt-in-Mouth Lamb Shoulder 214
253. Greek Spiced Pork Souvlaki . 215
254. Lovely Smelling Pork Loin .. 215
255. Elegant Pork Loin 216
256. Zero-Fussing Pork Meal 217
257. Grilled Steak 218
258. Spicy Roasted Leg of Lamb . 219
259. Dijon & Herb Pork Tenderloin 220
260. Grilled Lamb Gyro Burger ... 220
261. Pork Loin & Orzo 221
262. Lamb Chops 222
263. Roasted Lamb with Vegetables 222
264. Pan-Fried Pork Chops with Orange Sauce 223
265. Beef Spicy Salsa Braised Ribs 224
266. Chargrilled Mediterranean Beef Lasagna 225
267. Beef Cacciatore (Italy) 226
268. Green Curry Beef 227
269. Mediterranean Beef Pitas 228
270. Cumin Lamb Mix 228
271. Herb-Roasted Lamb Leg 229
272. Spring Lamb Stew 229
273. Pork and Mushroom Crock Pot 230
274. Buttery Herb Lamb Chops .. 230
275. Special Chops 231
276. Rib Roast 232
277. Spicy Lamb Rounds 232
278. Prime BBQ 233

279. Pork And Chestnuts Mix 233
280. Steak with Olives and Mushrooms 234
281. Greek Pork 234
282. Rosemary Pork Chops 235
283. Pork Rind Salmon Cakes 235
284. Worcestershire Pork Chops 236
285. Pork With Green Beans & Potatoes 237
286. Chicken with Peas 237
287. Chicken Wrap 238
288. Almond Chicken Bites 238
289. Garlic Chicken and Endives 239
290. Butter Chicken Thighs 240
291. Chicken and Olives Salsa 240
292. Chili Chicken Mix 241
293. Duck and Orange Warm Salad 242
294. Turmeric Baked Chicken Breast 242
295. Chicken Tacos 243
296. Chicken and Butter Sauce ... 244
297. Spicy Mustard Chicken 244
298. Walnut and Oregano Crusted Chicken 245
299. Coriander and Coconut Chicken 245
300. Chicken Pilaf 246
301. Chicken and Black Beans 247
302. Coconut Chicken 248
303. Ginger Chicken Drumsticks 248
304. Parmesan Chicken 249
305. Grilled Chicken With Lemon And Fennel 250
306. Chicken and Onion Casserole 250
307. Slow-Cooked Pot Roast 251
308. Chicken Quesadilla 251
309. Quinoa Chicken Fingers 252
310. Garlic-Parmesan Chicken Wings 253
311. Chicken Breasts With Stuffing 253
312. Turkey Sausage, Fresh Herbs & Feta 254
313. Chicken With Spanish Rice . 255
314. Italian Chicken 256
315. Turkey Meatloaf 256
316. Chicken And Tzaziki Pitas ... 257
317. Lime Chicken With Black Beans 257
318. Lemon Chicken Mix 258
319. Chicken Shawarma 258
320. Braised Chicken Thighs with Kalamata Olives 259
321. Buttery Garlic Chicken 260
322. Honey Almond Chicken Tenders 261

- 323. Chicken and Mushrooms 261
- 324. Blue Cheese and Mushroom Chicken 262
- 325. Lemon Chicken..................... 262
- 326. Greek Chicken Bites 263
- 327. Turkey Verde With Brown Rice 263
- 328. Lemon Garlic Chicken 264
- 329. Turkey With Basil & Tomatoes 264
- 330. Honey Balsamic Chicken..... 265
- 331. Mediterranean Chicken 266
- 332. Turkey Lasagna 266
- 333. Whole Roasted Chicken....... 267
- 334. Turkey and Cranberry Sauce 268
- 335. Sage Turkey Mix 268
- 336. Turkey and Asparagus Mix . 269
- 337. Herbed Almond Turkey....... 269
- 338. Yogurt Chicken Breasts 270
- 339. Coconut Chicken Tenders ... 271
- 340. Chicken Skewers with Peanut Sauce 272

Chapter 10.   Fish & Seafood..... 274
- 341. Shrimp and Lemon Sauce.... 274
- 342. Shrimp and Beans Salad 274
- 343. Pecan Salmon Fillets 275
- 344. Salmon and Broccoli 276
- 345. Dijon Fish Fillets 276
- 346. Marinated Tuna Steak 277
- 347. Garlic and Shrimp Pasta...... 277
- 348. Paprika Butter Shrimps....... 278
- 349. Mediterranean Avocado Salmon Salad 279
- 350. Tuna with Vegetable Mix.... 280
- 351. Salmon and Peach Pan 281
- 352. Tarragon Cod Fillets 282
- 353. Salmon and Radish Mix....... 282
- 354. Smoked Salmon and Watercress Salad 283
- 355. Salmon and Corn Salad 283
- 356. Cod and Mushrooms Mix 284
- 357. Sesame Shrimp Mix 284
- 358. Fish and Orzo 285
- 359. Baked Sea Bass..................... 286
- 360. Fish and Tomato Sauce 286
- 361. Halibut and Quinoa Mix...... 287
- 362. Lemon and Dates Barramundi................................... 287
- 363. Catfish Fillets and Rice........ 288
- 364. Halibut Pan........................... 289
- 365. Baked Shrimp Mix................ 289
- 366. Tuna Bowl with Kale 290
- 367. Greek Baked Cod 291
- 368. Pistachio Sole Fish 292
- 369. Baked Tilapia....................... 293

370. A Great Mediterranean Snapper 294
371. Mediterranean Snapper 295
372. Mediterranean Salmon 296
373. Heartthrob Mediterranean Tilapia 297
374. Herbed Salmon With Mashed Potatoes 297
375. Mediterranean Snapper With Olives And Feta 299
376. Moroccan Cod 300
377. Tuna Puttanesca 301
378. Fish En Papillote 302
379. Baked Fish Fingers 303
380. Shrimp Scampi 304
381. Mussels And Clams In White Wine 305
382. Shrimp Fra Diavolo 306
383. Sardine Pâté 307
384. Mussels In Tomato Sauce With Pastina 308
385. Easy Fish And Papillote Recipe 309
386. Calamari With Tomato Sauce 310
387. Salmon & Eggs 311
388. Nacho-Crusted Shrimp 311
389. Sriracha And Honey Tossed Calamari 312
390. Kataifi-Wrapped Shrimp With Lemon Garlic Butter 312
391. Fish Taco 313
392. Grilled Barramundi With Lemon Butter 314
393. Cranberry Cod 315
394. Cod Fish Teriyaki With Oysters, Mushrooms & Veggies .. 315
395. Salmon With Dill Sauce 316
396. Grilled Salmon With Capers & Dill 317
397. Black Cod With Grapes, Pecans, Fennel & Kale 318
398. Air-Fried Asian Style Fish 318
399. Salmon With Creamy Zucchini 319
400. Cajun-Seasoned Lemon Salmon 320
401. Salmon Croquettes 320
402. Salmon Asparagus Sweet Potato Nicoise 321
403. Mediterranean Fish Packages 322
404. Mediterranean Style Fish Stew 323
405. Mediterranean Trout With Sautéed Vegetables 324
406. Garlicky Branzino With Fresh Herbs 326
407. Shrimp With Black Bean Pasta 326

408. Spanish Style Salmon With Vegetables 327

409. Quick Mussels With White Wine Sauce 328

410. Breaded Fish 329

411. Tilapia With Egg 330

412. Marinated Shrimp With Orange 330

413. Poached Salmon With Mustard Sauce 331

414. Grilled Halibut With Romesco Sauce 333

415. Mackerel Niçoise Salad 334

416. Browned Salmon Cakes 335

417. Shrimp Mojo de Ajo 336

Chapter 11. Bread and Pizza Recipes 338

418. Rosemary-Walnut Loaf Bread 338

419. Tasty Crabby Panini 339

420. Sardinian Flatbread 340

421. Focaccia (Italian Flatbread) . 340

422. Taralli (Pugliese Bread Knots) 342

423. Testaroli (Etruscan Pancakes) 343

424. Pesto Vegetable Bread 344

425. Tomato Bruschetta 345

426. White Bean Crostini 346

427. Pizza Bianca With Spinach .. 347

428. Mashed Grape Tomato Pizzas 347

429. Sumptuous Vegetable and Cheese Lavash Pizza 348

430. Eggplant Pizza 349

431. BBQ Chicken Pizza 350

432. Caramelized Onion and Goat Cheese Pizza 351

433. Grilled Burgers with Mushrooms 352

434. Mediterranean Baba Ghanoush 353

435. Multi-Grain & Gluten-Free Dinner Rolls 354

436. Vegetarian Spinach-Olive Pizza 355

437. Chicken Bacon Ranch Pizza 355

438. Chicken Pizza 357

439. Shrimp Pizza 357

440. Veggie Pizza 358

441. Bread Machine Pizza Dough 359

442. Basil & Artichoke Pizza 360

443. Italian Mushroom Pizza 361

444. Broccoli-Pepper Pizza 362

445. Mozzarella Bean Pizza 363

446. Avocado Tomato Pizza 364

447. Mediterranean Whole Wheat Pizza 365

448. Fruit Pizza 365

449. Artichoke Pizza 366
450. 3-Cheese Pizza 366
451. Chickpea Pizza 367
452. Mushroom Pesto Pita Pizza. 367
453. Gluten-Free Zucchini and Walnut Pizza 368
454. Cheesy Fig Pizzas with Garlic Oil 369
455. Hummus Pizza 371
456. Pesto Pita Pizza 371
457. Veggie Pita Pizza 372
458. Mini Pizzas with Arugula & Hummus 373
459. Grilled Buffalo Chicken Pizza 373
460. Portobello Mushroom Pizzas 374

Chapter 12. Desserts 376

461. Blueberry Frozen Yogurt 376
462. Delectable Strawberry Popsicle 376
463. Deliciously Cold Lychee Sorbet 377
464. Easy Fruit Compote 377
465. Apple Couscous Pudding 378
466. Ricotta Ramekins 378
467. Papaya Cream 379
468. Orange Cake 379
469. Orange Butterscotch Pudding 380
470. Recipe for Ruby Pears Delight 381
471. Mixed Berry and Orange Compote 382
472. Streuselkuchen with Peaches 382
473. Black Tea Cake 383
474. Zingy Blueberry Sauce 384
475. Chocolate Almond Custard. 384
476. Honey Stewed Apples 385
477. Greek-Style Compote with Yogurt 385
478. Butterscotch Lava Cakes 386
479. Vanilla Bread Pudding with Apricots 387
480. Green Tea and Vanilla Cream 388
481. Picositos Brownies 388
482. Fruit Crepes 389
483. Crème Caramel 390
484. Revani Syrup Cake 391
485. Healthy & Quick Energy Bites 392
486. Creamy Yogurt Banana Bowls 392
487. Chocolate Mousse 393
488. Carrot Spread 394
489. Figs Pie 394

490. Poached Apples with Greek Yogurt and Granola 395

491. Jasmine Rice Pudding with Cranberries 395

492. Cherry Cream 396

493. Healthy Avocado Chocolate Pudding 396

494. Mexican Chocolate Mousse . 397

495. Chocolate Peanut Butter Cups 398

496. Banana Ice Cream with Chocolate Sauce 399

497. Raspberry Lime Sorbet 400

498. Baked Apples with Dried Fruit 401

499. Hemp Seed Brittle 401

500. Cardamom Date Bites 402

Conclusion 404

Measurement Conversion Table 406

Index of Recipes 407

Made in the USA
Monee, IL
06 November 2021